HOT
RELATIONSHIPS

Also by Tracey Cox
Published by Bantam Books

HOT SEX

HOT
RELATIONSHIPS
HOW TO HAVE ONE

TRACEY COX

BANTAM BOOKS

New York   Toronto   London   Sydney   Auckland

HOT RELATIONSHIPS
A Bantam Book / published by arrangement with
Transworld Publishers, a division of
Random House Australia Pty Limited.

PUBLISHING HISTORY
Bantam Books Australian edition published 1999
Bantam Books U.S. edition / July 2000
All rights reserved.
Copyright © 1999, 2000 by Tracey Cox.

ISBN 0-7394-1046-6

Published simultaneously in the United States and Canada

Bantam Books are published by Bantam Books, a division of
Random House, Inc. Its trademark, consisting of the words
"Bantam Books" and the portrayal of a rooster, is Registered
in U.S. Patent and Trademark Office and in other countries.
Marca Registrada. Bantam Books, 1540 Broadway, New
York, New York 10036.

PRINTED IN THE UNITED STATES OF AMERICA

To my family, for their endless love and support

Contents

● ●

Acknowledgments

· ·

So many people contributed to this book, it would be impossible to name them all. First billing, though, has to go to my family for their constant encouragement. A huge thanks to Mum, Terry, Dad, Mo, Nigel, Deb, Doug, and my niece and nephew, Maddy and Charlie, who make my heart thud with pride and give me supreme faith in the younger generation. Thanks also to all my friends, who put up with me saying no to almost every invitation but still called to say "hi" and slid chocolate cookies under the door.

Special thanks go to: Ute Junker, my clever friend, for spending her precious spare time proofreading and giving "Seriously—it's great!" pep talks; Janet Muggivan for to-die-for roast potatoes and girly chats when I needed them most; Pat Ingram and Mia Freedman for their friendship and overwhelming support of all my ventures; the entire team at Transworld, my publisher, but most particularly Larry Finlay, Diana Beaumont, and Emma Dowson in the U.K., Christine Brooks and Jessica Bellucci in the U.S. and Shona Martyn, Jude McGee, Louise Thurtell, Nerrilee Weir, and Karen Reid (my wonderfully wicked partner in crime) in Australia. You've all worked so hard to make my books a success, I can't thank you enough; thank you also to all the journalists and reviewers who said lovely things about my last book—you helped make this one happen; thanks also to all the psychologists who contributed via stories I've had previously published, particularly Dr. Nicholas Tarrier, Phillip Gorrell, Dr. Janet Hall, the much-adored Gerard Webster, Grant Brecht, and Eric Fleming; a HUGE thank-you to everyone who bared their souls and contributed real-life stories and quotes for the book: Deb, Steve, Leonie Robertson, Mark Watson, Nic McClure, John Graham, Craig Syphers, and others who didn't want to be named for fear of getting themselves in hot water.

Thanks also to the various magazines who let me pinch ideas, sentences, and small sections from my previously published stories. Small portions of text contained in this book originally appeared in:

Australian Cosmopolitan: "Jealousy," September 1990; "Women Who Love Sex and How Men Tell," August 1995; "Should You Give Him an Ultimatum," April 1996; "He's Back but Will He Stay?," May 1996; "Relationships in the '90s," May 1996; "The 20 Biggest Relationship Roadblocks," July 1996; "Will They Ever Get On?," January 1997; "Stop Being Sensible," February 1997; "Why He's Hurting More Than You," February 1997; "Why Your First Lover Affects You for Life," March 1997; "His Ex—8 Signs He's Not Over Her," June 1997; "Can Ex-Lovers Be Friends?," October 1997.

She: "Divorce," August 1996.

marie claire: "Supermarket Sex," June 1996.

Elle: "Two's a Couple, Three's Counselling," April 1997.

Mode for Brides: "Is There Sex After Marriage?;" "To Have or Not to Have Children."

Introduction

• •

When I told my best friend I was writing a book about relationships she spat wine halfway across the bar.

"You can't!" she said. "You're, you know, *divorced*!"

"Oh my *God*!" I said. "I'd completely forgotten."

Not. Look, I admit it. It doesn't make me feel terribly confident either when I'm described as "Sex and Relationships Expert. Divorced." It does sound like a contradiction in terms, so I thought I'd better explain myself up front.

What qualifies me as a relationships "expert"? Well, I've got a psychology degree for a start. I've also spent close to a decade writing, researching, and talking about sex and relationships. I'm *Cosmopolitan*'s agony aunt, I do a talk-radio show on relationships—and I've had . . . well . . . lots of practice. I've been married and divorced. I've had six-week flings, several two-year this-must-be-the-one live-in relationships, first-date fizzles, four-year triumphs (and yes, the odd one-night-stand as well). But if you want reassurance that I met, married, and am currently snuggled up on the couch with Mr. Perfect, you're reading the wrong book. I'm just your average 37-year-old who happens to know a lot about relationships on both an academic and personal level. (And I have to say, out of the two, I've probably learned more from experience and talking to real people than I have from psychological studies, however fascinating they are.)

What this book aims to do is answer all the questions people ask me about relationships, over and over and over again. What's wrong with the billion advice books already out there? Personally, I found most of them either mind-numbingly boring or tacky and sexist (How To Get a Woman in Bed within 60 seconds) or a bit too crunchy-granola and spiritual. Maybe chanting "ommm" and tinging bells does help, but I've always found rolling up to a great party in a stunning little black dress gets better results, if a date's what you're after.

This book is for singles and couples, men and women, heterosexuals, bisexuals, gays, and lesbians. While it's predominantly addressed to straight couples simply because constantly writing girl/boy or boy/boy or girl/girl all the time would have been confusing, all the advice applies to every couple combination. The book's format follows a relationship in logical sequence, so it's a good idea to start at the beginning. There's everything from self-confidence, standing out from the crowd, and spotting losers to jealousy, affairs, and past influences. There's cute little stats to wow them with at your next dinner party, lots of quotes from real couples and tons of practical advice on where to meet someone, what to do when you've found the right someone, and how to skid through those nasty ice patches so you end up in the His 'n' Hers towel section rather than on the scrap heap.

I'd love to claim all the ideas are mine but they're not. I've included lots of research and tips from people I admire (like John Gottman, Barbara De Angelis, and Dr. Maryon Tysoe) as well as information gleaned from psychological studies. I've tried, somewhat heroically, to cover every relationship problem, query, and situation I could think of but there are limits (like the number of pages I was allowed to do it in). The book's written in everyday language with lots of humor thrown in, so hopefully you'll have a giggle while you're learning.

Unfortunately, reading the book is the easy part. You could devour *Hot Relationships* cover to cover, be able to recite entire sections by heart, and still not benefit one iota. Knowledge will only get you so far: you've got to practice what I've preached. That's what people mean when they say, "You have to work hard at relationships." You do. But it's not really work, is it? It's more about finding out about each other, exploring each other's minds, hearts, and bodies, treating each other nicely and loving each other to death. If that's hard work, I'm volunteering for community service at whatever male modeling agency Calvin Klein uses.

While I was writing this book, lots of people said to me, "But how can you teach someone how to make a relationship great? It just is or it isn't. You either love each other or you don't." Alas, love alone doesn't guarantee a happy partnership. You both need good communication skills and relationship skills as well. You need to be able to express your wants, needs, and thoughts to each other, to argue without it ending with the door slamming. Both of you need to feel understood, supported, and respected. There *are* tried-and-true techniques which can help you achieve all of this. And (I like to think) all the good ones are in this book.

Hot Relationships will never be finished to my satisfaction because every day I discover something new about relationships. The temptation to keep on adding more is enormous but I had to stop somewhere. So this is it. I hope it delivers what you're looking for—and that *your* new relationship is so hot, it *sizzles!*

P.S.: To all my ex-boyfriends: If you recognize yourself and got a glowing reference, don't mention it, you deserve it. If it's not so fab, ditto.

1

The Smart Single

Why happy singles who know what they want end up in happy relationships

• •

I'm getting ready to go out. The party mix is pumping out of the stereo, I'm in the bathroom plucking, shaving, dyeing, exfoliating, fake tanning, moisturizing, blending, hiding, highlighting. I'm also getting drunk—the bottle of white is disappearing fast but I can't help it. I'm over-excited and can't *wait* to get out there. Deep in my bones (and other places), I've got the feeling tonight is IT. THE NIGHT I am going to meet a guy who's gorgeous, interesting, funny, intelligent, ambitious, and all-round wonderful. Never mind I've spent the last week moaning to my girlfriends about how there aren't any single men out there. How I feel fat/old/ugly/depressed. Tonight, I'm on a chardonnay-inspired optimistic high. This guy's going to knock my socks off. All my problems will magically disappear. My mother will never again have to give me ridiculously expensive Christmas gifts because "You've got no one, darling, and the other kids do." I'm off to a huge party: wall-to-wall men *and* the hostess has promised to provide at least a dozen single ones along with the seven-layer dip. *Fabulous!* I jump in the cab, smile beatifically at the cab driver and think, *"I'm not desperate, just hopeful."*

Around 3:00 A.M., I'm in another cab, cursing the inconsiderate bastard who appears to have moved my apartment. "Thancshhh," I say to the cab driver (when I finally find it) and walk sideways up the sidewalk. Alone. Somehow I manage to find the front door. Even more miraculously, I coordinate keys and keyhole so it opens. I head straight for the fridge, search for the highest fat-content food I can find, grab a Coke—not diet (what's the point of being slim, it doesn't get you anywhere), take everything to bed, defiantly attempt to read a book, then give up and cry. What's wrong with me? Why can't I find someone to love? Why is everyone attached? I should never have got rid of Brad. He wasn't that bad. Why am I too fussy? I wonder why I feel sick—I've only eaten one box of Chocolate Scotch Finger cookies. Oh God, my ass will be huge tomorrow. Do I intimidate men? How about that bitch who muscled in on the guy I *know* liked me? Why do I get little lumps on my bikini line after I shave? I wonder why the sky's blue and the grass is green? Should I have fruit salad and bran for breakfast or bacon and eggs? It's around then I fall asleep.

> When you're single, you drive yourself more. You force yourself to go out when you'd really rather chill in front of the television. There's always this fear that if you don't make the effort, you'll have missed the one opportunity you had of meeting Mr. Wonderful.
> Charlotte, 25, student

This is what usually happens to me when I'm in one of those down and depressed single phases and get asked somewhere that sounds full of promise. The reason for revealing straight up how pathetic I can be is twofold. Number one: you, like me, will never meet anyone when you're desperate to meet someone. Number two: before I launch into telling you how fabulous singledom can be, I want to acknowledge that I *know* it's sometimes a very lonely place.

While this chapter is all about *enjoying* being single (and I have to admit it, I'm happy 90 percent of the time when I am), let's be realistic here. Everyone feels down in the dumps sometimes because they're alone. It's *normal.* We've all done our fair share of pillow drenching after a night out where we'd hoped to meet someone special and didn't. And when you've lost your job, your dad's seriously ill, you've fought with your best friend, or just feel blah, being single *sucks.*

But let's look at things from a different perspective. Let's balance it out a little. One thing that never fails to jolt me back to reality when I'm in the midst of the single blues is to recall the *other* pillow-drenching sessions of my life: when I've been in a relationship but was desperately unhappy. That felt just as bad—if not worse. When you're down and single, being part of a couple seems *soooo* appealing. When you're attached and miserable, being single seems *soooo* appealing. There are pluses and minuses to both.

> Smiles, the most recognizable signal of happiness in the world, are so important we can see them far more clearly than any other expression: from the length of a football field.[1]

For instance, there's one thing no one can deny singles have over couples: freedom and variety. While a couple are flopped in front of the TV, their single friends are most likely to be skipping off to Cancún with a group of friends or taking up rock-climbing or discovering some fab new restaurant that does *amazing* things with rock-salted snails, balsamic pesto, and aged snow pea sprouts. You can't blame married friends for being envious when the most excitement they've had is washing out eco-friendly cloth diapers. Being single *is* fun if you let yourself enjoy it.

The happier you are single, the more chance you have of finding the relationship of your dreams. Sounds like a contradiction, doesn't it? But who do you think would be more interesting to go out with? The girl who does nothing much except wait around for a man to fill the big, empty hole that is her life—or the girl who's so busy getting on with her life, she only dates really special guys because she's got far better things to do than hang out with losers? This applies to both sexes, by the way. Energy, enthusiasm, sheer love of life: *that's* what people find attractive. It's got little to do with looks, money, what car you drive, or how big your boobs are. What it *has* got a lot to do with is how much you like yourself. If you look in the mirror and see a nice, attractive person with a lot to offer the world, people will see you that way, too. If you don't like yourself, no one else will.

And there's another reason why moping around won't get you

anywhere: people who think their life will truly start when they find a mate are usually the ones most disappointed by love. Even the best relationship won't get you out of a rut, solve your career problems, or make your relationship with your mother any better. It won't stop the cat from scratching your brand-new sofa, make you lose ten pounds, or suddenly decide lettuce is as delicious as chocolate. The same old problems you've always had will still be there.

And one other good reason not to base your happiness entirely on a relationship: love doesn't come with a guarantee. Saying, "I love you," doesn't mean your partner will love you for life; saying "I do," doesn't mean either of you will later. Children no longer necessarily ensure you're bonded forever, neither does a mortgage taken out in both names or co-owned stock portfolios. It really doesn't matter whether you've pledged lifelong commitment in front of a minister, your mother, or while diving out of a plane hooked up to a parachute and a Buddhist monk. Sometimes, relationships break up. Even a death threat won't stop someone from leaving if they're totally and utterly miserable. Cement boots and a trip to the bottom of the harbor can seem pretty appealing compared to spending the rest of your life with someone who gives you heartburn just from looking at him. No, I'm not a bitter woman, I'm simply telling you the facts for a reason. It's dangerous to base your entire happiness on a relationship with a partner.

Having said that, *sharing* your life with someone you love is a pretty wonderful experience—and there are ways to minimize the chances of it all ending in disaster. Like, knowing what you want. Before you can find Mr. or Ms. Right, you need to know (at least on paper) who that person is. Imagine you're out shopping for something to wear to a party that night. A sales assistant asks, "What did you have in mind?"

"I don't really know," you answer vaguely. "I'm just sort of waiting for something fabulous to grab my eye. I'll know it when I see it."

Five hours later, you're in a complete frenzy because you've got to buy *something* and suddenly that tartan print plastic jumpsuit seems like the best option. So you grab it and the minute you get it home, you think, *What the hell was I thinking?* Shopping and dating aren't dissimilar. Go out looking for a smart but sexy suit and chances are that's what you'll come home with: what you wanted. Go out looking for your perfect match, without a clue as to what or who that might be, and you'll come home with the human equivalent of the tartan jumpsuit. Hideous.

It's simple really: happy singles are people who feel good about themselves, who don't see a relationship as the source of all happiness, and are clear on what they want from one and what kind of person they'd like to have one with. And happy singles are the people who get dates! Here's how to be one.

SERENELY SOLO

Why it's good for you to be single (at least for a while)

I'm deeply suspicious of people who've never, ever been single. You know the type: they wouldn't dream of leaving someone, no matter how bad the relationship is, unless they have a replacement lined up and waiting in the wings. I know people who find this impressive. They say, "Wow! They're so fabulous they never have trouble getting a date." They don't see the fear behind the behavior, just the end result: a person who's *always* got someone hanging off his arm. But what I think is: *If he's always got someone hanging off his arm, he doesn't know how to stand on his own two feet.*

Because if you've never been single as an adult, you've never learned to survive on your own. You need someone to prop you up because you haven't developed the skills to do it yourself. I'm not suggesting you dump whoever you're presently hooked up with (unless you're *only* with that person because you're scared of being alone). But if you suddenly find yourself single—or are single right now— stay that way, at least for a little while. I'm serious. *Deliberately* stay single. Resolve *not* to date anyone seriously for at least six months. I swear, you'll be a different person by the end of it.

Meeting challenges solo, solving your own problems without any back-up, and knowing you don't *need* anyone to look after you, will not only make you stronger and independent, your next relationship will benefit hugely from it. You won't grab the first person who comes along and cling on for dear life because you're no longer scared of being on your own. You won't go out with losers. We attract people like ourselves: so the more confident and self-sufficient you are, the more likely it is your partner will be, too. You'll be together because you *want* to be, not because you *need* to be. Now there's a novel concept!

Love yourself first

Picture this. You're admiring a painting you think you'll buy, when the artist walks over.

"This is just fabulous!," you say.

"Do you really think so?" she replies. "Actually, I really messed it up there in the corner. Look, see where the proportion's all wrong? I never was very good at painting hands and feet. Oh, it's okay I guess, but *way* overpriced. I told the gallery no one would buy it for that amount."

Are you going to respond by slapping a credit card on the counter, shouting, "It's mine!"? No way! You'd walk away thinking, *Thank God I didn't spend next week's rent money.* You're selling a product when you're dating too—yourself. If you don't have high self-esteem and think you've got lots to offer, how the hell are you going to convince someone else?

Think of yourself as an onion (yes, really). The top layers are the tough parts—that's the part you present to the world. All confidence and bravado, nicely packaged in a suit. Keep peeling back those layers until you get to the middle of the onion. This is the part of you that your friends see: slightly softer, a few insecurities and vulnerabilities revealed. Peel off another one or two layers and you get to the intimate you, the part you reserve for your partner: the sexual and loving side. Now keep peeling until you're left with nothing but the onion's tiny core. That's the *real you:* the part of yourself no one ever gets to see, *except you.*

The core of the onion is where all our true feelings and attitudes toward ourselves are kept protected. We don't often get down to this level but we do on serious occasions. Like when we're lying in bed, terrified about giving a speech the next day. *I'll never be able to do this. What if I make a complete fool of myself? Don't they realize I'm a com-*

plete idiot? Did they really fall for all that upfront stuff without noticing I've got nothing to back it up with? If you've got good self-esteem, another little voice will answer, You're just nervous, that's all. If you really were incompetent, do you think you'd have gotten this far? If you don't think much of yourself, those negative thoughts keep racing around unchallenged.

When you're at the core-of-the-onion level, it's impossible to lie to yourself. You can try. Say, "Of course I've got good self-esteem—I'm always the life and soul of the party." But you know the most insecure people in the world are often the loudest, brashest, most opinionated. They cover up their low self-esteem with noise. The more noise they make, the less likely people are to get close to them. If they don't get close, they can't discover the real them, the inner core of the onion which has to be hidden at all costs because they don't really like what's in there. Same goes for people who say things like, "Of course, I like who I am! I'm successful, I drive a BMW, I own my own house." Liking yourself has nothing to do with material possessions.

Confidence will get you everywhere

That girl at the gym has it. You know, the cow who's always at the front of the aerobics class while you're hiding in the back corner. Never mind that you're in size-8 spandex and she's in a size-12 ratty old T-shirt: she looks great—and obviously knows it. My friend Jamie's also got IT. Turn up five minutes late at a cafe and invariably someone's standing there chatting her up. All she does is smile and people are drawn to her like ants to sugar.

So, it's not all about the outside, but since I'm already there, let me say a little bit about looks and that whole lot.

I know I'm okay on the inside, it's the outside that's the problem

So you think only good-looking people get dates. Oh, puhleeze! Of course looks are important. How often have you looked across the room at a party and thought, Gosh! He's sexy!, when the man in question badly needs dental work, has dandruff all over the shoulders of his lime-green T-shirt, a beer gut, and a bowl haircut? Our initial attraction to people is always based on appearance so there's an extremely good argument for making the most of what you've got and aiming to be as attractive as possible. Having said that, you *don't* have to be traditionally good-looking to be reeling 'em in.

An average or below-average looking person who makes the most of her looks, and is confident and comfortable in her own skin and around the opposite sex might not be the *first* person approached at the party, but she's the one you end up talking to all night. And the more you talk to her, the more attractive she becomes. You weren't in the front of the line when God was handing out good looks? Sure, it might have been easier if you had been. But it's behavior, personality, and presentation that really counts.

 ## FOR HER: IF I WAS THIN OR MY BREASTS WERE BIGGER . . .

While no one's denying a body like Pamela Anderson Lee's will have every guy in the room doing a fair impersonation of Linda Blair in *The Exorcist*, most men aren't as picky about body shape as we think they are.

It really doesn't matter what your breast size is or what size jeans you can squeeze your butt into because bodies are another case of "beauty is in the eye of the beholder." Some guys love really small breasts, others like watermelons. Some guys like that starved-and-on-heroin body type, 99.99 percent hate it.

Far more important than your body parts is the person they're attached to, and even *more* important is *your* attitude toward your body.

If you've got little boobs and you like them, he will, too. If you're constantly telling him you wish they were bigger, he'll start to agree with you. It's the same with men and their penises. Being comfortable with what you've got is the key.

> My dad always said, it's all well and good to say, "Accept me for who I am." Just make sure who you are is someone you like.
> Mike, 24, personal trainer

Ditto for how much you weigh. We all have "fat days"—even girls who disappear when they stand sideways. Just make sure you keep it in perspective. The truth is—and it's been proven over and over again—most females' idea of a "perfect body" isn't his.[2] While obesity isn't attractive (or good for your health), a few extra pounds add the curves that men find sexy. They don't think "fat" and "lumpy." They think soft, warm, female, and voluptuous.

Ask any man in love what he thinks of his partner's body and he'll muster up the best possible interpretation of whatever she's got. If she's overweight, she's got beautiful, big breasts. If she's skinny, she's athletic and lean. In fact, as much as they'll never admit it, most guys aren't as superficial as they like to make out. If you make the effort to take good care of yourself and make the most of what you've got, they're usually pretty satisfied. After all, they're not perfect either.

But there's one area where men and women do differ—there's absolutely NO WAY a man would let any insecurities about his body interfere with his sex life. Yet women do.

According to U.K. sexpert Susan Quilliam, 22 percent of women are uncomfortable naked in front of their partners and only one-fifth of the women surveyed said they'd be happy to strip for their partner. Quilliam says (and I echo) that common sense dictates the more at ease we are with our bodies, the more we will enjoy sex.[3] It stands to reason your sex life will suffer if you don't like your body because you're thinking things like: *Will my stomach look flat in this position? I'd better not get on top because my breasts will look funny. Shit—I'm dying to go to the bathroom but I can't because he'll see my fat butt.*

Sex is all about what's happening inside, not outside. If you're desperately trying to suck in your stomach, you're not mentally tuning into being turned on. Which means your vaginal walls don't expand, you don't lubricate, and you've got zero chance of having an orgasm. Good sex is about feeling confident. Feel sexy and you'll be sexy. No one looks good naked all the time during sex because you have to put yourself in some rather unflattering positions if you're going to make the most of it. Feeling good about your body will improve both your relationship and your sex life.

Get over a bad body image by:

- Looking at yourself naked in a full-length mirror regularly. Instead of focusing on your "faults," focus on the parts you do like.

- Write down every compliment someone gives you on your body ("I wish I had breasts like yours," "I wish I had your weight problem—you're skinny compared to me").

- Dress to play up what you perceive to be your assets but don't hide the "faulty" areas. Learn to accept them as part of the parcel.

- If anyone (your mother, best friend, boyfriend) makes negative comments about your body, tell them you're not interested in hearing their opinion. If your boyfriend persists in being nasty, get rid of him—not the supposed extra pounds.

- Throw out the scales and instead judge by how your clothes fit. It stops your weight from dictating what sort of day you'll have.

- Move your focus to other parts of yourself: your mind, your personality, your relationships—better still, your sex life!

Love your life and you'll love being single

In order to experience a state of relationship nirvana, you need to be happy with your life *right now*. Hate your job, loath your apartment, and can't stand your friends? Then *do* something about it! Here are some tips on how.

Surround yourself with happy friends

A friend is someone who makes you feel like a million bucks, who gives you the courage and strength to get out there and conquer the world. Friends don't put you down, make snide comments, tell you you're fat, or make you feel bad about yourself. If you've got "friends" who delight in criticizing you, stop seeing them. They're boosting their egos by stamping on yours. Same goes for the friend who's miserable

365 days of the year. It's hard to stay up and enthusiastic if someone's constantly pointing out the negatives.

Cultivate lots of different friendships with both men and women—and make sure at least some of them are single. Being "the odd one out" once a week is fine. But always? That's a bore. Give priority to functions that include people you don't know and when you meet someone you click with who's also traveling solo, make an effort. Get his phone number. Suggest you go out for coffee and take it from there. The more single friends you have the better.

> A girlfriend of mine drops all her friends the minute she's seeing someone. She cancels everything, holes up with this guy and then when it all falls apart, expects us to include her in everything again without so much as an apology. I look at her and think, *You consider yourself liberated? You're behaving like a 1950s housewife.*
> Rachel, 18, secretary

Find a job you love

Even if you're not particularly ambitious, it makes sense to find a career that excites you (unless you *like* being miserable five out of seven days). You're so underchallenged, you use more brain cells watching *The X-Files* than you do at work? Time to rethink or for a visit to a career counselor. It's impossible to be happy when you're in a job you hate.

Love where you live

Think about it. Why do we pay exorbitant rates to stay in posh hotels? Because you feel fabulous surrounded by all that luxury. It's pretty hard to be cheerful when your apartment's a pigsty, your office looks like a war zone, and your car's a portable trash can. A good spring-cleaning and purging will make you feel much more in control. A coat of paint works wonders: slap some bright yellow over that revolting hospital green and your soul will thank you (not to mention the landlord!).

Accept you'll have down times, too

No one walks around whistling "Singin' in the Rain," day in, day out. Sometimes, you can't help but wallow in misery. Once, I walked out of my apartment to buy some milk and had to turn around and go back home again because I'd forgotten it was a holiday. Holidays can be nightmares for singles because the streets are crammed with arm-in-arm couples licking ice-cream cones and landing kisses on the end of each other's nose. I simply couldn't face it. A permanent blissful state of happiness is unrealistic. But general happiness is attainable. That's what you should aspire to.

Make yourself happy

Don't expect other people to make you happy, do it yourself. Sure, a couple of glasses of wine with a girlfriend can lift your spirits, but basic happiness comes from within. Start a "feel good" folder. Fill it with records of your achievements, cards, or messages from friends saying how wonderful you are and look through it whenever you feel down.

Set goals

Ever felt like you're treading water financially—or worse, sinking deeper and deeper into debt? Money worries are the biggest robbers of happiness, so set yourself a budget and some material goals NOW. Lots of single people say they feel in limbo financially and left behind when they compare their assets to those of married friends. But while two incomes can buy a lot more than one, that doesn't mean you can't build a nice little nestegg on your own.

Think of all the time and energy you devote to a relationship (or trying to get one). Channel that into remodeling a modest house you've just bought and you'll be amazed at what you can accomplish. The days when single people (particularly women) couldn't get mortgages are thankfully over. And buying your own one-bedroom apartment or house isn't accepting defeat, it's smart. If your future partner has done the same, you'll be nicely set up for your future together. If you end up opting to stay single or don't meet that person for the next couple of years, you'll kick yourself for missing out on all that lovely profit.

Don't forget emotional goals and intellectual goals as well. Like resolving to see your friends and family more, enrolling in self-help courses, reading more, taking a class you've always wanted to take.

Make the most of every second

Corny, I know, but true: live every day as though it were your last. If you're as accident-prone as I am, it might be.

Solo and sorry for yourself? Turn around that bad attitude

Pick up an old *People* magazine and flick through the celebrity pages. Yes, there they are. That fabulously in-love couple you envied. He's gazing adoringly at her, she's snuggling in with that smug I'm-in-love-and-you're-not expression all over her face. "If only I had a love like that," you had sighed at the time. And the lifestyle! There they are skiing in Aspen, sipping champagne onboard a yacht, hobnobbing with the hotshots. Remember how depressed they used to make you feel? Funny how you don't envy them now, isn't it? Now they're suing each other over who gets the house in Malibu.

There's a simple point to this sad little tale: not everyone's life is as wonderful as it looks. And bags of money, a cellulite-free rear end, a concave stomach, and a drop-dead gorgeous partner don't necessarily make you happy (even if all that would help). Remind yourself of this the next time you feel yourself sliding into the single blues—or try any or all of the following.

Remember, 90 percent of people end up married

Do you honestly believe you're going to stay single *forever*? Single is usually a temporary state. If a computer program could mathematically prove that you'd be married with kids in two years, you'd be out that door in a millisecond, sprinting to the nearest nightclub. In other words, make the most of being single while you can. I can't *guarantee* this will happen to you in two years, but I'll bet money that you'll be

> Most of the 10 percent of people who aren't married are shacking up together.[4]

fighting someone for the remote control. So get out there and enjoy it while you can!

People don't feel sorry for you, so why should you?

I've got married-with-kids girlfriends who'd cheerfully hand over their first born to trade places with me for one weekend. Eating a leisurely breakfast in a cafe while reading the paper, collapsing on the bed for an afternoon nap after too many mimosas at brunch—I take all this for granted. They don't. Their lives aren't as spontaneous because they have to check in with their partners or take the kids to soccer practice. Feel sorry for you? If your attached friends are honest, they'll admit to envying you 50 percent of the time!

Stop thinking that all couples have perfect relationships

Couples don't all treat each other like royalty or never, ever get bored. Near perfect relationships are rare; they're not as common as colds.

Remind yourself why you're single

Because you *choose* to be. Imagine hooking up with someone, out of desperation, and how dreadful your life would be. A bad relationship would make things worse, not better.

Make the most of your friends

Got some great news and feel down because there's no "special some-one" to celebrate with? Call your best friend, grab a bottle of bubbly (actually, make that two), and get over there to spread the news. A good friend loves you just as much as a partner would (if not more!).

Ask your happily attached friends to tell you all the bad things about being a couple

Like her hogging the bathroom, him forgetting their anniversary, her mind-bogglingly revolting habit of picking her toenails while they're watching TV, his tendency to shove snotty tissues down the side of the sofa, and all those other charming I-swear-if-they-do-it-one-more-time-I'll-leave things couples do to annoy the hell out of each other.

(Be a little bit careful with this one. You might be envious but you don't want to split them up, do you?)

Turn the tape off

No, not the CD player, the one that's whirling around in your head saying, "Life would be so much better if I had someone to share it with." The next time someone says the same to you—"Why do I feel so empty when I've got a great job, lots of friends, and a terrific apartment?"—ignore the insinuation ("All this is great—but it would be better if I could share it with someone") and say instead, "I have no idea! Why do you feel empty when your life is pretty wonderful?"

TEN GREAT THINGS ABOUT BEING ON YOUR OWN

For him

1. You don't have to answer to *anyone*.
2. No one rolls their eyes when the remote accidentally sticks on the sports channel.
3. You can clip your toenails without someone vomiting in the background.
4. *Playboy* gets pride of place on the coffee table—and no one lectures you about how much porn degrades women.
5. You can wear your old football jersey and criticize the hell out of the players without someone saying, "You're kidding yourself. With that beer gut you'd be lucky to even catch the ball, so don't give him a hard time!"
6. You don't have to tell her she doesn't look fat/her butt's not big/more than a handful's a waste.
7. You can masturbate in the middle of the living room without fear of her walking in and saying, "Ohmigod! This must mean you don't want to have sex with *me*."
8. You can put ketchup on *everything* without "tut-tut's" and "Honestly, Harry, you're such a pig!"
9. No one tells you you're driving too fast.
10. You don't have to be nice to her stuck-up, snotty friends.

TEN GREAT THINGS ABOUT BEING ON YOUR OWN

For her

1. You don't have to answer to *anyone*.
2. You can walk in the door after a *horrible* day's work, throw your clothes in a pile, flop down in front of the TV in a disgusting, food-splattered nightgown, and eat junk while watching trash—without anyone surfing the channels just when the show's at the good part.
3. Fat days seem less important. So long as your stomach's flat by Friday night, who cares if you're bloated on Tuesday?
4. You can talk on the phone all night about absolutely nothing and lie outrageously about how wonderful Susan looked in her new outfit without someone saying afterward, "But you told me she looked like a fat cow."
5. You can change your mind every five minutes, just for the hell of it.
6. You can masturbate to fantasies of the gorgeous construction workers you passed on the way to the office, without feeling guilty.
7. Everything smells clean and fresh. There are no lingering boy smells (the obvious mixed with grungy socks, all vainly disguised with bad aftershave).
8. You can make your own smells—without feeling "unladylike."
9. You don't have to explain why it's essential to own 25 pairs of black shoes.
10. You can get drunk and cry over your hated-when-sober ex— without feeling totally silly the next day.

Indulge yourself

Drinking a frothy, yummy, fat-packed hot chocolate, reading a book in bed when it's raining outside, renting your favorite movie for the sixth time. Life's simpler pleasures are often the best. You don't need someone else to indulge you—do it yourself!

Smile so much your face hurts

If you like and respect yourself, it shows. Bound out the door happy, smile at everyone you pass and you'll notice a rather pleasant domino effect: you make them happy, they make you even happier by smiling back. Look for the best in people and you'll find it. Love life and it'll love you back. Believe all men are bastards, the system rips you off, and everything worth having is out of your budget and it will seem true. Of course there are times when being single is truly horrible, but when everything's cruising along nicely, it's criminal not to be happy just because you're not attached. Single isn't a life-threatening disease, you know!

> **Mr. Right is #13—or so say researchers. They claim once you've experienced 12 relationships, you'll know what you want and who's best suited to give it to you. With number 13, you'll finally get it right![5]**

WHAT DO YOU WANT FROM A RELATIONSHIP?

It's quite simple: you have to know what you want in order to get it. Most of us *think* we know what we're looking for, but few have actually made the effort to reduce those fairy tale ideas to specific needs and wants. The fact is, you've got a much better chance of finding someone who'll make you happy if you're crystal clear about what you're looking for. This is what this section aims to do:

- **Sort out what's really important from what's not.** In other words, what you really need to make you happy rather than what you *think* will make you happy.

- **Pinpoint the differences between what you wish for and what you could live without.** You need to know what to compromise on (external things like looks) and what you shouldn't budge on (values like trust and honesty).

- **Discover whether your wish list is realistic** or destined to keep you single for life.

Give it a try—you can't help but benefit from it!

The relationship wish list

It stands to reason that you've got to know what you want from a relationship before you can decide on the type of person who'll give it to you. Some things are pretty universal—like love, companionship, someone to look after you when you're sick—but there are drastic variations in other areas. For me, a relationship is important but it's got to fit in *around* my career or I wouldn't be happy. My friend Simon wants the opposite: total and utter devotion—the classic molded-to-each-other's-side partnership. The question is: what do *you* want from a partner long term?

How to do it

Divide a blank piece of paper in two before you start: write "wish for" on one side and "must have" on the other. You're going to write down what you'd like and what you insist on, in the relevant columns.

The questions

1. How long do I want it to last? Do you honestly believe you can meet someone at 20 and be sitting side by side in rocking chairs at 90? Or do you think ten years is pretty good? Perhaps you'd actually like two or three semiserious relationships before settling down for life.

2. What's your idea of commitment? Do you want to get married or would you be happy living together? What about when you have children—how would that alter it? Does it matter if your partner has been married before?

3. Do you want children? Are they essential to your happiness or are you a little ambivalent? What if they've got children from a previous marriage?

4. Do you want to be joined at the hip or independent? Do you want the sort of relationship where you do *everything* together or are you a bit of a free spirit and need an occasional separate holiday and lots of time alone?

5. Do you want a monogamous relationship? Ninety percent of us automatically tick "yes" but some of you might opt for, "What I don't know won't hurt me—so long as it's not flaunted in my face."

6. What level of intimacy are you looking for? A completely open, share-everything sort of relationship or are you happier cruising along at surface level?

7. How important is sex to you? A crucial ingredient in a good relationship or a bonus if it turns out to be good?

> When I was 18, I remember thinking, *Now I know who I am.* When I was 26, I thought, *I didn't know anything back then—now I know who I am.* At 42, I realize I'll never really know because I change constantly, depending on what's happening in my life.
> Craig, 42, lawyer

8. How secure do you need to be? Is being able to trust someone important to you (if it isn't, it should be!)? What about honesty? Do you believe in laying everything on the table or are there some things you think you shouldn't be *too* honest about?

9. How much support do you want from your partner? Do you need to know he is totally, 100 percent behind you?

10. Do you want your partner to be your best friend? Most of us would answer "yes," but some people don't mind if their partner doesn't share their life's passions. They're happy to satisfy those needs with friends.

The partner wish list

I have a type. Just picturing him makes my toes curl in anticipated bliss. He's tall, gloriously muscled. He's got olive skin and a permanent three-day growth. Chiseled cheekbones. Long, lean legs. Dark hair, cut short. He's successful but not ruthlessly ambitious. Generous but not clingy. Sensitive but manly. He doesn't exist.

I've been out with parts of him: I got the muscles, height, olive skin, and chiseled cheekbones all in one parcel. But that guy wasn't terribly intelligent or sensitive (thick as a cinder block and a complete prick, actually). I've also been out with manly (substitute semi-evolved) and generous (with his money but not his affection) men. Which probably explains why the men I've actually fallen for in real life have absolutely nothing in common with my fantasy man. The first step to finding your perfect partner? Accept that he or she isn't out there.

It's actually far more sensible to choose a mate the same way you choose your friends. Like, even if she does look so delicious you'd give up *ER* for her, you've really got to talk sometimes (though there are exceptions—see "Fancy a fling," page 67). All that stuff your mother harped about—common interests, similar backgrounds, age, and intelligence levels—they are important. But lovers need something extra that friendships don't—chemistry. Your lover has to do "it" for you. Anyway, enough of me telling you what's important. The point of this exercise is to work out *your* individual needs and wants.

For this exercise, I want you to write down all the things you want from a partner under the following headings: "wish for" and "must have." In other words, what you'd like and what you won't compromise on. Be as specific as possible and do it over a few days, not all in one sitting.

The questions

Physical: Stop right now! Forget the blond hair and stomach of steel, instead, concentrate on physical lifestyle habits. For instance, if you're a gym junkie and think of exercise as a pleasure, you're probably not going to find joy with a slobby couch potato. So you might write down "must exercise regularly and enjoy sports." Are you an avid anti-smoker? "Nonsmoker" is a perfectly acceptable thing to ask for. What about your alcohol consumption? Are you the type who enjoys sitting around chatting over more than a few beers? Someone who's a teetotaler would drive you nuts. If going out to dinner is your absolute favorite activity, a fellow gourmet would work well (probably make you fat, but hey!).

Example: *Nonsmoker. Likes exercise. Enjoys an occasional glass of wine. Vegetarian.*

Chemistry: Automatically write "must lust after me" under the "must have" side. There's only one stipulation: I want you to allot a time period. If the chemistry's not there immediately, how long are you prepared to wait and see. Two dates? Three weeks? Six months?

Example: *Prepared to give it two months for chemistry to develop* or *Must be instant or it'll never work for me.*

Relationship attitudes and skills: If you're a sentimental, sappy person who cries during the AT&T ads and thinks they should bottle puppy breath because it smells so divine, your ideal match isn't the person who didn't bother going to his mother's funeral and thinks nothing of flushing kittens down the toilet. So think about what your attitude to the word "relationship" is: romantic, realistic, pragmatic, cynical? Ideally, your partner should share the same views. Is marriage the logical (and highly desired) climax of a long-term relationship—or is it a worthless piece of paper?

Think about your potential partner's relationship skills. Do you want someone who's easily able—and willing—to wax lyrical about how much they love you? Who shares feelings openly and intimately? How much relationship experience do you require? Personally, I'd expect any man I dated to have had at least three or four serious relationships under his belt. That means he's had plenty of experience developing the relationship skills you need to make something work.

Example: *Romantic, gives relationships highest priority, wants to marry eventually.*

Social: What sort of person do they need to be to fit into your life? If you're a social butterfly and constantly entertaining, it helps if they enjoy it, too—and are good at making small talk. Is it essential that they're able to chat it up with the best of them so you can take them to work functions?

Example: *Outgoing, socially skilled—can get along with anyone.*

Intellectual: What level of education did you complete? Are you an academic or more street smart? What are your other achievements? For a blissful blending of brains, it helps if they're on the same level as you. How important is it to you to be able to talk on the same level?

Example: *University educated, creative, able to think outside the square.*

Sex: Do me a *huge* favor: decide what level your libido's on and *please* at least try to match up with someone on the same level. A high-libido/low-libido couple truly is a recipe for disaster. One of you is always left feeling unsatisfied; the other's constantly feeling pressured. There are things you can do to even the score but if you can avoid it, do. It also helps if you share the same attitudes toward sex. The adventurous, try-anything-once types should stick together. Ditto the "I'd really rather stay missionary" people. The icing on the cake would be to match in experience and skill as well.

Example: *High libido, adventurous, uninhibited, experienced.*

Communication skills: Are you a talker or a listener? Do you want someone who'll babble on as much as you do or would a listener suit you more? Someone who's easy to talk to—and who finds it easy to talk back—is crucial for most of us. But remember, communication skills can be learned. If they're shy, there's plenty you can do to help them open up.

Example: *A good communicator, likes having a chat, a good listener.*

Finances: It's not the amount someone earns that's important, but more a person's attitude toward money. Are you a spender or a saver? How important are material possessions to you? If your idea of an essential expense is a daily massage and theirs is generic cereal and milk, saving for that house down payment is going to be one argument after another. The same applies if you've built up a nice little bank balance and they've frittered their money away. A hell of a lot of resentment comes from unbalanced finances.

Example: *A saver, appreciates luxuries but doesn't waste money.*

Career: Again, it's not important what profession they're in but more your attitudes toward work. If you work simply to live, someone who lives and breathes their job will bore you senseless. If you give 200 percent to your career, you'll be more compatible with someone who's also ambitious.

Example: *Career-oriented, ambitious, supportive of my career.*

Aspirations: Make sure you're both treading the same path at the same pace. If you're a stroll rather than race person, someone whose energy level's on go-go-go won't suit you. If you're constantly trying to improve yourself, your ideal partner is someone who's equally as aspirational.

Example: *Lives life in the fast lane, aims high.*

Interests and hobbies: You're not going to be joined at the hip so it doesn't really matter if they're into squash and you prefer basketball. But a stamp collector and a rock climber? The sort of hobbies and interests you have usually reflect your general personality. And it would be nice to do some things together that both of you enjoy, wouldn't it?

Example: *Loves reading, into outdoor activities, likes sports.*

Religion: If you're not at all religious, it's probably not important to you what religion your partner is. Unless of course, they're very religious and it's important to *them*. If you're devout though, it's sensible to look for someone who shares your beliefs. One word of warning however: check that it's important to *you,* not your parents before

Ever noticed that beautiful people with ugly personalities seem to become less and less attractive with time? That's because they do. Research confirms cold, aloof people become less pleasing to the eye while friendliness makes us see people as more attractive than they really are.[6]

you write this one down. This is all about who *you* want, not who other people want you to be with.

Getting rid of the silly stuff

The moment of truth! Now's the time to go through your relationship and partner lists and check that they're realistic and achievable.

Check that the two lists match up

Look at your relationship list and compare it to the partner list. Can the sort of person you're describing fulfill the needs on the relationship list? Go through it painstakingly—if the two lists are asking for two different things, you'll never be satisfied.

Is it the right kind of wish list?

If you've got money, fancy cars, a man who's rich enough to take you to the right restaurants on the "must have" side, transfer them to the "wish for." Better still, cross them off completely. The ideal list doesn't have any qualities that don't relate to values or behavior. External things like looks and money aren't important; things like honesty, faithfulness, and kindness are. Make it a shopping list of values instead.

Check that everything you've asked for, you can give in return

Your partner's got to be witty, creative, intellectual, and a fab entertainer? Good luck finding them if you've got none of these qualities. You have no right demanding things you can't deliver yourself. Ideally, your wish list should be pretty close to a list of your own good qualities. The more like you the persons you want to attract are, the more likely you are to attract them.

How flexible is it?

If the "must have" side's got an enormous amount written on it and the "wish for" side hardly any, go through again and even them up a little. "Near-enough" might be as close to ideal as you're going to get.

Check the physical heading

Cross off anything that relates to appearance. It's pointless writing things like "must have long legs" because most of the time the person we fall for is packaged differently than we expected. My friend Cathy *despised* redheads. If she'd done this exercise, it would have been the first thing she'd listed—"must not have red hair." A year ago, she introduced me to the man who had "everything I've been searching for" and he had bright orange hair. "He's a redhead! You hate redheads," I told her in the ladies' room. "He's got red hair? I'd never noticed," she said. True love, mother nature, the X-factor, chemistry—call it what you like but it has a astonishing knack of completely ignoring the more ridiculous things on our list. Try to fight primitive instincts like these at your own peril!

How long are your lists?

Now cut back to ten points on each side on each list. Yes, you must.

Is it realistic?

Look at the sort of person you've described by looking through *all* your wants and wish-fors. Check you haven't fallen into the impossible-to-find-in-one-person trap. (Macho but likes cooking/A nice girl who likes taking party drugs.)

How to use your lists

These lists are for long-term partnerships, not when you're happily out there dating for the sheer fun of it. Keep them. Update them as you change. Look at them whenever you meet someone new. Check the lists again three dates into something and three months in. How close is this person to what you really want? Are they lacking in the wish-for department or the must-have department? Are there things you're

❚ Can't decide if he's right for you or not? Trust your female intuition. Scientists now say women who rely on gut instinct make much better decisions than people who rely on rationality and cold facts.[7]

now willing to forgo because they've got positives you hadn't listed? Or is this person way off target and you're kidding yourself? It doesn't matter if they're not a good equestrian and you are. Small things like that don't affect the base of the relationship. But if they're a womanizer and you want security and honesty, you're heading for guaranteed heartache.

> **Evidence shows we pair up with people who are roughly the same level of physical attractiveness as ourselves. We also look for partners who are similar in age, intelligence, interests, education, and social background.[8]**

YOU'RE READY FOR A RELATIONSHIP WHEN . . .

You're ready for a relationship when you're able to stand on your own two feet. Needing someone means you can't survive on your own. Wanting someone means you can, you're just looking to enrich your life further.

See how you score on the following. Answer "yes" to at least 13 of the following and you're officially approved to move onto the next chapter!

1. You're getting on with your own life. It would be nice if you met someone but in the meantime, it's not stopping you from moving forward.
2. You've got lots of friends—both male and female.
3. You're happy at work (or at least making plans to get to the point where you will be).
4. You've accepted responsibility for your own happiness.
5. You've set financial, emotional, and intellectual goals.
6. You're pretty happy with who you are.
7. Your self-esteem's in good shape.
8. You're not afraid to take risks, make decisions—and live with the consequences.
9. You're well and truly over your exes. You've left all the emotional baggage behind.
10. You feel in charge of your life.

11. You listen to the advice others give you, but ultimately make up your own mind.
12. You've discovered lots of positive things about being single.
13. You aren't in any great hurry to find Mr. or Ms. Right. A relationship isn't the goal of your life but an added bonus.
14. You don't just want a partner, you want the *right* partner for the *real* you.
15. You don't just want them to love you, you want them to love you for who you really are.
16. You're confident enough to be yourself. If being you doesn't appeal to someone, you're intelligent enough to know it wouldn't have worked anyway.

> This is the first time I've been single for any period of time. At first, it took a bit of getting used to and I was desperate to meet someone but I'm just starting to enjoy it. I met a really nice guy the other night and it was like, "Oh no! I hope I don't like you because I don't want to give up all this freedom just yet."
> Lynda, 34, journalist

2

Finding Mr. or Ms. Right-for-You

Likely hang-outs, how to spot a loser, plus tips on flirting, flings, and getting through the first few dates

• •

Finding a partner isn't easy for most people. But some go out for a loaf of bread and come back with flowers and six phone numbers. One of my best friends found love at a phone booth. She sauntered down the street to make a call, leaving her no-good boyfriend at home. The relationship was all but over—he was sick, she was bored, and their phone was out of order.

There was a guy at the phone booth, all dressed-up. He took one look at my friend, threw open the door with a flourish, and dramatically bowed in front of her. "Come live with me and be my love," he said, quoting John Donne, the sixteenth-century poet.

"And we will some new pleasures prove," she replied, delivering the next line.

They both laughed. "Want to come to a party?" he asked.

Why not? she thought. *I'll only be gone a few hours.* It turned out to be a little longer than that. She didn't go home at all. Like, never. Ended up living with the guy for close to a year.

If anyone else had told me that story, I'd be skeptical. Knowing her, it seemed perfectly plausible. She's one of those women who's got "it." Lucky her. And lucky *you* because, while some people seem to be born knowing how to attract the opposite sex, it is a skill you can learn.

Standing out from the crowd, sending out the right signals, flirting, and finding someone who'll make you happy—there's an art to "it." "It" has got a lot to do with good judgment: knowing the right thing to say and when to say it. Knowing who to steer clear of and who deserves a second try. That's what this chapter's all about: how to flirt your way into the arms and heart of someone amazingly special.

So how will *you* know when you've met *the one*? The sky will rumble and an angel will fall from heaven in front of you and say, "You have chosen wisely." Oh, and a lightning bolt will strike you on the head. *Not.* "I knew the minute I met him." "I felt suddenly complete." Excuse me while I vomit. I'm sorry, but there's nothing magical about it at all.

Funny how people always meet their "soulmate" when they're ready to settle down, isn't it? Funny how they never meet them when they're barging out the door, suitcase packed and ready to hit Club Med for a whoop-it-up bonkarama holiday. Timing is everything.

We all chatter on about finding our soulmate—but what *is* a soulmate exactly? I think it's someone who brings out the best in us, who we click with. Someone who has the same goals and wants the same things out of life as we do. In other words, "soulmate" is simply a romantic way of describing the person who's *the right choice for you right now.*

Sorry to dash those illusions but there're actually quite a few "soulmates" out there for everyone. (And so there should be. What if we all only got one shot and yours was locked away chanting in a Buddhist monastery?) But to find even one of them, you have to be open to finding him. For all you know, your soulmate sits right in front of you on the bus every day but *you've* never noticed because you've had so *many* Mr. and Ms. Wrongs you're worn out and more than happy coming home to your cat.

My point here is this: if you're still waiting around for that lightning bolt, you've been watching too much TV. Throw out that sappy romance novel because you probably *won't* know instantly when you've met "the one." But you will have a pretty good idea a few months in. Just as important as finding your soulmate is recognizing when you haven't. There are lots of warnings in the first section of this chapter designed to get your bitch/bastard radar turned on. Once that light's blinking furiously, it's safe to move on to the fun part. And have fun you will . . .

LOVE AT FIRST SIGHT

It happens in 5 percent of all relationships[1] and researchers say even that's usually more a case of wishful hindsight than anything else.[2] Women who fall in love instantly tend to fall out of love just as quickly. Men who fall in love instantly stay in love for longer. Why? Because men, bless their little hearts, fall instantly in love with what women look like.[3] Since physical characteristics don't usually change rapidly, he's happy for a while. Being more cerebral creatures, women fall in love with what they think a guy will be like—which is impossible to gauge within five minutes. When we discover he's not as intelligent/funny/charming as he looks, the feeling evaporates rather quickly.

Love at first sight can happen because you're open to it (the timing's right) or you meet someone who on surface level appears to have the main qualities on your partner wish list. Some experts think it's simply our subconscious choosing someone who reminds us of someone else we've loved dearly (an ex or even good old mom or dad). You feel a sense of recognition because a smell, a memory, or a gesture matches one you already know and love.

The brain is very sophisticated when it comes to recognizing familiar elements like the shape of a cheek or an elusive scent. When it spots one, it starts processing this information immediately, triggering a biological response in the body.[4] Your heart rate increases, blood pumps faster, and you feel like you've just downed six glasses of champagne. This also causes the brain to release dopamine and serotonin which make us feel happy and emotional.

Horrible thought, isn't it? You think you've met Mr. or Ms. Perfect when, in reality, you've fallen for your father's cheekbone.

CHOOSING WISELY: PICK A PARTNER WITH YOUR HEART *AND HEAD*

No one likes getting hurt, and one way to protect your heart is to be careful who you give it to. I'm all for giving in to chemistry, but don't turn off your brain while you're at it. I don't care how strong the attraction is, if the person you're feeling it for is looking at you through bars, forget it. On those first few dates, be sensible, look for warning signs and get out early if you see them. Watch yourself as well—we're all cheery little optimists at heart and *want* to think we've found true love.

> I rush to the phone each time it rings, hoping it will be her. I walk around smiling at everyone. I look at flowers growing and can't stop thinking about her. I now make tentative arrangements with the boys to leave myself open if she's available. If she dumps me now, I'm going to be devastated.
>
> Phillip, 31, technician

Spot the loser

People often say to me, "I always end up dating losers. But how can you tell in the beginning? Everyone looks good at the start." They're wrong. Most losers give themselves away within three dates. People look good early on because you *want* them to.

Meeting someone when you've been single for a while is a buzz. Regular sex is blissful and you don't have to stress about what you're doing on the weekend because, when you're a couple, well, you can do *nothing* and still have fun and not get lonely. It's so easy to get carried away with the great feeling of having a relationship, people forget to take a good look at the person they're having the relationship with.

Next time, pay attention. Most of the time, the signs that someone's a total loser are right there in front of you, you're just not noticing them. It's great to be optimistic, but you're wiser to take off the rose-colored Ray-Bans and pick up a magnifying glass in the beginning. *Don't see what you want to see, see what's really there.* And don't be gullible.

For starters, you're asking for trouble if you date people who are unavailable. Just for the record, unavailable includes: married people and people who are already involved with someone else (living together, dating someone, or sleeping with the same person once a week). Also unavailable are people who are getting over someone else or about to get involved with someone else. In other words, anyone who has *any* type of romantic involvement with another person.

These are some of the excuses unavailables will give you to make themselves appear available (translation—so they can have you on the side): "I'm going to leave soon"; "I don't really love her but I feel awful about hurting her"; "I'm just staying until the kids reach 15"; "It's an open relationship"; "I'm not *really* with him because it's very casual"; "It's definitely over but I haven't found somewhere else to live."

Lies! All lies! And even if they're not, wait until they've *done* whatever it is they're promising *before* you get involved with them. That's your first step to spotting a loser: check their availability.

We did partner and relationship lists in Chapter 1 so you'll have a good idea of what sort of person suits you. Now we're going a little deeper into character.

Barbara De Angelis, a major relationship guru, believes character is all important. Personality is the icing on the cake, she says, character is the cake itself. Don't ask yourself, "Do I love this person and will they love me?", says Barbara. Ask, "Are they *capable* of loving me the way I want to be loved?"[5]

It's a very high-brow, intellectual way of looking at love, but it's a damn good way of avoiding heartache. When you next meet someone, ask yourself that question. If you're constantly getting hurt, reduce the risk by putting things down on paper. Score a new date on the following *before* getting in too deep, so you're aware of what you're taking on. No one's perfect and we all have our foibles, but while some troubled souls are worth saving, others are just trouble.

How "in touch" with themselves are they?

Are they aware of their character and personality faults? Do they know their strengths? They don't have to be wearing an "I walked across hot coals with Anthony Robbins" T-shirt to have done a bit of personal soul-searching. Have they sorted out the emotional baggage from childhood and past relationships or are they dragging it along behind them?

Are they affectionate and able to express their feelings?

In *Men Are from Mars, Women Are from Venus* John Gray is all for letting men go into their caves and respecting the right for people to remain silent.[6] I say, if someone behaves like a caveman, let them be eaten by wild animals. The person who knows what he's feeling and shares those feelings with you is going to be a lot easier to share a bathroom with than the person who locks himself in it.

Want to find out if he's the faithful type? Take a long, hard look at his genitals. Scientists claim men with larger than average testicles and wide penises are the most likely to cheat. A case of if you've got it, flaunt it?[7]

Are they honest? Are they a "good" person?

Can you count on them to do the right thing by you *and* others? Do they treat their friends and family well? Do the right thing in business? Whatever your partner does to other people, he's more than capable of doing to you. That's why on-the-side people get really paranoid when their married lovers finally leave their spouses to be with them. They think, *They did it to them, what's to stop them from doing it to me?* (Nothing.)

Are they an adult?

A girlfriend of mine is 28 and acts 16. She's a scream as a friend but God help the guy who has a relationship with her. Does this person know how to cook, clean, look after themselves, pay bills on time, and manage their money? Are they mature enough to know they can't afford a Lamborghini when they're barely covering the rent? Are they responsible?

Do they love themselves?

The more they like who they are, the healthier your relationship will be. The more hang-ups they have, the more you'll be used as their therapist. Needy, clingy, scared-little-mice people suck all your energy and confidence until you feel like a balled-up, soggy towel.

Are they positive and happy most of the time?

Do they look for problems or solutions? Are they a doer or a procrastinator? I once went out with a guy who was constantly depressed because of all the starving children in Bosnia. He thought he was holier-than-thou because they were never far from his mind. I thought he was a hypocritical son of a bitch. His fretting didn't help one iota— but a big fat check from his very healthy bank account might have.

Little white lies and big, bad black ones

We've all done it. Reinvented ourselves a little (well, a lot) when we first meet someone. In nightclubs, I've been a ski instructor, taxidermist, midwife, vet, restaurant reviewer, and Freudian psychotherapist with Jungian leanings (that one stumped them). The temptation to paint a vividly fascinating picture on a blank canvas is just too tempting sometimes. Why do we do it? Aside from being a good laugh, we think it makes us more intriguing. Let's be honest here: which guy would you be most attracted to? A nine-to-five bank teller or a private detective who's currently trailing a well-known personality for an incredibly sordid reason but, unfortunately, they can't tell you what it is.

Most of the time (300 drinks later) we shoot ourselves in the foot anyway ("You don't know where Aspen is? But I thought you were a ski instructor?"). If we don't slip up most of us 'fess up when we find someone we really like.

Then we swap that set of lies for another. Roughly one-third of what we say to each other on the first three dates is either a straight-out lie or heavily exaggerated, especially if it concerns past lovers or recent indiscretions.[8] According to psychologists, the average person lies at least once or twice a day, but dating couples are the biggest fibbers of all.[9]

We all roll out the "I want you to like me because I like you" lies in the beginning. "Your apartment is charming!" we squeal, when it's really a dump. Those sorts of lies are pretty harmless and, most of the time, meant with the best intentions (protecting people's feelings while simultaneously painting ourselves in the best possible light).

Men lie for one basic reason: they want to sleep with you but not necessarily have breakfast with you (ever). Women lie for more complex reasons. Sometimes, it's for the same reason—we want no-strings sex. Other times, it's because we not only want to have breakfast, but dinner, and another breakfast and another dinner as well—but we don't want you to know that yet. But more often, it's because we're not really *sure* if we want to screw you *or* have breakfast *or* marry you and have your children, and until we've decided, we'll play it safe and paint a Ms. Pure-and-Perfect picture just in case.

Of course, not everyone just lies about little, inconsequential things, like the car they drive. Some people tell fibs about things that do matter—like the fact that they're married. So while some lies should be mentally filed for a good ribbing later on ("My last girlfriend was a model"), others are downright dangerous. Learn how to spot the difference.

> I used to have a thing going with my friends where we'd rate each woman by her CPI—cost per insertion—how much money you had to spend on her before she'd put out. The average was two dinners and one bunch of flowers.
> Simon, 34, nightclub owner

Harmless female fibs

- "Of course you're the best lover I've ever had."

- "I don't lust after your friend Tony at all."

- "Oh my God, that's the biggest I've ever seen."

- "I've got my period."

- "You're the third guy I've ever slept with."

- "This old thing? I've had it for years."
- "I used to drive a Porsche."
- "You're an hour late? I hadn't noticed."
- "I hate expensive restaurants. I much prefer places like this."
- "Flowers are totally overrated."
- "I think your clothes are great."
- "Your tummy's not fat, it's cute."

And the not-so-harmless: pay attention when—

- she says to call her at work—she's got a full-time boyfriend or is living with someone.
- she says she's too busy for a relationship—she doesn't want one with you.
- she says she just wants to be friends—she likes you but doesn't lust after you or you're already a friend and she doesn't want to lose the friendship.
- she says her husband doesn't appreciate her—she's the equivalent of the guy whose wife doesn't understand him.
- she says she wants to leave him but can't afford it—she's looking for a meal ticket.

Harmless male fibs

- "I love you [I want to sleep with you]."
- "I'll call you."
- "I've been looking for someone like you my whole life."
- "If you could only see how beautiful you look right now."
- "I really want to settle down."

- "If only it were summer we could walk hand-in-hand along the beach."

- "Your roommate's kind of cute." (If I hadn't met you, I'd want to have sex with her till I am blue.)

- "Isn't that funny? I hadn't noticed how good-looking my roommate Jane was until you pointed it out." (She turned me down.)

- "My car's in for repairs. A friend loaned me this old thing."

> Once you've had your heart broken a few times, you're much more careful. I tend to break up with men pretty early unless I can see a life-long future together. I don't want all that pain again.
> Nikki, 22, sales rep

And the not-so-harmless: pay attention when—

- he says you're too good for him—you are.

- he says he needs space—he doesn't want to go out with you.

- he says he doesn't want a relationship—he doesn't.

- he says his wife doesn't understand him—he's not just a sleaze but totally unoriginal.

- he says he's about to leave her—why would he when he can have you on the side?

- there's a pale band of skin on his left finger—he's married.

- he won't give you his phone number—he's married.

THE MEET MARKET: WHERE TO FIND MR. OR MS. PERFECT-FOR-YOU

You see him. You want him. You get him. It's a simple equation that somehow doesn't always add up in the real world. For a start, most of us get stuck on the first part—actually meeting someone we'd like to go out with.

Someone once said to me, "If you're not meeting the right person, you're mixing in the wrong social scene." There's a grain of truth in that. After all, if you're looking for a conservative academic with family values you probably won't find her snorting coke at the back of a seedy nightclub. But you might well bump into her outside because, truly, you can meet someone anywhere at anytime. Not just on the nights when you "go out."

"Where are all the single men?" women wail.

"Where are all the single women?" men moan.

Now, unless all singles are agoraphobics and refuse to budge from their own living rooms, it's obvious you're crossing paths at least some of the time. Nightclubs and bars aren't the only places singles hang out. Why not try . . .

Parties

When you're feeling fab and looking terrific, meeting people at parties is a cinch. Not so when you're frumpy, frazzled, or the competition is hot. But it's worth making an effort because parties force people to spend at least a few hours in one place out of sheer politeness. So you've got time to sit back and study your target, watch who they're talking to and for how long.

He's being chatted up by a girl with legs as long as a giraffe or she's being monopolized by a guy who's so bloody good-looking he must be gay? They could be brain-dead boring for all you know. (You, on the other hand, have personality and tons of style.) So find whoever organized the party and do some sleuthing. Single or attached? Nice person or steer-clear material? Find something you both have in common, then get them to introduce you.

"X, you must meet Sarah/Simon. They're as addicted to the movies as you are."

The host/ess is cornering someone they've just met? Find an excuse to do something near your target—change the CD, grab some hors d'oeuvres, or enlist a friend's help and just go and stand over there. Next, simply catch their eye and smile a few times. If they seem friendly, close the gap and introduce yourself. Once there, flirt like mad, completely monopolize them, and don't even think about going to the bathroom if the competition is hovering like vultures. (If you must, offer to get them a drink so you can come back to claim them.)

Nightclubs

In all the years I've been single, I estimate I've been to at least 50 different nightclubs around ten times each. Out of those 500 attendances, I've spoken to and flirted with hundreds of men. But you know what? I've only ever had a relationship with one that lasted past two dates.

"You're kidding!" said my girlfriends, when I revealed this astonishing fact. *Silence.* "But dead right—I've never ended up having a relationship with someone I've met in a club either."

The stats back me up on this one: less than 4 percent of people who meet in a nightclub, on holiday, or through the personals end up marrying.[10] Subtract the other two and it evens out to one out of one hundred.

But there are clubs and *nightclubs.* I'm talking the dimly lit, music blaring, dance floor, can't-talk-unless-you-shout type. Clubs with cosy little bars off to one side and fabulous outdoor drinking areas are a little different. For a start, you can actually see each other—and you can talk without all the veins in your neck popping out (most unattractive). So unless it's casual sex you're after, avoid the dark spots. Like your mother said, stick to the well-lit areas if you want to play it safe.

Pubs and bars (minus the dance floor)

Now we're talking—especially if it's a pub. The combination of a packed crowd, plenty of chances to take the long way around, and accidentally rub your way through the best-looking group in the place, a few beers to take the edge off, not too noisy so you can talk but noisy enough where silences don't seem uncomfortable . . . The only thing that could possibly make it better is a pool table. Personally, I would rather eat 12 hot chilies than pick up a pool cue, but I have to admire people who work the table: the old "lean forward to show off the cleavage" if you're a girl; the "push the cue really hard with your shirt sleeves pushed up so your biceps flex" if you're a guy. We know what you're playing at, fellas (and it isn't pool), but the floor-show works anyway!

The friend-of-a-friend

This is how most people meet the love of their life—they're introduced through a third party (most often your family or a friend). A cinch when it's someone you know well—not so easy when you've seen them over at your neighbors or at a distance at a sort-of-friend's party but never got to meet. You're too shy to ask them to set you up but if you don't act soon, you fear they'll be snapped up by someone else. Take a deep breath! There's nothing desperate about calling your friend or neighbor and saying, "X looked cute. Is he single? What is he like?" A gracious friend will immediately offer to set you up (assuming he's worth being set up with!). If they don't suggest it, you do—and remind them often until they're so sick of you hassling them, they finally do arrange that drinks party.

Don't play it coy once you finally do meet face-to-face. Sure, he might have figured out it isn't a chance meeting, but so what? If he's not flattered, he's not interested. Talk to him, pay him lots of attention, and make it blatantly obvious you're interested, but leave the ball in his court to arrange another meeting. You've done the hard work—if they don't pick it up from there, the attraction's one-way (yours). Guys—all of this works just as well for you, you know.

A class

Someone once told me to sign up for a course that usually only attracts men. Brilliant idea, I thought, and trotted along in heels and a mini to "Basic Mechanical Skills, Part I" at the local community college. There, sitting around in their chamois shirts and (where did they find

> ❗ Want to instantly boost your sex appeal? Put on a pair of sunglasses. Research shows people wearing shades are seen as sexier and more confident.[11]

them?) polyester slacks with permanent creases down the front, were all the nerds who lived in my area. Because let's face it: any *real* man who doesn't know how to check the oil and water isn't going to completely humiliate himself by admitting it in front of a bunch of strangers.

I was unlucky but that doesn't mean you will be. Night courses, especially, are a great idea. Two friends have 100 percent success ratings: one did a Thai cooking course, licking more than the spoon after school. Another signed up for an "Internet for People Who Still Use Pencils" course and landed herself a cuddly, bald but totally adorable college professor.

The office

Not surprisingly, around two-thirds of people meet their partners through work, because this is the one situation you know exactly what you're letting yourself in for.[12] Not only do you spend most of your time at work, you get to check out how people perform under pressure (that is, you see the *real* them rather than a dressed-up, well-behaved version). Plus, there's a million opportunities to chat them up—just make sure they're not already married to the boss's daughter first.

How to find out if they're single without risking a thing? It's easy. Just say, "Hi, I'm Jo/John and I work in—." After a few smiles exchanged down the corridor ("How's your day going, etc.") it's time to move in for the kill. Corner them in the elevator or the coffee room or wherever, sigh, and say, "What a week! I'm really looking forward to the weekend. How's your week been?" They'll answer, then you can drop in the all-revealing question: "How are you planning to unwind?" If their answer starts with "we," forget them immediately. "We" never means their mother, dog, or best friend, it means a lover/partner/spouse. Even if they don't drop the royal "we," you'll get a big clue from what they do have planned. A few parties or clubs? They're probably single or not dating seriously. Renovating the house? Almost certainly attached.

Got the green light? It's easy to follow it up with something like, "I'm going to check out X (a bar or restaurant). Have you been there?

Why don't you come along if you're not doing anything?"

If you don't want to be that forward and they work in your area of the office, ask them if they want coffee while you're passing their desk. Do they want to take ten minutes out to go *out* for a coffee? If they seem swamped, offer to pick them up a sandwich while you're out. Next time, ask them if they want to have lunch at that great new cafe.

Your own home

You just can't believe it. For six months, you've shared the dishes, toothpaste, and coffee. People keep assuming you're a couple because you do the shopping together, but it's a strictly roommate/friend thing—at least it was until now. Now you can't imagine why you didn't realize how stunning he or she was. Now you lie in your bed wishing you were in hers across the hall. A gift from heaven—or the beginning of a nightmare?

Personally, I'd think twice before sharing a bed with a roommate. For a start, you become instant de factos—the relationship's serious before it's even started. If you split up, one usually ends up moving out (leaving one of you with the problem of finding a replacement); if she doesn't move out, bringing home a new partner is never going to feel comfortable again. Having said all that, more than one married couple met when one answered a "room for rent" ad.

> I went to a Desperate and Dateless Ball and got matched up with this complete moron. He started by banging his bread roll on his plate, shouting, "Where's the food!" and got worse from there. I escaped to my girlfriend's table and spent the night looking nervously over my shoulder, expecting my "date" to materialize at any moment. Despite being matched to someone so awful though, I've always found D & D and Bachelor and Spinsters' Balls loads of fun. Everyone's out to have a good time, you all walk around the room and it's like, "Gosh! They're cute!" No wonder they're so popular.
> Alison, 25, photographer's assistant

Dating services

Oh no, has it really come to this? Hold on one second. You might be surprised who's using dating services these days. Busy people. Career people. *Intelligent* people who realize they're unlikely to meet someone at a bar or a nightclub or don't have the time or energy. Isn't it logical to have a computer (because that's how it's done) match you up with someone with similar interests and aspirations? Sure, they can't predict chemistry but you might get lucky at a big dating service. Your "how we met" story possibly won't thrill the grandkids but, truly, is it more dignified to say you met in a bar? Dating agencies do the legwork so they're especially useful for people who are in their late thirties or forties when your options or avenues may have decreased. They can't promise miracles but a good, professional dating service is well worth a try.

> I live in the country and have a child so I find it difficult to meet people. One day, I was flicking through the paper and stopped at the personals. I thought, *Why not?* Then a little voice said, *Jesus! I must be a bit of a loser if I'm stooping to this.* But I gave it a go and I ended up meeting a really nice guy who I went out with for eight months. Another I went out with for two years. Pretty good odds really.
> Judy, 35, single mom

The personals

They used to be for men who couldn't go near a girl without tripping over their shoelaces and for women called Beryl and Marge who wore twinsets before they became fashionable again. Now people use them because there's no need for corny pick-up lines, nasty rebuttals, and red, bleary eyes from smoke-filled bars. You can spell out exactly what you want from a partner, screen them over the phone, and get to know them via the receiver without ever having to press flesh.

But there are drawbacks. Be careful what you write in your ad and learn how to interpret other people's. It may come as a shocking surprise but not everyone uses the personals to meet life-long partners: lots are after sex. So keep it simple and steer clear of adjectives that could be misinterpreted (like "fun-loving"—usually means up for casual sex). Give the basics of your appearance (tall, slim, petite) and that's it. Don't say "lonely" or "open-minded." "Sexy" will only attract sleazes. If you're a professional person, say so, but don't advertise your income unless you want someone who wants a free ride.

The Internet

If I had my way, I'd still be typing on my beloved typewriter with the sticky "h" key. This is when you go into a private "chat room" and type sentences like, "Ummmm," and, "That feels great, baby," very fast, using one hand. Not all Net nutters are after an intergalactic orgasm, however—plenty use their computer as a dating service. All you do is log on to a local dating site (or an overseas destination that appeals) and choose from the options available. There's everything from singles chat rooms to cybervow weddings on offer as well as an Internet version of the personals. Fill in a form on the computer, describe yourself, attach a picture if you like, then sit back and wait for the e-mails.

It's safe (no one can track down where you live by your e-mail address) and, even I have to admit, really convenient. Once you've connected with someone you like, use the same rules that apply to personal ads and dating services. In other words, chat on screen until you feel you've got a sense of the person. There are as many loonies (possibly more) on the Internet as in your average nightclub so if you meet in the flesh, do it in a public place and tell people the details beforehand.

The chance meeting

They're in line at the deli, sitting alone in the next row at the movies, across the aisle on a plane, snivelling into a tissue at the doctor's office.

Cybersex seems to be super popular. Approximately 47 million people worldwide are currently surfing the Net at this very instant. Call me suspicious, but I honestly don't think the majority are exploring the *Math Can Be Fun* site.[13]

It takes guts and confidence to go up to a complete stranger and the rejection factor is about 90 percent (they're gay, married, or just met the love of their life). But what have you got to lose?

Chance encounters call for drastic measures—especially if they're only going to be around for a few minutes. Swallow all pride (there's no way to get around this one without putting yourself on the line), walk up to them, and say, "Hi. I know this is ridiculous, but I've got the weirdest feeling we're meant to meet." This will prompt either a warm, intrigued smile or a cold "Get away, wacko." If it's a smile, follow it up with, "Have you got time for coffee or a drink just so I can satisfy my curiosity?" Now, good looks and a tingly feeling in your tummy won't guarantee they'll turn out to be what you desperately want them to be, but at least you won't spend the next six weeks dreaming about a total stranger!

Ever noticed how the talent looks better at closing time? It's not just the alcohol, say psychologists. We unconsciously inflate our opinions of others late at night to make ourselves feel better about the dwindling options. At 10:00 P.M., singles judged the average attractiveness of opposite-sex club patrons as 2.3 on a scale of 1–5. Ratings soared to 3.8 an hour before the club shut. Unfortunately, the effect evaporates in the harsh light of the morning after.[14]

If they're trapped on a plane, train, or bus, ask a question. Do they know which stop to get off at if you want to get to X? Where is the bathroom? Could you borrow that paper? While you're doing it, make it obvious you're looking for an excuse to talk to them. Smile every single time they look in your direction and look them straight in the eye. Bar writing "Come and talk to me" in black magic marker across your forehead, give them a definite green light (and I wouldn't rule out the former if it's an emergency). You think they're interested but

DIAL-AN-ORGASM (BUT NOT A DATE)

I did a radio show on 1-900 lines and figured I'd better give it a go first. They're supposed to be "the nineties way to meet someone" but, quite honestly, I wasn't convinced to begin with (and sure as hell wasn't at the end!). You'll find them in the back section of any free weekly paper: tons of them. I, rather predictably, chose the one with the biggest ad.

Most date lines work on the same system: you leave a message to say you're on the line, then you're allowed to scan through the other messages, left by the opposite sex, who are also sitting at home, telephones pressed to their ear. If you like the sound of someone, you send them a message saying you'd like to talk. If they agree, you're put through. If someone wants to speak to you, a voice tells you to check your mailbox—not that I'd know from first-hand experience.

Despite leaving a deliberately provocative message ("Hi, I'm Susan. I'm five feet nine, rich, slim, and people tell me I look like Julia Roberts" [who said I was going to be honest?]) not one person called me. Humiliating. But I soon found out why. Ninety percent of people who use phone lines are after a little more than just coffee.

Like Rolly. "Hi. I'm Rolly. I'm six feet two, blond, athletic, intelligent, rich, and want to make you feel good right now." (Like, if he's that good, why isn't he out with a supermodel instead of calling a phone line at 10:00 A.M.?) But I couldn't resist and, funnily enough, Rolly was free when I requested a chat with him. This is how it went.

"Hi, I'm Rolly."

"Hi, I'm Susan."

Then Rolly cut straight to the chase. "What are you wearing, Susan?" (Who was this guy? Head of the fashion police?)

"Eerr, just old track pants," I answered rather lamely.

"Susan, I want you to pull those track pants down, pull your panties to the side, and put your fingers—"

I hung up. Holy moly! Now, I might be a little naive sometimes (especially before I've had my coffee), but wasn't this an *introduction* line rather than live phone sex? Seems not. The verdict from the regular users: phone meeting lines aren't fab for finding a long-time soulmate but as Dial-an-Orgasm, they're terrific!

shy? Use the old "haven't we met?" trick. "Sorry I keep staring at you but you really remind me of my friend, X. I don't suppose you're related?"

Places you just might get lucky include:

- **The supermarket:** Those new, wide aisles aren't for easy cart access, they're for flirting in. Admittedly, you feel more confident date-hunting with a few stiff drinks under your belt than hovering around the Pine Sol in your sweats, but don't underestimate the supermarket as a potential hunting ground. Whether people add "one blonde with big knockers" to their shopping lists is one thing but more than a few singles have connected while reaching for the same toilet paper. Besides, you can tell a lot about someone by what's in their shopping cart. Like, it's a pretty safe bet the man stocking up on disposable diapers and tampons is married with child; the guy with chocolate cookies and 25 frozen pizzas is most definitely single. Just one word of warning: couples frequently split up while shopping. Just as you're chatting nicely about Colgate versus Crest, the other half comes thundering down the aisle clutching dinner rolls.

- **The beach:** To be avoided at all cost unless you have a similar body type to Elle MacPherson or the new Levi's guy. On the other hand, if someone shows interest when you've got sand all over your butt, zinc oxide on your nose, and sweat dripping from every pore, they've got to be genuine.

- **The laundromat:** A terrific chance to check out their underwear without having to peel it off. Pick one that has a coffee shop just around the corner to satisfy both your caffeine cravings while your clothes are swishing around in the dryer.

HOW TO FLIRT THEIR PANTIES OFF (WELL, ALMOST)

It's a fact: confidence and a great sense of humor will score you more dates than good looks (though, I will admit, you're way ahead if you've got all three). Chatting people up really is quite easy: all it takes is the right attitude and the willingness to take a few risks and make things happen.

Getting noticed

There are ways to stand out from the crowd *and* retain a sense of dignity. Attract his or her attention by using any (or all) of the following tricks.

Have a good time

Look around any crowded single's venue and you'll see groups of two (sorry, girls, but it's usually us), their chairs facing outward, faces peering hopefully into the crowd, waiting for someone to come and talk to them. This sends two signals: "I'm bored, come and entertain me" (hard work); or "I'm desperate" (the supreme no-no). If you're smiling, laughing, and thoroughly enjoying yourself, people notice. They think, "I wish I could be with them. They're having fun."

Attract attention

Pull out a Filofax or start writing intensely on a napkin at a cafe and people have something to talk to you about. "Is this going to be your first novel? What are you writing?"

Use the old "look-then-look-away" trick

It's the best way to let someone know you've noticed them without feeling like a twit if they aren't into you. Look at them until they look back, then drop your eyes and smile to yourself. This says, "I think you're cute but I'm too shy to come over."

If you're with friends of the opposite sex, make it obvious you're not lovers

My brother and I are best friends. Which is fabulous—but not so great when we're out hunting. We're around the same age and everyone assumes we're a couple. Bar wearing "I'm her brother" and "I'm his sister" buttons (which we considered), the only other thing that seems to work is very definitely saying, "This is my *brother*, Nigel," whenever we are introduced to, or introduce, anyone.

Don't worry too much about your opening line

People clam up when they see someone they're interested in because they think the first thing out of their mouth has to be witty, charming, or funny. It doesn't. A short "Hot, isn't it," or "Great pub!" will do the job. Keep it simple and keep it logical. The best lines are often the obvious. "Have you tried the chicken salad?" while you're standing in line at a sandwich shop. "Do you know how to work this machine?" while you're at the gym.

Be impulsive and unpredictable

Most people aren't terribly creative so they're awfully impressed when they meet someone who is. It's not hard to be seen as unpredictable and wildly interesting. Thrusting a cold, frosty beer into an unsuspecting male hand while saying, "Hi. My name's Lucy," will be seen as highly impulsive and wonderfully eccentric. Telling a girl you love her earlobes will guarantee you a smile.

If you're not getting anywhere, take drastic measures

I was into this guy for ages, but every time we met (he was a friend of a friend), he'd look straight through me. After trying every single ploy I could think of, I decided I didn't really care that he didn't lust after me, I just wanted to find out *why*. I plunked myself down beside him and said, "So—what's the deal? Are you gay, hate brunettes, or just don't find me attractive?"

He burst out laughing and his roommate piped up with, "He *is* into you—he just didn't think you liked him."

We ended up going out for eight months. The point is, sometimes you really do have to take the bull by the horns.

If all else fails, blame it on a friend

"My friend and I have got a bet. She thinks you're an investment banker, I think you're a surfer."

"My pal told me I wouldn't have the guts to come over and ask you if you've ever been on TV. Aren't you the girl in the toothpaste ad?" (Come on, we'd all love it!)

While you're watching them, they're watching you

The way you walk, what you're wearing, how you hold your drink (in all senses): make no mistake about it, you'll be judged instantly on all of them.

Make sure your clothes reflect the real you

A white mini teamed with thigh-high boots will brand you a party girl (and that's putting it nicely). A shirt undone to your waist, hairy chest, and a gold medallion means womanizer (add crotch-hugging pants and women will start wearing garlic around their necks and making cross signs with their fingers when you approach them).

Not sure what to wear when you're out on the hunt? Two rules: wear something you feel comfortable in and make sure it suits the occasion. If in doubt, dress down rather than up. The girl who shows up at a barbecue, picking her way across the lawn in heels and a Chanel suit, instantly earns the label of "pretentious snob." A girl in jeans and a T-shirt is seen as carefree and down-to-earth when she's surrounded by standard black.

Feel desperate and you'll look it

Your biological clock is ticking like a bomb, you're dying to get over an ex, haven't had a date in ten years, or are simply having a fat day: those "I'm desperate for attention" vibes send out waves that spread over a ten-mile radius. If you're walking out the front door praying to God that this *is* the night, stay home. Murphy's Law guarantees not even the bar staff (and they're *paid* to be nice to you) will give you a smile when you most need one.

The better looking you are, the more work you have to do

This is what people automatically assume when they spot someone who is drop-dead gorgeous. He thinks: *She'd never be interested in me/Bet her boyfriend's rich, powerful, and built like a gorilla/What could I say that she hasn't heard a thousand times before?* She thinks:

Anyone that good-looking has to be vacant between the ears/Bet he's a bastard and really high on himself/Bet he only dates models, he'd never go out with someone like me.

The good-looking person is thinking: *Why doesn't anyone ever talk to me?/Why doesn't anyone ever ask me out?/What's wrong with me?* If you're above average in looks or have something particularly spectacular (a great set of knockers for instance), no one will come near you unless you make it incredibly obvious you want them to.

If you're a confident female, some men will find you scarier than Godzilla

"Confident" in boy talk translates to any female who earns more than he does, has a more prestigious job, is more articulate, has a better sense of humor, is more attractive—and I'm really not kidding. A woman who knows what she wants and is confident of who she is, is as attractive as hell but requires a lot more courage to approach than your average girl. If you're getting lots of looks but no action, this is probably what's happening. The solution? Smile a lot and look friendly. Or approach guys yourself.

Now you're talking . . .

OH MY GOD! They've taken the hint and are on their way over. Relax, take a deep breath, then:

Pretend you're talking to your best friend

Skip the small talk and clichéd "do you come here often?" stuff and talk about what you normally would. Adopt a relaxed, friendly, attitude even when you're screaming inside, *"Gorgeous!"* When you're both a bit more relaxed, then you can move into full-on flirting mode.

Don't leave your brain in the backseat of the cab

That little black dress will be appreciated, but you need more than a Wonderbra and great legs to keep someone's attention. Same for men. A jaw that looks like it's been carved with a chisel is what dragged us over but you need to open your mouth for us to hang around. A male friend of mine put it perfectly. Men are looking for a best friend with breasts. Someone they can share the good and bad times with—and bonk afterward. Women are also looking for a best friend—with benefits.

Say your target's name three times in the first conversation

Repeating the name of someone you haven't met before not only shows you're interested, it makes them feel noticed and important. An added bonus: you'll actually remember it.

Give a compliment

But only if you mean it. Sincere flattery will get you everywhere. Insincere flattery sounds like a line (because it is).

Tease but not too much

Some people love a challenge and adore it when someone instantly takes up a contrary position to whatever it is they're talking about. If you're clever and articulate, go for it. Just make sure it doesn't turn into a match of wits where you're both trying to score points. Trading insults isn't sexy.

Make them laugh—but only if you've got a good sense of humor

Body language experts believe women should use more humor while flirting, men less. Why? Because men like to keep things on a more superficial level (and what better way than with a joke?), while women like deep conversations. Similarly, men laugh more among their own sex, women talk more and laugh less.[15] It's something to think about, but if humor's not your strong point, don't push it. There's nothing worse than delivering the punchline and seeing a sea of expectant faces still waiting for it.

Always leave when it's going well

Ahh, here she goes, sounding like those dreadful women who wrote *The Rules*. I don't mean to, but any performer will tell you you should always leave your audience wanting more. Flirting requires energy and 100 percent undivided attention. Even the best flirt can only keep it up for a few hours—leave before you run out of steam.

GUARANTEED TO TURN OFF BOTH SEXES

- **Traveling in packs:** If they have to wade through 16 drunken friends to get to you, they won't bother.
- **Being inflexible:** If they ask you out but you're not free on the night they suggest, suggest another. The old "I'm not changing my plans for anyone" isn't challenging, it's rude and unflattering.
- **Not paying attention:** Look over someone's shoulder while they're talking to you and you might as well have said out loud, "I'm keeping my eye out for someone better."
- **Being too eager:** Give off a "wow! I really like you" too soon and they'll feel suffocated and manipulated. It's unflattering. Like, "How can they think I'm so wonderful when they don't even know me?"
- **Suggesting a date too early:** Saying, "We should go out next Friday" when you've only been chatting for five minutes, is jumping the gun.

THE SIX SECRETS OF WOMEN WHO GET MEN (AND MEN WHO GET WOMEN)

There are certain qualities that make *anyone* appear attractive and all reduce to this simple equation. If you love sex and love people, you're probably sexy.

All of us have a subconscious "sexy" radar that automatically tunes in to people who've got "it." Our looks radar sets off first—instantly scanning for the best-looking person in the crowd—then the sexy radar clicks in, looking for more subtle (and surer) indicators that someone's worth talking to. Men have exceptional sexy radars (most have them fine-tuned before they've mastered shaving). The average guy can spot the sexiest woman in the room before she's finished her first cocktail, even when she's *not* wearing neck-to-thigh spandex. How? They know the other giveaway signs:

1. **They're enthusiastic.** It's infectious—you can't help but smile and respond to someone who's full of life. It doesn't really mat-

ter what it is you're passionate about (though plankton and gray-speckled tree frogs are pushing it), so long as you're throwing your arms around and getting excited about something. As one guy put it, "The girl in the corner whose facial expression doesn't change and talks in a monotone isn't appealing, even if she is discussing how to give a great blow job. It's the girl who's gesturing madly and talking a million miles an hour who you want. Even if *she's* discussing what color to paint her bathroom." Sexy people aren't afraid of life. They live it to the fullest and drag everyone else along with them.

2. **They make you feel like you're the only person in the room.** Jerry Seinfeld's just walked in, the girl at the next table has just taken off her clothes, and the waiter just dropped a $100 bill at his feet, but his eyes haven't moved from your face. The person who looks you directly in the eye, really listens, calls you by name, and focuses on what you're saying wins every time.

3. **They know who they are and are proud of it.** A person who isn't scared to express an opinion even if it's the opposite to everyone else's, even if it *does* turn into a screaming match, might be called opinionated, or even rude, but there's one thing they'll never be branded: boring. Stick up for your beliefs and believe in yourself. We all respect and admire people who are capable of holding their head up and fighting their own battles.

4. **They touch a lot.** The person who really hugs hello, who puts a concerned hand on your arm if you're upset, gives a firm handshake to say "Congratulations!" is making warm, sexy gestures that make them seem approachable. When someone touches us, it instantly makes us like them more.

    Don't forget to touch yourself, too. Smoothing your stockings, wiping your hands down the front of your jeans, pushing back your hair, hugging yourself if you're a bit cold—it's all very sensual and inviting and draws attention to whatever body part you're touching. If you're stingy with your affection, others assume you're cold, hard to get to know, uptight. None of which are adjectives you particularly want applied to you, right?

5. **They're aware of their body language—and their body.** The more you like your body, the better you'll present it to the world. Sit with your arms crossed, clutching a pillow across your stomach and the message is obvious: I feel fat and I'm trying to hide my stomach. A woman who does a big, lazy stretch, lifting

her arms up, sends a very different message: I'm proud of my body. Not only is she well aware what gravity's doing to her boobs, she knows people will look at her body as she does it. Ditto for men. Grimace and roll a shoulder and she'll notice how broad they are.

6. **They aren't looks-obsessed.** "My girlfriend is sexiest when she's got lipstick smeared everywhere from kissing me." "I love Brad first thing in the morning when his hair's sticking up all over the place, he's got sleep in his eyes, and morning breath. He looks so gorgeous and vulnerable." It's hard to accept someone will find you sexy when you've got spinach wedged in the cracks of your teeth, but it really is true. That's why the just-got-out-of-bed tussled look never, ever goes out of fashion.

GETTING THROUGH THE FIRST TWO DATES

While first dates are stressful for women (like, who can ever decide which black dress?), I have to say men have it tougher. Approaching a woman, risking rejection by asking her out—it's not easy. If you're overconfident, she thinks you're cocky. If you're a shoe shuffler, she thinks you're a twit. And when's the right time to do it? If she's told you her ex dumped her last week, she might think you're insensitive if you rush in too soon. But wait too long and some other guy will get there first.

No matter how ordinary a girl looks, she becomes Super Woman if you want to ask her out. For every woman who has waited by the phone, there's a man sitting by one trying to pluck up the courage to dial that number. So, girls, unless the guy who's asking *you* out is drunk, rude, sexist, or outrageously egotistical, be nice. Don't go out with him out of pity, but *do* be polite.

Moral lecture over, let's move on to the nitty-gritty.

That desired but dreaded first date

I'd rather tell a wedding congregation the groom's run off with the maid of honor than repeat some of my first dates. There you are, trying to give this fabulous first impression and you end up doing quite the opposite. You never have trouble parallel parking but when *they're* in the car, you simply can't do it. You're so jumpy you become clumsy, you're so worried about saying the wrong thing you get tongue-tied. You're both trying to be sexy but not *too* sexy, intelligent but not boring, and the pressure's just too much. And some things really are out of our control—like the restaurant's awful or you run into your ex.

First dates make us nervous for good reason. They *are* a test. What we're really asking each other is, "Am I likable/attractive/rich enough/thin enough/successful enough for you?" Even if we don't like them, it's a blow to the ego if they don't like us.

What to wear?

Wear something you feel good in, that suits you and the venue. If you've forgotten to ask, call back to find out what the dress code is. While dressing down is cool in most situations, first dates are one occasion where I'd dress one notch up from what's expected. Their definition of casual might be your slightly dressy and you're better off slightly overdressed than under (especially if the venue has dress rules). More important, looking like you've made an effort makes them feel the date means something to you. It's a compliment. (A word of warning if you're female: keep in mind that if you overemphasize the outside, he'll never get past it. Wear that tight, black mini and plunging neckline and you can't blame him if he doesn't hear a word you say.)

Where to go

There's a reason why dinner nearly always wins. Parties are a nightmare (you end up eyeing someone else or they do), movies are pointless (two hours of sitting in silence doesn't tell you a thing about them), and anything creative is destined for disaster (your parachute doesn't open, for instance).

Dinner gives you the chance to talk, but there's enough going on to cover up those awful silences. Choose a mid-range restaurant or a cheap eats with loads of atmosphere rather than that expensive place with the starched linen tableclothes. You feel nervous enough without snotty waiters frowning when you pick up the wrong fork.

What to talk about

Anything. Babbling on about how the beavers in Canada build dams with their teeth is still preferable to sitting there, gazing at the floor. As a basic rule, it's always good to ask lots of questions: where did they grow up, how many kids in their family, what's their job like, how did they get into it. After all, you're curious, most people like talking about themselves and even the socially inept can take the lead from questions like that and ask you the same questions back.

Don't censor your conversations (there's no use pretending to be something you're not—they'll find out soon enough anyway) but there are three danger zones. Ripping apart your ex (or anyone for that matter) will make you seem mean and bitchy, launching into your sexual fantasies (especially the one about honey and the football team) isn't appropriate when you've only known each other an hour, and telling your entire life history in under three hours is no good either. At the end of the night, you want to have a sense of what someone's like, not know every single thing that's happened to them. Who needs a second date if you do?

> I find women incredibly confusing—I don't think they even know what they want. Sometimes, she wants me to act like a man—open doors and stuff—other times she wants me to be her girlfriend and sit there and listen to all the stuff girls talk about. She wants me to be both male and female, but doesn't give me any hint as to which role I'm supposed to play when.
> Jeremy, 28, small-business owner

Who pays?

When it comes time to pay, both of you should fish for your wallets. But the general rule is whoever asked the other out picks up the bill. (After that, split the bill, take turns, or pay according to your respective salary levels.) His paying for you doesn't mean you owe him anything (sex or a second date). Ditto for her.

Guaranteeing a second date

Just when you think all the hard parts are over—you're getting along famously and are finally relaxed—comes the hardest part of the first date: the end of it. If you can't wait to get out of there, you're frantically thinking of how to say, "Had a great time but let's not do it again." But if you really like them, it's tempting to take it through to a different level (that is, sex).

Let's deal with the first scenario first. You've had a pleasant time but were ready to go home at 9:00 P.M. This is all you need to say: "Thanks, X, that was great. It's always nice meeting new people. Maybe we'll run into each other again sometime. Bye!" If they try to pin you down to another date say, "Look, I'm frantic at work right now but give me your number and I'll give you a call sometime." That way no one's waiting by the phone but you haven't been rude.

For the couple who've already moved on to an intimate bar to have "one for the road," thighs touching and lips itching to mesh, sometimes, it's the right thing to give in, make-out passionately, desperately hail a cab, and take each other's clothes off the minute the front door shuts. But you're taking a huge risk. Apart from the obvious safety issues (rape, assault, passing on STDs if you don't wear a condom), there are emotional implications. Will he think you're easy? Will she think you were only out for a roll in the hay? Sex moves things rapidly into intimacy mode, and in the bright light of day, when the alcohol's worn off, you might not feel like you know each other quite as well as you thought.

If your attraction to each other is strong, saying, "Good-night," and sealing it with a promise-of-things-to-come kiss is by far the better bet. Plenty of people regret sleeping with someone too soon. I don't know one person who wishes they'd done it earlier. When you sleep with each other depends on how well you're getting along, the circumstances, your individual morals, and what you want from the relationship. Forced to put some sort of time frame on it, I'd say the consensus is at least three dates. If you're hoping for a long-term relationship, I'd *strongly* recommend waiting longer, until *both* of you feel comfortable and reasonably secure that you both want the same things from the relationship. That might take one date, three weeks, or six months. By all means put your best undies on for the first night out (it'll make you feel sexier), but you don't have to take them off. (See "Between the sheets," page 63, if you're still not convinced.)

In short: be yourself, have a sense of humor, don't drink too much, and don't make snap judgments—first impressions are often wrong. Instincts, on the other hand, rarely are, so trust your gut feeling.

> One girl took me to an ice-skating rink for a first date. She was a great skater and very impressive but it didn't do much for my confidence. I felt like a complete fool flailing along behind her like a novice. It gave her way too much power.
> Nick, 27, bartender

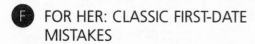 **FOR HER: CLASSIC FIRST-DATE MISTAKES**

- **Sleeping with him:** It might be the only time you've ever done it but he thinks you do it every time.

- **Spilling all your secrets:** Revealing too much too soon moves him into a space he's not comfortable with. He suspects you must really like him to trust him that much and feels trapped already.

M **FOR HIM: CLASSIC FIRST-DATE MISTAKES**

- **Getting drunk:** You're nervous and keep downing drinks to gain confidence. Slurring isn't attractive. Neither is offering to drive her home when you're well over the limit.

- **Clamming up:** You're so desperate to make the right impression, nothing seems witty or intelligent enough so you sit there in silence.

- **Talking about yourself too much:** You think you're impressing her by showing off all your expertise. She thinks you're big-headed.

The acid test: date two!

The better the first date, the more nervous you'll be for the second. He's thinking, *She's far too pretty/intelligent/cool/classy to bother with the likes of me. Especially after I dribbled soup down my shirt.* She's thinking, *He's far too good-looking/intelligent/cool/sophisticated to ask me out again. Especially after I babbled on like an idiot.* If there's going to be a second date, both of you will spend the next day analyzing every word and gesture to convince yourselves the other person enjoyed the first as much as you did.

Who calls whom?

Usually, one of you (often the guy) will say, "I'll call you," at the end of the first date. If that's how it was left, leave it a few days to see if he does. You swapped phone numbers but it was left up in the air as to who'd call whom? If *they* called *you* for the first date, it's perfectly acceptable for *you* to call *them* for the second (assuming it all went swimmingly well).

But don't say I didn't warn you if you're a girl calling the guy. Some of my girlfriends don't think twice about calling men—with terrific results. The guy's knocked out to find a girl confident enough to put herself on the line. But every single time I've done that, it's backfired. Miserably. I convince myself that they're just too shy, that I didn't give enough green lights, there's been something wrong with my phone, or they've lost the number, and I call them. The minute I say, "Hi. Just wanted to say thanks for such a great night," I *know* I've done the wrong thing.

I ended up friends with a guy I did this to (we met later through mutual friends) and asked him why it freaked him out so much. "You were too eager," he said. "You removed the challenge. Men like the chase most of all."

> The average person lies once or twice a day but dating couples lie to each other about one-third of the time. Eighty-five percent of couples surveyed admit one or both had lied about past relationships or recent indiscretions.[16]

So there—you're warned, but good for you if you decide to do it anyway!

If you're a coward like me and opt for the waiting game, give up if the person who said they'd call hasn't after three days. If you had sex on the first night, give up after one.

What to wear, where to go

The pressure of what to wear and where to go eases a little on date two. Most couples still opt for dinner or drinks out, though it's usually at a more casual venue than the first. Don't be surprised if you find yourself acting like shy schoolchildren when you first link up again. You probably won't snap straight back to the same level of intimacy you last left on. Give it an hour or so, because if you thought the first date was loaded with expectations, the second's even worse. After all, here you both are again, which means you've admitted you like each other and want more!

What to expect

Date two, if you're still both into it, usually turns into a talkathon, the old "let's stay up and tell each other all the stuff you never tell anyone" scenario. You part (reluctantly) and, despite having had half an hour's sleep, float into work having hitched a ride on cloud nine. Either that or it's been a total disaster. You both realize date one was a fluke, the best behavior starts to slip and you get a glimpse of what you're both really like. Brave couples will struggle on to date three to make sure it wasn't just a case of clashing biorhythms or the moon rising in Scorpio. Sensible couples give up when date three's equally as bad.

In short: don't panic if you get tongue-tied, don't reveal *all* your secrets, no matter how tempted you are. Remember that date two is the "heavy infatuation" date: take everything they say as a compliment but don't treat it as gospel.

F FOR HER: CLASSIC SECOND-DATE MISTAKES

- **Assuming you're now an item.** Don't launch into, "My parents will love you," and "What are you doing for Christmas?" It's acceptable to suggest date three—but that's it.

- **Planning the next three dates.** Same deal as above but for different reasons. Women are natural social organizers so we think nothing of organizing him. You want to know when you're next going out so you can plan your week; he interprets it as being overeager.

Ⓜ FOR HIM: CLASSIC SECOND-DATE MISTAKES

- **Backing off big-time because you're embarrassed about how intimate you got by the end of date one.** She'll take it as a sign you're not interested and also take ten steps back, leaving you both nowhere.

- **Relaxing too much, too soon.** You know she likes you or she wouldn't have agreed to date two. But believe me—she's still not quite ready for that really funny party trick you do with the match.

HIS IDEA OF A GREAT DATE

A girl who holds her own—and holds her drink. Who greets him with a huge smile, enjoys her food, is spontaneous, and goes with the flow. Who says, "I know exactly how you feel," and means it. Who relaxes and is herself. Who laughs at his jokes, offers to split the bill, and makes him forget he's "dating" because he's having such a great time. She leaves him wanting more.

HIS IDEA OF A DISASTER DATE

A woman who is indecisive. Who drinks too much or takes party drugs. Who is overeager, clingy, and starts planning the wedding reception after the first five minutes. Who doesn't let him get a word in edgewise. Who sleeps with him then calls every day afterward, even though he's blown her off. Who is stuck up and criticizes the restaurant and him.

HER IDEA OF A GREAT DATE

A guy who arrives with flowers—and arrives on time. Who makes her feel special without feeling patronized. Who really listens and gets past the small talk. Who treats her as an equal but still makes her feel feminine. Who's willing to talk about his feelings. Who laughs when things don't quite go as planned. Who doesn't pressure her to sleep with him—but makes it clear he's really into her.

HER IDEA OF A DISASTER DATE

A man who arrives late without calling. Who dominates the conversation. Who is rude to the waiter and throws money around in an attempt to impress. Who gets drunk and punch-happy. Who expects her to do all the talking. Who hasn't got a sense of humor. Who demands she put out because he paid for dinner.

BETWEEN THE SHEETS

When should you sleep together, and how do you make it fabulous when you do? Don't rush it. (There, I got it out before you could skip to the good parts.) I *know* you're just dying to rip each other's clothes off and you're both adults and what's the big deal and all that, but the fact is, sex with someone you think you might just fall in love with *is* a big deal. Even in our liberated times.

Sleeping together too soon is the most common mistake most couples make. It truly can destroy a relationship before it's even started. Why? Because despite the fact that, these days, we recognize that we can have good sex (fabulous sex) with someone we don't love, when it comes to someone we *do*—or *think* we could—sex gets thrown straight back into the "special" box.

That "old-fashioned" gene starts tapping us on the shoulder, saying, "Wait. Save it. Make it special." And usually, it's good advice. As I said earlier: make no mistake about it, if you're a girl and you "put out" too quickly, men will judge you. They really will think "less" of you. Why then, do men try to sleep with us if they don't really want us to say yes? Maybe he thinks *you'll* think he doesn't like you if he doesn't give it the old college try. Maybe you're being tested. Whatever it is, even if he is hyperventilating with lust as he's pushing that bra strap off your shoulder, take it from me, he's secretly wanting you to say, "No, not yet." That is, if you're someone he wants to see long term. If it's a fling he's after, he's praying for the opposite.

Sixty-eight percent of men like the way they look naked— compared to 22 percent of women. Which may explain why we cry five times more often than he does.[17]

I'm not saying I condone this attitude or necessarily think you should put up with it *or* agree with it, but it is a fact. I know plenty of "liberated" men who hate themselves for thinking like this, but they still do. I know three times as many liberated women who also detest it. But they also admit the attitude's out there. So, at this point it's something you need to factor into the relationship equation.

There's another reason for not jumping into bed until you know the name of each other's childhood pets. Once you sleep with someone, there's no excuse for not doing it again. You're instantly thrust into a far more intimate space than you were. If you're looking long term, ideally, you should date each other (minus sex) until you're reasonably sure you're compatible, want the same thing out of the relationship, and, most important, think you might make each other happy. This requires logical thinking and objectivity. Good sex rather effectively robs us of both instantly. It's extremely difficult to look at your new partner sensibly and objectively while their tongue is working its way up your inner thigh.

Experts call it "lust blindness."[18] You get so involved with your partner's body, you forget to look closely at the person inside it. This is how people end up emotionally involved with people they later find out are bad for them. That "I know he's a bastard, but I love him" thing. No one falls in love with a bastard when they're thinking straight. But if you put your brain on hold and get involved with their body, you stumble out of that glorious, lust-infused haze, rub your eyes, and find you've made all sorts of promises and commitments to someone who wasn't worth getting intimate with in the first place.

Look, I'm a huge fan of sex. I know I sound like a boring old fuddy-duddy by telling you to wait but I see so many people getting hurt by committing themselves to the wrong people. There's no magic way of guaranteeing this won't happen to you, but you can reduce the risk by putting off sex until you're confident you've got a handle on the type of person your partner is. The more confident you are of your judgment in people and the less you've been burned in the past, the sooner you'll know when it's safe to have sex. If you *haven't* made great choices in the past, force yourself to wait another six dates *after* you're convinced you're ready.

Eight steps to orgasmic first night sex

Tonight's the night and you both know it. Here's how to turn that butterfly in your tummy to a tingle in your—*ummmm*, toes?

1. Pick the time

Wait until you're both reasonably relaxed with each other—and the idea of having sex.

2. Get the condom(s) ready

The minute it's obvious you're going to have sex, say, "I'll get the condoms now because I know we're not going to want to stop later." Thinking each other's special isn't protection against HIV or other sexually transmitted diseases.

3. Create a mood

Lighting is crucial. Dim them but don't make it so dark you're bashing into furniture on the way to top off the drinks. Music helps enormously but make sure it's not going to stop suddenly at a crucial point. (Load as many CDs as your player takes.)

4. Spend a long time on foreplay

Kiss a lot, take it slow, and take your time exploring each other's body. Don't panic too much about your underwear: if the time's unexpectedly right, it's better to go with the flow than squirm your way out of it because you've got once-white-now-gray baggy, unflattering panties on (actually, if they're that awful, encourage your partner to take them off while they're hidden by your top or skirt). I wouldn't suggest going without underwear on the first night. If he's a little nervous, his erection will disappear faster than he can think, *Oh God. This one really expects me to perform.* Help him remove your clothes if he's having trouble (and feeling like an idiot). Besides, it shows you want sex as much as he does.

5. Don't expect too much

Ideally, you'll have joked about your first time beforehand to relieve the pressure. It's really not make-or-break time: if you really like each other, you won't split up over one bad sex session (though you will find out if the chemistry is there). If you lose your erection or orgasm too soon, just say lightheartedly, "Sorry! I'm a bit nervous." Don't panic if you can't make her orgasm—lots of women are too shy to tell you what they need to make it happen the first time you're in bed.

6. Relax about your body

There's nothing you can do about it now anyway! If she really likes you, she's not going to run from the room when she sees that sock tan line—and he's not on cellulite patrol. You're the only naked woman in the room and he'll think you're gorgeous.

7. Guide each other but not too much

You're both under enough pressure first time around: wait until the second run before you start directing.

> The problem with having great sex with someone you've just met is that it stops you getting to know each other. From then on all you do is "it." You stop talking.
> Katie, 34, customer service

8. Don't worry if you feel embarrassed afterward

You've both exposed yourselves—literally and emotionally—and the relationship's now on a new level. Men, especially, go into a strange space after they've "done it" for the first time. He's uneasy, *you're* uneasy. She thinks, *Is this it? After all, he got what he really wanted.* He thinks, *I bet she thought I was awful.* Some guys do take the nearest exit ramp (the front door) after sex—no matter how long you've waited. But most—God love them—seem miserable because they're waiting for some kind of thumbs-up sign. He's not thinking of leaving you, he's self-conscious. Like, did you notice his love handles, that his penis was a tad small, that he lasted all of four seconds?

MR. AND MS. RIGHT-FOR-NOW: FANCY A FLING?

Not all relationships last forever—and neither should we want them to. A lusty three-week fling with a brain-dead but body-beautiful might be just what you need to get over that ex-obsession for good. The person who's cute and clever but about to be transferred to another city in three months? So what if the only aisle you'll walk down together is at the movies?

There are lots of different types of relationships and each has its own appeal. But you wouldn't know it. Most of us tend to divide relationships into two, mutually exclusive categories—serious (will end in marriage) or not serious (sex and that's about all). There's also a perception that somehow you're "wasting time" or "being cruel" by dating someone when you know it's not going to be long term. Silly. Really silly. As long as you're honest (and not pretending to think white picket fences), there's absolutely no reason to refuse a date on Saturday night just because you know it won't last past a week. In fact, I thoroughly recommend it. Not just because first impressions are often wrong (and that one date could turn into a life-long love) but because relationships are like everything else in life. Practice makes perfect.

The more people you go out with, the more you get to hone your relationship skills. The more diverse the people you date, the more likely you are to know exactly what type of personality suits you best. A just-for-the-hell-of-it fling is good for the heart, soul, and spirit!

Date outside the box

I once went out with a man who was dead-set perfect "marriage material." Nick was tall, good-looking, and earned enough money to single-handedly rescue all Ethiopian orphans. He was polite, stopped to pat dogs and children, and wouldn't *dream* of parking in the handicapped spot even if he was ("There's always someone worse off than you"). I dutifully ditched my miniskirts for the sort of clothes Nick preferred (conservative coordinates), spent my money on facials and manicures instead of wine and smokes, and hosted very proper dinner parties without ever forgetting to scoop my soup from the opposite side of the bowl. A few months later, as I reluctantly pulled on yet another blah beige ensemble, I suddenly thought, *What the hell am I doing here?* I was going out with a guy who did zilch for me, pretending to be someone I wasn't, simply because he was Good Marriage Material. And guess what? I didn't even want to get married! I dumped him real quick and ended up going out with a totally unmarriageable (and rather nutty) psychology student. He made me laugh more in one week than Nick had in three months.

Like every other female I knew then, I'd fallen prey to the only-date-men-who-could-be-prospective-husbands trap. I wised-up quickly after that. Long-term relationships and marriage aren't just about salaries and stability; they're about liking someone, chemistry, and "clicking." What's right is what feels right for you *right now.*

I'm not suggesting you date everyone who asks you, but I am suggesting you open your mind and your Filofax to someone you probably don't want to share your room with at the old folk's home. Date outside the box. Don't stick to the same type over and over. He seems a little out there? Give him a chance—you're going for a drink, not about to bear his children. The more motley your collection of exes the better—it shows you're adventurous and open enough to step outside your personal square.

> When you're in your 30s and date women the same age or older, there's definite pressure. Both of you are well aware that if she wants children, she can't just date for fun.
> John, 36, stockbroker

Great reasons to play the field

- **You build a rather useful network.** Need your car fixed? Call the mechanic you once dated. Your computer's acting up again? That nerdy tech-head comes in very handy.

- **You can't have a serious relationship right now.** You're not ready for (or don't want) one but you do want someone to have fun (and sex) with? So long as you make this perfectly clear to your partner, there's no need to feel guilty.

- **You've just recovered from a long-term split-up and are easing back into dating again.** Resisting the urge to replace one long-term partner with another immediately means you'll give yourself time to work through the fallout properly.

- **You aren't sure what sort of person would suit you long term so you're dating as many different types as possible.** Bravo! The best reason of all!

- **You haven't kissed (let alone had sex) for six months.** Assuming you're not grieving for a past relationship or person, haven't been in intensive therapy or intensive care, or haven't just been made managing director of your company, that's way too long without erotic contact. It's fling time—get out there!

Good reasons not to even consider it

- **To boost your self-esteem.** Even the word "fling" sounds jaunty—and it's meant to be. You're there for fun and games, not deep psychological stroking.

- **To get back at someone.** Sleeping with your ex's friends won't show the arrogant so-and-so a thing or two—it'll just convince your ex you're still heartbroken.

- **Because you feel pressured into it.** Don't listen to your friends, your family (or even me for that matter): if you're not ready or don't want to date someone, don't do it.

- **To ease the pain of loneliness.** A stranger in your bed, who doesn't really care about you and whom you'll never see again, isn't the person to pour out your troubles to.

- **You don't honestly agree with no-strings sex.** If your morals or religion mean you'll wake up feeling "dirty" and "used" after sex that doesn't have a could-develop-into-something tag on it, stick to sex within serious relationships.

3

I Think I've Met "the One"—Now What?

Getting from bonking-each-other-senseless to couplesville (without losing the urge)

● ●

Y ou're intoxicated. You can't stop thinking about last night. Images of "the one" smiling/laughing/sleeping, flash up out of nowhere to dance in front of your eyes. A Mariah Carey song comes on the radio and *you don't turn it off*! Either you're "in love" or you're experimenting heavily with party drugs.

Assuming it's the former, good for you! If you think you've found someone worth hanging on to, hold on hard. But there's something else you should also hold on to: objectivity. Sorry to squash that soaring-above-the-clouds feeling but there's a long way to go before you're shopping for queen-size sheets and his 'n' her towels.

This chapter shows you how to make it last when you've hooked up with the *right* person—and how to know when you haven't, so you can stop it right there. I know you don't want to even *think* about the second option right now because it's like all your Christmases have come at once (or, more accurately, you've come so often it feels like Christmas). But it's not a *real* relationship yet. You're still in that goofy, "You like me? Aww shucks!" first stage, and there are plenty of obstacles to dodge, jump, or squeeze through before you're officially a couple.

Even worse, there's another influence on your relationship you have absolutely no control over: other people. Sometimes, you'll meet the person you've been waiting for all your life and be foiled by someone *else* screwing it up for you: an interfering friend who spreads rumors; an overprotective parent who insists on knowing your partner's "intentions" when the only one he or she has at this point is to lick the inside of your thigh the minute you get home; a sibling who thinks your new fella isn't good enough for you.

We can't control other people's reactions to our new partner—and don't I know it. I met my husband-to-be about one month before Christmas. So besotted were we, I invited him to stay with my family when I found out he had no family here. All went swimmingly well, until the traditional Christmas Eve get-together. My mother ushered us into the living room, packed with people. "This," she said proudly, "is Tracey's latest boyfriend." Chris, my now ex-husband (did I ever have a chance?), was rather put out.

"*Latest* boyfriend? What does that mean? Do you trade them in like cars?" he hissed at me.

"Perhaps it's easier if you just give me a number," he said to Mom.

"What darling?" she answered, blissfully unaware of her faux pas.

During our stay, she called Chris by the name of every significant ex I'd ever had. Lucky for me, Mom just happens to be one of those totally adorable types who gets away with complete murder, so it all turned into a massive joke. But I have to admit it, I was holding my breath for a little while there.

The only way to completely avoid having things like this happening to you is never to introduce your partner to anyone (tempting but unrealistic). Like the rest of us, you're going to have to risk it—but you can minimize the other pitfalls. We're now going to talk about how to build a healthy relationship—right from the tentative, both-on-best-behavior beginning. I warn you—there's a lot in here that isn't terribly romantic, and I've included some exercises that require you to put your heart on hold and use your head instead. But would you parachute out of an airplane without checking your equipment first? Bungee-jump without a cord? That's exactly what you are doing if you let yourself fall in love and turn your brain off while you're doing it.

It's fine to doodle your love's name and bore your friends stupid with "Brad said/Judy said" stories but keep a little part of yourself—just 30 percent—objective. While the rest of you is walking hand-in-hand along that beach, let that 30 percent watch, analyze, and form accurate conclusions about this person. You wouldn't go to a doctor unless he was qualified. Why commit to spending your life with someone without checking out *their* credentials?

Let's start by looking at how a typical relationship usually runs, so you can see where (hopefully) you're going, and what you'll need to do to get there.

THE SIX STAGES OF A RELATIONSHIP

While each and every relationship is unique, most move through the same love stages. If you're a typical couple, you'll probably experience them in the order I've listed; other couples may skip a stage and go straight onto the next. Or the opposite. If you've just found out your partner's cheated or work pressures keep you apart more than usual, you might slip *back* one or two stages before moving forward again. Whoever said the path to true love is never smooth was exactly right!

Stage 1: *yahoo!*

Timing: anywhere from date one up to three months

They're available and interested, so are you. There's chemistry both above and below the waist. You go out, you like each other. Euphoria! Stage one is that lovey-dovey, gooey stage. You're reacting to primal instincts from your heart and your groin. You give each other those goofy grins. She spends a fortune on sexy new lingerie, he buys four new shirts. Where and how you met is a constant topic of conversation.

"I can't believe I didn't want to go to the dinner party," he says. "Imagine if I hadn't."

"I nearly didn't go because my mom was sick," you say.

The thought of not having met fills you with dread. Life before seems dull and boring. The future is deliriously, ridiculously bright.

Sex

The only time you stop having it is when you lie back, snuggled in each other's arms, to talk about "us."

Keep it going

Treat your date the way you'd like to be treated. Be yourself as much as possible. Don't push for intimacy too soon.

Check for

Chemistry: Does it *feel* right—do you lust after as well as like them?

Stage 2: fairytale fantasies

Timing: around two to six months into the relationship

In stage two, you still haven't found one thing wrong with each other; in fact, everything's just perfect. This is the heavy idealizing stage. You know enough about your new love to feel you know him well but you haven't been together long enough to see his faults, so there don't appear to be any. If friends point out a glaring incompatibility (you're a brain surgeon, he's the pool guy; you want ten kids, he wants none), you tell them, "Have faith! True love conquers everything!" You lie to each other constantly. You force down hot curry because she loves Indian; you sit through each other's favorite films and pretend you adore them. You hate spending even a night apart, and if you do, call each other three hundred times just to say, "I miss you."

Sex

It's still fun, fresh, and exciting but a little less frenetic. Instead of having it twice a night, once is enough. Sometimes you even manage to eat first.

Keep it going

Let your heart rule your head but don't do anything rash (like get married or quit your job to live in Saudi Arabia). Don't make long-term promises. It's okay to say, "Wouldn't it be nice if this lasted forever," but not, "Let's get married so it does last forever."

Check for

Compatibility: Do you share lots of similar interests, look at life the same way?

Stage 3: you officially emerge as "a couple"

Timing: three to six months

This is the time when things start going wrong. The just-you-and-I-alone video nights are starting to wear thin—or your friends have threatened to disown you if you don't come out with them—so you and your love venture out to be judged by others. You've met each other's friends before, but they now realize it's more than just a fling so they look harder. And so do you. You start to see each other through other people's eyes. You watch your mom lift an eyebrow at his rattly old car and realize he earns a quarter of what you do. Your best friend says, "She's great—but I wouldn't have picked her as your type," and you realize she's blond and you only ever go out with brunettes. The lies start to be exposed: his childhood home's not quite the mansion he'd described, her ex couldn't possibly have been a model. You pick him up at work and see a different side.

What's happening is this: you're both reconciling your glorified images of each other with a realistic idea of who you really are. Plenty of couples take the exit at this point when they realize the person isn't all they'd hoped for or find out they don't want the same things out of life. If you decide you do want to continue, you both drop the best-behavior act and feel safe enough to expose not-so-lovable sides, like a bad temper, insecurity, possessiveness, and impatience. You start having a few arguments and question each other's judgment and opinions on things that really matter.

Sex

If you like the "real person," sex shifts from the lusty, "forget the bed, let's just do it right here" variety to a more loving, intensely romantic stage.

Keep it going

Don't panic when you discover your perfect lover's not so perfect after all. Give each other time to get used to the "real" version, and you might just slide through. If it is obvious you've made a bad choice, however, now's the time to cool it. Split or agree to be friends.

Check for

Timing: Are you both ready for, and want, a long-term relationship—because that's where it's heading.

Stage 4: why are you acting funny?

Timing: six to twelve months

You're starting to think long term, so you start examining your partner with a microscope. In stage one and two you focus only on the good points; in stage four you focus only on the bad. "You've changed," you say accusingly. He hasn't—you're just looking at him from a different perspective. Sometimes this is the end of what you thought was going to be "the relationship": you can't move past the nitpicking or don't think it's worth it. Even committed couples feel a letdown. You're not as spontaneous. It's starting to feel familiar; maybe you're a little bored in your lover's company sometimes. The arguments intensify as you both struggle for power and control. You drop almost all pretenses: if you

> A very old, very wise lady once said to me: you don't know if you love someone until you've seen through each season, twice over. This literally translates to two years but it also means going through the bad times as well as the good.
> Jeff, 26, chef

really are going to be together, there's no way you're eating sushi for the rest of your life. If you survive this stage, your faith in the relationship zooms higher. You know a major argument doesn't mean you'll split up and you start to believe your partner actually loves *you*, warts and all.

Sex

You may be arguing more, which reduces the frequency, and differing libidos become apparent. It's around now you'll realize if one of you wants sex much more or less than the other.

Keep it going

Because you're arguing more frequently, planning a few good times is essential. Now's the time for a few relaxing, pampering weekends away from it all. Be honest with each other about what you're not happy with, but be tactful as well. Try to balance any criticisms with compliments.

Check for

Pace: Are you both "fast" people and do things a million miles an hour or both stop-and-smell-the-roses people? The fights could be caused by mismatched energy and intensity levels.

Stage 5: the readjustment

Timing: around one to two years after you met

You both know exactly what you're letting yourself in for. You see each other as "wholes"—good points and bad—and if the commitment's still there, start compromising on things you don't agree on. When people like me say you need to "work on" your relationship, this is the stage at which you'll usually do it. Because it seems likely you will stay together long term, you both take a careful look at the relationship to decide if it really is what you want forever. You'll both need advanced communication skills to move farther (see Chapter 4). You need to "think for two," come up with win–win solutions to keep both of you happy, listen properly, and be open about your needs.

Sex

You've established a pattern by now and settled into some sort of routine. If you've sensibly worked on your sex life as well as your relationship, you'll have reached some compromise on frequency and be able to let go of inhibitions without fear of being judged. If you haven't, sexual tension is starting to build. The low libido person is feeling pressured; the high libido person is frustrated.

Keep it going

You need to instigate *serious* discussion on what both of you want from life and relationships. Listen carefully and don't kid each other or yourselves. It's around now friends, family, and perhaps your partner expect a deeper commitment like moving in or marriage. Make sure you're doing it for the right reasons, and not because it seems like "the right thing to do."

❗ Dating couples want to be adored; married couples want to be understood. Why the shift? Being uncritically adored feels great at the start but it's far more flattering to be loved warts and all when someone knows you well. Married people feel most intimate when partners see them as they see themselves.[1]

Check for

Common goals: Have you planned mutual goals for the future and are you equally excited about reaching them together?

Stage 6: true commitment

Timing: three to five years from your first date

Whether you marry, move in, or live apart still, you make some sort of public statement that you intend staying together permanently. If it's a healthy match, you'll start to focus less on your relationship and more on your lives. You feel a deep, secure sense of satisfaction when you're with your partner but are equally as secure when flying solo. You hone your relationship skills to perfection. You can tell from across the room she's unhappy, simply by the way she's standing. She knows you're bored when you do that hand-through-the-hair thing. You feel comfortable sharing your most humiliating, embarrassing fears and don't criticize unless it's really important. You're kind to each other and there for each other. The bonds are strongest now: external events like the death of a parent, shattered career dreams, the realization that you won't ever earn a million/get your waist back may cause friction but it won't shake your faith in each other.

Each couple is unique in what true commitment and intimacy means to them. Some marry and never spend a night apart for the rest of their lives. One couple I know say it's given them the freedom to separate for up to six months of the year, pursuing work projects on different sides of the world. Another very happy match have decided living together doesn't work. They rent apartments next to each other.

Sex

Your sex life reflects what else is happening in your life. If you have children, sex gets put on the backburner for a while (maybe even years). Ditto if something major happens—one of you gets a promotion or loses a job or a parent. Most couples drift in and out of great sex and no sex stages but if you've both given sex a high priority, especially since stage four, you're happy. You might occasionally yearn for new flesh but certainly aren't dissatisfied with what you're getting at home.

Keep it going

Love, respect, and treat each other as the most important person in your life. Never take each other for granted. Remind each other constantly how lucky you feel spending your lives together.

Check for

You should be well and truly connected in all areas of life by this stage. All you need to do now is keep the communication lines open so you *stay* that way—forever.

LOVE REALLY IS A DRUG

Why can't we stay in the really good "in love" stage forever? Some experts claim it's biologically impossible: our natural "love chemicals" dry up after 18 months.

When we're infatuated, our brain produces a range of intoxicating chemicals, says U.K. sexpert Sarah Litvinoff. Great sex (and lots of it) keeps the hormone surge fizzing. But in 18 months — around the time a Saturday night in has definitely lost appeal — the "love buzz" chemicals run out and the "in love" feeling disappears.

The most potent love chemical is phenylethylamine (PEA). There's also a snuggle-up chemical called oxytocin, which scientists believe is responsible for the urge to hug your partner so much at the start. As with any drug, the longer you have it, the more of it you need to get "high" and the newer the love, the more chemicals produced. This could explain why love junkies constantly move from one lover to the next: they're addicted to the chemical rush, which is strongest at the start.

But if you do make it past 18 months, your body rewards you with another drug dose. This time it's endorphins: soothing substances that make us feel warm, content, and peaceful. This is the stage when you can most trust your feelings, both biologically and psychologically (couples who get engaged around the two-year point have the best chance of avoiding divorce). In fact, the longer we stay with a partner and the happier we are, the more endorphins we

ARE THEY RIGHT FOR YOU? THE FIVE CRUCIAL CONNECTION POINTS

Through decades of intense study of all sorts of relationships, psychologists appear to agree on five key areas which make or break a relationship:

1. chemistry
2. compatibility
3. common goals
4. pace
5. timing

Couples who remain blissfully bonded for life tend to connect on all five. Those who match on three or four still enjoy very happy, satisfying relationships, but the couples who struggle to hit two inevitably find they are barking up the wrong trouser legs and split. How soon will you know how you and your lover score? Pretty much instantly on one (chemistry). As for the others, only time will truly tell—and *that's* essentially what dating is all about. It's also the reason why those whirlwind meet-then-marry relationships rarely work: you *can't* tell immediately whether you'll click on all these levels. Jump in head-first and you could be forced to walk the same path through life with someone who's desperate to turn left, while you want to go right.

To find out how well you connect, you need to start initiating open, honest discussion about your feelings and relationship, and the sooner the better. Practice makes perfect. After three months of intense dating, it's sensible to talk honestly about where you're headed and to make it clear what you want from the relationship and what the rules are. (If they're out the door and down at the local bar after you say you'd like a future, better to find out now.) During the discussion, check that you agree what words like "serious" and "monogamy" mean. Some people interpret monogamy as no physical contact at all with anyone but their partner. Others think it means no penetrative sex. Everyone's different and we all put our own interpretations on things. (If you want to know more about communicating effectively, see Chapter 4.)

Dating is—and should be—a try-before-you-buy exercise. Unless you're just in it for a good time not a long time, it's sensible to keep an objective eye focused on your long-term compatibility. Knowing what to look for along the way obviously helps, and this is what this section is all about. It's not a bad idea to check how many areas you're connecting on (and how well) at one month, three months, and one year into a relationship. Keep reading so you know what to watch for, then drag this book out and read this section again at various points.

I know, I know, you're starting to think a computer would have a better chance at finding you the perfect mate. The truth is, it probably could predict a fairly accurate survival score if fed all the relevant information. But there's no way it'll ever to be able to predict the most mysterious connection point of all: chemistry. Ain't love grand?

Chemistry: does it *feel* right?

Finally, the good-looking guy Kate had been eyeing all night took the hint and came over to talk to her.

"Hi, I'm Pete," he said. "Oh— and this is my friend Dave."

Pete looked like all he had to do was pull on a g-string and he'd be a "Chippendale." Dave was short, balding, and looked as though he'd been dressed by his mother, but Kate was besotted within minutes. "It was so *weird*," she says. "Here was this gorgeous hunk paying me attention and all I could think of was how much I wanted to kiss his unattractive friend."

Caught flirting at a party by your loved one? Your reaction will depend on what sex you are. Women are more likely to apologize and reassure in a desperate bid to save the relationship; men are more likely to pretend it doesn't matter, particularly if others are watching. They're far more concerned with saving face.[3]

Lust at first sight. Instant attraction. Feeling really comfortable around someone after exchanging two words. Suddenly feeling awfully hot and restricted by having to wear clothes. *That's* chemistry. And there's a simple way to tell if you've got it with your partner: if you have to think too hard about it, you haven't. Chemistry is instant: it's either there right from the start or it develops rapidly.

Apart from being none-too-subtle, chemistry is illogical, irrational, and out of our conscious control—which is why it can land us our perfect match *or* in scalding hot water. Chemistry doesn't care if this person will dump you after three nights, taking the family heirloom with him, or whether he'd make a fabulous parent for future children. It works on a primitive level—like whether your body wants to get close to his. It's involuntary and feels delicious, which is why it's so frustrating when we find chemistry with people we know we shouldn't (your best friend's husband, for instance).

Find it with the *right* person, however, and you're lengths ahead in the relationship stakes. While chemistry alone won't guarantee you a great relationship, it's essential for a long-term happy liaison. If it's not there in the beginning, it's likely you're not going to be aroused by your partner in the future. Lose the chemistry—or never find it—and you've lost the relationship.

Which begs the question: is it a bad sign if you're not ripping each other's clothes off in the beginning? In a word—yes! If you've only made love once or twice and a deep, tonsil-touching kiss doesn't end with both of you ripping your gear off in the living room, it is *not* a good sign. Burning loins, frantic underwear removal, making out in inappropriate places—if you're not doing it in the beginning, you sure as hell won't be six months down the road (let alone 20 years on, when every couple goes through that "I'd rather eat slugs than sleep with you" stage). Love without lust is friendship. Some experts disagree with me, but I honestly don't believe it's possible to have a passionate relationship for life unless the passion's there in the beginning.

Can chemistry develop over time? If you're both emotionally healthy and don't have any hang-ups, my honest answer is, not usually. But there are exceptions. If you've had bad sexual experiences that have made you afraid of sex, you might be too scared to feel passion. You probably won't have "chemistry" with any partner, not just this one. Or perhaps you've been hurt one too many times and fear that if you give all of yourself (commit your heart, mind, *and* body) you'll never survive if it happens again. In those situations, it's worth getting some counseling and seeing how you feel afterward. Otherwise, think about whether this person should really be a friend rather than a lover.

The other question that people often ask me is: what if it's the opposite and there's nothing *but* chemistry? Can a good relationship develop when all you have in common at the start is the frantic urge to shred the sheets together? You bet it can! Sexual attraction is incredibly powerful. If you're shooting off the Richter scale for chemistry, it's well worth hanging around to see if there's any other areas you click in. Besides, what have you got to lose? If it does turn out to be just sex and both of you didn't expect more, you've lost nothing except a few dozen weekends locked in each other's bedroom.

How long before you'll know? If you're working through the Kama Sutra for the sixth time and still don't know the names of your partner's brother and sister (or even if they have any), it's a pretty safe bet it's lust. If you're still spending *most* of your time having sex but have at least emerged long enough to meet each other's significant friends and family, hang in there.

You've got chemistry if:

- You find your lover very, very attractive. She definitely does it for you.

- You feel a little intoxicated when you're with him. Even in a crowded room, it still feels like you're alone because you only have eyes (and ears) for each other.

- You feel like you "click": your initial gut instinct on meeting was a very definite "Yes please!"

- You're either having lots of sex or you can't wait to start.

Compatibility: how much do you have in common?

When your mother told you to "go out and find a nice boy or girl," what she really meant was, "Go out and find someone who's like us." My friend Nathan did quite the opposite. He's a 25-year-old medical student from a privileged Australian background. His girlfriend was 32, came from a poor, religious Italian family and worked in the family business, a laundromat. The chemistry was certainly there—they couldn't keep their hands off each other—but compatible they weren't.

"The sex was great," says Nathan. "But on almost every other level we disagreed. The age made a difference, but it was our backgrounds that caused the squabbles."

Most of us have strong cultural beliefs and values, even if we aren't conscious of them, and we tend to match up with someone whose views correspond with ours. Compatibility is about past experiences and future expectations—it's an identification that makes us feel comfortable with someone. Without it, relationships flounder—unless one person consciously adopts the other person's values, which can lead to a whole *different* set of problems.

If you're ridiculously incompatible, you'll find out early in the relationship (you can't even agree on which restaurant to eat in and what night to do it on). Most couples discover whether they're basically compatible within a month or so, but it obviously takes years to discover if you're compatible enough to last a lifetime together.

Rolled up in the compatibility package are our secret expectations of life and what we want out of the relationship. One of the biggest causes of break-ups is when expectations don't match. It's like a vacation fling. You loved him when you were lounging around on an island but when you see his *real* life—working at the bank, dinner with mom on Wednesday, football every Sunday—you may start thinking, *There's no way I'll fit into this lifestyle!*

HOW COMPATIBLE ARE YOU?

Okay, so you've been dating a few months, done a few *Cosmo* quizzes together and talked enough to decide you think pretty much along the same lines. Now put your relationship to the real test by rating it and giving honest answers to some of those "big" questions you've been avoiding.

Each of you should answer the questions separately on a sheet of paper. Rate each question on a satisfaction scale of 1–6, 1 being very unsatisfied, 6 being extremely satisfied. For the second section, use the same scale to rate how important the named issues are for you. When you've finished, prepare for a few home truths as you compare scores and answers, then talk about any major discrepancies. Can you fix them or come to some sort of compromise?

How satisfied am I with:

- my partner's appearance
- the way my partner manages moods
- the routine that we follow

- the split of household chores
- my partner's attitude to life in general
- my partner's commitment to telling the truth
- my partner's commitment to fidelity
- how often we have sex
- the quality of our sex life
- the common goals and interests that we share
- how we handle money issues
- the amount of time we spend separately
- the amount of time we spend together
- the amount of independence we give each other
- my partner's family and friends
- the level of communication we share
- the way we solve problems and resolve arguments
- the amount of affection we give each other—both physical and verbal

How important is:

- having a child at some point in our relationship
- having several children
- having children immediately
- my career
- my career versus the relationship (which has first priority?)
- a satisfying sex life
- a partner who understands me
- being in love
- loving someone deeply for the rest of my life
- being surrounded by friends and family

Common goals: how many do you share?

When people think of common goals, they think of things like buying houses and children. But while agreeing on where to live and how many children to have is very important and can keep you both focused and moving in the same direction, it doesn't do much for the excitement factor. There's a difference between keeping busy and having fun together.

You need to make sure that the common goals you share aren't just the big, boring ones. Saving for a down payment on a house isn't much fun, even if buying the house is. It needs to be balanced with things like wanting to travel together, because planning an overseas trip *will* keep the fun factor high. Throwing parties, taking a class together—these are the things that keep partners motivated and interested. The more common goals you have, the better. Set another goal the minute you complete the first one. It doesn't take long for a relationship to go very flat. Obviously, this connection point applies more to long-term relationships, but there are early clues to watch for.

You're progressing nicely if:

- You work well as a team. One of you picks up the video and take-out, the other's in charge of the wine and dessert.

- You both place the same importance on planning "special" nights or weekends away. Anniversaries or birthdays hold the same significance for both of you.

- You both make an effort to make the other feel special with impromptu presents or phone calls out of the blue.

- You both put effort into keeping the relationship fresh and exciting by suggesting new things to do.

WHAT IF WE AREN'T "MATCHING BOOKENDS"?

The most successful relationships are usually those that are balanced: both of you rate pretty much the same on the scale of attractiveness, wealth, intelligence, and background. But there is an argument for hooking up with someone who's not quite as fabulous as you are. It's commonly called "down-dating," and some say our perception that the rich should marry rich, the beautiful should go out with beautiful, and intellectuals should date intellectuals isn't necessarily true or sensible.

Sometimes oddly matched couples find their own balance. If you're an ambitious career woman, a guy who's less ambitious and domesticated could be perfect. You've got yourself a "wife," and you are simply trading places in a formula that's worked for centuries: one goes out to earn the bacon, the other stays home to butter the bread.

Most oddly matched couples are getting some sort of trade-off—it's just not apparent to others. The gotta-have-him looking guy who chooses Ms. Plain Jane? She could have more personality in her thumbnail than all the bimbette beauties he's ever dated combined. The Harvard graduate who married someone from the wrong side of the tracks could be getting a much needed grassroots perspective on life.

Down-dating only works, however, when both parties are secure in themselves and their relationship. Society (that is, "friends") will constantly point out to one of you that "you could have done better." The other will be told, "you're very lucky someone like X has chosen you." The "lucky one" needs to know they're not going to be thrown over for someone "better"; the person who could have done "better" has to watch they don't become resentful. You both need to be in the relationship for the right reasons so that comments like these don't destroy you.

Also make sure you're not *deliberately* choosing someone who doesn't measure up to your own standard out of insecurity. *Always* having to be the one that's richer, more attractive, more intelligent and articulate means you're picking people who make you look good by comparison *and* it's highly unlikely they'll dump you, isn't it? Ask yourself: is it fear of rejection that's got me here or a genuine love and respect for someone who just happens not to measure up in society's eyes?

Pace: are you moving at the same speed through life?

The chemistry's there, you're compatible, have lots of common goals, but still having problems? Chances are, it's a pace problem that's causing it. We all live our lives at a different pace—how fast we think or move or the rate at which we want to realize our dreams. If you're a "fast" person—juggle a dozen projects at once, talk on the phone while you're typing on your computer, rarely sit down for five minutes, and plan to be the boss within five years—it's not a good idea to choose a partner whose idea of excitement is watching *Cheers* reruns on a Saturday night. Eventually, you'll either both decide you're not matched or the fast person will move on. Fast people are the ones who constantly crave excitement, and if they aren't getting it, they'll create it (that is, through an affair). Pace is also about ambition. If you're aiming for a six-figure salary, you'll need to devote a great deal of time to your career. If your partner doesn't share or understand your drive to succeed and rates their leisure time above their job, you're definitely headed for some rough spots.

You're travelling at the same speed if:

- Your energy levels seem matched. You either both want to slob in front of the TV or both want to get out there and *do* something.

- Your attitude to work is similiar. You both place the same importance on career.

- You think and talk at a similiar pace.

- You seem to need and want similiar proportions of quiet time and excitement.

Timing: are you at the same stage in your lives?

You can have all four previous connection points—chemistry, common goals, compatibility, and pace—but if your timing's wrong, forget it. What stage in life is each of you at? There are certain times in anyone's life when a long-term, serious relationship is the *last* thing you want—or need.

The timing's not great if either of you:

- Have just come out of another long-term, serious relationship. Lurching straight from one relationship to another isn't sensible.

- Are at crucial stages in your careers. It's less of a problem but you need time to make a relationship work.

- Have unfinished business. You haven't quite gotten that ex out of your system or gotten over a trauma.

- Just aren't ready to settle down yet. You still feel there's a lot you want and need to do on your own before sharing your life with someone else.

Sometimes, you'll meet the right person at not quite the right time and think, *Screw it! I'm doing it anyway.* Your feelings are so powerful, they override whatever it was that stopped you from wanting to commit. Other times, you'll meet the right person at not quite the right time and think, *I wish I could stick you in the deep freeze for five years while I traipse around Europe.* Even if the person seems perfect for you, your need to be solo is greater.

One point I want to make crystal clear here: timing doesn't always relate to age. What you want at 18 is different from what you're looking for at 28 or 38, but being around the same age doesn't guarantee synchronicity. You could easily be ready at 25 for what they want at 35—or vice versa.

When you're ready to "settle down" depends very much on what you've accomplished, your personality, expectations, and morals. So while age is a rough predictor, there are numerous exceptions. Check your maturity levels rather than birth dates, and don't get too hung up on the age thing. If you're both over 25 and your age difference is 5 years or less, I wouldn't give it a second thought. Even if there's a ten-year gap between you, it can work—especially if you're older. The older you are, the less important age differences become. (There's less of a generation gap if you're 40 and he's 30 than if you went out when he was 16 and you were 26!)

Having said that, you do need to prepare for some problems if the difference *is* ten years or more. First there's the issue of kids. If he's 25 and you're 35 and you both want children, will he be ready to change diapers before your biological clock stops? If you're the younger partner, you're in the "pupil" position. Your partner's lived longer so they probably (hopefully) know more. The power's automatically on the elder's side and there's a tendency for you to view him or her as a teacher or parent: someone to hide things from if you've been "naughty." You may feel like you can't have fun for fear of being thought immature. Plenty of younger partners say no to boozy all-nighters or weekends away with the girls or boys (you know, the *fun* stuff), then regret missing out later in life.

If you're the older partner, your lover's lack of experience and wisdom can be frustrating. You've been through all those experiences and some people don't *want* to go back for round two. You probably earn more, so once again, the power is skewed in your favor. Major decisions will probably be left up to you and sometimes it would be nice if you didn't have to carry all the burden. Just as your lover will try to act older, you'll feel obliged to act younger. Instead of going out to dinner, you'll drag yourself along to the hottest nightclub and feel like a geriatric up on the dance floor.

Another common timing question is: what if I'm ready to settle down and my partner isn't? Should I wait?

It depends very much on why they're not ready and when they will be. If you've just met and they're about to go traveling for a year, I wouldn't spend the next 12 months hanging around the mailbox and looking longingly at planes flying over. (Though I would trade phone numbers so you can contact each other when he or she comes back.)

It's a different scenario if they're not ready because they've just split from someone else. Play it cool, don't pressure them, give them lots and lots and *lots* of space and in six months or so, they might change their mind. Ditto if it's a time problem rather than tim*ing*. If they need to concentrate on their career for a year or two and you're happy being slotted in whenever they can, again, it's worth a try.

The one I'd be most wary of is the guy or girl who says they're just "not ready" to settle down yet. It's not a concrete reason so there's no end in sight. Besides, "not ready" often means "not played around enough yet," so unless it's just (safe) sex you're after, personally I'd run for the hills.

I've fallen in love with my partner's friend. What now?

Oh help! You've decided you're not only *in*compatible with the person you're dating, you're convinced Mr. or Ms. Right-for-you just happens to be Mr. or Ms. Wrong's close friend?

If it's not that serious between you and your partner

Sure it's not a case of the grass being greener on the other side? When you say "in love" do you mean love or lust? If it's lust, give it a few weeks: those wicked desires might well disappear when you start to see the "real" person (that is, picking their nose when they think no one's looking). If you honestly have fallen for the friend, the first thing to do is break off your existing relationship, because dating someone to get to someone else isn't nice. Explain, quite truthfully, that you don't think it's going to work out long term and *don't* suggest staying friends; it'll make it even more difficult long term if something does transpire.

Before you do this, make sure you have some way of contacting the friend independently, but don't divulge the reason you're splitting up to Mr. or Ms. Hope-you're-next. A week or so after the break-up, call the friend to say you're no longer seeing so-and-so but would like to keep in contact with him or her. Make it pretty clear you'd like more than just coffee, then leave your phone number and the ball in their court. If the feeling is mutual, they'll make a date instantly or call to ask you out within a few days. If they don't, they're either not attracted to you, or your ex is upset and their loyalty to them is stronger than their feelings for you. If you do end up getting together and it looks like it will continue, it's courteous though not essential for you to ring your ex and tell them what's going on. Not to ask for permission, but to assure them the relationship started *after* you split.

If it's very serious between you and your partner (you've been going out for years or you're living together or married)

A psychiatrist once told me, "When making a crucial decision, stay at the point of confusion for as long as possible." Why? The longer you're frantically tossing up this side and that side, the more pros and cons you'll think of and the better decision you'll make. I can hear you groan from here: this is exactly what you *don't* want to hear. You're already feeling stressed, guilty, and so upset by it all, you want the world to stop spinning so you can get off.

But he's got a point. This is not a decision to be made overnight. It requires a lot of time and thought, because if you leave your partner for a good friend, the fallout will be *enormous* and the guilt difficult to bear. You're robbing them of a long-term lover *and* possibly the person they would have turned to to help them through it, simultaneously. They're being betrayed on two levels at once. By removing both support systems, you're not just pulling the rug out from under them, you're polishing the floor so it's nice and slippery. They can't help but fall flat on their face.

Even if you didn't so much as kiss the friend before confessing, your partner will imagine you've been having an affair, right under their nose, the entire time. They'll feel stupid and totally lacking in judgment. Why didn't they see it coming? They'll think back to all the heart-to-hearts they had about you to the friend and about the friend to you and think, *They must have been laughing at me.* Their life will feel like one big lie. They'll find it extremely difficult to trust again, both friends and partners, and probably need six months of therapy.

That's what you have to accept. I'm not saying all this is your fault (*no one* deliberately falls for a friend), but this is what's going to be thrown in your face once you confess, by your partner and people who love your partner who will hate you for causing them this much pain.

The only way you and the friend will get through all this is if you both feel so strongly for each other you honestly can't imagine living happily without the other. So make sure you're 150 percent sure it isn't lust or idealized romanticism that'll fall flat the minute it's out in the open. You need to be absolutely sure you won't regret leaving your partner if it doesn't work out with the friend.

Both of you should assume the worst: they'll lose their friendship with your partner *for good*; you'll lose your partner *for good*. Be prepared for friends and family to judge you. Some will stand by you, knowing you didn't set out to hurt anyone, and that there was no point in your staying when love had left. Others will call you names, slam the door in your face, and never, ever see you again. All your friends will have to choose between you and your long-term partner: you stand to lose 50 percent of them. If you're very, very lucky, and handle it extremely diplomatically, they might well forgive you in the future. But in the meantime, you'll be the "bad person." The one who caused the whole damn mess.

You know all this and have given it time but remain utterly convinced it's the right thing to do? Set the wheels in motion. Sit down with the friend and decide when you're going to break the news and where you're both going to live. Is it better to live separately for a little while? Organize accommodations discreetly and start thinking through practical matters: who's going to keep the house, the cat, and

(God help you) the children. In fairness to your partner, it's reasonable for you to be the one to move out initially, even if a later settlement does award you the home you own together.

If you have a good relationship with your family and trust them to keep quiet, consider warning them before you deliver the bombshell. Close friends may also need to know, though it goes without saying that if you have any concern whatsoever they'll deliver the news to your partner before you can, keep quiet.

As for what to say on D-Day, there's no alternative but the truth. Tell your partner you need to talk, sit them down and say, "I'm so sorry. This isn't working out for me and hasn't for a long time. I don't know what happened (if you do, say what) but I don't love you anymore and haven't for a while. I stayed hoping it would work out but in the meantime, I fell in love with someone else. You will possibly never forgive me for this but it's X. No, we haven't been having an affair but (however long ago), we had a talk and both realized we felt the same way. I am not leaving you for X, I'm leaving because it's over between us. But I do intend to pursue a relationship with X and I think you should know that."

Their reaction could be any one of a number of things. The talk will probably end with both of you crying hysterically and one leaving. When that happens, make arrangements (as best you can) to ensure your partner isn't alone. Ring a close friend of theirs or relative of your partner who you know will be supportive of them. Fill them in quickly, put up with whatever abuse they fling at you, and tell them you're worried about your partner and think he or she needs support.

The first place your partner will go after finding out will probably be the friend's place. Personally, I'd make sure I wasn't there: this is between the two of them. It goes without saying you'll have warned them when you're about to confess, and it's a good idea if they also have some sort of prepared speech ready. Not that your partner will take in much of what either of you say—they're in shock—but it may sink in afterward.

What happens now? You'll both spend the next few months feeling guilty, being abused by everyone from the drycleaner to your parents, and worrying yourself sick about your partner. The friend will blame him or herself for causing all this. You will blame yourself.

Friends will sort themselves into for-her and for-him camps. You'll start the painful process of splitting up mutual possessions. But, *if you honestly have done the right thing*, you'll also feel relief. No more hiding, it's out in the open and while your new relationship will be strained—you're constantly saying to each other, "I'm so happy to finally be with you but Christ, this isn't easy, is it?"—the sheer pleasure of being with the person you love will help ease the pain.

WELCOME BACK TO THE REAL WORLD

Your problem's more of the don't-want-to-share them variety than fancy-someone-else? Well, sorry, but you have to come out sometime. When friends and family ask, "When are we going to meet him?" quit the vague promises and instead set a date. After all, if you are to be joined at the hip, it's got to happen at some point!

Meeting the family

It's the moment you've been simultaneously dreading but desperate for. After all, if your partner takes you home to meet good old mom, dad, and the rest of the clan, he *must* like you! Dying for it all to run smoothly? Here are some tips for that first meeting:

- **Smile like you're in a Gap ad:** Smile until your face hurts and you'll be forgiven a multitude of sins (except maybe for wearing a bottom-skimming mini and thigh-high boots).
- **Be polite but try to act naturally:** "I found myself saying things like, 'Would you care to pass the sugar?' and 'I'm just going to powder my nose,' " said my friend Anabel, who was desperate to impress her new lover's parents. "After a glass of much-needed wine, I stopped behaving like I was visiting the Queen and started being myself. They visibly relaxed and did the same."
- **Be nice and show interest:** Even if his mom's a frump, she might have beautiful skin. If his dad collects something, ask him to tell you about it and he'll be on your side instantly.
- **Stick to safe topics:** Now's not the time to tell them your university thesis is about female ejaculation. Politics, religion, sex, anything remotely controversial is out until you know them better. It should go without saying that swear words and slang won't get you invited for a Sunday dinner.
- **If you don't think they like you, don't panic:** Sure, your last

boyfriend's folks treated you like a daughter, but some people find it easy to express emotion and affection while others don't. Give them time to get used to you and warm to you.

- **Don't bitch in the car on the way home:** Let's be honest here, it's a lot easier to go out with someone if she likes your family and your family likes her. If you're complaining before you've even pulled your seatbelt on, it's obvious any future family get-togethers are going to be a free-for-all.

Meeting friends

Meeting mom is nerve-racking but friends probably have more influence. Here's how to survive and win them over.

- **Dress for success:** Think about what image you'd like his friends to have of you. Want to be one of the crowd? Wear jeans and a big smile. If it's respect you're after, arrange to meet after work while you're still in a suit.
- **Don't get huffy if your partner acts weird:** He's anxious for both parties to get on because it'll make life a lot easier if you do. If his friends are protective, he's nervous you're being scrutinized and judged. If they're the type to give him a hard time, he'll avoid being affectionate for fear of being ribbed later.
- **Ask questions:** Where did they meet your partner, how long have they known each other, where do they work, what did they do last weekend? Ignoring them and insisting on playing footsies with your partner won't score points with either.
- **Don't flirt:** Even if her best friend is supermodel material, flirting is bad form, humiliating for her, and you'll end up on the scrap heap (along with all the other exes who couldn't resist).

EARLY WARNING SIGNS YOU'VE FOUND MR. OR MS. *WRONG*

Not all of you will be patting yourself on the back, thinking, "Wow! I chose well!" at this point. If you've absorbed most of what I've been talking about and know, deep in your heart, that somehow your relationship's not measuring up to the standards I'm suggesting, it's time to face reality. Even if you have invested a great deal of time and energy (and possibly cash) into making it work, you're still better off cutting your losses and getting out NOW if your relationship's got all the signs it's not going to last. See if you recognize your relationship in any of the following.

Too many ups and downs

We tend to equate stormy, tempestuous relationships with grand, passionate love. Cathy and Heathcliffe. Romeo and Juliet. Most of us are suckers for up-and-down relationships when we're younger (we've got the time and energy). When we're older (and have work commitments and other pressures), they're usually not worth the effort. Relationships of this type usually mean you've got tons of chemistry and passion but are hopelessly incompatible in every other area, hence the constant arguments and miscommunication. The highs are addictively delicious but they'll wear you out eventually.

Get out now if:

- You're having as many bad times (or more) as good. The first five dates at least should be fun; preferably you should hit ten before having a bad time or a major argument.

- You constantly misread each other: you say tom*ah*to, he says tom*ay*to. You're saying things like, "No, I didn't mean that at all," every second sentence.

- Your partner is moody, defensive, and overreacts to situations.

- Your partner seems to *like* arguing and deliberately pick fights.

- The only time you really seem happy together is when you're making up after an argument.

> **Never go out with a guy thinking, "When we're serious, he'll change." He won't.**
> Carla, 32, pharmacist

Too many stops and starts

Instead of "How's Richard?" people are asking, "Are you seeing Richard at the moment?" because one week it's on, the next it's over, only to be kick-started afresh the following week. You're long-suffering; he's unreliable. She's awful; then she's nice. Just when you think you've had enough, he turns up with flowers, apologies, and a smile that melts your heart.

Why are you sticking around? Because of the poker machine effect, officially known as "variable-ratio reinforcement."[4] Just as addictive as gambling, you're hooked on the if-only principle. If, every time you put your hands on a hot stove to warm them, they burn, you'll leave. But if it's intermittent—sometimes they burn, sometimes they feel deliciously toasty—you'll keep going back for more. It's the same with relationships. If occasionally, your partner comes through *just* when you're at the point of giving up, all that effort was worth it after all. The "if only" has been realized—until the next time. The longer you stay in a relationship like this, the more trapped you are. If you've worked hard to fix unsolvable problems, you're even more vulnerable to the poker machine effect. After all, you've put all the hard work in, why should his next partner reap all the benefits?

Get out now if:

- In the three months you've been "going out," you've broken up twice.

- Your partner is not consistent in how he or she treats you. One minute you're treated like royalty, the next like dirt.

- Your partner tries to buy you back after an argument. Instead of talking through the issue, she brings in champagne and says, "Let's not rehash the whole thing."

- One minute you feel secure and cozy about the two of you, one phone call later you're convinced it'll never last.

Your partner treats you badly

We've all seen it. The couple standing next to us at the bar. She's picking hairs from his coat jacket, he's brushing her off in more ways than one. Even from ten paces away, it's obvious he's flirting with the bartender. Your heart goes out to her as she slinks off to the bathroom for the hundredth time that night to have a cry or to look at herself in the mirror and ask, "Why am I putting up with this?"

It's a good question. Nothing makes me angrier than when I meet attractive, intelligent people, bursting with personality and love of life, only to find out they've hooked up with Ms. Bitch or Mr. Bastard who walks all over them like a well-worn doormat.

I was at a wedding recently where there were two different entrees, which were plunked down in front of us without a choice as to which you preferred.

"Yum!" said the girl opposite me. "I scored the seafood. I love seafood and hate tortellini."

"I want the seafood," said her boyfriend, and swapped, putting the hated pasta in front of her.

She smiled brightly at me. "Never mind," she said.

Later, she confessed she was "dreaming of her wedding."

"When is it?" I asked.

"Whenever I can get Jason to ask me," she said.

Jason smirked and said charmingly, "Keep dreaming, babe."

She shrugged, smiled at me again and said, "One day."

I would have handled the situation somewhat differently. First, the tortellini would be dumped over his head and mashed in with two fists. Next, an oyster (on the shell) shoved up his nose. Had someone slipped something into her drink? Was she a masochist? Who in their right mind would be dreaming of marrying such an arrogant, rude person who treated her so badly?

I'd really love to say it's rare to see this sort of thing, but it's not. I've often met women matched up with men who, quite frankly, aren't worthy of kissing their feet let alone smugly sitting beside them. And it's not just females who put up with bad treatment: men do it, too.

"Yes I know it's her 30th birthday and I'm not invited," says Phil. "But the numbers were restricted and she promised she'll make it up to me tomorrow." Where's his brain? He's been dating this girl for six months!

If you're staying with someone who, even early on, is already treating you badly, you're possibly codependent. Codependent was a buzzword in psychology a few years back. The textbook definition is a pattern of behavior and/or personality that causes people to stay in relationships or situations which are unhealthy and bad for them.[6] In other words, a codependant thinks their partner is God when they're behaving like the Devil. (See Chapter 8 for a more in-depth look at bad relationships.)

Psychologists aren't sure what makes people codependent, but there are theories. The first says if you've been treated badly by your parents and/or previous lovers, you're so used to being put down, it feels odd if someone is nice to you. You subconsciously choose nasty over nice because it feels familiar, it's what you're used to. On the opposite end of the scale are people who've had such idyllic childhoods and past relationships, it doesn't occur to them that people might be mean.[7] You'll excuse atrocious behavior because you honestly don't believe it's directed at *you*.

Get out now if:

- You suspect you're a codependent person and have made yet another bad choice.

- Your friends are saying things like, "I can't believe you're putting up with being treated like this." No one seems to like your partner but you.

- Your partner puts you down or criticizes you. At this early stage, he should be showering you with compliments, not pointing out your faults.

- Your partner's emotionally abusive: She shouts at you, calls you names, and makes disparaging remarks about your appearance, personality, or abilities.

> People who blurt out their entire life story on the first meeting don't just remove the mystery, they're likely to be troubled souls. They have no "boundary" around themselves as protection and are likely to be hurt easily—so they carry lots of baggage.[5]

- Your partner is showing violent tendencies (like hitting walls during arguments). If you feel even slightly physically threatened, leave immediately. (See Chapter 8, if you feel unable to.)

ARE YOU READY TO COMMIT?

Congratulations! If you've gotten this far (and been paying attention), you're reasonably confident you've chosen well and can see a future together. The next step is commitment: making a pact with each other that you're ready, willing, and able to move the relationship into a more serious stage.

The first commitment most couples make to each other is monogamy: promising you won't play footsie under the sheets with anyone else. "I love you" tends to follow fast. (While not technically a commitment, most of us translate "I love you" to mean "I intend to stick around—at least for a little while.") Moving in together is usually the next stage, followed by marriage and (the most serious commitment of all) deciding to have children together. (More about those in Chapter 6.)

If you're traveling along like two peas in a pod, you'll both want the same level of commitment at the same time. Others (like, most couples) wouldn't qualify for the synchronized swimming relationship team. One's ready to move forward, the other wants to wait. Or you're both ready but too scared to suggest commitment just in case the other isn't. Think you're ready to take the plunge? Hopefully the following will make the transition from casual to committed a little easier.

The first commitment: monogamy

Few people can love someone and still happily share their partner with others. Right or wrong (and there are plenty of people who'll argue that humans aren't designed to be monogamous), it's a basic human instinct to want our lover all to ourselves. A few brave souls try "open" relationships, but even they have rules (you're allowed to sleep with other people but only if the partner knows/it's not a mutual friend/you do it between 5:00 P.M. and 6:00 P.M. on Mondays/it's a super-model). In my experience, most open relationships don't work. Usually one partner secretly wants monogamy but goes along with the free-for-all idea because he or she would rather have part of their lover than none at all. In exceptional cases, however, it does work for both. Whether this means the people involved are truly exceptional individuals or were abducted by aliens as young children and tampered with, who knows? But this book's aimed at the majority of couples, and because most of us want and need monogamy, I'll assume you do, too.

> She broke it off because she said I wouldn't open up to her. What she didn't know was that I'd told her stuff I'd never told anyone else. She knew all my secrets. That was as open as I can be.
> Evan, 25, apprentice

How to bring the subject up? If you're convinced you've given it enough time, you're ready to commit to one person and pretty sure the one you've been dating is, too, simply say to your partner, "X, are you happy with our relationship? Do you want to continue going out together?" If he says yes all you need to follow it up with is, "That's great because I'm really happy. Does this mean we won't be seeing other people?"

You'll get one of two responses to this. Either, "Yeah. I guess it does. But I thought that was pretty obvious anyway." (Mission accomplished!) Or, "Look, I'm really enjoying this but I want freedom to see other people." It's up to you how you react to that answer. You can decide it's not worth it (the correct answer then is "Get out") or ask when he would be ready. Don't kid yourself though. If he says, "Look I'm not interested in a serious relationship and I don't want a commitment," believe him. He's not playing hard to get, he's telling the truth. Accept this or find someone else.

Saying (gulp!), "I love you"

They're the three most significant words in the English language. Deliver them at the right time to the right person and the first time they're said out loud calls for champagne. Blurt them out at the wrong time to the wrong person and you need a stiff drink for totally different reasons. It's like the siren just sounded on *Showtime at the Apollo*.

Most of us have a justifiable phobia about being the first to say the "L" word. Why? Because we don't know what the hell we'd do if our partner didn't say it back. There is only one correct response to "I love you" and that's "I love you, too."

So, what if he says, "That's nice. Anyway, as I was saying . . ."? Or looks at you with pity and says, "Sharon, you're awfully sweet but . . ."?

Timing is everything. Say "I love you" too soon and you not only look desperate, you instantly lose power and dignity. Leave it too late and you risk missing that magic moment that could launch you both on to the next relationship stage. One couple I know have been in love for at least six months. I know it. They know it—but neither of them can get up the courage to say it to the other. They say things like, "I really miss you. I really, really, *really* miss you," and "God, I love being with you," but you can see the frustration mounting. Sometimes, often, no other words but "I love you" can express how you're feeling. (In fact, if they don't say it soon, I'll betray both their confidences and tell each what the other has said, in front of the other.)

So how do you judge when it's appropriate to let the cat out of the bag? Only you can truly answer that one, but these are some things you might like to think about:

Make sure you both speak the same language

Your "I love you" might mean, "I think this is special, let's give it a go." His interpretation might be, "When's the wedding?" If you think your partner will overreact, tack something on to the end like, "Don't panic—I'm not about to propose. I'm just telling you how I feel."

Wait until you're absolutely bursting

Like, you'll explode if you don't say it right now. Wait until you're 150 percent convinced you mean it. And no, you can't possibly mean it after three dates.

When I was 12, a kid at my school came up to me and delivered a message. "See that guy over there?" he said, pointing to a kid from my English class. "Well, that's Brad and he sent me over here to tell you he loves you and wants to go steady."

"Okay," I said.

Brad and I went steady for a whole week. We didn't speak once though we did sit together on the playground for a full five minutes and look at our feet. True love? You betcha! Telling someone you love them on the second date or second week is just as ridiculous. It's silly—and that's what they'll think you are if you do it.

The fact is, the first time anyone says, "I love you," he or she usually doesn't. Not really. True love takes years to develop and if you're lucky, it's always growing. You look back and think, *I really thought I loved him when I said it back then but it's nothing compared to how I feel now.* That's not to say you can't feel "in love" after three months of serious dating, and it probably is acceptable to trot it out then. For absolute maximum impact, I'd wait six. If someone says, "I love you," after you've dated for six months, that person's thought long and hard about it and there is truly long-term potential because it's often harder to say it later than it is earlier. Saying, "I love you," when you're in the infatuated part of the relationship is easy: you aren't aware of any faults. Saying it when you've got a pretty good idea of what you're letting yourself in for is far more of a compliment.

A much-loved ex of mine told me he loved me when I stumbled back to bed after throwing up for the sixtieth time that night because of food poisoning. Call me strange but I was far more moved than if he'd said it across the candlelit dinner table earlier that night, when both of us were all dressed up and looking fabulous, totally unaware I was about to swallow a bad oyster.

> **I just called to say—**
>
> • **"I love you": 70 percent of lovers have called simply to say those three words.**
> • **"It's over": 12 percent have taken the coward's way out and ended it over the phone.**
> • **"Marry me": 2 percent have proposed, or been proposed to, over the phone.**[8]

If you're saying it first, sneak it into conversation

Who says it first? Whoever's bravest I guess. The coward's way out is to say, "I *think* I'm falling in love with you." If your amour looks at you in horror, you can always say, "Don't panic, I know it's just casual with us. I was only *kidding* . . ." Another less traumatic option is to pop it at the very, very end of a conversation when you can disappear immediately after saying it. Like just before you walk through the doors to catch a plane or at the end of a phone call. "Love you," then *clunk*. Dropping the "I" off it also makes it less heavy. "Love you" is what you say to your mom. Again, if the object of your affection looks uncomfortable, you can always add, "As a friend, of course."

If you're unsure of whether it's reciprocated, try putting something on the end of the sentence. "I love it when you do that," "I love it when we spend time together." If she looks wide-eyed and gazes at you hopefully, it's safe to say the big three words solo.

Don't ask

Never ever follow up "I love you," with, "Do you love me?" If she does she'll tell you immediately. If he doesn't, he'll be forced to say something like, "Gee. Uhhh. I guess so." Dignity demolished.

Don't do it with sex

Don't say it just before (especially before) or after sex—you won't be able to trust the reply. Some people will say anything to get laid, and even if it's afterward, it might feel forced to say, "I do, too," because they've just had sex with you, for God's sake. Few of us are courageous enough to ravage someone then say, "Actually, it was just the sex I wanted." Even if it was, you'll mumble something appropriate just to be polite.

Getting more serious: moving in together

Think it's time to move in? DON'T think about it without doing a reality check first. I'll discuss the emotional ramifications of moving in and marriage in Chapter 6, but if you insist on rushing things (and you are if you're only in the early stages of a relationship and considering living together), it's time to put on your objectivity hat and see how many of the following you can honestly answer yes to. If you can't answer yes to the majority, give it a bit more time.

Essentials

1. Your partner makes you feel good about yourself, you're happier since you met him, and you're able to be yourself.
2. You've seen how she behaves in all sorts of different situations: day-to-day, happy events, under pressure at work, with her family and friends. In other words, you've seen her survive a few crises.
3. You're similar in most things: tastes, views, what you like to do.
4. You connect on at least three, preferably four, of the crucial points: chemistry, compatibility, common goals, pace, and timing.
5. You communicate well (or at least think you'll learn to in time).
6. You trust your partner to be faithful. How does he handle temptation? If she goes out alone, does she reassure you with details of who she saw, where she went, who she ran into? In other words, does your partner make it clear he's not straying from the rules?
7. You get along with each other's friends and families. If neither of you can bear each other's significant people, it's not a great sign. The old saying "we are the company we keep" has a grain of truth to it.
8. You both want the same things out of life at around the same time. You have similiar career aspirations, thoughts on marriage, kids, and the future.
9. Your gut instinct tells you it's right.
10. You like as well as love your partner.

Lost in space: commitment phobia

"I need *space*." Anyone over the age of 14 knows what *that* really means. It means, "It's over and I don't quite know how to tell you yet, so I'm going to start seeing you less and less in the hope that you won't notice when I finally don't show up at all." That's what most of us mean when we trot out those three not-so-magic words. But not everyone.

There's a certain type of person who means exactly what he or she says when they say they need space. If they can't have space, they can't be happy in a relationship. In a sense, that's all of us, because we all need time apart as well as together. Space and intimacy are on opposite ends of the relationship spectrum, and healthy couples settle a little right of center. They give each other freedom and time alone but the need for intimacy is stronger, so they end up spending two-thirds of their time together. That's normal. It's normal even if you prefer to settle a little left of center—so long as you *both* agree. What's not so normal is needing so much space, if your lover lived in another country it wouldn't be far enough away. This is what psychologists call commitment phobia: fear of commitment and intimacy.[9]

We're all a little bit commitment-phobic these days. But while we'll certainly weigh up the pros and cons before committing ("Jane and John didn't make it—but then again, Sarah and Mark did"), most of us do end up closing our eyes and taking that leap of faith. Giving it a go anyway. Better to have loved and lost and all that stuff.

But not the commitment phobe. That person finds it incredibly difficult, if not impossible, to take relationships into that "sign here" stage. Whether it's a mortgage, marriage certificate, or a six-month shared lease on a car, he or she just can't say, "I do." Some people take it even further: being unable to commit to a date next Saturday night, let alone make plans for Christmas.

If you're going out with someone like this, it's not much fun. But neither, by the way, is being a commitment phobe. Just about all of us would like to find someone to share our lives with. Commitment phobes are just big scaredy-cats—often for good reason. Look at the past of most commitment phobes and you'll usually find the reason why they've ended up that way. They've been married or in a long-term relationship that ended badly. Their parents divorced and they saw the fallout. Even worse, their parents are still together but utterly and completely miserable or venomous. In other words, their experience of relationships isn't fab. If all *you'd* seen in the past was people hurting each other, you wouldn't be too thrilled to put yourself in that situation either.

A lot of commitment phobes get over their fears once they find someone who gives them time to get used to being part of a couple.

But I'll be honest here: think twice before you let yourself fall in love with a long-term sufferer. If that person is over 40 and has never, ever settled down for more than a few months, it's going to take a lot of hard work to overcome the embedded disillusionment. Unless you particularly like people who want more space than NASA, beware.

How to spot commitment phobes

- **They've had a bad experience in the past.** Find out if they've experienced any of the situations above.

- **They like to be in control.** If your partner hates being told what to do, watch out. Commitment phobes often become really defensive and argumentative if you take control of a situation because they like being the ones in control. If they're in control, they can control their emotions and they can't get hurt. That, of course, is ultimately what they're scared of.

- **They're irresponsible.** Often, commitment phobes have problems committing to *anything*, not just relationships. They're the people who are always late because they resent having to be somewhere at a certain time. It's the same with money. They don't pay bills until they're stamped red with "overdue."

- **They don't like making plans.** If your partner hates tying himself down to things even a few days in advance, be afraid.

- **The absolute giveaway—they panic when you mention the "c" word.** C-o-m-m-i-t-m-e-n-t. Spell it out nice and slow for them as you mention the other two no-nos—the "l" word and the "m" word (moving in *or* marriage)—and watch for terror. There's no need to put yourself on the line—simply say something like, "My friends Jane and Brad have decided to move in. How sweet!" or, "My best friend's getting married this weekend. Would you like to come to the wedding with me?" The true commitment phobe will: a) be out that door so fast, your head will spin; b) look as though he or she has an intense diarrhea pain; or c) change the topic immediately.

One word of warning! Don't tar everyone with the same brush. People who need time to make big decisions—like marriage or moving in—aren't commitment phobes. Not being 100 percent sure of something doesn't make you one either. With most of the Western world living with a high divorce rate, anyone with half a brain cell looks around and realizes no relationship is guaranteed. What's even more frightening is we *know* most of those couples floating down the aisle really do think it's forever at the time, yet only a little over half will make it.[10] That's a sobering thought. Even people who are happily married still have those moments after an argument when the doubts creep in ("Yup. I *knew* it! I've made a mistake.").

We live in a very uncertain world, we're never 100 percent sure of anything. So if your partner's waiting for God to come down and say, "Look. Let me reassure you this person's definitely the one for you," it ain't going to happen. None of us knows what the future holds; all you can do is make a sensible choice and put all you've got into making it work.

Having said all this, it also depends on what their doubts are. If it's just the "what if in 20 years' time you stop loving me" stuff, that's natural. But if they have serious doubts—like they truly aren't sure you're compatible or want the same things out of life—that's a different story. That's not being commitment phobic, it's being sensible.

What to do if you want a commitment and your partner's not sure.

You've been going out for what seems like ages and while all your friends are buying houses, having babies, and painting the white picket fence, you're still struggling to get your partner to commit to Christmas with your family. What to do? Try the following.

Check you've got the diagnosis right

Is your beau really commitment phobic or are you asking for a commitment too soon? Some people have the opposite problem to commitment phobia—they're commitment junkies. So desperate to be wanted, they find someone who's equally as desperate, then they latch on to each other like they're drowning and have just discovered a plank of wood floating in the ocean. It's not the person they want, but the relationship.

All relationships need to grow and move forward in order to last. That's why people move in, get married, renovate houses, and have kids—you need to do things together to keep it interesting. But don't be in such a rush to get to the finish line. If you're both young—25 or under—I'd be very careful about making lifelong commitments until you've been together at least five years. I know that's an awfully long time but most of us are still maturing right up to the grand old age of 30. If you really do want to have the best possible chance at making it, you'll wait until after that to make sure you're still compatible. If you meet when you're older, say in your late twenties or early thirties, you're in a better position because at least then you've got experience and hopefully some wisdom behind you (like, you can both change the duvet cover without ending up inside it). So the first thing to ask yourself is: am I asking for a commitment too soon?

Find out why they're not ready

If you're absolutely convinced that what you're asking is reasonable and your partner comes back with, "I'm not ready to make a commitment," the obvious questions to ask are: "Why aren't you ready? What are you waiting for?" You'd be amazed how many people don't ask those two very obvious questions.

You'll get one of two responses to this. True commitment phobes will say something like, "I don't know but that's all there is to it." In other words, end of discussion. If that's the answer you get, bail out, because there is no solution if they don't know what the problem is.

If they say something like, "Look, I'm not ready now but I might be in the future," that's more promising. Again, ask what it is they're waiting for. Do they have doubts about how they feel about you? Or is it because their parents broke up and they're scared they'll be hurt if you two split? If they'll open up and tell you the reasons why, I'd stick around. Maybe they're frightened of commitment because they've been in a relationship where they did commit and it all ended in tears. If that's the case, they probably just need time before they truly trust you.

Something else to keep in mind: although we all say we're terribly liberated these days, old stereotypes still hang on. If your guy doesn't want to get married just yet, he might be waiting until he's more financially secure. It seems silly because you both work, but he might feel he's still got to be the breadwinner and take care of you. Same goes for women. If your girlfriend's crossing the street to avoid bridal boutiques, it might be because she's terrified she'll turn into a mom and lose her independence—have to stay at home with floury fingers and make biscuits all day. The way to get around all this is to spell out, very clearly, what marriage, moving in, monogamy, or whatever it is you're discussing means to each of you.

Reassure them

Is it a simple case of lacking courage? It takes guts to say to someone, "Okay, I'm choosing you and only you as the person I'm going to spend the rest of my life with, regardless of who I might meet." That's a tall order! Let them know it's normal for everyone to have doubts. Some commitment phobes are simply too idealistic. They think they should have a solid-gold guarantee the relationship will work forever. If your partner thinks like that, point out, ever so gently, that relationships don't come with warranties like the TV does. They're being a bit unrealistic.

Follow your instincts

What's your gut instinct on it? Are you sure you're not pushing for commitment out of panic because they're pulling away? If they're seeing you less often, going out with the girls or boys more, and muttering about needing time alone, they're headed for a nightclub, not the jewelers. Your asking for a commitment will only push them out the door sooner rather than later. Force someone to think about whether they want to be with you long term and you run the risk of their using it as the ideal time to say, "Actually. I've been meaning to talk to you about this—I think it's time we broke up."

Compromise

If you want a commitment from your partner to spend more time with you, aim for a compromise. Draw a straight line with zero at one end and ten at the other. Zero means time alone ("space"); ten means time together ("intimacy"). Put a cross where you are on the scale, then do the same for your partner. Then show them and talk it through. If you move back a point or two, will he move forward a point or two?

Work out your bottom line. What's the minimum level of commitment you'll accept? Spell this out to him very clearly and give him a week to think about it. If he can't oblige, move on.

Why men have more trouble committing than women

Most women know a serious relationship *doesn't* have to mean all of the things I'm about to list. Either that or they're not as important to us. Again, we're a lot more advanced in the intimacy game. But he's still secretly paranoid that:

He'll have to "give up" things

He notices you've stopped going to the gym on Wednesday nights to see him instead and thinks, *Does that mean I have to give up my Thursday night squash game?* Relationships involve sacrifice, and he hates the word. Just because she wants to stay home and watch videos, why should he give up a night out drinking with the boys? Committing to someone is like saying, "Here's a big chunk of my life—it's yours." He takes it one step further and imagines a life with *only* you and him in it.

He's worried about sex

There are lots of horror stories out there. Like the girlfriend who gave a hell of a blow job right up until the wedding day and hasn't given one since. Men worry women will stop putting out once that ring's on the finger because they don't truly believe we enjoy sex as much as they do (silly boys).

He's worried he'll rate a poor second

He thinks: *She could do much better than me. Some guy who earns more, is funnier, wears better clothes, drives a better car.* Rolled up into the magnificent men she's bound to meet in the future is a fear of the past. That ex who "went on all night"—what if he turns up again? What about the rich one—could he lure her away? If he commits and it all falls apart, he knows how devastated he'll feel.

He'll miss out on meeting the perfect woman

He can't help but wonder if there's someone better out there, and the more you boost his ego by telling him how fabulous he is, the more he thinks, *Maybe I could get a babe from* Baywatch.

He doesn't like criticism

Before, you'd tease him in a nice way about his addiction to TV. Now it's delivered through tight lips. Which leads straight into his top fear—

He doesn't want to be tamed

My friend Simon put it wonderfully. He said he caught himself putting dirty clothes in the basket instead of on the floor and was horrified. "The next night I said no to drinks with the boys—not because she wouldn't let me go but because I'd rather stay home with her. The realization that I was becoming domesticated scared the hell out of me."

He doesn't have to commit as early as women do

A man can decide to have kids at 50. So long as he marries someone younger, he can play daddy much later.

He's worried he won't measure up to what women want from men these days

This is the biggie. It's true—women *do* want different things. Instead of someone to look up to and look after us, we want companionship, good sex, emotional support, a partner who'll stand by our side, not over us. He felt comfortable with the breadwinner bit (his dad taught him that one very early on). But that other stuff? Phew! That's hard. He hasn't been trained for it and honestly doesn't know *how* to deliver things like "emotional support." That's why you have to teach him.

Women are asking men to take a more traditionally female role in relationships because we've taken on lots of male characteristics. We're more assertive, independent, and financially secure, and that has to be a good thing, right? He doesn't have to worry about making enough money for the whole family. He doesn't have to worry about *us* because we can take care of ourselves. In return, we figure he can even the score by becoming more tolerant, expressive, and understanding. Many perceptive men are working hard on delivering the goods—and doing it. Others feel like relationships have changed and no one's given *them* the rule book. (Want some hints on what the rules really are? See Chapter 4.)

Jane was the third of my friends to marry that year. I remember standing in the church, alone as always, thinking, "What's wrong with *me*? Why aren't *I* ever the one that's up there?" I met Alex about two months later and grabbed on like he was a lifeline. One year later, we got married. Two years later, we were divorced. I wasn't in love with him, I just wanted someone.
Katherine, 30, painter

4

Keeping Each Other Happy

Want your love's dentures soaking next to yours when you're 80? The essential ingredients in the recipe for life-long love

● ●

It's not just your imagination: it *is* harder to find and keep a good long-term relationship than it was in our parents' day. The divorce rate is soaring, infidelity has reached an all-time high, single-parent families are commonplace, and almost everyone over 30 has seen friends swap wedding vows for a divorce contract. Given such gloomy statistics, it's surprising we're still dating at all! But despite the break-ups, the friends with half a dinner service and one of two matching sofas, there *are* couples out there who give the rest of us hope.

My sister Deb and her husband Doug are one such couple. They're coming up on their 20-year anniversary and *still* call each other about six times a day. I watch them at parties. Deb's at one end of the room, Doug's at the other, yet, while they're rarely by each other's side, there's no doubt whatsoever they're connected. Every few minutes (average five, I've timed them), one will look up and check on the other. Not out of jealousy but to make sure they're still okay, still smiling, that they don't need saving or a fresh drink. They've achieved an enviable balance of independence and intimacy, and God knows they deserve to enjoy it and each other because they've worked damn hard to get to that point. Like other couples, rare as they might be, that we look at and think, *Aren't they lucky!*, luck has little to do with it. It's hard work, communication, and compromise that get them to this state of relationship bliss.

Couples who survive the distance today are there for different reasons than before. You no longer need to be married to be accepted by society. There's no stigma attached to "living in sin" and you're not an "old maid" if you're not married at 30. Even having a child on your own is okay. Rather than being taboo, it's accepted, even advised, to sleep with several different partners before settling down. Women might want a husband, but they don't *need* one. We're more independent financially, emotionally, and sexually: we enjoy successful careers and casual relationships, earn substantial incomes, buy our own homes. We don't require a partner to provide or care for us, we do it ourselves.

This equality has bred a new respect between the sexes but also problems. On the up side, many men are happy to relinquish the burden of being the breadwinner: they enjoy playing second fiddle to wives or girlfriends in more prestigious, higher-paying jobs so they can pursue *their* dreams without financial pressures. Other, more conservative, traditional men find it threatening. They've been brought up to believe the man is "boss" and are confused by the fact that today's couples function more as a team, with both partners sharing equal importance and responsibility.

Some women, as well as men, yearn for the old style of relationships. They were certainly simpler! Each sex knew exactly what was expected (not much). Most of us though, have embraced the new style of relating to the point where we find it hard to understand the old. "My accountant, who's in his late 50s, sent me a questionnaire recently that included the question, 'Do you talk to your wife about your finances?' " said Andrew, a 27-year-old businessman. "I laughed out loud. What a ridiculous question: my wife manages the money, not me! Then I thought about it and realized that, in his generation, that didn't happen. My mother had absolutely nothing in her name— she doesn't exist on paper. All her credit cards are linked to my father's, all the store accounts and property are in his name. She's never, ever filed a tax return. She has no idea how much my father earns or how much things like electricity cost."

Appalling! we think. But along with a new openness in our partnerships, we've created some new pitfalls. For a start, juggling two careers isn't easy, and a shortage of time is the biggest threat to modern relationships. Sex is ignored as we tumble into bed, exhausted from work. The workplace is still the number one venue for affairs.[1] As many women as men are being tempted at late-night meetings and on business trips by colleagues whom we spend more time with than we do our partners. People split up more easily and often. There's no stigma attached to divorce and we're surrounded by a score of newly single friends to play with. It's hard to keep perspective and work hard at our relationships when it's less effort to keep trading in for new models.

So how do you manage to resist the temptations, shoulder the burdens, sort out all the differences, and still curl up satisfied together at night? I spoke to a selection of long-term happy couples to find out the secrets to their success.[2] It came down to the following five points:

1. **Talking things through and being "heard":** Talking openly and honestly with a partner, knowing they're interested and listening hard, was listed as of number one importance in every single case. Being able to reveal all, without fear of being judged, is, in a nutshell, the secret of long-lasting love. If you get that right, the rest is easy.

2. **Commitment and trust:** These were also up there, with commitment defined as "I know he or she's in it for a long time, not just the good times" and trust defined more as "he or she will do the right thing by me" rather than faithfulness.

> He's the person I turn to when I'm in strife. I can do anything when we're together because he gives me strength and total support.
> Carla, 23, shop clerk

3. **Freedom:** All couples gave each other space to see friends and pursue interests separately, but also made an effort

to do lots of things together. They made time for their relationship and consciously planned pleasurable "dates," away from work and chores.

4. **Support and friendship:** When asked what they most liked about their relationship, almost all the couples listed support as one of their top reasons. "She helps me and I help her—we guide and advise each other in our careers and our problems," was a typical answer. Most had "gotten over" that initial in-love stage, and while they still loved each other, companionship and the joys of having a "live-in best friend" were as important as sex. "Because I love her so much, I'd rate my sex life as ten out of ten—though I've probably had better sex in a technical or lusty sense with other people," said one happily involved man.

5. **Working at it:** Not one of the couples expected their relationship to coast happily along—all were prepared to put the effort in to get through the rough patches.

If communication is the most important, it makes sense to tackle it first. After that, I'll move on to discussing all the other elements that are essential ingredients in the true-love recipe.

COMMUNICATION: THE KEY TO EVERYTHING

When I was a kid, we had a party game. One person in the group wrote down a simple story on a piece of paper. They then had to whisper the story to the person sitting next to them, who whispered it to the next, and so on until it reached the last person in the room. They retold the story and the original "correct" version was produced. We used to roll about the room laughing at how different the end version was. (Why, I have no idea.) But it was an early lesson in how information gets garbled very quickly.

The same thing happens when you talk to your partner. Even simple messages can get horribly confused because words have different meanings and connotations for different people. You say to your partner, "Phew! What a bloody awful day." To you, it's obvious that means you had a bad day at work, need a bit of TLC and a large glass of wine. Your partner might think it means a) you're prewarning them—no sex tonight; b) you had a dreadful day because they didn't call and were supposed to; or c) they should steer clear to give you time to cool off (when you'd rather talk to let off steam).

Couples who stay together learn how to "read" each other. They don't just listen (really listen) to the words, they look for accompanying body language and are sensitive to each other's moods and soft spots. They speak clearly and specifically. They let their partner know where they're at, even if they're not really sure themselves. Instead of "I don't know why I'm moody. I just feel funny, that's all," they'll say, "I feel a bit weird, honey, but it's nothing to do with you. I'm just a bit flat—maybe I'm coming down with a cold or something." If they can't provide a reason for feeling "off," they'll make sure each other knows it's nothing to worry about.

Communicating couples are also sensitive to "problem issues" in the relationship: they sit up and pay attention if they're discussing a topic they've argued about before. But even if it's a volatile area, they're not afraid to reveal their feelings or fears and keep talking until they feel understood:

"I hated seeing you chatting up that girl at the party."

"What do you mean chatting up? I wasn't chatting her up."

"Oh yes you were! I know when you're chatting someone up. You didn't take your eyes off her face for a second and you didn't offer to get me a drink when you went to the kitchen."

"No, because you had a full one. I checked. And as for looking at her for too long. To be totally truthful, I was trying to work out if she had caps on her teeth."

Silence. Both laugh.

"Did she?"

Argument averted. She made it clear what "chatting up" meant to her. He was then able to explain his behavior.

Communicating is all about being specific. It's okay to trot out words like "hurt," "angry," or "jealous," but you need to provide much more information to really be heard. Does "hurt" mean you'll never trust them again and are going upstairs to pack your bags? Or that you feel you deserve an explanation and an apology? Is hurt really the right word? Perhaps what you mean is ignored, didn't feel special, slighted in front of their or your friends.

The *real* differences between men and women and why we communicate differently

I didn't want to write this section but felt obliged to. While I agree there are differences between men and women (I wouldn't have to write separate sections "FOR HER" and "FOR HIM" if there weren't!), in my experience, problems in relationships are caused by individuals rather than genders. So while you'll find lots in this book that says, "Women are more likely to be victims of this one," or "Sorry, guys, this relates to you more than her," I'd rather focus on how to meet in the middle than promote the battle of the sexes.

Also, I'm loathe to expand on what John Gray, author of *Men Are from Mars, Women Are from Venus*, has created: the concept that men and women come from different planets. Gray fans, forgive me (and he does have a few valid points in his books), but I don't think it's healthy to think of your partner as an alien. It's negative and also incredibly sexist.

These are the sorts of statements made by Mr. Gray that make me want to do nasty things to his photo. They're from the original *Mars and Venus*, under the section "101 ways to score points with a woman."

No 20. Occasionally offer to wash the dishes, especially if she is tired that day.

. . .

No 28. If she washes your socks, turn your socks right side out so she doesn't have to.

. . .

No 56: [My fav!] Drive slowly and carefully. After all, she is sitting powerless in the front seat.

. . .

No 94: Take her for a walk without the children. [On a leash perhaps?]

Puhleeze! It reads like an excerpt from a 1950s issue of *Housekeeping Weekly*.

Sure, men and women think and act a little differently but the edges are blurring all the time. I have plenty of male friends who'll talk about nothing but relationships, when I might be more interested in discussing career or what stocks to invest in. While we're counting the wrinkles around our eyes, he's counting the hairs he finds on the pillow each morning. If women are the romantics, how come men fall in love quicker and out of love slower (even if they do fall in love less frequently)?[3]

Now I've got that off my chest, I'll happily admit there is one area where Ken and Barbie do have problems connecting: communication. Rolled up into the communication parcel is expression of emotion and how we relate to other people. Women and men *do* talk a different language sometimes, women *are* more adept at expressing emotion and tend to worry about others more. Which is why . . .

If you were a guy turned into a girl for one day, you'd:

- **Listen more.** Women make more "listening" noises, like "Really?" and "Wow!" Because they're not as comfortable with deep and meaningful discussion, men try to turn the conversation back to themselves and on to lighter topics. Alternatively, they'll cut the conversation short by trying to solve whatever's being discussed, not realizing women like verbalizing fears and anxieties, even if they already know what the solution is. Men are also prone to interrupt more, especially when a woman is talking. In one study, men interrupted 75 percent of the time with women they'd just met and 96 percent with women they knew.[4]

- **Feel much more comfortable with expressing emotion.** Men are taught not to show feelings because it's unmanly or "weak." "Manly" emotions like anger, indignance, or pride are okay, but fear or vulnerability isn't. This is one reason why men think women have more emotional problems than they do. We don't—we're simply more open about talking about them.[5]

- **Be able to tell how someone feels just by looking at them.** Women are twice as good at finding hidden meanings simply by reading people's expressions. So now might be the time to suggest that poker game . . .[6]

- **Search for deeper messages.** Men take words at face value; women read between the lines. What men say is what they usually mean, but we'd rather delve into the *meanings* of human actions ("Why does Sue always end up with men who are bad for her?"). Besides, we love analyzing. Men tend to be more curious about sports, politics, history, or how things work. Women tend to like dissecting relationships.[7]

If you were a girl who turned into a guy for one day, you'd:

- **Be angrier.** There's one emotion you won't have trouble expressing: anger. Women are taught anger is "unladylike" so we tend to get "hurt" rather than angry. We also value our relationships more, so we're far less likely to shout at someone in case we hurt their feelings.[8]

- **Dole out advice rather than sympathy.** Tell most guys a problem and they'll try to fix it before you've even explained what it is. Practical and solution-oriented, as a man it seems logical to focus on the facts rather than talk through every possible emotional consequence. Women, on the other hand, are often just looking for a sympathetic ear. The act of talking out loud to someone who understands is often all they're really after.[9]

- **Put friends down—straight to their face.** Nasty, eh! Actually, it's the opposite. When men do it to other men, it usually means they like them. It's all part of the teasing and jostling that happened during his adolescence. Women aren't angels: we put down people, too. But seldom to their faces because we show

> I used to go to restaurants and watch couples who didn't have a thing to say to each other and I just knew I'd never have a problem with Sylvia. I never tire of her company. I can sink my teeth into a conversation with her though we've been going out for four years. She gives me the zip to get out of bed in the morning and confidence on my down and vulnerable days. I can put myself in her hands to look after for life and she'll do the right thing by me.
> Brad, 27, accountant

affection more directly. To insult a friend face-to-face for us means we really *don't* like them.[10]

GETTING HIM TO OPEN UP

Relationships expert Dr. Maryon Tysoe says one of the strongest binding elements between two people is their ability to reveal intimate thoughts and feelings to each other. She cites one study that tried to predict which couples would stay together over a four-year period by just one factor: how much they shared their feelings. The results were as expected: the more the couples shared, the more likely they were to be together four years later. Another survey of 400 therapists showed the largest single reason they thought marriages failed was the husband's inability to communicate his feelings.[11]

Unless your guy's spent the last five years locked away in a dark room playing computer games (come on, he must have come out sometime), he's probably got the message that he should be opening up. Then why doesn't he? Because it may not be that easy for him. Most women consider a good, long, deep conversation one of life's pleasures. It's up there with walking into your favorite store with a spare $500 to blow. For some men, a deep conversation isn't enjoyable at all because it's hard work. Men are "doers." When he meets up with the boys, they don't sit around in coffee shops chatting. They play pool, go to a game, go for a jog or a swim. He's not that practiced at talking intimately so it requires effort. And say he messes it up? "I worry I'll give the wrong answer." "It all comes out wrong and I upset her." "I don't know what she wants me to say." These are the comments I got from male friends who don't find it easy to talk to their partners. If talking doesn't come naturally to him, it's not surprising he's all for going to the movies rather than out to dinner (where you're bound to want a conversation).

My idea of a good time is a good chat. My ex's idea of a good time was playing tennis. Personally, I would rather clean all the public toilets at Yankee Stadium the day after opening day than hit a ball around the court. Why? Because that doesn't come naturally to *me*— I'm embarrassingly pathetic at it. My boyfriend would say, "I know— let's play tennis!" expecting me to jump up with an enthusiastic "Yes!," rush into the bedroom and pull on a short white skirt. Instead

I'd do *anything* (even watch football on TV) to avoid it. The last time I was forced to play a game of social tennis I spent most of the day before throwing up. If a "deep" conversation for men is the equivalent to tennis for me, they have my sympathy.

Unfortunately, being able to have an intimate conversation is slightly more crucial to relationships than perfecting a backhand. Besides, once they do get the hang of it, most men admit having a good chat is an incredibly rewarding experience. Which is more than I can say for tennis.

How to help him open up? Encourage him by:

- **Letting him know talking is important to you.** Say, "I know you don't feel comfortable talking about your feelings just yet, but it would mean a lot to me if you'd try." Explain why. Get him to read this section of the chapter and other sections in the book that talk about communication issues.
- **Rewarding even the slightest hint of intimate talk.** If he usually says, "My boss, Bob, is a bastard," then one day comes out with, "I don't know, Sally, sometimes I think Bob isn't happy with my performance," let him know you're thrilled. I don't mean jump up, throw your arms around him and say, "Honey! At last! You're talking to me" (he'll clam up for good). The trick is to acknowledge it but not make a big deal. Let him know a) you don't think "less" of him for revealing a fear; b) it's normal; and c) it's great he let you in. Say something like, "I think all of us worry about that sometimes—I sure as hell do. What makes you think that?" Let him tell you, then say at the finish, "I'm glad you let me know. It's nice to know how you're feeling."
- **The more open you are, the more open he'll be.** If you're comfortable with talking about "embarrassing" things—topics that make you look a bit foolish—he'll take your example.
- **Ask him questions.** If you think he's worried about something, say "Are you worried about this? Tell me," then truly listen to his reply. Guide him along by saying, "What did you feel then? Angry? Confused? Frustrated?" Yes, you are putting words in his mouth, but you're also teaching him *how* to talk intimately.
- **Don't assume silence means disinterest.** This is the main difference between how men and women talk: women tend to think out loud, men tend to work things through in their heads. He might mention a problem he's got ("My boss is really on my

back"). The next time he mentions it, you'll probably hear the conclusion ("I've decided to apply for a job with another company"). The middle part—weighing the pros and cons—he does privately. That's why, when you ask his advice about something, he might say, "Let me think about it." He's not brushing you off, that's just the way he handles problems. Women, on the other hand, verbalize thoughts. In fact, we're extremely fond of expressing *every* thought that enters our head, not just important ones. So we might say, "Okay, I've got to go to the bank, then the drycleaners. No, I'll go to the drycleaners first because it's on the way. Jesus! I nearly forgot! I have to drop off that presentation to a client, even though it is Saturday. Honestly, sometimes I feel all I do is work, work, work. Where *is* that black sweater? Oh—here it is. Great. Now, sweetie, what do you want me to pick up for dinner? Sweetie? Honestly, I might as well talk to myself!" (You are.) Here's what he'd say in the same circumstances: "I'll be back in an hour." When he thinks or says, "I wish she'd get to the point," this is what he's talking about.

How to talk and listen to each other

All the happy couples I spoke to said they talked intimately ("We fill each other in on what's been happening") for around one hour per day. If you're answering, "Hi honey. I'm home" with "Shut up, *Ally McBeal*'s on," you aren't going to be sitting side-by-side in rocking chairs at 80. If you don't talk constantly to each other, you lose sight of how the other person is thinking, feeling, and looking at the world. You stop connecting because you don't know where you're both at. If he doesn't tell you he's irritable because his mom's just been tested for cancer, you'll give him a hard time about it. He withdraws even

> **Women typically make three times as many personal phone calls as men, with the average conversation lasting 20 minutes. Men phone purely to convey information with their calls lasting around six minutes.**[12]

further, and before you know it there's a gulf between you that's bigger than the Grand Canyon.

Words are the glue that sticks couples together. The more you talk and share what's happening inside your hearts and heads, the more you'll get out of the relationship. Let's face it: one reason why all of us want a special relationship is the joy of being able to share all our worries and fears and get reassurance.

Listening is even more important. After all, there's not much point in either of you rattling on about this, that, and the other if it's all falling on deaf ears. It's insulting if someone's reading the paper while you're talking to them. Ditto people who switch channels on the TV or are obviously lost in their own thoughts, even though they're looking straight at you.

> **Think like the opposite sex and you'll solve problems more efficiently. Take what he says at face value: what he says is usually what he means. Let her analyze: she's not finding fault, she just wants to discuss the issue thoroughly.**[13]

A good listener isn't someone who sits there quietly, letting you talk. It's someone who *actively* listens. Their body language shows they're interested. They lean forward, eager to hear your next words. If you're telling them something funny, they laugh along with you. If you're worried, concern is etched on their face as well. They acknowledge the conversation every few sentences with an "uh-huh" or comment on the subject. They ask questions and offer opinions. When you've finished the conversation, you know they've not only heard every word you said but tried hard to experience it with you.

Like most relationship skills, talking and listening properly requires a bit of effort at the start. Keep the following in mind until it all starts to come naturally.

Ⓑ FOR BOTH OF YOU

- **Be aware of each other's body language.** Watch your partner's body language and facial expressions and you'll learn to "read" each other more accurately. Close couples can list each other's "giveaway" signs. "I know he's worried about something even when he doesn't admit it because he gets this red, angry line between his eyes from frowning." "I know when Sarah's uncomfortable when we're in company because of the way she stands. She's stiff and doesn't move her hands around as much as she normally would." "I know when he's lying because it's like shutters come down over his eyes and they go blank."

- **Give each other time.** Sure, we're all busy, but if you truly can't spare an hour a day to sit and listen to someone you supposedly love, you shouldn't be in a relationship.

- **Ask lots of questions.** "How did that meeting go? Did your idea get through?" is better than, "How was your day?"

- **Offer solutions, not problems.** There's nothing more satisfying than having a good, long whine about something, but constantly bitching about life to your partner drags both of you down. If you want to complain about something, at least finish it with, "So I've decided in the future I'm going to . . ."

- **Try not to let emotions stop you from listening.** Your girlfriend says, "There's a problem with our sex life," and even if she continues talking for an hour, you're stuck back at the first sentence thinking, "Shit! I'm a dud in bed." If you are stuck, ask them to stop explaining and give some reassurance before continuing.

- **Be discreet.** What you reveal to each other isn't anyone else's business. Intimate secrets aren't fodder for your next meeting with best friends, no matter how discreet they are.

(F) FOR HER

- **Don't interpret silence as disinterest.** He's simply thinking about what you just said.

- **Touch, along with talk.** It helps keep him focused and it's easier for him to get in touch with his emotions.

- **Let him know you're not going to get angry** if things do come out "the wrong way." Don't get defensive, just ask him to repeat what he said using different words.

- **Tell him if you want to talk just for the sake of it.** Say, "I'm just going to ramble on here because it helps me to work it out by talking out loud. I don't expect you to solve it for me."

- **Don't finish his sentences.** It's not as easy for him to express emotion, so he takes longer to "search" for the right word or phrase or even think about what he does feel. A woman may analyze her relationship every few minutes, he might not have thought about the issue at all. Give him time to think—don't expect instant solutions.

Ⓜ FOR HIM

- **Be patient.** Women tell long stories, men summarize. Accept that she'll take the long way around. Don't say, "Can you get to the point?"

- **Don't jump in with solutions.** She's probably just letting off steam. If you're not sure what's expected of you, say, "Do you want my advice or are you just talking this through?"

- **Start small, aim high.** If you're uncomfortable expressing emotion, start by revealing not-so-intimate stuff ("I was so angry with my boss today," "I really enjoyed last night with you") before working up to biggies ("I'd be devastated if we split up," "I'm worried I'm not successful enough for you").

Talking through important issues

The next time you want to talk about something important, try systematically following these steps until they become second nature.

Before you talk to your partner

- Work out how you communicate best. Do you find it easier to explain yourself verbally or to write things down? If you're about to tackle something that usually ends in a screaming match, you might get further by handing them a letter, then discussing what's written. The beauty of the written word is that you can get it exactly right. Read it first thing in the morning and last thing at night before handing it over, to make absolutely sure it clearly and specifically states all the points you want to get across.

- Work out what you want to say before you say it. Start with what you think the problem is: "I swear I'll go stark raving mad if I have to sit through another boring work party with him." Then think up at least three reasons to answer, "why?" You might discover it's not the work dinners that concern you but the fact that you're not spending enough time together, just the two of you. Maybe you don't like taking second place to his career. Maybe you don't like the person he becomes when he's around his work colleagues. These are the real issues. The work dinners are a symptom.

- Put yourself in your partner's shoes. Every time you talk about something important, imagine how it sounds on their end. Not how *you* would react if *they* said it to *you*, but how you think you'd react if you *were* them. Take into account their personality, their past, their vulnerable points: do they have a tendency to take a negative slant on criticism? Is what you're going to say or write worded in such a way that they won't feel criticized and put up defenses? Insult someone and they'll immediately stop listening.

- Think up solutions. What is it you want to achieve from this? What would stop this from troubling you in the future? Is your solution practical or a wee bit selfish? Will it make both of you happy?

During the discussion

- **Wait until you're both calm.** It's crucial. The old saying, "Don't go to bed angry," doesn't always apply. Sometimes you're better off huffily sticking to opposite sides of the bed and talking it through in the morning than saying things you really don't mean in the heat of the moment.

- **Don't accuse.** Instead of saying, "You're a———" or "You made me———," say, "I felt———when you behaved in that way." Start sentences with "I" and criticize the *behavior*, not the *person*.

If you ignore all the rest of my advice in this section and only take on board these two points, you'll still notice a huge difference.

- **Be specific.** Deliver your speech or letter and ask them to repeat back to you what it is they think you just said. When you're satisfied they've received the message you wanted to send, then move on to discussing the issue.

- **Take turns.** Give them full attention for five minutes and don't interrupt. Then repeat back what you think they've just said. Then it's your turn and they do the same to you. It's called "validating": showing that you understand (even if you don't share) your partner's viewpoint. Repeating back what each other's said has another advantage.[14] If what you're asking or arguing over is silly, it'll sound even sillier coming out of *their* mouth.

- **Talk through the solutions.** Give a bottom line: "I'm prepared to do X, but won't put up with Y." Keep going until you reach a compromise you're both happy with. If it's incredibly important to you, your partner might decide to give up something. If they do, make sure it evens up. The next time something is important to them, you do the compromising.

SHOULDN'T COUPLES IN LOVE BE 100 PERCENT HONEST WITH EACH OTHER ALL OF THE TIME?

It's a sweet thought but horribly naive. Think about it. I don't care how angelic you are, would *you* want your partner to know your every thought? Because that's what being totally honest would entail: hooking them up to a 24-hour mind-reading device.

Total honesty means every time they ask, "What are you thinking?" you'd have to tell the truth. "Actually, I was thinking you look a bit pudgy and wondering if you'll end up with a beer gut." Or, "I was thinking I wish you'd bloody well stop going on and on about Christine. I couldn't care less what she said." You ask what he thinks of your best friend, Michelle, and he'd be forced to say, "Brilliant! If you weren't around, I'd bed her in a second." He cooks you dinner and asks how it is. Your answer would be, "It tastes like dog food but

---

I suppose I have to eat it or you'll get offended. If I throw up, I throw up." I could go on and on (and on), but I think you get the point by now.

No matter how much you love someone or how compatible you are, there are times when your partner drives you completely nuts. There are times when they don't look so hot. There are times when other people do. If you make a pact to be truly honest with each other, you'd have to admit to these thoughts. I don't know about you but I don't particularly *want* to know if my partner's spent all day imagining what the girl at the next desk would look like with her hair spread out over his pillow. So long as he has no intention of acting on it, that's his business, not mine.

Total honesty would reduce most of us to paranoid, blithering heaps within a day. Those fleeting desires and momentary doubts should be left unsaid. Spoken out loud, they're painful and hurtful and destructive. I'm not advocating lying to each other about big issues or issues you've been concerned about for a while, but I see no advantage whatsoever to making a pact to tell each other every thought. (Don't laugh: lots of couples *do* pledge to do this. It usually lasts about five seconds until one says something the other definitely didn't want to hear.)

There's one area in particular where it doesn't pay to be honest: your past sex life. "What's the best sex you've ever had?" you ask them, smugly confident it's bound to be with you. "Gosh!" they answer, truthfully. "That's hard. I had sex in a elevator once—that was *fantastic*—but if I had to pick just one I guess it'd be the time Trudy and I had sex on the steps of her parents' house. Just thinking about it makes me want to——" Like, this is *not* the answer you want to hear. The answer you want is, "The time you and I——" If someone asks you that question, I don't care if your nose grows like Pinocchio's while you're saying it, that's the answer to give.

If you and your lover get into that "how many people were there before me" discussion, stop it before it goes any further. It's pointless, anyway, because you'll be none the wiser at the end of it. Men subconsciously up the figure because they think it makes them more of a stud; women reduce it because they're worried they'll seem "easy" or "slutty." (In fact, if you *really* want to know how many men a woman's slept with, researchers say you should triple the number she admits to. One study found women tend to "forget" significant sex encounters, particularly one-night stands.[15] Whether that's because we've deliberately blotted them out or they meant so little we just forget them, is beside the point.)

There's a huge difference between talking about your past and reducing it to a statistic. Telling each other about significant past relationships is healthy and necessary to get close to each other. Most people start asking the ex-lover questions when it's starting to get serious, and the reason we do it is to check how special we are. Like, am I as important to her as she is to me or does she act like this with every guy? We need and want to know what's happened to our partner's heart. If some girl led him along then dumped him, it explains why he's a bit nervous about commitment. If she's never had a relationship that's lasted more than two weeks, it says something about her. That's not prying, and you need to share stuff like that. If you focus on the feelings for the person, not your sex life, you probably won't get into too much trouble.

COMMITMENT AND TRUST

There are two levels of commitment: making a public statement you intend to stick around (moving in, marriage, the stuff we talked about in Chapter 3), and what I call *true* commitment. True commitment is making an emotional commitment to do the right thing by each other and the relationship. Just because you've got the first, don't assume you've got the second. Plenty of people commit to marriage and walk up the aisle eyeing the bridesmaids. Others go through the motions of a relationship on such a superficial level, they don't even know their partner's favorite color.

True commitment is about deciding you're going to make the relationship work, no matter what. It's called looking out for someone, being their number one biggest fan and best friend. Listening to their dreams, protecting them from "the big, bad world," traveling through life together as a team. If you're truly committed to someone, their happiness is as important to you as your own. You say no to the "this would be so easy to get away with" sex on the side because you couldn't face *yourself* in the mirror afterward, let alone them. In essence, it's about treating your partner with love, respect, and kindness. The very best relationships are those where both partners are not only truly committed to each other, they both know it.

It's the same deal with trust. Trust isn't just about knowing someone won't fool around on you. It's knowing they can be trusted to take responsibility, live up to expectations. Like, you know they're not going to blow next month's mortgage payment on the horses. Or forget to feed the cat while you're away. Or organize a stripper when asked to provide entertainment for Aunt Betty's eightieth. In short, you respect their judgment and can count on them to do the right thing in any situation. This sort of trust tends to be taken for granted in good relationships—you just assume your partner will behave responsibly and they do. It's when it's missing that you notice.

Then there's a deeper, more intimate level of trust that's equally as crucial. It's about being able to trust your partner with your innermost thoughts, about feeling comfortable enough to expose your vulnerabilities, reveal those nasty and/or incredibly painful secrets from your past, and know none of it will be used against you later. This type of trust is earned and it takes time to develop. One of you starts the ball rolling in the beginning by disclosing something personal, the other responds by sharing something equally as intimate. Both of you hold your breath and wait a little while to see if it's safe to go further (you don't read it in the gossip pages, their friends don't look at you oddly, it's not thrown back at you in an argument). Once you've got the all-clear, you go a little deeper the next time, and so do they. For a relationship to be healthy, trust needs to be reciprocated. Lopsided relationships don't work. If they know everything about you and you know nothing about them, you feel exposed and powerless. Not a great feeling.

It's impossible for me to give practical pointers on how to truly commit to and trust someone or get them to commit to and trust you. Only you know whether your partner's worthy of both. Only you can make these private pacts with yourself and each other. What I can tell you, though, is this: if you want a *really* good relationship, commitment and trust are both part of it. So if you or your partner have problems with either or both, I'd think about getting some professional help to get to the bottom of it.

According to Dr. Maryon Tysoe, most people fit into one of three categories. *Secure* people find it easy to get close to others and to trust them. *Anxious* types commit and trust a little *too* easily, become obsessively preoccupied with their partner and worry excessively that they don't love them back. *Avoidant* people are uncomfortable with intimacy and closeness and fight against both.[16]

If you're a secure person, you're in an enviable position. (In fact, if you are having problems trusting or committing to someone, sit up and pay attention. If the act of committing and trusting doesn't usually frighten you, the problem obviously lies with the person you're nervous about committing to.) You're the anxious type? Back off and calm down. You tend to perpetuate your worst nightmare and drive your partner away by being overly jealous, possessive, and clingy (see "Freedom," below). If you're an avoidant person, you constantly run away from good relationships or deliberately sabotage them to justify leaving. Read Chapter 8 for some clues on why you've ended up this way, or schedule an appointment to see a good therapist.

FREEDOM

Not one of the happy couples I interviewed lived in each other's pockets. They all saw friends separately and enjoyed activities solo as well as making an effort to do lots together. It's natural to want to Velcro yourselves together in the first few months; not so healthy if you're still doing *everything* together a year later. Freedom in a relationship is allowing each other to keep your

> She had a bowl near the door where she'd dump change and business cards and stuff. Every time I came over, I'd sneakily look through it. One day I found a note that said, "All those lunches meant the world. I love you. David." I thought the worst and dumped her without giving a reason. A few months later, we ran into each other and she asked me why. Turned out the note was from a gay workmate whose partner was dying of AIDS. She'd take him out every day to cheer him up but promised not to tell anyone. I apologized but she hasn't forgiven me.
> Alan, 31, personal trainer

sense of self. Thinking for two as opposed to thinking *as* two: there's a huge difference.

"Come out to dinner with me tonight," says your friend Sarah.

"I'll pass this time because Mike's a bit down," you reply, "He missed out on the promotion." That's thinking for two: you're considering your partner as well as yourself.

Thinking *as* two is automatically assuming Sarah's asking *both* of you to dinner. "We can't come because Mike's working late," you say. It doesn't occur to you to go solo because, well, you're a couple, right?

Don't laugh—I've met several Tweedle-dee Tweedle-dum, couples: they come as a matching set or not at all. Quite frankly, they're the ones you only ask to a dinner party if you need a nice, pleasant pair to fill seats while you're entertaining that "Oh God, when are they going home?" visitor. They're boring! I mean, if you haven't got the balls to say, "Honey, order in some pizza and beer. I'm out with a friend tonight," you're hardly likely to be one of those witty, vivacious, mesmerizingly passionate types who's on *top* of everyone's must-invite list.

The healthiest, happiest relationships are those where both partners give each other the freedom to enjoy life apart from each other. She spends a week in Bali with a girlfriend with his blessing. He says, "Count me in!" to the boys when they suggest a weekend fishing trip, knowing he doesn't have to ask permission. Just because you're now part of a couple doesn't mean you don't spend an occasional Saturday night watching videos and gobbling chocolate with your best friend. Or he cancels his Tuesday night squash game with his. Quite apart from maintaining precious friendships, seeing people separately gives you the chance to vent. Let off steam when your lover's driving you nuts. Get a fresh perspective on how to handle a relationship problem. Talk about how delicious the man in the video store is and you couldn't help but notice him noticing you when you happened to have to return a video on the way to the cocktail party when you looked pretty fab in that tight black number. And how (Jesus!) if you were single, Harry's secretary would be doing a lot more than taking dictation if she worked for you. Let's face it: talking about doing something can be just as good as doing it (with far fewer complications). Saying it out loud makes you think, "I *could* do that if I wanted to." And you realize you don't really. You just wanted it acknowledged somehow.

Freedom's also about not expecting your partner to be a clone of yourself. You respect each other's rights to have different opinions, likes and dislikes, and don't get all huffy because you were both on opposing sides during a raging debate with friends. You appreciate that just because you want something, it doesn't mean they will, too, at the exact same moment. That goes for everything from wanting to eat Indian that night to wanting to have kids before your partner's ready. You can't wait to play dad but she's concentrating on her career right now? Fine! She's got her own life, you respect that and give her time. Freedom's about not expecting to be the number one priority in your partner's life every single day of it. If studying four nights a week while working full-time will help them get their dream job, you'll encourage rather than complain. Remember those posters that were all the rage during the flower-power years? The ones that had naked bodies silhouetted against sunsets, with the slogan, "If you love something set it free. If it returns it was yours, if it doesn't it never was," blah blah blah? Sure, the person who wrote it was stoned at the time, but it actually does make a lot of sense.

Of course, letting go of someone you love desperately isn't that easy for some people. If you're insecure or the jealous type, there's a temptation to keep them on as tight a leash as possible.

I went out with a guy once who couldn't bear to be separated from me. When I went to the bathroom, he'd stand outside the door talking to me. Initially, I was flattered. He was so besotted and devoted, my ego skyrocketed with all the attention. Flowers every week, phone calls to say how wonderful I was, how he'd never met anyone like me before, notes shoved in my wallet, under my pillow, inside the fridge. He'd come over to cook for me when I worked late, clean my apartment if I was too busy to do it, ask my opinion on *everything*. Yup. It all got *too, too* much. After two months, it felt like he couldn't breathe without consulting me first. I pulled back and the phone calls went from two to ten a day. If I dared to go for a night out with the girls, I'd come home to find 12 messages on my machine, all saying how much he loved and missed me, when I'd only seen him a few hours before. I felt like I was being stalked.

Relationship guru Barbara De Angelis calls people like him emotional vampires. She says they're people whose hearts are like empty containers they desperately want *you* to fill up, except there's a hole in the bottom and it's never, ever enough. Emotional vampires feed off their partners, sucking up their energy, affection, and attention like hungry puppies.[17] Why do they do it? Usually it's because they've been hurt badly somewhere along the line and think being loved by you will make the pain go away. It won't. Counseling will. Do yourself a favor if you've hooked up with someone like this: send them off to a therapist and then disappear to the Bahamas for a few months. (Maybe for good.)

SUPPORT AND FRIENDSHIP

Clock up a decade as a couple and you realize romantic relationships are based as much on friendship as they are love. "It's not about gazing into each other's eyes and whispering sweet nothings, it's about two people who are best friends." "It's about liking your partner as well as loving them. I'd choose Michael as my best friend even if we weren't going out."[18] "We're best friends": pretty well all the couples I interviewed said this about their relationship. And the same rules that apply to platonic friendships apply to romantic ones as well.

Closely linked to friendship was support. Support means helping each other out: taking half the responsibility for everything to do with the relationship. Sometimes, support means carrying the *entire* load on your shoulders to give your partner a break, knowing they'll do the same for you when you need it. In short, it's about thinking for two. If you can't put yourself in your partner's shoes, see how life and the relationship feels on their side, you haven't got a hope of making them happy. A psychologist friend of mine takes this even further. She says the true secret of great relationships is when each partner lives their *life* as if they *were* in the other's shoes. Every single thing they do and say they look at from their partner's perspective rather than their own. "If everyone concentrated on keeping each other happy, we'd all be happy," she says.

I say, "Bullshit!" It sounds awfully romantic and some couples could pull it off (the sort that say no to an all-expenses-paid trip to their dream destination because it wouldn't be fair to go alone—ridiculous). Most of us would have major problems being that selfless. My version of thinking for two would be to first think what would make you happy, *then* see it from their side. What objections are they likely to have to what you're suggesting? Are you taking their feelings into account?

Thinking for two also has a calming effect in arguments. The bastard completely forgot about your anniversary so it—and you—obviously mean nothing to him? From your side, this would be true. You place great store by significant dates. But looking at it from *his* side, you realize he's just not a "date" person and never has been one to make a fuss about birthdays and Christmas. It might still piss you off like crazy, but you know it *doesn't* mean he doesn't love you. Instead of confronting, you'll say, "John, I know anniversaries don't mean much to you but they do to me. It upsets me that you forgot. Can you put it in your diary for next year so it doesn't happen again?"

If your partner doesn't think for two, ask them to. Say, "Look at it from my side, just for a minute," or "Think about it: how would *you* feel if I did that to you?" The more you remind each other there are two sides to everything, two ways of looking at things, the more natural thinking for two will become.

WORKING AT IT

This whole book's about working at it because "at it" simply means putting effort into the relationship to keep each other happy. Working at it includes satisfying each other sexually, splitting the household chores evenly, and dividing finance commitments fairly. It's about being interested, attentive, and thoughtful. Expressing affection by telling and showing your partner you love them through words and actions. Loving each other warts and all. Turning a blind eye to things that annoy you about your partner, focusing on things you do like. Solving problems before they turn into crises. Partners who actively work on their relationship constantly check with each other: "Are you happy? Is there anything you're not getting that you need?" It's about putting all the things I talk about in this book into practice. Again, the energy both of you put into the relationship should be fairly even, or resentment creeps in.

Working at it is a lot about making each other feel special. It seems trite to say be nice to each other, but you'd be astonished how many couples aren't. Some spend their lives playing a game of one-upmanship, in a constant struggle for who's got the power. Others *think* "I love you" often but rarely say it. There are two ways to let someone know you think they're special: through words and actions. I'd suggest you use both.

At the start of relationships, couples spend an extraordinary amount of time talking about how they feel about each other. "The relationship" is often the favorite topic of conversation. Unfortunately, this tends to wear off rather rapidly once a major commitment is made. One study dramatically demonstrated how affectionate behavior decreases after marriage. Within the first year of "wedded bliss," saying "I love you" dropped by 40 percent, approval and compliments by 30 percent, doing something nice for each other by 28 percent, and touching and cuddling (non-sexual) by 39 percent.[20] Don't fall into the same trap.

You consider yourself a tennis pro, he wins the match. Do you a) slap him on the back and say a genuine "Congratulations!" or b) secretly seethe? According to U.S. researchers, your reaction to a partner's win could predict the long-term future for the two of you. If you take joy in their achievements (especially if they beat you in an area you excel in), start booking the reception. You're happy with reflected glory and think of the two of you as "one." Feeling resentful and wanting to outdo each other means you're still sorting out the power balance—a long way to go yet, guys![19]

Say, "I love it when you laugh, it makes me laugh." Say, "That's so sweet of you, darling. It's just one of the things I adore about you." Give loads of compliments about your lover's physical appearance as well. "I was watching you walk back to the car and thought, *Yum!*" and "Do you know how fab your arms look in that shirt?" Every time you *think* something nice, say it.

Say thank you as often as possible: "Thanks for being so patient, darling," "Thanks for listening," "Thanks for being so nice to me." It's the equivalent of giving the dog a pat when he's been good. The more positive feedback you give, the more they'll keep on being nice to you. There's a reward at the end, which makes *them* feel good!

The other way to make each other feel special is to *do* nice things. I'm not just talking flowers and inpromptu chocolates, even though they *are* wonderful, but also caring enough to find out what your partner's idea of heaven is. Do you know what their all-time favorite thing to do is? Do you know their favorite food, which of your (and their) friends they like best, what they'd like to do more of together or less of? If you don't know, ask—or watch. Does their face light up when you suggest dinner out? Or do they look longingly at the video store and takeaway when you drive past and wish they were curled up on the couch?

Also keep an eye out for the little things your partner does that maybe you don't notice. Like his getting up half an hour early so he can drop you at work. Her coming home early from a night out with the girls because you were feeling down. These small, seemingly insignificant gestures are the things that hold couples together. Men, especially, are more prone to showing love than verbalizing it. In one study researchers asked a group of men to show more affection to their wives. One man decided to wash his wife's car.[21] Hardly romantic, but the intention behind it was.

Working at it also means keeping the fun happening. We all need routine in our lives and there's definitely something appealing about knowing you'll be tucked up in bed asleep by 10:00 P.M. this Friday, arms wrapped around your partner, when the week's been a nightmare and you're knocked out. But if you can predict pretty accurately what the two of you will do every night this week, every week of the year, you're heading for a fall.

Psychologists call it "emotional deadening."[22] The average person calls it being bored out of their brain. Both mean the same thing: let your relationship get *too* routine and life takes on a hum that is comforting and pleasant sometimes but dull for the rest of it.

It's not so much *what* you do together, but how often you vary your routine. If you've eaten out every single night for the last three weeks, a night *in* can be unbearably exciting. In fact, couples who are always running out the door to yet another social event aren't any better off than those who stay home. The idea is to aim for a balance. Just the two of you, stress-free evenings combined with novelty and what I call kick-up-the-heels outings.

Go places together where there are people you don't know of the opposite sex. It's necessary to remind each other of how attractive your partner is out there in the big wide world. I'm not talking singles bars, it could be a dinner party for four: anywhere you're forced to dress up, get out there, and socialize. It's good for you to see your partner across a crowded room and realize you'd still go home with them every single time.

Money's tight? No excuse. If finances or time mean you only go out once a month, just vary when you do it. Make it a boozy brunch on Sunday instead of Saturday-night dinner. Don't mix with the same old friends, over and over. Throw in a few people neither of you knows very well or mix friends in different combinations. Do things apart as well. Do they really have to come to that family get-together? If they don't get along with a group of your friends, see them on your own. If you do everything together, what are you going to talk about that's fresh and new?

Set aside one weekend a month and take turns to plan it. Deliberately turn it into a game of who can come up with the most interesting itinerary. The more situations you put each other in, the more interesting you'll both seem. Watching her screaming with hysterical laughter while riding the rollercoaster reminds you how much fun she is. Watching him build a campfire reminds you of how resourceful he is. If the only time you see each other, you're both in bum-around clothes saying things like, "Honey, hurry up, *ER*'s about to start," you'll end up in the emergency room yourselves. Comatose.

SEVEN SIGNS YOU'RE GOING TO MAKE IT

1. **After arguments you feel closer.** You both feel raw, exhausted, and a little fragile but closer than you did before it. You've managed to talk it through rationally, listen to each other's viewpoints and come up with a solution that suits both of you.

2. **Jealousy isn't a problem.** Instead of losing it and storming out or trying to get even by flirting with someone else, you confess jealous feelings and allow yourself to be reassured. You become less jealous of each other the longer you're together. While both of you dabble in a bit of harmless, occasional flirting, you try not to do it in front of each other. If one does get caught, you turn it into a joke because you *know* it's harmless.

3. **If in doubt, you'll take it as a compliment.** If your partner says something that could be misconstrued, you'll put the best possible light on it and ask if that's what they meant. She says, "All I want to do is curl up and read a book. I'm sick of everyone." Instead of getting huffy and assuming he's included in "everyone," he says, "I know what it's like. Take some time out, sweetheart, then let's go down the road for dinner and a glass of wine." If your partner doesn't feel like sex, you think, *They must be tired*, not *They don't want me anymore*.

4. **You think first, react later.** Everyone sees the world differently, through a different filter. If you truly accept each other, you'll allow for differences. If your partner's being extraordinarily critical of someone or something, you'll listen first to what they have to say, take into account any stresses and how tired they are, *then* throw in your two cents—if at all. Important issues are worth fighting over; trivial differences aren't.

5. **You don't change to suit each other, you work with each other.** You're both aware of each other's bottom line—what each will and won't put up with—but allow each to be an individual. There's a certain standard of behavior that's expected, but you're not rigid. Neither of you compromise *those* standards, but you are prepared to put their needs before your own occasionally.

6. **You know how to say goodbye.** They're about to head off for a two-week work conference overseas. You don't cling, sob, and feel miserable and resentful they're having time away from you. You take them to the airport, kiss and hug, then wave them off

cheerily. A graceful exit is the best preparation for the next grand entrance. Smart lovers keep each other hungry for more.

7. **You both feel you're getting a fair deal from the relationship.** Ask yourself this: Who's getting the best deal from this relationship: me or my partner? Are they getting much more out of it than you or vice versa? You're on the right track when you can honestly answer, "It's fairly equal."

5

Sex: Do It or Kiss Goodbye

Why hot sex makes for a hot relationship and what to do with loony libidos, lousy lovers, or if you're both too zonked to bonk

••

"To tell you the truth, Trace, I'd much prefer to read my book," said my boyfriend of three years, lifting the blanket to peer down at me.

Call me sensitive, but when you've got your mouth wrapped around some guy's penis, it's rather insulting to be told to stop. It's sort of like a shivering street kid holding up the fur-lined leather jacket you're offering, when it's snowing and minus 30 degrees, saying, "What's *this*? I wouldn't be seen dead in it!" Mustering up all the dignity one can when forced to emerge, *un*triumphant, from the darkness, I tried desperately not to be offended at being passed over for Stephen King. I failed.

"Sorry, honey, what was I thinking? I forgot we'd had sex once this month already," I snapped.

"When are you going to grow up?," my lover (actually, scratch that and make it "roommate") retorted, waving the hated book madly about. "Honestly, we're not 17 anymore, in case you hadn't noticed."

No. Twenty-eight—practically in our graves.

"*No one* has sex all the time when you've been together as long as we have," he said with that superior "I'm trying very hard to be patient" look.

"John and Alice do," I ventured.

"Well"—big sputter—"Phhhhtttt! You're holding *them* up as an example!!!! The couple who *tongue*-kissed in front of our guests at the last dinner party? They're . . . well, they're . . . sex maniacs!"

I knew there was a reason why I liked them so much.

"Perhaps," said the about-to-be-dumped-big-time boyfriend, "you'd be happier living with *them*, if you think they're so great. You can all have a . . . a threesome or . . . something."

Actually, that's not a bad idea, I went to bed thinking (the living with them bit, not the threesome). And I did shack up with John and Alice (though, I hasten to add again, not in the sense *he* meant) for a month until I found another apartment. Solo this time. That way I could have sex as often as I wanted to, even if it was just with myself. Funny enough, I'm still friends with John and Alice but have lost contact with Mr. Sex-Is-for-Teenagers. After all, us sex maniacs have to stick together, and anyone who expects it more than once a month (I really wasn't joking), obviously qualifies as one. *Not.*

At this point you're (hopefully) having a bit of a giggle but may be feeling a tad guilty as well. Like, you can sort of identify with the wanting-to-read-rather-than-bonk part? Relax! It really is normal. *Everyone*, even that hussy who works in the liquor store and licks her lips and thrusts her chest out at *anyone* in trousers, occasionally thinks, *If I have one more cigarette maybe he'll give up and start snoring.* She, like you, isn't always as eager when she's worn out from carting around one-too-many cases of Budweiser. Believe me, after a long day writing about sex and/or relationships, the *last* thing I want to do is actually do it or have one. The only stiff thing I feel like at the end of a long day is a drink.

But—and it's a BIG but—while it's OK to give an exaggerated yawn now and again when your partner turns to you with that unmistakable twinkle in the eye, constantly and consistently saying no to sex is not a good idea. For you, your partner, or the relationship.

Making love isn't a luxury, it's essential for your relationship to survive. According to research, we get about a quarter of our total enjoyment of a relationship from sex.[1] That's if you're having *good*, regular sex and the rest of your relationship's in pretty good shape. If you're having bad sex, or none at all, the other three-quarters of the relationship that *was* good gets canceled out. Why? If your sex life is in drastic dire straits, it spills over into the rest of it and ends up poisoning everything.

What's the one thing that differentiates good friends from lovers? Sex. Think about it. These days, when we see friends separately and share lots of ourselves with same- and opposite-sex friends, it's the *only* thing we do with our partner that we *don't* do with anyone else. Good sex builds a close, intimate relationship—and it does a lot to smooth over the rough parts. Sex is good for us, both physically and mentally. It decreases stress, boosts the immune system, and gives us a sense of well-being.[2] We feel loved and nurtured when we're having satisfying, regular sex. More relaxed with each other and prepared to put up with more.

Stop having good sex and you stop feeling connected to your partner. If someone doesn't want to make love to you, you don't feel sexy or attractive. Your self-esteem plummets. Sexual frustration makes you irritable. Resentment means you start getting angry over things that previously didn't worry you. Without sex, intimacy disappears. Both of you feel increasingly isolated. You start fantasizing about other people. You may take it further and actually have an affair. Or you might just up and leave.

Bad sex really is bad news. Put the relationship first and sex last and you lose the most effective way of nourishing yourself and each other. Give it the same importance as the relationship itself and everything falls into place much more easily. I'm not saying you should expect great sex *all the time*. Sometimes career and children have to take priority, and all couples go through phases when sex isn't as good. Just don't ever give up on *trying* to make it as good as humanly possible.

> ❗ We're always hearing that men are always ready for sex, anytime, anywhere, with anyone, but one study shows it's quite common in relationships for a woman to want sex and the man to blow her off.[3]

I found this chapter incredibly difficult to write because my first book, *Hot Sex: How to Do It*, afforded me 400 pages to dispense advice. This is but a mere snippet of what I'd like to tell you, so if you're interested in more, you might like to check that out as well. I'm not shamelessly self-promoting (well, maybe a bit)—I honestly think sex is such an important part of your relationship it deserves the full treatment. So, if you don't already have a few good sex books tucked in behind the *Intellectualization of a Modern Species* stuff you bought for show, do yourself a favor and buy a couple. Even if it's not mine (sob!).

FIVE STEPS TO A GREAT SEX LIFE

Sex is a bit like typing. Anyone can sit down and bash something out using two fingers, but you'll never be as good as the person who uses ten fingers and took the touch-typing course. This quick step-by-step guide is the equivalent of the touch-typing course (except a hell of a lot more fun). Once you're firmly established as a couple, it's a good idea to work through the following program to set up a strong foundation for your sex life and open the lines of communication. You don't have to do this in order, just pick whichever suits the mood at the time.

1. Put it on paper

Each of you grab a notepad and pen and write down, being as specific as possible, what you do and don't like about your sex life. You can do this together or separately, but no talking as you're writing! Divide the page into sections with different headings: "What I need to get in the mood for sex"; "What I'd like more or less of during foreplay/oral sex/intercourse/during orgasm/after sex." At the bottom write general comments: are you happy with when, where, and how often you have sex? Are there any new things you'd like to try (acting out fantasies, sex games like tying each other up or renting an erotic film)? Also include relationship issues: what you do and don't like about the relationship, areas you think need work. Be as honest as you can but be a little tactful. Try to think up as many positive things as criticisms, and word it carefully. "I'd like more foreplay" rather than, "You don't give me enough foreplay."

When you've finished, it's not a case of swapping lists and skimming to see how you rated as a lover. Instead, read them to each other, talking through each point as you go along. Obviously, the best time to do this is when you've got time to talk and both of you are in good moods. Attempting it after a weekend with your mother (lovingly nicknamed "that old bitch" by your partner) is asking for trouble. You'll be crucified. So pick your time. One goes first, then the other. Try to be as clear and nonjudgmental as possible when you're talking. Saying, "I hate it when you're too rough," is guaranteed to make your partner prickly. Saying "I like it when you're really gentle" (even if they never are) is a nicer way to give the hint.

When both of you are finished, each summarize what the other has said so there's no room for miscommunication. The more specific you are during the discussion, the more you'll get out of it. Saying, "I'd like intercourse to last longer," isn't enough information for him. You need to spell out exactly *how much* longer, or he'll still be thrusting away six years from now after buying a lifetime supply of Stay-Hard-Forever.

Give each other a few hours to digest what's been said, then come back with at least five ways you think you could make sex better for your partner, based on what they've told you. Don't try to put all ten suggestions into the very next sex session—you'll end up confused (not to mention exhausted). Instead, consciously try to introduce one new thing each time you make love in the future.

It's a good idea to repeat this exercise a few times during the first year or so. After that, you should be in the habit of talking openly and honestly and able to tell each other what's working and what's not, as it springs to mind.

2. Give each other permission to let loose

When you sleep with someone purely for sex, you can be as wicked as you like because you don't really care what they think of you. Once you fall in love, it's like the censors moved into the bedroom. Will he think I've been around if I suggest that? Will she think I'm kinky if I do this? We switch from being lovers to auditioning as potential Mr. and Ms. Rights. Hell, if she could bake a few muffins during intercourse, she probably would. The only way to stop the censorship is to talk to each other. Confess your fears, have a laugh about them, and reassure each other that there'll be no judging going on. Each of you has the green light to suggest whatever wild, weird, or wonderful activity you'd like.

3. Don't stop masturbating

In fact, do it more. Lots of people think they shouldn't need to masturbate once they're getting regular sex, and if you've just had it 25 times over the weekend you probably *won't* be locking the bathroom door Monday morning. But when your partner's away, they're not in the mood, or you just feel extra sexy, masturbating's a great way to keep your libido running hot.

I'd also strongly suggest you take it one step further and do it *in front* of each other. Yup. That's right: a live performance of something you usually do in private. Why? Because partners can't read minds. Body language can speak volumes, talking to each other is essential, but a picture really is worth a thousand words. Watching each other masturbate, you get to see firsthand what technique you each use— the pressure and speed, how you speed it up or slow it down on approach to orgasm, how you stimulate yourself (or stop) when you're actually having one. All you need to do then is copy each other.

You'd like to try but are too scared to suggest it? If your partner's pretty open about sex, simply start touching yourself the next time you make love. Chances are, they'll sit back and watch, entirely fascinated. If they ignore you or don't notice, say, "This is how I do it when you're not around," or, "I've had fantasies about masturbating in front of you. This feels great." As you're doing it, get them to put their hand over yours so they can feel the pressure and rhythm you're using. Then remove your hand and let them copy you and give lots of (hopefully positive) feedback.

If you or your partner is a little shy, talk about it first. Tell them you read a magazine that suggested you can improve your sex life by watching each other masturbate. Follow it up with, "I'm sure they're right, but as much as I'd like to, I think I'd be too embarrassed." If they admit they'd also be a little uncomfortable, say, "This is silly. Why don't we at least try next time?" The more confident partner goes first, prefacing it with something to break the ice ("If you laugh, I'll kill you"). If your lover's really embarrassed, ease them into it. Get them to put their hand on top of yours as you're stimulating them. Once things heat up a little, move your hand out of the way and say, "Show me, it's easier." Let them keep their eyes shut if they want: it's *you* that needs to be watching, not them. And, by the way, don't be surprised if you can't orgasm in front of each other when it takes a mere two seconds solo. It's just because you're self-conscious. Persevere though—there are plenty of reasons to give it a try. Watching her masturbate is a popular male fantasy and plenty of women also enjoy the experience. More important, it's a guaranteed way to find out how to give your partner an orgasm.

4. Take a guided tour of each other's body

To be the best lover they've ever had, you have to know *all* their hot spots, and this is how you'll find them. Each take turns, but I'll presume here that you're the one doing the exploring first. Get them to lie back, naked and comfortable on the bed. You then use your hands and tongue to explore each part of their body, while they give you a running commentary on how each sensation feels. They don't have to call it like *Monday Night Football*—just say, "Ahh, that feels great," or, "That would feel nicer if you did it gentler." You, of course, are listening and watching intently, discovering what sort of touch turns on what part of their body. One touch won't do for all. Lots of women like their breasts massaged quite firmly, but want a so-gentle-it's-like-a-tickle touch on their clitoris. Start from the top and work downward. And no cheating: skimming straight to the good parts isn't

> Men are able to recite, in detail, what they do once they're in the bedroom, but it's women who remember each and every step in the flirtation game that got them there.[4]

allowed. Slide palms up and down their arms, lick their armpit (shower first), stroke and kiss their neck, run your fingers through their hair. Move down to the breast area, using fingers, mouth, tongue (maybe even teeth) to find out what they enjoy. Stroke their stomach, down the outside of the thighs, explore behind their knees. Massage feet, suck toes, then slide your palms up their calves and the inside of their thighs. Now—and only now—can you go to work on their genitals. Remember: the idea isn't to make them orgasm, it's a learning exercise. If you feel they're getting too close, switch to a less sensitive area. Once they've climaxed, they won't be half as interested in playing the game.

5. Show him how to stimulate your clitoris

What worked for Jane won't necessarily work for Mary, and it's crucial he gets this right for you to orgasm easily. If you did the masturbation exercise, he'll know how to manually stimulate you. But it's dark down there during oral sex and it's also easy for him to lose his bearings during intercourse. So let him have a good look in daylight.

If you're one of the majority of women who can only orgasm during intercourse with extra clitoral stimulation, speak up NOW. Explain it's just the way women are built—a matter of biology rather than penis size or his technique—then, the next time you have intercourse, take his hand and guide him to the spot. Choose positions that allow easy access. It takes more than a few seconds of stroking, so make sure his hand's not twisted or cramped. He should be comfortable while he's doing it so it doesn't detract from his enjoyment. Share the workload: stimulate your clitoris yourself sometimes so he doesn't have to. Or put your hand over his while he's stroking it. You can guide his strokes better and it seems more of a together, two-way thing.

YOU LOVE YOUR PARTNER TO DEATH, BUT . . . : SOLUTIONS TO SOME COMMON SEX SNARLS

The same couple who'll sit down and talk for hours to solve their relationship problems, sometimes adopt an ostrich approach when it comes to sex snarls. "I'm too embarrassed to say something." "Say I

WORKING AS A TEAM

If you're having hassles with your sex life, it's not your partner's fault or yours, it's a problem both of you share—so solve it together.

- **Stop blaming.** Don't persecute the less "sexy" partner. Don't accuse the other of being a "sex maniac."
- **Be honest with each other.** Work out how often you'd like to make love per month. Ask your partner to do the same, then compromise. If you say six times and they say twelve, settle on eight one month, ten the next.
- **Make sex as good as possible.** Sorry to keep harping on it but if I get nothing else through, I'm determined you'll remember this: the more you enjoy sex, the more you'll want to do it. If your partner's libido isn't as high as yours, it's in your interest to make sex so absolutely fantastic, you override their "natural" urge.
- **Keep healthy.** Get enough sleep, exercise, eat healthily. The better you feel physically, the more energy you'll have for sex.

upset him/her?" "Oh, it'll sort itself out somehow . . ." Hmm. *How* exactly if *you* don't do something about it?

The right time to fix sex problems is when they arise (or don't). The longer you leave it, the harder it is to speak up and the worse the problem gets, leaving you both even more sensitive than you were at the start. I agree, it's not pleasant telling a much-adored partner they're possibly the lousiest lay you've ever had. But what's the alternative? Put up and shut up and the frustration and resentment will simmer nicely until one day, on your fiftieth wedding anniversary, the pot will runneth over and *you'll* run off with the milkman or in-home nurse.

Here's a few hints on tackling delicate subjects like clueless lovers, mismatched libidos, and sex drives buried under the pressures of everyday life.

Your partner's awful in bed

You're crazy about your love but think you really will go mad if you have to put up with ho-hum sex for the rest of your life? Take heart—and take action by trying the following.

Pick your time to talk

Make sure it's out of the bedroom. The absolute worst thing to do is erupt into a frustrated, fiery stream of criticisms while the bedsprings are bouncing. Wait until you're both comfortable, happy, and chatting freely. Then say, "Darling, I really love our relationship and adore making love with you. Is there anything you'd like me to do in bed that I'm not already? There are so many things we can explore together." It's less threatening to kick off the chat by talking about new things you'd both like to try, *then* you can gently work it around to how satisfied each of you is. If your partner's not terribly forthcoming on this point, speak for him/her. "When I give you oral sex, I never know whether to keep going while you're climaxing or stop?" After responding most people are polite enough to then ask, "What about you? Are you happy?" If your partner doesn't, turn it around yourself by saying, "I love it when you—"

Concentrate on what they're doing right

Saying, "Harold, if you keep on doing that weird thing with your tongue I'll go completely nuts," won't get you very far. Saying, "Honey, it feels fabulous when you do X, but it would feel even better if you moved a little to the left/did it for longer," will. Even if your partner truly is pathetic, there must be something nice you can say. Even if it's "It turns me on so much watching your muscles flex when you're on top of me."

Let your body talk

Back this up with body language and you'll get the point across far more effectively. When they do something you like or they're on the right track, exaggerate your response: moan loudly, move closer,

For years, I put up with truly awful sex. It was like being served up broccoli and peas for dinner every night when you hate the stuff. Eventually, I plucked up the courage to tell him I wasn't happy. Predictably, he stormed out. But he came back in an hour and said, "Okay, let me have it." We talked for hours and haven't stopped. I'm happy and he's enjoying sex so much more as well.

Fiona, 39, journalist

kiss them harder so they can't help but get the message you like what they're doing. If you don't like something, make that obvious as well. Twist away, lift your body away from their touch, or (better still) redirect their hand or mouth or whatever. Most people do to their partners what they'd like done to them. If you like having your neck kissed or bitten, kiss and bite theirs. If they don't get the hint, say, "Do you like that? I love it, too." Remember to ask, not order. Boss them around with, "Do this, do that," and they'll feel resentful. Besides, it's about as satisfying as asking someone to tell you they love you.

You thought everything was fixed but after three sessions they seem to have forgotten all you've said? It's very easy to get carried away in the heat of the moment and forget your partner needs their left toe sucked at the crucial moment. If this happens, just remind them. Whisper in their ear, "Honey, remember you said you'd—"

You're too zonked to bonk

Who's got time for sex? Juggling jobs, friends, bills, housework, families: is it any wonder a lot of couples end up having it about once a month unless they consciously make an effort? You're both working hard to establish your careers. You're *desperate* for that to-die-for-but-horribly-expensive couch so take on overtime. Stripping the paint off the walls of your brand-new apartment seems more important than stripping each other. Just as sex is given a low priority after having children, it can get pushed to the bottom of the heap *way* before then by young couples who've just moved in or married.

Putting sex on (what you're convinced will be) a temporary hold seems justifiable when you're both totally exhausted by life. But if you want to stay together, it's possibly the stupidest thing you could do. Because if sex is given a low priority, even for a little while, it rarely creeps back up again unless both of you make a concerted effort. And who knows when you'll have time to put *that* much effort in? We all talk about how we'll have more time when this is done or that happens, but it never quite seems to eventuate, does it?

Ironically, couples starved for time tend to think the little they do have left for each other is better spent talking and communicating. Wrong. If you've only got five hours a week to devote to the relationship, put a good portion of that into your sex life. Sex is by far the quickest way to feel connected to each other, and if you're after maximum closeness with minimum time, that's the way to go. Talk all you want, but one good sex session can achieve the closeness you get from four hours of intimate conversation in five minutes flat. And yes I did say five minutes.

You don't have to have marathon sex sessions every single time. You're better off having three quickies a week and one long session a month than four long sessions a month and nothing in between. The more your body has sex, the more you want it. The more sex you have, the more time you'll make for it. The more effort you put into making sex great, the quicker you can both have orgasms. If you roll into bed dog-tired but know there's one hell of a reward for five minutes of effort, you'll be far more inclined to keep your eyes open just that little bit longer. I'm not saying *all* your sex sessions should be that short, just that you're better off having a quickie than nothing at all.

! Where would you most like to make love? In the world's most romantic cities, of course! Book tickets now to Paris (voted #1), Rome (#2), or New York and London (both shared third place).[5]

Grab it whenever you can

A quickie is fast, hasty sex of any kind. Get the hang of it and you might find it can be equally as satisfying as those long, drawn-out sex sessions. Apply lots of lubricant (a quickie doesn't allow time for the vagina to produce its own lubrication) and you're on your way. She's tighter than usual without foreplay so it feels great on his end, and the quick, instant shock of pleasure is great for both of you. Even better, you've only taken three minutes out of sleeping/decorating/feeding the kids time. If you're *only* having quickies, you're missing the point but they are a great way to supplement a time-restricted sex life. Don't restrict them to intercourse either. Oral sex, when you're still clothed, also feels fabulous.

Make sex a priority

Even during *serious* stress times, when you can't face a mid-week session or don't have the time for one, you should make time for sex on the weekends when you're not so tired. Set aside one hour—come on, even the busiest couple can manage that one!—and spend it having sex.

Try something new every third time you have sex

It really doesn't take much effort, just get in the habit of varying one thing. It can be as simple as lights on or lights off. Music on or off. Clothed, half-clothed, naked. A different position. Different location.

The fact is, the better sex you have, the more you'll make time to do it. If it's boring, it hardly seems worth finding the energy for. Constantly changing the scenario ensures each time's as hot as the last, so you'll be more eager to have it the next.

WHEN I WAS SINGLE, I WAS DESPERATE FOR REGULAR SEX. NOW THAT IT'S ON TAP, I'M NOT INTERESTED. WHY?

It's a bit like Thanksgiving. You can smell that turkey cooking and you're practically *drooling*. Come the day after, you'd rather eat mashed up grasshoppers than face another slice. You really *can* have too much of a good thing. Most couples gorge themselves on each other's body when they first get together. They've overfull, but they keep going back for refills.

When you're single, sex isn't always available so that's all you think about. We want what we can't have. When you live with someone, you can have sex whenever you damn well please. Add to that, *he's* (I'm not being sexist but it is usually the guy) almost always ready, willing, and able for sex—and you start to see why desire can wane. At first, being woken up by hands on your breasts and an erect penis sticking in your back is sexy. You think, "Awesome! Regular sex again." Six weeks in, it's like, "Oh for God's sake. Does that thing ever go down? Get *off* me!"

If your partner *always* wants sex, you never get time to build an appetite for it.

"I never, ever get the chance to initiate sex because Mark's always suggested it before I have the chance to *think* a sexy thought, let alone carry it through," says a girlfriend of mine. "We never go without it, so I never have time to miss it."

If you never get the chance to reach out first, if you're always asked before getting an opportunity to do the asking, your sexual feelings wither. You start to feel pressured and used and lose interest all together.

"I was totally bored with our sex life until my boyfriend lost interest because he was working so hard," says Annette. "After a week of him falling straight to sleep instead of hassling me, I suddenly realized I missed sex and started kissing him hard.

He said, "Sweetheart, I'm too tired," which fired me up even more. Suddenly, I *desperately* wanted sex and did stuff I'd never do normally in an attempt to turn him on. Not only did it make me realize how it feels on his end, I've never felt sexier because it was me wanting sex first. I was the seductress and he was the seduced—and he loved it. Now we play this game where he feigns sleep and I have to wake him up . . ."

Your libidos don't match

Some people have naturally high sex drives: given the choice between winning the Lotto and hot sex every day of their life, they'd kiss the cash goodbye without a moment's hesitation. Sex is as essential to them as oxygen, food, and water. Deprived of it, they're like dogs in heat and just as likely to start humping your leg. For others, sex is a pleasant enough experience but not one they'd give up a nice, hot cup of cocoa for. They enjoy it when it's offered, but tend to forget about it if it's not. At the bottom of the desire scale are people who are so uninterested or put off by sex, they'd be quite happy if their last romp was their last for life.

In an ideal world, we'd all find our libido equivalents. After all, if you only want to have sex every two months and that suits your partner, it's not a problem. Hook up with a twice-a-day person and it's a huge one. If you find you're a perfect match outside of the bedroom but not in it, this section's for you. It's all about evening up mismatched libidos so you're both a little happier.

They're hot, you're not

You're the one saying, "Not tonight, honey, I've got a headache"? The first thing I want to say to you is this: it's not your fault. There's a tendency to blame the low libido person for any sex problems, and that's not fair. Sex drives are influenced by genes, hormones, and past experiences, and not all of it is in

> Whenever I came near her, she'd push me away, even if all I wanted was a cuddle. She made me feel like there was somthing wrong with me, like I was immature for wanting regular sex. We split and I'm now with a woman who enjoys it as much as I do. I'm marrying this one.
> Aaron, 27, plumber

your control. Having said that, there *are* ways to kick-start a naturally lazy libido so you'll feel like having sex more often. The idea, as always, is to meet your partner in the middle. You boost your desire while they learn to manage theirs (and stop hassling you).

I've aimed this section at both men and women. "What???!!!" I can hear you splutter. "A man passing up sex?" True, it never happened on *Melrose Place*—but it does in real life (as I humiliatingly confessed earlier). Men aren't sex robots: they're human, and they're affected by stress and feelings just as much as women are. Besides, we're demanding little beasts these days, and some men find the pressure of having to perform puts them off entirely.

1. **Pinpoint the reason why you don't often feel like having sex.** It's the obvi-

> Ever secretly think you enjoy sex more than your parents did when they were young? You might be right! Thirty-two percent of over-40s said first-time sex was a letdown for them, yet four in ten 16- to 19-year-olds say it lived up to expectations, and a further 34 percent said losing their virginity was better than they'd expected.[6]

ous place to start. Plenty of people who think they've got naturally low libidos actually don't. With the right partner, under the right circumstances, they're as randy as the rest of us. So do a bit of soul-searching. Are you simply bored by sex and happy to let other things in life take precedence? Most of us move out of that can't-get-enough stage after a few months. Unfortunately, we replace it with lovemaking that's as predictable as Aunt Martha's gall-bladder operation story. In other words, if steamy, sexy, raunchy sex with George Clooney or Pamela Anderson Lee was on offer, would you be more interested?

Men with symmetrical features give their partners more orgasms, but they're also more likely to be unfaithful. Why? They're more attractive to women, so they're spoiled by all the choices.[7]

Are you tired and physically rundown? Working long hours, staying out too late, having too many drinks and cigs, eating a diet based around McDonald's—none leaves us feeling terribly energetic. Is it temporary disinterest or permanent? At some point, all of us have found the thought of sex about as appealing as filling in a tax return, so think about what else is happening in your life. Are you putting all your energies into something else? If you're trying desperately to score that promotion or working extra hours to pay off the mortgage, there's not much energy left for romping around the bedroom. Stress and exhaustion affect our hormones, blocking those that give our libidos a kick, increasing those that make us anxious. (Taking time out, making priorities, and planning for sex can solve the problems in a flash.) Are you happy with your body? If you don't feel sexy, it stands to reason you won't feel like it. If you don't like what you see in the mirror, either see a dietician and start exercising or get help if you've got body image problems.

Another biggie: are you in the right relationship? Hooked up with a nice person who does nothing for you below the waist but plenty above? Or trying to force desire for someone who treats you badly? Sex slumps aren't usually just about sex, they're a sign your relationship's gone awry as well. If you have problems outside the bedroom, they leak under the door. Equally as important is your partner's skill as a lover. A bad lover is a common cause of sexual disinterest for women. If he's selfish, inexperienced, or incompetent, in other words a bore or boorish in bed, why would you want to initiate a session?

If you've never enjoyed sex, only ever have it because "you have to," and it rarely satisfies or arouses you, there could be deeper psychological factors at play. An earlier traumatic experience, a strict religious upbringing, or growing up being told "nice girls don't do it" could be responsible, and a visit to a good sex therapist might help. If the thought of sex frightens you or you often feel as if you're "watching yourself"—you're there but not really there—again, go and see a counselor.

2. **Get back in touch with your sexy side.** If it's a temporary lack of desire, consciously concentrate on feelings and sensations when you are having sex, and don't get too hung up on having an orgasm. Start masturbating if you've stopped: the more orgasms you have, the more your body will crave them. Deliberately focus on your erotic self. Read some sexy books, watch erotic movies. Buy a book on sexual fantasies (*The Joy of Sexual Fantasy* by Andrew Stanway is excellent). Start writing down your favorite fantasies and use them to turn yourself on before sex. Prepare for it mentally. Anticipate what's going to happen. Have a bubble bath instead of a shower and read an erotic book while you're soaking. When you're out with your partner, imagine what that tongue will do to you later. How much better his fingers would feel cupping your breast than wrapped around a beer glass. How she'll look when that sexy little black dress is stripped *off*. . .

3. **Make sure you know what turns you on, then tell your partner.** Read the Five Steps to a Great Sex Life (see page 147) and work through each. Initially, it'll be an effort. You're not used to giving sex a high priority so you'll need to do it deliberately. Ask yourself regularly: what would I like more of in bed? What would I like less of? Keep a diary and jot down thoughts over a

two-week period. Think back to sex you've had in the past that you enjoyed. What was it about it that turned you on? How can you re-create this with your partner? Then pass on what you've discovered. Don't be scared to speak up, to ask for more foreplay or a different oral sex technique. Think outside the box. If you don't feel like intercourse, offer to give your partner oral sex instead. More than one person has changed their mind once they see their partner having such a good time (while they're missing out!).

4. **Learn to receive pleasure.** If your problem's long term, you may have grown up feeling guilty about sex and never been "awakened" erotically. In other words, you simply don't know how to respond to sexual sensations in your body. A sensate focus program is what sex therapists use to help you learn to receive pleasure. This simply involves replacing sex with a series of sensual massages, spaced over a month or so. During the first, you rub oil over your *own* body, to find out what feels good and arouses you. In the next stage, you and your partner massage each other, avoiding the genitals and breasts, reporting back on what feels good and what doesn't. During stage three, you're allowed to touch each other's naughty parts, but still no intercourse. The grand prize at the end is a long overdue, deeply satisfying, good old-fashioned fuck.[8]

5. **Ask your partner to be supportive.** Explain that you're trying new things to boost your desire but they can help by not pressuring you to have sex when you don't feel like it (see Why doesn't she initiate sex more, page 164. It applies to both sexes). Get them to help you relax and feel sexy by reducing the stress level in your life. Sexual desire appears to originate in the brain. If you're juggling so much your brain feels like an amusement park, there aren't too many cells free for fantasy. Ask for some "pampering time": an hour or two a week when they massage and stroke all the stresses away. (You can return the favor. Just because their libido's not affected, it doesn't mean they won't appreciate a massage.) Ideally, you'd both take a vacation. A few weeks just lying around can revive a lagging libido quicker than *you* can say, "Let's skip dinner and have sex instead."

HONEY, WAKE UP! I JUST HAD AN ORGASM

Make no mistake about it. That *was* an orgasm, even if one hand is wrapped around your partner and the other's clutching a teddy bear. It might take ten arduous minutes to masturbate yourself to orgasm in real life, but in your sleep—"Look, Mom! No hands!"

Around 40 percent of women experience wet dreams, according to sexologist Alfred Kinsey.[9] It's just more obvious when he's had one (do I really need to explain?). Men have erections once every 90 minutes during the Rapid Eye Movement (REM) stages of sleep, coinciding with the dream period. It now appears women's sexual rhythms mirror those of men: our genitals also become swollen and lubricated. For some women, night-time orgasms are the only ones they'll have.[10] British sex expert Anne Hooper says she's encountered women who could orgasm in their sleep, but couldn't through masturbation or with a partner. Why? It's the old cliché—the brain is the ultimate sex organ, and when we're asleep any emotional blocks (like sexual hang-ups) are removed.[11]

According to Hooper, we're more likely to have a wet dream when we're not having regular sex.[12] If we're single, our partner's away or been too busy with work to indulge, wet dreams are a wake-up call: you're not getting enough in real life. They can also be the result of having unsatisfying sex with a partner before falling asleep. Your body, very politely, finishes the job for you.

If you can remember the content of a dream that resulted in a bonus orgasm, pay attention. Force yourself to wake up and write down everything you can remember: where was it, what were they doing, how were they doing it, what were you feeling? When we dream, our subconscious allows us to fantasize guilt-free: you'll come up with scenarios you'd blush at if you'd daydreamed them. Often, it's your subconscious desires tapping you on the shoulder, saying, "Hey, boring, be a bit more adventurous, will you?" You dreamed of making love outdoors? Introduce some alfresco sex into your real life. Being seduced forcefully? Play out a slave–master fantasy. The only thing you *shouldn't* pay too much attention to is *who* you were having sex with in the dream. Dreaming of sex with a member of your family or of someone the same sex as you, for instance, doesn't mean you've got secret incestuous desires or gay tendencies. It's more to do with what they represent. If you adore your brother, he could simply represent sex with someone you feel comfortable with as opposed to

You're hot, they're not

"Is that all you ever think about?" "Stop mauling me!" "I get it, you're pissed off because you didn't get it this morning, aren't you!" Just as your partner's feeling the pressure of not wanting sex enough, you're getting a battering for wanting it too much. And since we always want what we can't have, constantly being pushed away only seems to fuel your desire more. What to do?

1. **Take matters into your own hands—literally.** Masturbate often to take the edge off. And drop the "why should I have to when I'm in a relationship?" attitude. Your partner's not there to service you, it's not their *job* to keep you sexually satisfied. You're together because you love each other and want to make one another happy. Constantly hassling them for sex does the opposite. Masturbate every second time you feel like sex. Ideally, you'd tell your partner what you're up to so you don't have to lock yourself away, but make sure you don't make them feel guilty. There's a difference between stomping off ("I suppose I'll have to do it by myself—again") and giving a wink as you head for the bathroom with a sexy mag ("Be back in a minute, sweetheart. Get ready for a cuddle"). Even better, get into the habit of doing it in front of them. Your partner might be more than happy to watch you pleasure yourself, even if they aren't in the mood for sex themselves.
2. **Don't force your partner to have sex.** Stop putting pressure on someone to have sex and you'll give them time to actually feel like it. That doesn't mean you can't be affectionate or sensual, just make it clear when you *are* innocently kissing or touching your partner that there's no hidden agenda. You should be able to

snuggle up on the couch and watch a video together without immediately suctioning your hands to her breasts. Ditto his penis. Stick to stroking arms, shoulders, and neck and you'll ignite desire rather than squash it.

3. **When you do make love, focus on their pleasure, not yours.** The better lover you are, the more enjoyment they get from sex and the more likely they are to crave it. Encourage them to open up and tell you what they need to get turned on. Do you need to brush up on your technique? Do they need more foreplay? Are you picking the wrong time for sex (like Saturday mornings, the only chance they get to sleep in)? Suggest you take a bath together or give them a massage first. Ask for feedback during sex and above all, give them *time* to get aroused. Lower libido people take a little longer. Just because your genitals can spring to attention while reading about cross-pollination in *Green Foliage: A Guide* doesn't mean their arousal system is permanently on automatic.

WHY DOESN'T SHE INITIATE SEX MORE?

It could be because you jump in before she's had a chance to make the first move herself. Or maybe it's because she's worried she'll come across as "unladylike."

When I was at college, every psychology student had to "volunteer" to participate in a number of psychology experiments in order to pass the course. For one, we were all seated in a classroom, arranged in boy–girl format, then presented with large, blank notepads and a pen. The professor beamed down at us from his lectern and asked, very politely, for us to write down all the slang words we'd ever heard used to describe the male and female genitals.

Now, at 20, all of us knew plenty. The guys scribbled ferociously, constantly checking the competition in a bid to be the last in the room to stop writing. The more he knew, the more sexually experienced he'd seem. The girls did the opposite. Twirling our hair and gazing innocently out the window for supposed inspiration, we made the odd pathetic scribble, then crossed out whatever it was we'd written. After eavesdropping on my big brother for years, I could have filled the entire notebook. Sue, queen of dirty jokes, could have filled six of them but even she feigned disinterest and a complete lack of knowledge. Why? Because it wasn't nice for females to be seen as too in touch with the raw, primitive side of sex. None of us could bear being thought of as a "slut" by filling the page.

That's what may be at the bottom of your girlfriend's reluctance to initiate sex. If she grew up in a religious, strict household, I'd bet that is at the root of the problem. Tell her you'd love it if she was the one to make the first move and see how she reacts. If she opens up and confesses she's worried about being judged, reassure her profusely. You could also try buying her some erotic fiction, written by a female (try Anaïs Nin as well as modern writers), so she'll get the message it's okay these days for women to feel and be sexy. Incidentally, you're not alone in wanting her to initiate sex more often. Relationships expert Dr. Maryon Tysoe cites a U.S. study where psychologists asked dating or newly married couples what they'd like more of in bed. Men, much more than women, wanted their partners to have more experimental sex, spontaneous sex, initiate sex more often, and play the dominant role.[13]

FIRESTARTERS: REIGNITING PASSION WHEN THE FLAME'S GONE OUT

There are two common reasons why sex dies: 1) your relationship's gone sour (in which case, read the whole book); 2) sex has become so routine and predictable, it's just not fun anymore. I know plenty of couples who just give up at this point. "Sex? Oh, we stopped doing that years ago. Done everything. What's left to explore? Right, honey?" "Honey" usually grunts and decides now's the time to freshen the drinks. Quite frankly, I'm with them. If sex is no longer offered up, you might as well drink yourself stupid.

Now while I accept it's *common* for long-term couples to lose the sexual fizz, it's not written in stone. You won't find, "And in the seventh year, thou shalt no longer desire thy partner," painstakingly etched into some ancient granite tablet somewhere. It *doesn't* "happen to everyone eventually," only to those too lazy and disinterested to put the effort in. Sure, maintaining a great sex life isn't easy when you've been together for years. As we've already discussed in this chapter, you need to give sex priority, spend time thinking of ways to make it better, and be able to talk to each other about what you need to keep *your* fire burning brightly. But it can be done and there are plenty of couples out there (the ones who always leave the dinner party early *and*, incidentally, John and Alice) who are still shredding the sheets 20 years on.

How? For a start, they focus on what's great about couple sex rather than focus on what's not, namely, the "I'd kill for some new flesh" thing. Believe me, even happy couples complain about that one. It may come as a shock to you, but falling in love doesn't provide bullet-proof protection against finding others attractive. *Very* attractive. Saying "I love you" or even getting married doesn't mean you've signed a contract that says, "I will never desire anyone else," and window shopping is fine. It's when you start handling the merchandise, buying it, or taking it home with you that there are problems.

But think about this for a moment. What if you succumbed and got caught? Would you really swap all the other pluses of being with someone you love just to satisfy that momentary craving? For a split second now and then (after being chatted up by an Elle MacPherson or Billy Zane look-alike), you'll probably answer, "God yes!" Force yourself to think about it for a full five minutes, however, looking into your partner's face and imagining their finding out, and you may find *that* fire burns out pretty quickly.

Just in case you need reminding, couple sex has it over singles sex in some areas. First off, if you've put effort in, orgasm is pretty well guaranteed for both of you. You know each other's body so well, it's a matter of pushing a few buttons to make each other climax. You know each other's preferences and are comfortable enough to speak up and say what you feel. You've got a vested interest in pleasing each other. You want them to enjoy sex as much as you do because you care about them. You trust each other. You can share those kinky sex fantasies because they know in real life, you're not weird or perverted, it's just a fantasy. My research indicates that couples enjoy more varied sex than singles. As well as lust-driven sex, there's lazy, sleepy Sunday-morning sex, romantic sex, and sex when you both laugh each other stupid.

The trick to not letting the urge to stray turn into reality is to keep an erotic edge going long term. The trick to doing *that* is to constantly re-create, rediscover, and reinvent sex.

Re-create

Sex with someone new is naughty—that's half the appeal. Re-create and satisfy the "naughty" craving by being "bad" together. Act out fantasies, have sex where there's a hint of being caught. Behave like you're having an affair with each other. Plan what you're going to do to them that night, then tell them about it as you wave them off to work. Anticipation can be just as heady as newness.

Rediscover

Remember in the beginning how you used to try *anything* just so you'd both climax together? Continue the quest to slow his orgasm down and speed hers up. Ideally, give her a head start by making her climax through oral sex or masturbation before intercourse. If he orgasms too fast during intercourse, give him one orally, then let him give you oral sex to allow him time to get another erection. He'll last longer if he's onto orgasm number two.

Have more foreplay, not less. It's not a luxury, it's necessary for the women's vagina to physically prepare for intercourse. Relax, take your time and enjoy it for what it is. It's not something you do in the beginning; it's even more essential later when the "newness" has gone.

Spoil each other with massages. It's a sadly underused way to reignite the laziest libido. Women, particularly, like the slow build-up. Again, take your time. A five-minute massage isn't fun,

> As much as we don't like to admit it, women are as turned on by porn almost as much as he is. Our testosterone level shoots up by 80 percent when watching a flesh flick. His goes up by 100 percent.[14]

that's just a token gesture. Instead of rushing, put something slow and sexy on the stereo, grab some oil (a water-based oil, sold at sex shops, is best because you don't need to wash your hands before touching the genitals—oils can cause things like yeast infections), a few towels, and settle in for at least 30 minutes. Start with non-erotic touching, sliding your hands over their back, shoulders, and neck, massaging all the tension away. After 20 minutes or so, you can start teasing. Slide your palms up and down the inside of their thighs, across their stomach, skim the breasts. Don't even think about touching the genitals until they're straining toward you.

Also, up her orgasm quota. Men usually climax each time they have sex, women often don't. If you're the one always hitting the jackpot, it's understandable you'll be more eager for sex than the less lucky one. Devote a lot of time to foreplay and keep searching until you find that secret spot or technique that guarantees it for her.

Reinvent

Saying you're bored with sex is like saying you're bored with reading because you've read all the books in your library. There are as many varieties to sex as there are new authors to discover. Swap roles, for instance. If they normally seduce you, you seduce them. Even if you've already done the tie-each-other-up thing, try a twist. Add a blindfold—or take it off. Masturbate for them *while* they're tied up. Or both of you wear blindfolds and make love "blind." Your sense of touch is tripled, you're much less inhibited about what you're doing because your partner can't see you and you can let your fantasies run riot. Speaking of which . . .

Fantasize like mad. Sexual fantasies are the cheapest, most effective sex aids around. Pretending you're doing the construction guy or the girl in

> I got dragged along to one of those dreadful parties where they sell sex toys, but once I got there, I thought, *Why not?* I came home with crotchless panties, a vibrator, and a pair of rather pathetic-looking handcuffs. Mike was still up when I got home and he stayed up all night, if you get my drift. It was brilliant!
> Sophie, 28, producer

the cafe isn't being unfaithful (though best to keep your mouth shut), it's a way of introducing variety into your sex life without the disastrous consequences of actually doing it.

Enlist some help. Buy a few good sex books and how-to videos and try out some of their suggestions. If nothing else you'll have a good laugh together.

LIGHTEN UP A LITTLE: EROTICA CAN BE EROTIC

Oh come on! I don't care how upscale you are or how intellectually brilliant or politically correct, I bet *you* sneak furtive glances in the window of those sleazy but oh-so-fascinating "adults only" stores, just like the rest of us do. There's something macabrely fascinating about sex shops. Even when you are inwardly cringing, the urge to pick up that huge, black, throbbing, "talking" vibrator and switch it on is pretty appealing. (Not to mention hanging around the entrance hoping your stuck-up neighbor will emerge with a hot pink vibrator sticking out of a brown paper bag.)

If I'm offending anyone, I'm terribly sorry. Sort of. But seriously, I'm not talking about hard-core pornography that involves children, animals, or violence, more the saucy stuff even your family video store stocks. And I'm not talking make-your-eyes-water torture gear either (though, if you're into it and use it sensibly, I'm not bagging that). While there are a lot of sex aids out there that are a complete waste of money, I personally think the kick you'll get out of blowing $100 at a sex shop is well worth the cash. It's naughty. It's forbidden. Sneaking into a sex shop, a few sheets to the wind, is *not* what your average well-to-do couple does. And that's exactly why you *should* do it. It's fun, and sex is supposed to be fun. So don't be prudish. Have a laugh. Have *fun*.

At the risk of making fellow feminists' hearts pound with fury, I really think us "girls" should lighten up a little with regard to erotica and pornography. I'm *not* talking about the truly nasty stuff. But I don't think the sisterhood stuff needs to be dragged out just because your guy happens to like freeze-framing Kim Basinger during the strip scene in 9 1/2 Weeks. Sorry to be sexist here but I have yet to meet a man who's outraged to discover his girlfriend watches an occasional sexy flick. It's women who usually have problems with it. Some think their partner is comparing their body to the woman on the screen, and they're worried they're not measuring up. Others believe if their partner watches or reads porn, it means he doesn't love them or they're not satisfying him sexually. Not true.

Let's set a few things straight here. The majority of men don't watch porn for the sinister reasons women think they do. They watch it because it's fun. Porn to men is no big deal. They honestly can't see how watching a sexy film can be any sort of reflection on their love for their girlfriend. Most don't understand why she takes offense because, as far as they're concerned, *every* guy does it.

They're right. Research shows the infrequent porn user is your average guy—90 percent of them.[15] He's not a deviant, he just likes looking at sexy pictures. It's got a lot to do with what turns each sex on. Usually, men are turned on more by pictures and visual images, women are turned on more by words.[16] Now, that's a massive generalization, but true in a lot of cases. That's why we prefer to curl up with a steamy blockbuster and he prefers to look at pictures. In most cases, it's pretty harmless.

Your partner not only watches it but—OH MY GOD!—wants you to watch it with him? If you truly have vehement moral objections to pornography, you're well within your rights to tell him you're not interested and not to pressure you further. If you just feel a bit embarrassed about it, try it once. You wouldn't be the first couple to use mainstream erotica to spice things up a little. So give yourself time to get used to the idea and then at least give it one try.

Start by watching an R-rated movie rather than diving straight into X-rated. And it's one thing watching a sex scene together, quite another having sex while watching it. Get over the awkwardness before moving into the more explicit stuff (and if you don't want to go further, fine). If you get one out and find it laughable or horribly boring, just have it playing in the background and look up at the good parts. It's more the thought of doing something naughty than what you're actually doing that's the turn-on. You could also try renting some women's erotica (films made by women, for women—it's made pretty clear on the back). They're pretty mild and—surprising, I know—actually have a plot.

If you give it a go and don't like it, be honest. Tell him what he does in private is his business but it's not something you want to share: you tried it but it's not for you. If your partner hassles you constantly or puts the pressure on after that, *then* feel free to put him and his videos out on the street.

NO SEX PLEASE—WE'RE MARRIED

Picture a happy husband and wife. It's a rare person who'd imagine the couple in bed—unless, of course, they're reading books and sipping tea. Why does marriage have such a bad reputation when it comes to sex? Well for starters, you're living with the label. If you lived together before getting married, you were "living in sin" as "lovers." Slip that band of gold on your finger and you become "husband and wife." You're respectable, and for some couples that's the equivalent of pouring a bucket of cold water all over the bed. What is marriage if it's not official permission to shred the sheets to your heart's content? God won't mind, your mother won't mind, the neighbors won't mind because you're married—you're *supposed* to have sex.

"People say it's just a piece of paper, but marriage is a mental attitude," says Anna, a 32-year-old receptionist who's been married for six years. "Before, John and I would think nothing of spending all Sunday in bed. Now we're married and have bought a house, it's like we feel obliged to get up and do something like work in the garden. Sex seems frivolous, it's almost like we should be over that by now."

Anna's not the only one who thinks of sex in marriage as the Saturday-night-only-and-don't-disturb-the-children variety. Check out the bumper stickers that scream, "No sex please. We're married." The plots of TV sitcoms that constantly reinforce the get-in-bed-with-PJs-on rather than slinky lingerie. How many times was he slapped on the back by his friends at his bachelor party and told, "This is the last time you'll have fun, dude. Make the most of it." Why do girlfriends organize a male stripper for your "last night of freedom"? There's a definite perception that fun—and that includes sex—ends once you're married. And this is where the secret to a good marital sex life lies.

All the couples I've interviewed who are still romping about the bedroom have a healthy disregard for traditional views about marriage and sex. In the bedroom, they cease to be husband and wife and, instead, revert back to being individuals with very real needs and desires. In other words, they refuse to act "married."

These are other pitfalls to be avoided at all cost:

Make the most of the "recharge"

Make-or-break point for a lot of marrieds is when the newness of sex wears off—again. Getting married can add a nice, new edge to it for the first few months of being Mr. and Mrs. The trick is to keep it going rather than let it lapse and fall back into the same old sex ritual. Think, *That's what happens*, and put up with ho-hum sex from now until death do you part or start working at sex as hard as you should be working on the rest of your relationship.

Speak up if you're not happy

When Mandy, 27, found she was dreading going to bed with her husband Andrew, she confronted the problem head-on. "When we first got married it was wonderful—then it quickly slid into familiarity. I knew we had to explore our sexuality or it was all over." She told Andrew how she felt—that she was bored and wanted more—and they ended up talking for three hours about their fantasies and expectations. "The result is we now let ourselves go and try stuff that would have made me hot with embarrassment at the start." It is possible to pull your love life out of the deep freeze, all you need to do is reach in there and get it.

Don't get complacent

Most couples who rate their sex lives highly say they are proactive in sex. They think about when, where, and how they'll have it and think up new things to try. They spend time thinking about sex and what they'll do that evening. It's like a gourmet who'll spend half an hour deciding which dish on the menu to choose. They imagine what the

Turn on the stereo to turn on each other. When researchers asked men and women worldwide, "What gives you the most pleasure in life?" the majority said listening to music. Sex came a close second. For the ultimate pleasure experience? Jam while you slam.[17]

food will look and taste like. Their senses are heightened. Savoring what's coming is almost as good as eating it (both puns intended).

Don't think of sex as just intercourse

Move away from the all-roads-lead-to-intercourse theory and make a conscious effort not to follow the same pattern in lovemaking. It's not all about orgasm, it's about giving and receiving pleasure—orgasm and intercourse are but a mere part of that. Substitute oral sex for intercourse more than occasionally. Manually masturbate each other to orgasm. Enjoy a deep kissing session without feeling pressure to "finish it off" with anything.

In short, marriage isn't a sexual death sentence and monogamy doesn't have to be boring. It's all in *your* control. Devote time and effort to making your sex life as varied as possible and it will reward you back.

REAL LIFE: A SEX SUCCESS STORY

Catherine: "It's really quite amusing that people seem so astonished that Rob and I still enjoy good sex despite being married for 22 years. We simply put a lot of effort into our sex life and always have.

"I was 20 when we got married and Rob's the only person I've slept with. But both of us are sexual people and we've given it a high priority. We had sex for the first time about six months before the wedding and it was predictably dreadful. After we got married, we bought a few sex books and videos and educated ourselves as much as possible. In the first few years, we had a lot of sex. We were still in that "can't keep our hands off each other" stage when I got pregnant. That was the first shock: for two years, sex was something we did for about three minutes once every two weeks. When the worst of it was over—the sleepless nights and constant demands— we dumped Claire on my mother and took ourselves away for the weekend. We had nothing else planned but to enjoy sex again—and we did. We tried a few new things (those sex books, again!) and remembered how good it used to be.

"We also didn't stress out too much about the lack of quality sex during the children's younger years; we just accepted that we'd have time for that later. I think we work harder at sex now than we ever have. I'll try to think up little surprises for Rob—pack the kids off and wait for him to come home in the bedroom, champagne and snacks laid out on the bed, a sexy video in the VCR. If I had to sum up our recipe for sexual success, I'd say it's never taking the other person for granted and making time for sex in your life."

Rob: "From the moment I met Catherine, she did it for me. The first few years were amazing—we had sex about five or six times a week and it was always good. Catherine made a real effort: she'd make me read books about it and always tried to think up something new for us to try. The more imaginative she got, the harder I'd try to beat her at it. It turned into a competition but a friendly one with a great reward!

"When Claire arrived, I remember feeling jealous because all her energy went into being a mother. But I was always confident our sex life would go back to normal and it did. There was only one other time it's suffered and that was when my father died. I slid into depression, but Catherine was brilliant. She didn't complain, just talked and listened and gave me lots of TLC and massages. She knows when to be sexy and when to be understanding.

"My advice to other long-term couples would be accept that sex can't be wonderful all the time but always try to make it so."

Love Landmines

Getting through the inevitable blow-ups over house-work, families, money, and just about everything else

● ●

You meet her parents and they're as cool to you as the chilled potato soup they're serving. It's 5:00 A.M., and the bastard's still out partying with his friends. She's turned out to be a workaholic. You open the cupboard and discover his idea of washing the dishes is rinsing off the really big food chunks and now there's an entire ant colony whooping it up on the pots and pans. Yep—the blinders have fallen off and you're seeing your partner for who they really are: human.

One minute you were cruising happily along, the next you're lurching from one argument to another. Remember all those lonely nights in bed when you dreamed of finding someone to share it with? Now's the time when you start dreaming of being single again. We've all got faults (yes—even you!) and, not surprisingly, most center around the same old troublespots, like housework, money, not getting along with friends or family, and when or whether to get married and have kids. The rough spots are what sort the flings from the in-it-for-a-long-time-not-just-a-good-time couples because you need a lot more than deep breathing and counting to 100 (Ten? You've got to be kidding!) to survive. Chapter 4 taught you about communication skills—this is the place where you'll get to use them. I'll start with how you handle arguments generally, then talk about the specifics of what you're arguing over.

I WIN, YOU WIN: FIGHTING FAIR

The first step to surviving fights is to remember that every couple argues. If you don't, there's something very wrong with your relationship. You're either the first human clones out of the lab (and gosh, you grew up fast!) or one of you is agreeing for the sake of it. Arguments are healthy: they show you're secure enough to question each other's beliefs and behavior. So long as they're balanced with good times (relationship guru John Gottman's theory on a healthy relationship is five good times to every one argument), you're doing just fine.[1]

On the other hand, arguments aren't up there on anyone's "how I'd like to spend next Saturday night" list. So the aim of this section is to try to change the *way* you argue, so there are fewer of them. Plenty of couples argue about the same old problems, over and over again. Hopefully, this will help you solve things the first time around.

There's a right way and a wrong way to argue. You won't get anywhere by:

- Being aggressive and attacking your partner verbally
  "Sorry I'm home late again, honey."
  "Do you realize what time it is? You're such a selfish bitch/bastard. You care more about your job than you do me! Asshole!"

- Avoiding the argument by walking out and refusing to discuss it
  "Sorry I'm home late again, honey."
  "That's fine," as you storm into the kitchen, lips pursed.

- Trying to smooth things over simply for the sake of peace
  "Sorry I'm home late again, honey."
  "It's nothing really. You're only an hour late. I didn't mean to upset you by complaining."

- Being sarcastic
  "Sorry I'm home late again, honey."
  "That's okay, darling. Of course work should take first priority

over a night home with me. After all, we did have those two hours together two months ago."

- Looking for solutions too early: instead of discussing the emotions behind it you skip straight to the end
  "Sorry I'm home late again, honey."
  "Right. Look, in the future, I'll eat dinner before you. How does that sound?"

- You *will* get somewhere by problem solving. Discuss feelings directly and openly, look at the reasons behind the argument, and search for a solution both of you are happy with.
  "Sorry I'm home late again, honey."
  "That's fine. Have a shower then let's have a drink."
  Later: "Do you think we could talk about this a little? I know your job is important to you, but sometimes I feel like I'm second priority. I need some reassurance and we need to come up with ways to stop the arguments we've been having when you arrive home later than expected."

Think you can get the hang of it? Here's a step-by-step guide to how to have an argument *successfully*—and survive.

HOW HAPPY COUPLES ARGUE

In one study, researchers looked at the difference between how happy couples argued compared with unhappy couples. Here's what they found:

Happy couples:
- Talked more and revealed more about their feelings. They gave clear, direct messages that weren't riddled with double meanings.
- Actively listened to each other (lots of nods and uh-huhs) and peppered their arguments with expressions of respect and encouragement ("I see where you're coming from," "I still love you even though I'm upset by this").
- Were calm and able to be rational.

- Were sensitive to each other's feelings, and often ended arguments with private, intimate jokes ("Come and give me a hug, snooky bear").

Unhappy couples did the opposite to all of the above, then topped it off by:
- Talking over each other with one partner constantly having to fight to be heard.
- Reading negatives into everything. If there was a double innuendo, each would take the negative slant immediately.
- Ridiculing and abusing. They used more expletives and spent most of the argument calling each other names and criticizing rather than solving the problem.

Seriously, which fighting style do you think is likely to get you further?[2]

The five-step plan for the ideal argument

I don't expect you to sit there, book open at this page, and solemnly work through this step by step. But if both of you give it a quick read at some stage and try to memorize the key points, then check back *after* arguments to see how you've done, it'll soon become second nature. Don't worry if, to begin with, you feel a bit stiff and as if you're reading from a script. The way I'm asking you to word your criticisms does sound formal and excessively polite. It's not—it just looks that way written down. While it may feel a little unnatural in the beginning because you're deliberately choosing words, it's amazing how quickly you'll find yourself adopting "win–win" speak.

1. Define the issue

Make sure you know what you're arguing about. Ask, "Why is that important to you?" and "Why do you want that?" and the argument could be over before it's started. A psychologist friend of mine explains win–win perfectly: "If you have an orange and both of you are arguing over who'll get it, the obvious thing to do is to cut it in half—with both of you losing half. If you ask each other what you want it *for*, you may find he or she wants the pulp for juice and you want the rind for a recipe. That's win–win. It's not always that simple, but quite often it is."

Rate how important the argument is. Each of you give the issue a mark out of ten for importance. Whoever gives it the highest score should get the lion's share of talking time.

If it's something you're sensitive about, admit it. Say, "Look, this is a sore point for me because of something that's happened in my past. Maybe I am overreacting so forgive me if I am but it's still really important that we talk this through."

> We argued about everything from whose car to drive and whose turn it was to do the shopping through to how much his mother hated me and I hated his profession. It was like dating your worst enemy: neither of us was allowed to get away with a thing.
> Jan, 29, secretary

Be specific. Make sure your complaint includes three elements: a) what it was your partner did or didn't do; b) what situation(s) it happened in; and c) how it made you feel. "When you didn't pay attention to me in front of your friends, it made me feel ignored and not very special," rather than, "You don't make me feel special anymore." Instead of, "You never give me compliments," say, "Last night I wore a new outfit and I felt upset that you didn't notice or comment."

Word it so you're giving the reaction you would have liked, rather than what you didn't like. "I'd really appreciate it if we could spend more time together," rather than, "We don't spend enough time together."

Don't automatically lash out if your partner says something unkind or tactless. Force yourself to wait five minutes before responding. Research by American psychologists Nancy Yovetich and Caryl Rusbult found when men and women are asked to say what they'd do if a partner behaved badly, they're more likely to respond destructively if asked to give a fast response. A pause of as little as six seconds was enough to make them think more constructively, calm down, and weigh the consequences of what they were about to say.[3] Fighting fire with fire often doesn't work: you need to pour water on the situation instead. It's not a sign of weakness to react to an insult rationally, it's a sign of strength.

2. Move into discussion

Take turns. One of you gets center stage for a full five minutes (time it). They talk, you listen (no interrupting). It's cheating to spend that time mentally planning how you're going to word your part. Instead, try really hard to give them full attention and listen to what they're saying—you'll have your chance, uninterrupted, at the end. When their five minutes is up, repeat back to them what they've just explained to you. If they feel you understand, it's your turn. If you've got it wrong, keep on asking questions until you get it right. *Then* it's your turn.

Keep reminding yourself: stop pushing my point, listen to theirs. Resist the urge to take over the conversation, even if you're better at articulating. The key to solving problems isn't about making your partner understand your feelings, it's understanding theirs. If each of you shifts the emphasis from talking about how you feel to listening when the other speaks and asking questions, you'll get a lot further.

Stick to the issue. If you find yourself saying, "And another thing . . ." or, "This is just like how you behaved with Linda," stop right there. One problem per argument.

Criticize the behavior not the person. Keep your criticisms focused on what your partner did (or didn't) do, not on what sort of person they are. "I felt upset when you . . ." not, "You're so self-centered, you didn't even notice when . . ."

Stop blaming by removing "you." Say "I feel," not, "You made me feel."

Don't say, "If you hadn't slept in, I wouldn't be late for work. Now I'm in trouble and it's your fault." Instead try, "I was late for work this morning and it caused no end of problems. We need to look at ways to ensure it won't happen again."

Don't use threatening statements. "That's it then, we might as well call it quits," or, "Well, I don't know why we're even bothering going out if we can't agree on this." It instantly makes the argument seem much more serious and hackles rise. It's very easy in the heat of the moment to come back with "Fine! Leave then!" if someone threatens to.

Listen for trigger phrases that make the other's blood boil. Just last week, a pleasantly stimulating debate with my boyfriend about relationships turned into a raging argument. He told me I was being condescending and patronizing. I thought I was simply letting him know the latest research on the topic we were discussing (after all, I was in the middle of writing a book about the topic!). One simple phrase turned out to be the problem.

This is how I thought I was coming across:

"Do you know, I read a study recently that actually said quite the opposite."

This is what I was saying:

"Listen, honey—the research actually proves quite the opposite."

The phrase "Listen, honey" does sound condescending. I don't know where I got it from but whenever I used it he'd stop listening to what I was talking about and think, *Bitch thinks she's smarter than me!*

Check you mean what you say and say what you mean. Most of us pull words out of the air, particularly when we're angry, that sort of express what we mean but not accurately. We'll call someone "stubborn" when we really mean "You're not acknowledging that I have a point even if you don't agree with it."

Don't mind read. If you're not sure what your partner's trying to say, ask them to put it another way. Don't assume you know what it is.

Recognize that men aren't as good at arguing as women are. Strange, isn't it? Men are supposedly more aggressive, yet they're the ones who'll do just about anything to avoid having a fight. Why? It's probably because arguments involve discussing feelings and we're usually better at that than they are. Psychologist John Gottman also thinks it's because men suffer more from "*flooding*" when arguing with their partners. Put simply, "flooding" is when you become so distressed and upset by the negative emotions flying around during a fight, you're swamped by distress. The emotional shutters come down to protect your feelings and you become hostile, defensive, or withdrawn. Needless to say, it's not a very pleasant feeling and according to Gottman's research, men become "flooded" far easier than women do when arguing with the love of their life. Yet another reason why they'll avoid it if at all possible.[4]

3. Check your progress after 20 minutes

Who's doing the talking? Are you both getting enough time or is one dominating the conversation? Do you feel the other person's still really listening to you?

If you're feeling really angry, take a 20-minute break. Relationships expert John Gottman's research proves discussions fall apart when heart rates soar. If your blood's pumping furiously and your heart's racing, talking is pointless—you're too angry to listen. Gottman suggests taking your pulse every five minutes during an argument. If it starts racing, take some time out. It's probably not enough to just get a glass of water or go to the bathroom—it takes at least 20 minutes for one's body to return to normal.[5] Spend it doing something that soothes you. Go for a short drive, a walk, or call a friend and make small talk (don't sound off about the argument). *Don't* spend the time out planning what to say when you resume the conversation. Instead think calming thoughts like, "This is just a bad moment. We'll work it out."

Check your body language. British relationships expert Susan Quilliam believes happy couples use very different body language when fighting compared with unhappy matches. Even though they're angry, their attention is still focused on each other: they face each other, make eye contact, and talk. The body language says, "We still love each other so let's face this now."

Unhappy couples do the opposite. They jab fingers at a partner's chest while trying to make a point: annoying as hell and also quite threatening. They cross their arms and roll their eyes, which sends a clear signal: "Talk all you want but I'm not listening to a word of it." Gazing around the room means they're not just disinterested, they're looking for an escape route.

Quilliam suggests the following to ease tension during an argument. Lean forward toward your partner, leave your arms loose by your side, and nod your head: that way they'll feel you're listening. If you're talking and your partner seems to be drifting off, take their hand and *ask* them to look at you. Use soothing gestures if they're getting overheated. Lay a hand on their arm and say, "I know you're angry and I wish we weren't arguing." Let them know you also want the argument over with even though you're prepared to discuss it and resolve it for good.[6]

4. Continue the argument, this time looking for solutions

By now, the anger should have evaporated a little. Try including conciliatory phrases. Saying, "I see your point even if I don't agree with it," will get you a lot further than, "I don't agree with you." Let your partner know you've at least heard and understood what they're trying to say. Include phrases like, "I see where you're coming from," and, "I know you probably won't agree with me but I just want you to understand why I feel this way."

If you now think you're in the wrong, admit it. It's natural to want to defend yourself but if you really have messed up, your partner will be much more inclined to listen to your reasons if you apologize *first*, justify later. Say, "I apologize for not calling to say I was going to be late. I should have made the effort. But the meeting ran late and I raced out of the door so I could get home more quickly. My intentions were right but I can see now I'd have been better off taking those extra few minutes to let you know." Put it this way and your partner's likely to come back with, "That's okay, sweetheart. I know you did your best."

Ask each other: "How do you think we can avoid this happening in the future?" Listen to their side. If you're confident you can do what they're suggesting and are happy to, simply agree. If not, put your solution forward. Then talk about how they feel about it. You might well combine both ideas or ditch both and come up with another. Alternatively, the solution might well be to think about it over the next few days so you can rationally think it through.

Don't play shrink. "You're defensive about this because your father left you," or, "This is all about your ex-wife, isn't it? She's made you this way." There's a difference between exploring underlying reasons together and feeling like you're on a couch and your partner's taking notes.

5. End the argument

Once you both feel understood and have found a solution you're both happy with, stop talking about it. Sometimes you'll agree *not* to agree on something: you understand each other's viewpoint, have worked out how to deal with it but it's clear you have differing opinions. It's tempting in that case to keep thinking up evidence to support your side. Don't—no matter how fab it is. Drop it.

You don't have to solve the argument to end it. Even if you haven't come up with a solution, don't beat it to death. If you've been at it for two hours, that's enough. Call a truce and resume the conversation later.

Don't expect to kiss and make up immediately afterward. You've both taken a few steps backward from each other and feel emotionally exhausted, maybe even a little frightened ("For a moment there, I really thought we *were* going to split"). Personally, I think it's best you stay together: even if you turn on the TV and the other reads a book. But if one needs to be alone for a little while, that's their way of getting back to normal. Don't object—but do set a time limit. One hour is enough (any more and paranoia sets in: you'll think the relationship's damaged for good. Either that, or feel abandoned and get angry all over again).

If you're fighting about the same thing, over and over, try taping your arguments. This is incredibly effective for two reasons. First, if you know every word that comes out of your mouth is being taped, you'll think before you open it. Second, playing back the argument gives both of you a chance to hear what you *really* said rather than what you *thought* you said.

Do something nice for each other the day after an argument. Give a small gift or a nice card, or, even make a phone call to say how much you hated arguing and how much you love each other. Failing that, just give each other an extra big hug when you wake up the next day. Smile and say, "We survived. We're stronger than ever before. Isn't it great!"

Do ultimatums ever work?

Exactly two years after Lisa met Paul she received an eviction notice from her landlord. Secretly, she was delighted. For months, she'd been hinting to Paul that she wanted to live together and this was the perfect way to cement the issue. That night, she insisted they go to their favorite restaurant, held his hand across

> She'd clam up the minute an argument started, making me feel like a complete ogre. But she was passively aggressive. While she wouldn't come right out and criticize me, she'd make smart, snide comments, then tell me I was being over-sensitive when I picked up on them. Give me a partner who screams and yells over someone like her any day.
> Tom, 36, designer

the table and told him her rental was sold and she had two weeks to move out.

"That's a drag," Paul said. "But hang on, I might just have an idea."

Here it comes, thought Lisa, *he's going to ask me to move in.*

Except he didn't. Instead, Paul suggested she call a friend of his who was looking for a roommate. "I was so utterly humiliated that it didn't even occur to him, I just mumbled something and ran to the ladies' room," Lisa said. "Once I'd gotten myself together, I decided it was now or never. The minute I sat back down I gave him an ultimatum: either I move in with him or it's over."

In Lisa's situation, many of us would be tempted to do the same. Most people don't enjoy issuing ultimatums, absolutely no one likes receiving them but just about everyone has opened their mouths at some point to say, "Do this or that or it's over." Sometimes, ultimatums are logical, well-mulled-over requests delivered in a calm I-mean-it tone. More often than not they're outright (often outrageous) demands, heavily peppered with expletives, that spill out during a hot, vicious argument. When all else fails and frustration reaches the boiling point, ultimatums seem the most effective weapon we have, bar a loaded gun. Unfortunately, they're just as dangerous. Not only can ultimatums be turned and used against you, they have a nasty habit of backfiring. So if you're about to read your partner their last rites, do so at your own peril—and take a few tips first.

Why we give them

On one level, ultimatums work. They bring a situation to a head and show your partner how important something is to you. Trouble is, they're the poor man's means of communicating—and one of the least effective methods around. People who constantly dole out ultimatums are usually emotionally immature and aren't very good at communicating or working through problems. Top that off with poor listening skills.

If you're always saying, "Do this or else," you lose power and respect. Most times you don't follow through with your threats and your partner starts to see you as pathetic. There are far better ways to solve a problem. My friend Melanie agrees. "I stopped delivering ultimatums because they proved mortifyingly embarrassing. Once I was at a party and told my boyfriend it was all over if he didn't leave with me there and then—in front of a huge audience. He refused and I stormed out and went home only to discover he had the keys to my place. I had to slink back in, in front of all those people, and ask him for them. They all laughed and I felt like a complete idiot. Now, if I feel strongly about someone's behavior, I tell them calmly that I won't put up with it but leave off the "or else.""

Why they backfire

Word them as nicely as you like but ultimatums are still thinly disguised threats. Which is why our natural reaction is to do the opposite of what's being asked, if only to maintain some sort of pride. If someone delivers a "you do this or else" ultimatum, people often refuse even if it is reasonable. It's so demoralizing to say, "Okay, dear."

The fact that you're forced to issue an ultimatum usually means your relationship is in dire straits anyway. Sometimes it's a symptom of basic incompatibility. It's certainly a sign neither of you is clear about what you want from the relationship. If you're doling out ultimatums over trivial things—like taking out the garbage—you really should ask yourself, "Am I overreacting here?" Better still, "Should we be together if I have to issue an ultimatum over something so stupid?"

Ultimatums aren't necessary in healthy partnerships with strong communication because problems are discussed and solved before they get to a make or break point. If you can't solve a problem by talking about it, you're unlikely to solve it by threatening. As Karen found out—the hard way. "I'd been going out with Karen for about three years and we spent the last one arguing bitterly," says David. "It was obvious we were headed for a break-up, which is why I was so astonished when she told me, 'Marry me on my birthday or it's over.' How she could even consider settling down when we were getting along so badly astounded me. In a sense it gave me an out: on D day I told her it was over." Karen's ultimatum was a last-ditch attempt to save a dying relationship. She put her cards on the table and lost the game.

Never say never unless you mean it

Never, ever give an ultimatum unless you're prepared to follow through. You won't be taken seriously again and you strip yourself of any power in the relationship. "My girlfriend issues loads of ultimatums and never means them so I don't notice anymore," says Robert. "Like she's hardly going to dump me for showing up five minutes late! It's the old boy-who-cried-wolf scenario: one day, she might be serious but how am I supposed to know?" Packing your bags today, then turning up on the doorstep tomorrow doesn't just make you look silly. By coming back you've effectively said, "I'll not only put up with this situation against my will, I'll hang around no matter what you dish out because I don't have the strength to leave."

Commitment ultimatums—move in/marry me/say you love me or else—are perhaps the diciest of them all. There's a reason your partner's not moving the relationship forward: he's not ready, he's still thinking about it, or you're not "the one." Giving him a jolt, trying to shock him into realizing how much you mean to him by imagining life without you, will certainly give you an answer. Problem is, it might not be the one you want. Pressure someone too early and you could lose a partner who would have been ready a year later, when she felt comfortable and ready for commitment. Behavior ultimatums—stop putting me down/stop looking at other women—are usually more successful, but even then, use them as a last resort. You don't start by dishing out ultimatums, you finish with them. There's a whole load of things you should try first. Let's say your boyfriend flirts outrageously at parties. Instead of ending the evening with "Flirt with that blonde once more and your clothes will be on the pavement," keep calm, go home together, and talk about it over lunch the next day. (How? See the section above, pages 178–187.)

When an ultimatum is the only way

Tried talking, exhausted all angles, and your partner's behavior is still intolerable? *That's* the time to give an ultimatum. If it's serious—your partner is hitting you or has a severe drinking or gambling problem—issuing an ultimatum isn't just a good idea, it's advisable. What's imperative is that you follow through.

And if there's one situation that *only* an ultimatum will solve, it's when your partner is having an affair or you're having one with someone who's married. Most people with a spouse and a lover won't change anything unless one of them says, "It's them or me," and stands by their word. This time, you really don't have anything to lose except someone who's making you miserable anyway. Even if it's not the answer you want, at least you know where you stand.

Which was precisely how Lisa felt when her boyfriend said no to her ultimatum of moving in. "If he wasn't ready by then, I knew he never would be," she said. "At least I wasn't hanging on forever, wasting my time."

If you must give an ultimatum, do it the right way

- **Don't deliver one without forewarning.** They're a last resort and should only be used after many discussions have failed. If you've spent several weeks (or months) talking about the problem with your partner, they'll at least have given it some thought before being forced to make a decision.

- **Write it down.** Think hard about what you want to say, then write it down as clearly as possible. Use nonthreatening language, and talk about changing the behavior not the person. Instead of, "I'm leaving if you don't see me more often," try, "I feel the relationship can't progress if we don't see each other more often. If you can't give me more time, I can't really see the point of continuing." Tell them what you'd like them to do more of, rather than what you want them to stop doing. "I want you to be sober," rather than, "I want you to stop drinking." Word your demand as best you can, then leave it for a few days. Does it still seem reasonable? Is there a better way of saying it?

- **Don't deliver it when you're angry.** If need be, leave the situation until you've calmed down. Ultimatums issued in the heat of the moment, when you're both tipsy or tired after a long argument, won't be taken seriously. Leave it until you've both calmed down, can talk reasonably, and think logically.

- **Don't drag other people into it.** Tacking on "and all your friends agree with me" won't get you anywhere: your partner will feel even more ganged up on and defensive. Checking that your ultimatum is reasonable with someone you trust and who also knows your partner, however, is a good idea. Do they think you're overreacting or is your stand understandable and necessary?

- **Leave yourself room for compromise.** Tell them honestly that you're not prepared to put up with the current situation but if they have any other solutions, you'd like to hear them.

- **Be prepared to follow through.** Think about the worst possible outcome (they refuse to do what you're asking) and decide if it's worth it. If it is, be prepared to stick with your decision and have some good, supportive friends on standby.

- **Put a time limit on it.** If you want to get married or move in, tell them how long you're prepared to wait. There's a big difference between "immediately" and "six months."

- **Pick the right time.** If they've just lost their job, have the flu, or found out their best friend's moving away, they may say no to whatever you're suggesting simply because they're emotionally exhausted.

- **Reward your partner for changing.** If they do make an effort to get their act together, give some positive feedback. Pay attention and let them know how much you appreciate it. Otherwise, they'll slip right back into old patterns.

> Myth: Women nag more than men do. Reality: It's true. And we do it twice as often. Researchers say it's because women have got more to complain about, especially if we're married. Even if you both work, it's still usually the wife who's saddled with most of the housework (and the kids). He doesn't nag because he's got little to gripe about![7]

CAREER CLASHES

I freely admit it: I'm a workaholic. It's not that I wouldn't prefer to be snuggled up watching trash TV with a partner than bashing away at my computer, it's just necessary at this point in my career. (Actually, sometimes I *would* prefer to be writing. Sick, isn't it?) Some of the guys I've gone out with understand this commitment and encourage it, probably because they're equally as busy and ambitious themselves. Others think I'm unhealthily obsessive about my job (which is probably true) or a selfish pig (which hopefully isn't). I talked about the importance of matching career aspirations and attitudes toward work in previous chapters. But even if you did do as you were told (add bossy to selfish), circumstances change. The laid-back and disenchanted can turn into mad career-heads if they hit on the job of their dreams; some put their feet on the top rung of the corporate ladder and realize they suffer from vertigo. Whatever, if your relationship's suffering from unbalanced work schedules and commitments, the following will hopefully help even it up.

If one of you is a workaholic

If it's you who's being accused of working too hard, don't dismiss any career complaints without giving it a lot of thought. Few people complain for no reason in these sorts of situations and they might be right: you may well have become a workaholic and a martyr. Ask others you trust if your partner's got a point, then make up your own mind about what career sacrifices you're willing to make. The fact is, you have to spend time doing enjoyable, relaxing things to bind you and your partner together; if you've lost sight of that, rework your priorities. If the relationship is important to you, be flexible—but don't be coerced. If it's not justified, talk together about why they're feeling ignored. Are they insecure about your feelings for them? How much time do they want with you? Be understanding, but don't relinquish your career for demands that aren't reasonable. You'll only end up resentful later.

If you're the one putting up with a partner talking into a dictaphone at 8:00 A.M. on Sundays, ask how long they expect to be working weekends and evenings. Say you realize their job is important but it's also important to have time together. Work together to try to achieve more balance in their life and be flexible. If their job requires them to work weekends, spend quality time during the week: meet for lunch at a cafe near their office or get up a bit earlier to have breakfast together. But don't put your life on hold just because they're entrenched in work. If you're never, ever given priority and there's no light at the end of the tunnel, you might want to reconsider whether the relationship's worth it. After all, it's not really a relationship if you don't see each other, is it?

If you're doing better than he is

If it's you saying, "Honey, I'm home," and dropping your briefcase on the floor while he's in the kitchen preparing dinner, you encounter your own set of problems. While it's hardly unusual for the female to be the one with the company car, expense account, glamorous job, and high salary, it takes a liberated guy to cope with it. A traditional man might feel he's lost power—particularly if you were both even-steven at the start of the relationship.

Women tend to feel proud of their partners when they achieve success; men often feel threatened. "Whenever we went out, it was always Katie who got the pats on the back," says Pete, a friend of mine whose partner scored a highly desirable promotion. "Her career was flourishing, mine was stagnant. I found it really difficult to smile when people asked me if I was proud of her. Of course I was, but I wondered if they were really thinking, *What's she still doing with him? She could score someone much better now.* Her success became my failure." Often, men won't even approach women who are more successful than they are because they think, *How can I attract a woman like that? She's too good for me.* (Which goes a long way to explain why lots of successful women are single.)

And it's not just him who feels weird. Women often feel put out if they're paying the lion's share of the bills, because there's a little part of them that still says, "Hey! Isn't *he* supposed to be looking after *me*?" Resentment increases if they're not just the breadwinner but prime caretakers of the relationship and chief cook and dishwasher. "I'd work my ass off, I was paying the bills, he'd have been home for hours and yet it was me who was expected to look after him and the house as well," says Patricia. "It wasn't fair."

It's a lot harder for couples who started out on an even job status than those who met when she was more successful or financially well-off. After all, if he's the sort of guy who can't handle it, he probably wouldn't have asked you out again once it became apparent. If it is a case of your career taking off suddenly, approach him tactfully. Saying, "Honey, I know you're a bit put out that I earn ten times as much as you do," will have him immediately on the defensive. Don't play down your own achievements, but boost up his. Remind him constantly of all the reasons why you love him so much, how much you appreciate his support. Encourage him to chase his own career dreams but don't push. Forcing him to go for higher-paid positions will make him even more paranoid that he's not measuring up to your standards. Broach the subject tentatively when he's relaxed and in a good mood. Kick off the conversation by saying, "I know you realize how important my career is to me and you're incredibly supportive, but are you happy with the amount of time we spend together?"

You've come a long way, baby—if you're a woman, that is. A recent survey comparing gender stereotypes common in the 1970s to those held in the 1990s show our image of women has improved while his has soured. Twenty years ago, women were viewed as indecisive, passive, unworldly, and feelings-focused. Now, we're seen as intelligent, logical, independent, adventurous, and dependable. Men got positive adjectives first time round—objective, savvy, assertive—but not-so-nice ones have been added to the list: jealous, moody, narrow-minded, and deceptive.[8]

Keep it light and nonthreatening and he might well open up and talk about any fears created by your success.

HASSLES OVER HOUSEWORK

I can't say I've ever met anyone who said, "I broke up with my boyfriend because he wouldn't wash the dishes," but men not sharing domestic chores is a major cause of resentment in relationships. So while it seems like a trivial topic, it's not. You both make the mess, it's logical that both of you should clean it up, and being treated like a servant is not fun.

Before I go any further, though, I have to say all the responsibility doesn't rest squarely on the shoulders of that lazy bastard who never makes the bed. Women are half the problem. We mother men. We're always saying things like, "Don't forget to pick up your drycleaning," and, "Did you remember to pay the electric bill?" and, "How many times have I told you not to leave wet towels on the floor." If you treat someone like a child, you're giving them the message that they aren't capable of looking after themselves. If someone always cleaned up after me, I'd be inclined to sit back and let them do it, too! Men get lazy because they're used to us doing the running around. Conditioning's also part of it. Young girls are encouraged to "play house." In fact, three things predict whether you'll share the housework equally with your partner: your upbringing, income, and how well you want things done. If you come from a home where mom did everything for the family, you're likely to think housework is "a woman's job." The more you earn, the less likely it is to worry you (you can afford hired help!). Lastly, there are a lot of women out there who refuse to "let" their partner help because "they don't do it right" (i.e., the way a woman would). Lighten up, girls! You can always straighten the bedspread and fluff the cushions up after he's done the bulk of it![9]

It sounds crazy, but not splitting the chores fairly is incredibly bad for your sex life. (There, that got your attention!) For a start, the quickest way to kill passion is to mother your partner. He starts behaving like a son, you start thinking of him as one; you start behaving like a mother, he starts seeing you as his. And who wants to sleep with their mother or their son?

Sex and housework are the two things just about all couples argue about at some stage. Generally, men want more sex and women want a fairer division of the housework. Relationship guru John Gottman believes one feeds the other.[10] He's right if you think about it. Both sex and housework require energy, and most of us have only got so much left at the end of a hard day. In plenty of relationships, *he'll* come home from work, flop in front of the TV and relax with a beer while *she* organizes dinner. She'll cook, clean up, do the dishes, work out what's needed for the next night's meal then—Gee!—it's time for bed. Guess who'll feel more like sex?

The quickest way a man can boost the amount of sex he's having with his partner is to do his share of the housework. It's a fact: men who do more housework and involve themselves with the kids have better sex lives and happier relationships than those who don't.[11] If he does his part, she not only has more energy, she feels more valued and respected. The spin-off? She's in the right head space to feel sexy. Treat her like a servant and she'll feel resentful as hell and carry *that* feeling into bed with her. Ever noticed how the garbage feels heavier and the pile of dishes seems higher when you're thinking, *Bastard! He should be helping me with this!*? Ever jumped into bed after feeling like that and said, "Give it to me, big boy!"? I didn't think so.

I bet if you're a New Age sensitive guy reading this you're feeling rather smug. Don't. Gottman did a survey on 50 guys who considered themselves "liberated" and compared them to 50 guys who admitted they thought it was a woman's job to do the housework. Do you know how much more housework the liberated guys did compared to the chauvinists? Four minutes a day![12] Like, wow, what a tremendous help that'd be.

Housework isn't a woman's job, it's a couple's job. You aren't "helping" her by making the bed, you're sharing the necessary chores that make both your lives more comfortable. So it's a very good idea to sort out the housework thing the minute you move in together. Don't just assume you'll each pick up your fair share—it rarely happens. Instead, grab a pen and paper and write down all the things that need doing every week—not just the cleaning but stuff like grocery lists, washing, ironing, shopping, and who plans the weekend's social activities. Everything you do as a couple should be shared. Women tend to be the social organizers. We're the ones who remember someone's birthday, buy the present, wrap and write on the card, arrange a dinner, and bake the cake. We're also the ones to organize whom we're seeing on the weekend, when, where, and what time. We juggle friends so they're all happy. That takes time and effort as well, so it's imperative this is also taken into account.

Write it all down, then each go through and pick what you like doing best (or rather, what you dislike doing least). If you don't mind doing laundry and he doesn't mind ironing, split it that way. If you detest cleaning the car and the other doesn't like it much either but hates it *less* passionately, that chore goes to them. So mark what you both don't mind doing or hate doing so you can split things fairly.

Finished that? Now go through the list and make it as even as possible. Take into account the time it takes to complete the chore and likes and dislikes until you're both happy it's split evenly and fairly. It doesn't have to be 50–50. If one person works full-time and the other part-time, you might decide a 70–30 split is fair. Some couples swap chores from week to week to even it up that way. Others take one look at the list and decide they'd rather fork out for a cleaning person and get their ironing done than waste precious weekend time.

Also remember you can use trade-offs. You might put up with doing all the washing and ironing if he gives you a weekly massage. He might take on more cleaning if you do all the social stuff like keeping up with friends. The bottom line is as always: compromise and communication.

FED UP WITH EACH OTHER'S FRIENDS AND FAMILY

I asked a psychiatrist friend of mine what advice she'd give to a couple who love each other but can't tolerate each other's family. "Move to the other side of the world," she said wryly. "If you can't do that, at least keep a sense of humor."

Squabbles over parents and siblings are both common and damaging. It's very easy to get into situations where you and your own family side against your partner and vice versa. So it's important to work out any differences—or at least ways of handling them—early, so there is no ganging up. I touched briefly on the initial meeting in Chapter 3. This is a more detailed version (for the truly petrified) plus some tips on handling the relationship once it progresses.

Meeting their family

First up

- When you're introduced, smile, shake their hand, and say warmly, "I'm so glad to meet you. I've heard so many nice things about you." If the relationship with your partner and their family is so strained they'll know you're lying through your teeth, drop the "heard so much about you" bit. But still smile and say "Nice to meet you." A tactful, well-liked partner can work wonders to resolve family tensions.

- Try to treat them like you would anyone else you've just met. If they start firing questions at you, calmly answer them. Assume they're nervous rather than attacking you. Try not to get defensive.

- Lay on the compliments. What a great job they did raising someone as wonderful as your partner. How delicious the meal tastes. What a nice house they have. There's no need to be gushy but a few white lies designed to ease *their* discomfort go a long way.

- Ask questions. Who are the photographs of? How long have they lived in the house? If you're getting along well, ask them to tell you what sort of child your partner was. He or she will be as embarrassed as hell but you'll win the parents over immediately.

Later on

- If they start nagging your partner (they don't see enough of them), resist the urge to join in. It's not your business to interfere and you're in a no-win situation. Side with their parents and your partner will feel resentful; side with your partner and they'll feel put out.

- If any member of the family is openly hostile, take a deep breath and try to steer the conversation to safer topics. Ignore the chill and see if they warm up over time.

- If they compare you to an ex, making it clear that's where *their* loyalties are, swallow all pride and say, "I know how much you loved Linda/Lyle and it is a shame they broke up. But it's over and who knows? You might grow to like me as well." Only the truly cruel won't be disarmed by that sort of statement.

- Don't forget it's your partner you're in love with, not them. You don't have to adore them, though it's certainly easier if you do. If you've truly tried but can only manage a superficial politeness, fine. That's enough to get through the family get-togethers.

- Don't criticize their family, even if they do. The unwritten rule is this: it's okay for them to find fault but not okay for you to agree. Say, "Oh well, honey, that's brother/sister/mother/daughter-love for you," even if you are dying to say, "I agree— your mother should be shot at close range. Can I be the one to pull the trigger?"

- No matter how much you dislike them, you owe it to your partner to be polite. They owe you the same courtesy. If their family was particularly vicious and destructively protective of their offspring, you're well within your rights to simply refuse to see them again. If you behaved like an obnoxious brat, it's totally acceptable for them not to see you again.

- You both get on with each other's family to the point where you feel torn between the two? Aim for a compromise that satisfies you both and keeps the peace. If both sets of parents expect you for Sunday lunch, visit one set together one week, go separately to your own parents the other, and do the other set the following (not forgetting to save the occasional Sunday just for the two of you).

Introducing your partner to your family

- Fill your partner in on any family eccentricities. Your dad probably won't even take his eyes off the TV? Warn them so they don't feel slighted. Your mom's a little over-the-top? They're both liable to assume the wedding's planned for next year? Forewarned is forearmed.

- Fill your family in on your partner. If they're a little shy and cover up their shyness by talking a billion miles an hour. What they do for a living. Any significant vulnerable points: a parent who's recently died, a promotion that's just fallen though. That way, they'll know to steer clear of certain subjects. It's also a good idea to let them know how serious the relationship is, especially if your partner's more serious than you are. They'll already think meeting your family is the green light for commitment. Your parents smiling and saying things like, "Well, you're part of the family now," will have wedding bells ringing in their ears.

- Grin and bear it. If your mom accidentally calls them by an ex's name, give your partner's hand a squeeze and laugh. She's not trying to sabotage, she's just ditzy. If they drag out highly embarrassing photos, laugh along with them.

- If you're going to stay the night, make sure you've had the where-you're-both-going-to-sleep discussion beforehand.

- Don't quiz your partner afterward to find out what their impressions were. Give them all time to get used to each other.

It may come as a complete surprise but researchers have discovered men like to dominate conversations, hate being interrupted, and want to be seen as the "expert." Women, on the other hand, cooperate with each other to tell a story, finish each other's sentences, and make more encouraging noises than men.[13]

Juggling friends and lovers

You book the restaurant and warn the waiter your table's likely to be the rowdiest and the last to leave. After all, you love your friends, you like your partner—they're all bound to get along, right? At 9:00 P.M., you're in a cab, sitting in stony silence. "I don't know what you see in them," your partner says. *I think they're wondering the same about you*, you think. *What the hell do I do now?*

Why those first few meetings are tricky

Being able to get along with each other's friends doesn't just make life easier, it's a good indicator you've chosen well. We surround ourselves with people we like and admire. If your partner doesn't like your friends, there are probably things they don't like about you. Having said that, don't be too hasty to jump to conclusions. There are lots of other reasons why those first few meetings might not go as well as you'd hoped. Here are some of them.

Your partner feels like he's under the microscope. Some friends deliver a very obvious message to new partners: you're on trial until *we* decide whether you're good enough. If they're sitting on the edge of their seat waiting for your friends' seal of approval, it's no wonder they're a little nervous. If you think your friends will be ridiculously overprotective, take the pressure off by ensuring you all *do* something together first time around. Invite a friend over to watch a video with you and your partner, play a game, get both to help you prepare dinner. Get them focused on a task rather than on each other so they're working as a team rather than fighting for your attention. Don't make your partner the centerpiece—especially if they're shy and reserved. A big group of friends is sometimes better than the two of you and one best friend. Warn them if they're likely to be overprotective. Tell your friends to back off if they give your partner a hard time. Say you realize they're trying to protect you, but you are quite capable of doing it yourself.

Your partner feels she don't measure up. Are you "dating down"? Is your partner less intelligent/trendy/financially secure than your usual dates? If you and your friends all have master's degrees and your partner didn't finish high school, she'll obviously feel out of her depth. *You* might not rib her about her lack of education or bad grammar but friends often aren't as tactful. If they treat him or her like the village idiot and are patronizing, your partner's understandably going to feel rather insecure.

Your friends will contrast and compare. Your partner knows your friends have seen all your other dates and is being measured against them. Help ease the situation by making it very clear they don't have to impress your friends, just you: it's what you think about them that matters.

If it is a case of "pick the person who doesn't belong," pay attention. If your friends are very different from the sort of person your partner is, it's not a great sign, because it means you probably are, too. An introvert matched with a party animal; dating someone who's so shy you need a can opener just to talk to them—it's worth reassessing whether it's worth it. Statistically, people who are alike have a better chance of making it than people from completely different worlds.

Your partner sees something you don't. Friends that only see you when they want something. Friends that put you down. Partners are more objective and they'll sometimes see what should be glaringly obvious: this person isn't a friend, they're an enemy in disguise. Partners give us another angle and perspective. If they love you and feel you're being taken advantage of, they've got good reason not to be rapturous over the friend you treasure so much. The trick is to weigh the comments and make sure your partner's not motivated by jealousy but your well-being. Then make up your own mind whether you want to keep the friend in your life. Some friends are worth making allowances for. One of my friends is notoriously unreliable and breaks two dates out of three. But she's there in a flash when I need her, and to me, that's more important. Boyfriends have never understood why I put up with her, but who cares? The bottom line is she's my friend, not theirs.

It's none of the above and they still don't get along with anyone? If your partner despises every single person you've introduced them to, sirens should be wailing and red lights flashing WARNING! WARNING! They're on an ownership trip: the "I love you so you shouldn't need anyone else" one. If their comments about your friends are getting nastier and nastier, get out. It's one thing to say they don't like Sarah but quite another to call her a fat slut. Ragging on your friends mercilessly is your exit cue.

How to make it easier on everyone

Be loyal. If a partner forces you to *choose* between them and your friends, choose your friends every time. If they simply grumble each time you want them to go out with them, ask why. Is it the whole group they don't like, one particular person—or the fact that you ignore them? Usually, there's at least one or two people they'll take to (or at least tolerate), so see those friends together and the rest solo.

> I remember going out with the boys one night and all I could think about was how much I wished I'd stayed home with her. I bought some flowers at a convenience store, let myself in, and spelled out "I love you" with the petals on the living room carpet. In the morning, they were all withered and rather pathetic but she thought it was just wonderful.
> Phil, 25, law student

Set limits. Can't tear him away from the boys? It's healthy to have time apart for girls' or boys' nights, but if they want to do it *every* Friday and Saturday night, it's immature and unacceptable. You think you've got a relationship, but you haven't. How much leeway you give each other depends on the relationship and where it's going. But do let him out once in a while. "Relationships are hell," says Pete, a friend of mine. "You have to be polite, politically correct, and charming. On boys' nights out you can relax, swill beer and bourbon, joke around, and punch each other in the shoulders. All the stuff she thinks is childish."

Spell out expectations. Talk through how much time spent seeing friends solo is acceptable, and what's not. Also, what activities are off limits. She might think a night playing pool down at the pub is fine, a night cruising the strip joints isn't. He might give the thumbs-up to dinner out but not be quite as understanding about you and the girls hitting the nightclubs till 5:00 A.M.

If there are fights over time, think about whether they've got a point before getting defensive. Are you spending too much time with friends and not enough with your partner? Are their demands reasonable or childish? A mature partner will say, "Can you change your night out with your friends tonight? I'm working all weekend and won't get to see you otherwise." That's a different story than, "What are you seeing them for? You should be spending time with me!" Some partners expect their partners to sit at home and be constantly available.

Sometimes, it's a good idea to give each other designated nights. Say, "I'm happy to see you Wednesday nights and over the weekend, but I need to see my friends during the week." For a relationship to work, you need to make time to be together, alone, with your partner and their friends, and with you and yours.

Accept there will be personality clashes. People clash for all sorts of reasons but there's often nothing sinister about it. They subconsciously remind us of that abusive teacher, nasty cousin, or dreaded ex. We also slot people into existing stereotypes, sometimes on sight, for silly reasons like what they're wearing. If it's instant dislike, your friend/partner/both may well get over it once the real person starts to take over their preconceived perception. If they've met five or so times and still can't get along, accept it's not going to work. Mix the two together as little as possible and see the hated friend on your own.

Don't stress too much. Is it really that important they get along? Not every relationship is meant to run for a lifetime. We're drawn to people throughout life, go down a little road with someone for a few months, realize we're at cross purposes, then split. If they're only going to be around for a little while, does it really matter if he hates Mandy or she hates Joe?

Demand respect from both sides. You can't force people to like each other but you can demand respect. Both should be polite to each other.

Allow for first-time nerves. A little bit of nervousness around friends is a compliment: it means it's important to your partner you all get on. Avoiding even meeting them isn't. It could be a sign of commitment phobia: meeting your friends means the relationship's moving forward.

Make your own judgments. Don't be swayed by a friend's judgment of your partner but do think about what they've said. It's normal for friends to offer an opinion and for you to ask for one. Listen to what they have to say—they might well see things you don't—but don't buy into the "so when are you going to leave them?" game.

Remember you have the benefit of time. Partners often don't see friends the way you do. You think they're supersuccessful, he thinks they're career-obsessed and stuck up. You think they're a laugh a minute, she thinks they're vulgar. Give both time to see the person behind the façade.

Don't drop your friends every time you meet someone new. Juggling best friends and a new lover takes the tact, military precision, psychological analysis, and maneuvering skills of a foreign diplomat. If they're squabbling over your time and affection like two hungry seagulls fighting over a crust of bread, it's tempting to tell both to fly away. Instead, make the effort to keep both happy. Your friends will understand you both want to hide away from the world in the beginning, but will be peeved if it lasts more than a month. Catch up, even if it's just for coffee, and don't spend the entire time raving about your new love affair. Show you're as interested in them as you were before you became a couple.

See best friends and partners together sometimes. If Tuesday nights were TV night with a girlfriend, invite him along. If Fridays were drinks with the boys, get her to bring along a few girlfriends.

But remember to give friends time separately.
There's nothing worse than always having to see your friends with their other half, so be a little sensitive. If a friend calls and wants to talk, go solo. Most of the couples I know see friends alone at least two nights a week: your friends are happy, you get breathing space from each other.

I'M BORED ALREADY

Arguments aren't your problem because you're so bored you can't be *bothered* fighting? Maybe you're wondering if this is the relationship for you after all but think it'd be a shame to give up now. How do you tell if your relationship's over or just going through a rough patch? First of all, be thankful you have a choice at all.

For most of human history, the question of whether to leave a long-term relationship was almost irrelevant. Marriage was seen as an unbreakable contract, and it was often impossible economically for women to survive solo. Divorce was unsavory, so most people made their bed and lay in it, even if on the very edge.

Today, it's not only acceptable to leave spouses or live-in lovers, you're viewed as a bit of a loser if you stay in a relationship that's not going amazingly well. Which is just as unrealistic as the old formula. No one's happy all the time. *All* relationships go through bad patches and down stages. So it doesn't necessarily mean it's over or will never get better if you're more interested in polishing the chandelier than swinging from it.

If you've entered the so-so zone—your relationship's not bad enough to leave but "if this is the future they can stick it"—it might well be an indication you really aren't as compatible as you thought. But it could be you've both simply settled into Dullsville: you do nothing but routine things together, you do fun things apart and you rarely make love. If this sounds all too familiar, give each other a swift kick in the butt and *instantly plan six fun things you can do together this week. Continue doing this for a month.* If you're still not enjoying each other's company four weeks later while lounging around that fabulous five-star resort, yes, you're in trouble. It sounds like an overly simple solution to the problem, but according to most of the couples' counselors I know, if the relationship can be saved, that saves it in 70 percent of cases. Make the relationship the #1 priority in your lives for a little while (if not permanently), instead of placing it behind family, friends, and career.

Think about reasons *other* than the relationship that could be responsible for your feeling this way. Are you both under extreme pressure from work? What's your past relationship history? The reason why many of us hover in relationship limbo-land is that we doubt our judgment. Perhaps previously, you've left when others would have stayed, or stayed when others would have left. If this applies to you, my advice would be to do the opposite of what you usually do. If you're the sort of person to up and leave at the first hint of trouble, stay—at least for a while longer. You might be pleasantly surprised to discover relationships *can* recover from hiccups and grow stronger. If you have a tendency to drag relationships out until they're hanging by a thread, it's probably wise to get out. Here are some other things to think about.

The leave or stay checklist

1. **Don't base your decision exclusively on retracing the history of your relationship.** Your memories are biased by what you're feeling at the moment. If you're feeling pessimistic about your partner, says psychologist William Doherty, you'll put a negative slant on things. This memory bias means you'll color the relationship history when repeating it to friends and family, which of course means the advice *they'll* dole out is inaccurate. They might tell you to pull the plug on what's essentially a good relationship or, if you've painted a rosy picture, stay in a bad one. Take this into account.

2. **How willing are you and your partner to work at making the relationship better?** It's all part of our throwaway lifestyle: if something's broken, don't fix it, buy a new one instead. How much energy and effort have you both already put into trying to make the relationship good? If the answer's hardly any or none at all, stay where you are. You haven't even tried yet!

If you've spent months trying to fix things but your partner's made no effort at all, even though they're aware you're not happy, it's a different story. Ask yourself, "If I stopped working at this, would it fall apart?" Try it for two weeks and find out. You *both* have to be prepared to work on the problem and come up with viable solutions.

3. **Are you staying because you can't bear to give up on all that hard work?** If you've been together for years, it can seem like such a waste to throw it all in and start again. If that's the *only* reason you're staying, get out. Cut your losses and leave now, so you're not wasting even more time.

4. **What if you leave and don't find someone else?** If you find yourself asking this question and it's the *only* thing that's stopping you packing your bags, again, you're definitely hanging around for the wrong reasons. It's not healthy to cling on to something that's over just because you can't bear the thought of watching TV alone. (Get a cat.)

5. **Have you outgrown the relationship?** Two years ago, you might have been compatible, but different life events sometimes force us in different directions. Ask yourself, "Are we such different people now we really don't have anything in common? Or could we bridge the gap by talking more and letting each other in on our lives?"

6. **Make two lists.** The first: what do you have to gain by staying? Emotionally, your lover might make you feel secure and loved, be a great shoulder to cry on, dispense terrific advice, give great orgasms. Practically, they might pay half the mortgage or rent, give you a better lifestyle than you'd have alone. Write down all the good things your lover brings to your life. Ask, "Am I in it just for the—?" Sex? Something to do on the weekend? Be honest with your reasons for staying. The second list is: what do you have to gain by leaving? Repeat the exercise from the opposite perspective: write down all the advantages of leaving. More time to spend on you? The chance to meet someone you're truly compatible with? The freedom to travel? You never have to sleep with your partner ever again? List all the pluses for flying the coop.

7. **Do you need more information?** You may decide you would like to stay with your partner but want to travel solo for six months. It's worth asking rather than assuming they'd say no.
8. **Does your decision feel right?** If you've decided to leave, do you feel a bit excited about the future, like once the painful part of telling your partner it's over, you'll feel a massive relief? If you've decided to stay, do you feel a renewed commitment to your partner? Are you looking forward to the relationship becoming all you've wanted it to be?

It's time to go when:

- You only share one or two things in common: a hobby, sex, the dog.

- They're unwilling to change or compromise. They don't think you have any problems even though you've confessed you're not happy.

- Your partner treats you badly.

- Your partner takes you for granted or you're so bored you can barely work up the enthusiasm to kiss goodbye before leaving for work.

- You love them but don't like them much. It sounds bizarre, but love isn't a reason to stay. You can love your partner on one level but still not be suited long term. If you've been with the person a long time, of course you still care desperately about them and have lots of shared history and good times. But if your head tells you you're not only both moving in entirely different directions but very happy about where you're headed, it's time to kiss each other tenderly and change the relationship to friendship.

Torn between two lovers: how *not* to be a fool

We tend to think we're immune to falling in love with more than one person, but it's definitely possible to love two people at the same time. The human heart is a wonderfully generous organ (yes, it's not the only one) and if you're a warm, open person who adores meeting new people, you could fall in love with ten people at once if you let yourself! We've all got the potential. What stops us is commitment to the relationship we're already in and time and energy. It's hard enough making one relationship work let alone ten of them simultaneously!

Usually, someone is choosing between an established relationship and a new one. There you are, quite contentedly sailing along with a partner until *Wham!* out of the blue someone appears who makes your heart thump out of your chest and liquefies your loins. Then you're faced with a huge dilemma: which one should you choose? Try the following five-step plan:

Step 1: give yourself breathing space

Stop seeing the person you've met most recently and put everything you've got into trying to make it work with the person you've been with the longest. Why? Because the biggest mistake you could possibly make is to leave a good relationship—one that could have been saved with a bit of work—for someone who turns out not to be quite as fabulous as you thought. Break up with your old lover because there's no hope for the two of you, not because of someone else. I swear you'll regret it otherwise. Most relationships seem promising in the first month or two but few make it past that.

Step 2: decide what you really want from a relationship

Do the relationship and partner wish lists in Chapter 1. Also think about whether you really want a long-term serious relationship. Perhaps this new person is simply a symptom: you'd prefer to be single and date casually than be settled down right now. Take a good, long look at these lists before moving on to step 3.

Step 3: look objectively at the relationship you've been in the longest

On one side of the page, write down all the things you like about the relationship. On the other, write down all the things you don't like. Beside each *don't like* point, check those things you think you could change if you both worked hard on the relationship. Put an "X" beside those you don't think will alter, no matter what both of you do. For instance, "Doesn't get along with my friends" is something you could sort out (even if it means seeing your friends without your partner), so that gets a check. Go back up to the start of the "don't like" side and start again, this time rating each on a scale of one to ten on how important it is to you. (One is not important, ten is extremely important.) "Find my partner unattractive" might rate a ten, "Not getting along with friends" a four.

When finished, this list represents the state of your relationship and what hope there is of saving it. If the "don't like" side also has mostly X's and tens, it means there's a lot you're unhappy with, it's all important to you and largely unfixable. If that's the case, it probably is time to move on.

If it's the opposite: the "do like" side has lots of points and the "don't like" side lots of checks and low numbers, stay where you are, at least temporarily. There's plenty left to work with, your gripes aren't that important to you, and your attraction to the new person is probably because you're in a rut with your old lover.

Step 4: focus on the new person

List the things you like about your new lover, then areas you suspect might cause problems. If you're honest with yourself, your gut instinct should give you a few clues. Write down ten reasons why you think a relationship with this person would be better than the one you've already got. Are they logical, sensible, long-term reasons, or do they look flimsy to you, even in this deliriously optimistic stage?

Step 5: trust your gut reaction

In most cases, the lists will point you pretty obviously in one direction or another. What's equally as important is your reaction to the decision they're telling you to make. Say the odds are definitely in favor of staying with your old lover. Does the thought of it fill you with joy—or dread? It's not going to work if, in your heart, you don't want it to. You haven't put your finger on the reason yet, but it's there all right.

It's pretty obvious you should leave your lover and give it a go with the new person but that makes you terrified? You're probably scared to take a risk because you're frightened you'll end up alone. And don't forget there is a third option: don't choose either of them. Stay single for a while until you're really sure where your heart lies.

MONEY MATTERS

Money can't buy happiness. I absolutely agree. There's no way I'd marry some old fart with a red, bumpy nose and shiny head just because he happened to be loaded. On the other hand, I know I'd be much happier typing this in a penthouse apartment than the two bedroom space I'm living in. It's a dilemma but I look at it this way: I decided years ago that the only way I'd ever have money is to make it myself. Even if I did marry someone rich, it would still be *their* money, not mine. Having said that, I have to say it would be rather nice to hook up with a partner who's got at least as much as I have (which isn't difficult). I've worked hard for the little I've got and I don't really relish the idea of handing over half of it to someone who hasn't. That doesn't seem fair to me. Also, I reason, if we're around the same age and have accumulated similar assets, it shows we share the same attitudes toward money and are responsible about it.

I know plenty of women (and a few men) who think differently. I met one girl at a function who openly admitted she'd never date anyone who earned under six figures. (I couldn't quite see what she had to offer in return, but perhaps under that hard veneer there was a heart of gold. Actually, scratch that because she'd have cashed it in already.) But, let's face it, money's always been attractive. Rich men and women always top the "I wish he/she'd ask me out" list because it's a lot easier to be happy, loving, and affectionate to someone while sipping champagne on board a yacht than watching TV on a lumpy couch, eating baked beans out of a can.

Money affects relationships at all stages. If you're rolling in it, you've got the cash to dress well, look after your appearance, and treat people to nice things so you're instantly more desirable to date. Two or three dates into a relationship, even couples who haven't a clue what the other earns find out fast because your incomes determine what you do together. If you're both reasonably affluent, eating out at nice restaurants is de rigueur. If they go deathly pale as you order the lobster, it's a fair bet they're mentally counting the bills in their wallet to check they've got enough. Date for long enough and situations like these can breed resentment. "You're such a snob," the poorer partner says. "I had enough of cheap eats while in college," the other snaps back. "I deserve better now." The relationship's particularly vulnerable if she's the richer of the two. The old "he should earn more" attitude might be buried, but it's still there at the back of people's minds. He may feel "less of a man" because he can't afford to take her to places she'd prefer to go or spoil her with expensive gifts. She'll be told constantly, "You could have done better for yourself." Income determines lifestyle. If you decide to move in together and one's looking at $2,000 per month apartments while the other's checking out $600 studios, it suddenly becomes horribly apparent you're used to different standards of living.

Even if your incomes don't differ, your spending styles might. Match a penny-pincher with Ms. Splash-it-around and there's bound to be trouble. She's insulted by his "cheap" gifts; he gives her a hard time for "wasting" money on designer clothes. Then there's the saving-up-for-a-down-payment part of the relationship—guaranteed to cause arguments. One of you is 100 percent committed, taking lunch in a bag to work. The other's still buying three new CDs a week.

Let me give it to you straight: just as matching libidos mean less problems in the bedroom, matching incomes and attitudes toward money mean less problems out of it. Unfortunately, Cupid has a nasty habit of shooting arrows into financially noncompatible hearts. Fortunately, there are ways (as always) to solve the problem. The first step is to identify your spending styles and the cause of the fights.

Spending styles of the rich and not-so-rich

The money miser

They'll drive two hours out of their way to get 20 cents off a box of cookies. They don't just watch their finances, they're obsessed with them, tallying up every cent which they hand over (begrudgingly). Usually from homes where money was tight or mom and dad were also penny-pinchers, often they'll have the last laugh: while you're still living in a rented, run-down apartment, they've bought their second investment property. You, however, had a lot more fun along the way. It costs money to travel, look good, socialize with friends, and have a good time.

The over-generous spender

You bought them a card and a piddling bunch of flowers for their birthday; they buy you a TV. You drop in for coffee at their house clutching stale cinnamon buns from the local bakery; they drop in for a drink clutching Veuve Cliquot and caviar. Amazingly, they often earn the same as you do. How do they do it? Let's put it this way: entire forests are felled just to print their credit card bills. Usually, their parents splashed money around. Sometimes, it's the opposite: their parents were scrooges and they're totally sick of not having nice things. Over-generous spenders also tend to equate money with love. The bigger and more expensive the present, the more liked they'll be by the recipient.

The skin-of-their-teeth spender

They're always just a few dollars short of meeting their budget so borrow from friends/family/the bank to make ends meet. They use one credit card to pay off another, have six different personal loans going and, understandably, feel anxious whenever money is mentioned. Living anywhere from slightly to way above what their income allows, they're not prepared to make the lifestyle sacrifices to live within their means because somehow, they always scrape through.

The money lover

While other kids were throwing a football around, they were on the sidelines selling soft drinks and sweets and making a tidy profit. Fascinated by money, their hobby is watching it grow. They make smart decisions because they research their investments but are prepared to take risks, so get higher returns. Entrepreneurial, they're to be admired if they're not obsessive about it. If they are, the terms "heartless bastard" and "shallow" are probably more accurate.

Why couples clash over cash

If you're arguing over money, it's usually because of one of the following:

There's a power imbalance

In plenty of relationships, the person with the money has the power in the relationship. They're seen as the better "catch." If they're constantly paying for you, you're constantly thanking them, and you're expected to feel eternally grateful and dependent on them for the lifestyle you're leading. In short, you feel like the poor cousin dressed in their hand-me-downs.

You have mismatched incomes

If one earns way more than the other, it's usual for your lifestyles to also be worlds apart. The simplest decision—like whether to go to the movies at night (full-price) or wait for the (half-price) matinee, causes conflict. Also, the more money you earn, the more likely it is you've developed more expensive taste. The lower earner is used to "making do" and can't quite understand why it's imperative you serve Belgium caviar. Who likes smelly old fish eggs anyway?

You spend at different rates

Even if she does earn a quarter of what you do, she'll spend more in one day than you would in a week. Some combinations of spending styles are disastrous: Over-generous will bankrupt Skin-of-the-teeth in a week as they struggle to keep up. Money also has different value depending on your salary. If you're earning $25,000 a year, "expensive" to you might be Indian takeout. If you live on $150,000 a year, "expensive" might be splurging on the $150 bottle of wine, rather than the $50 vintage.

Gender-perception problems

He earns less and she still thinks the man should pay (as mentioned previously). The obvious answer to solving this one is to have a long, hard think about how important it is to you. If he's got enough other positive qualities to overlook it, do so—and be gracious about it. Don't rub it in or make snide remarks. If you decide you can't accept the situation, do him a favor and stop the relationship so you can search for Mr. Money-bags.

Managing money as a couple

In the old days, the minute you got married all accounts became joint accounts. These days, most couples keep their own personal accounts and open up joint accounts for shared expenses and/or future goals. It's a nice blend between retaining individuality and working together, and it also allows for different spending styles. (If you both agree on an amount to deposit in the joint account, it shouldn't really bother you what they do with the rest of it.) It makes sense to me, so this is the model I've based the following exercise on. If you decide to do it, set aside a few hours for part one: you'll learn a lot about each other, so settle in and enjoy it. Part two is the boring mathematics part. Don't attempt it without a calculator and prepare to be depressed afterward (You earned *that* much and now have *that* much left? What happened to it all?).

Setting some ground rules

Work out your spending style. Decide which category best describes each of you, referring to the section above. Talk about what influences have made you both this way. If you know your partner's overly careful with money because times were tough during their childhood and they seriously did survive on bread and gruel, you'll be far less inclined to get angry.

Define the problem. See the section "Why couples clash over cash" and work out which problem best describes your

The joint account idea was a nightmare. He spent hundreds on frivolous things like drinking with the boys and CDs. I did the opposite and was scared to spend too much grocery money. The fights almost broke us up. Now we have a shared "bills" account and that's it. Maria, television producer, 28 situation. Write down your own version of it. Her side might be: "I get upset when John wastes money drinking down at the pub with the boys because that could be used to put toward a house down payment." His side might be: "I resent it when Sarah nags me when I've been out. I know we're saving, but aren't I allowed to relax once in a while?"

Look for underlying reasons. Is the argument *really* about money? In the above scenario, it could be that Sarah interprets John's "wasting money" as a sign he's not as excited about buying a home together as she is. That makes her nervous about his commitment to the relationship itself ("Doesn't he want a home so we can start a family?"). Couple that with his wanting to drink with the boys instead of being with her and she starts to think, *He'd prefer to be single.* John and Sarah aren't arguing over him wasting money—they're arguing over a commitment issue.

Make a pact to solve fights over money once and for all. Once you know each other's spending style, you know the reasons behind it and you've isolated problems that really are about money, the next step is this: to work *together* to come up with a financial compromise that both of you can live with. If you are prepared to do this, write down how you think you can improve your spending style and how you think your partner can improve theirs. Then swap lists and talk it through. Keep talking until you're both happy with the solutions and, whenever possible, try to meet in the middle. For example: he wants to buy a $60,000 BMW; you think a car's to get from A to B and want him to buy a rattlingly runaround worth $5,000, putting the rest toward an expensive vacation. The compromise might be to settle for an average-priced new car worth $20,000 and a less-expensive vacation destination.

Remember to take into account people's passions. If fresh flowers once a week make all the difference to her, let her trade something else. She might cheerfully agree to cut back on clothes spending to keep her "indulgence."

Decide who's best at managing money. That person gets the job of being in control of the budget. This doesn't mean the other person hands over their paycheck and closes their eyes, simply that one's usually better at remembering when things are due. If you want to share responsibility evenly, set aside one hour at the same time each week or month to sit down together to pay bills and revise where you're at.

Decide when you need to check with each other. While no one wants to answer to their partner for every dollar they part with, you might like to "check" on major personal purchases. Decide what's none of each other's business (presents for best friends) and what is (a $10,000 stereo system for the car).

Practical stuff

Do a budget. Once you've done all this, you can get down to the nitty-gritty, that is, work out where your money is going and how much is left over. I'd strongly suggest you ask your bank for a budget planner to get the most accurate picture. It's basically a chart that you fill in. On one side, you list your monthly income, on the other what you spend it on. Most planners also include information on how to calculate expenses (wild guesses tend to be pathetically wrong). The budget planners are also great because they remind you to include things like vacations, presents, gym fees, and medical expenses. (Not accounting for the "little things" is why most people blow their budget.) If in doubt of what something costs, overestimate. Some expenses can't be altered (like electricity), others can (cell phone bills, daily facials). Decide what both of you are prepared to cut back on.

Set some goals. Do you simply want to free up some cash so you don't both have coronaries when the gas bill arrives or are you saving for a major purchase? If you're saving for something together, it makes sense to plunk that cash into one account specifically for that purpose. The balance will rise twice as fast and it's a nice bonding exercise.

Make a savings plan. Once you have a good idea of what each of you needs to contribute to cover shared monthly expenses, you'll know how much cash is left over for saving. (If there isn't any, you might like to make an appointment with a financial planner to help you consolidate any debts and manage things more efficiently.)

Decide what accounts you need. Most couples open several joint accounts. The first is to cover shared monthly expenses (electricity, phone, car insurance), the second is usually a savings account for future goals. If you've got a shared mortgage, that counts as the third. Decide what accounts you need to open and what facilities you require (do you really want ATM access on the savings account?)—but don't get too carried away. Keep an eye on bank charges.

Decide who contributes what. If you both have roughly the same income, it makes sense to split things down the middle. If one's making $35,000 and the other $135,000, it doesn't. Make it proportional to be fair.

Check it's livable. Go through your budgets and make sure they're realistic. Are the amounts you've agreed to contribute fair and attainable? Are you both comfortable with what you're committing to joint accounts?

Consider income protection. Could you afford to support each other if either became ill or lost their job? Would you want to? Income protection will cover your salary for a specified period against unemployment or illness. (Read the fine print very carefully—policies vary hugely.)

Put the plan into action. Open the joint accounts, arrange for the specified amounts to be deducted straight from your existing bank accounts so you don't forget—then sit back and congratulate each other on taking the first step to financial freedom!

MOVING IN AND MARRIAGE

Plenty of people consider marriage an outdated, religious institution that's quaint and cute but pretty irrelevant these days. I mean, all that standing up there before God stuff—isn't it a bit old-fashioned for us? Others would crawl on hands and knees for a week in return for the chance to play princess for a day and flounce around in a big white dress. Which is best for you? Only you know that—but read these statistics anyway.

The number of couples who opt for playing house minus the gold ring has increased sevenfold since 1970.[14] Living together is more popular than marriage—but de facto couples split up quicker, usually in the first year. If you're married you tend to split (if you are going to) within five years.[15] The perception that it's far more sensible to live together before marriage and that you've got a better chance of it lasting if you do isn't backed up by statistics (even if most of us, including me, still believe it). The most recent studies show that if you live together before marriage, you're 50 percent more likely to divorce than those who don't live together first. But don't rush up the aisle just yet, because it's actually not the living together part that's the problem. It's more that the *type* of people who choose to live together first tend to be less traditional and less likely to believe in marriage as a concept. If you don't have any religious or moral objection to "living in sin," you're not usually as committed to the institution of marriage and are much more likely to leave if you're not happy. Couples who head straight

> **Thinking of getting married after years of living together? If you're doing it because all your friends are, your friends and family want you to, you think it'll fix your relationship problems, or simply because you want to have kids, you're on the way to joining the 50 percent of couples who split within five years once they become Mr. and Mrs.[16]**

for the altar often stay together just for the sake of "the marriage" and because they made a vow before God. But although they have fewer divorces, whether they're *happily* married is another story.[17]

People are pretty cynical about marriage and it *is* a little offputting when you know half of all marriages end in divorce.[18] Just about ready to slit your wrists with that engagement ring? Why not look at it this way: One out of two marriages *does* succeed and who's to say you and your partner won't be one of them?

Convinced you'd make it but your partner's not so sure? More on that and marriage later. First, let's talk about moving in together because the same advice applies even if you do head down the aisle beforehand.

"Let's live together"

You're sick of trying to find something, then realizing it's at *their* place. You're tired of carrying a change of underwear around in a plastic bag. Suddenly it seems like a complete waste of money to be paying two rents when you're spending every night at each other's place anyway. You love each other, the idea forms, and then it's said out loud: "Perhaps," one of you says tentatively, "we should think about finding a place together."

Break out the champagne—you've officially moved the relationship forward about six million paces. But don't be too hasty: there's much more to moving in than finding a place to move in to. Like, are you really sure you're ready to give up the courting period just yet? "One minute, we were dating—I'd doll myself up, he'd arrive on the doorstep with flowers—the next, we were flopped on the couch eating takeout with greasy hair," says Anna. "We fast forwarded through those fizzy, sparky times into domesticity. I felt ripped off. I know it would have happened eventually, but it happened too fast."

He sees you plastered in night cream instead of make-up; you see him out of his suit and trimming his toenails. Hardly the stuff of lust but all part of being human beings who can't look or act perfect all of the time. (One word of warning: don't get *too* comfortable together. It's okay to pull on the sweatpants some of the time but break out the glad rags occasionally.)

Apart from noticing what slobs you both are, you'll also notice a loss of privacy. It's one thing to be going out and spending just about all your time at each other's place. It's quite another officially moving in. Before, if you felt irritable or tired and fancied a night by yourself, you simply stayed home. Give up your own place and there *is* no time out from the relationship.

The first week or two of living together is heaven. You throw a house-warming party, feel all grown up, cook lavish meals for each other, snuggle at night. Then you move into the "who left the cap off the toothpaste" period and it's *hell*. There's a massive adjustment period for both of you. You might think you're "one" but in reality, you're two individuals with different ideas on how to run a house and your lives. You'll fight about the housework, sex, general cleanliness, moan about money and who takes the garbage out. Each of you will be struggling for power, trying to be the one who's boss. Which is one reason why I wouldn't suggest either of you move into the other's house unless it's so wonderful you'd need your heads examined if you gave it up. Finding a new place together, with both names on the lease, puts things on an even power keel. "It seemed obvious to move in with Maryanne because her place was bigger," says Matt, 24. "But I never ever felt like it was my home because it had always been hers. I think she also found it difficult because she was so used to living in the place alone."

Prepare, also, for a change in your sex life as first-time roommates. Your sex life could improve dramatically once you move in—or fall in a big heap! "After years of sneaking around corners—hiding from his roommate or my parents—to finally be able to have sex somewhere other than bed was a fantasy come true," says Leonie. "Our sex life definitely improved when we moved in simply because we were free to make love when and where we wanted to." Other couples feel somewhat different. "Jess and I definitely had more sex before we moved in because we'd grab the chance whenever we could. Now we know we can have it every night—and that's sometimes a huge turn-off," says Jake.

This whole chapter talks about practical ways to sort out moving-in matters like housework and money, but I suspect you'll need to read the entire book to get through all the tough parts. *Expect* to argue, *expect* to feel resentful, sulky, and irritable for the first little while and you won't be disillusioned. Give it a good four months before throwing in the towel (in the laundry basket, please!): it really does take that long to settle in.

So here are some things you might like to think about *before* rushing straight to the real estate agent, pens poised to sign a shared lease. If you can't agree on issues like this before you move in, you haven't got a hope afterward.

- **Spell out very clearly what moving in means to each of you.**
  Is it for convenience and a temporary thing? Is it because you want to spend the rest of your lives together? Is it a trial run to marriage? If it is, how long do you want to live together before tying the knot? Personally, I wouldn't advise moving in with someone unless the intention is to move the relationship a stage further on. If it's money problems that are forcing you to move in, get a roommate—that's what you're truly after. It takes great tolerance to live with someone else and cope with all their personal habits. It's difficult enough when you're madly in love, let alone when you barely even like each other.

- **What furniture do each of you have?** Can you stand living with each other's stuff? If one person's got designer taste and the other mismatched hand-me-downs, will one of you feel resentful? If the bad-taste partner doesn't mind, squirrel away the not-so-nice stuff in storage for a year or so (and good luck deciding which of you has the bad taste). Don't sell it until then: you never know, it may not work out and that bright purple coffee table might come in handy.

- **Decide on what you need to buy and who's going to foot the bill.** It's romantic to go halves on things like fridges and sofas, but a complete pain to split it all up if it doesn't work out. Instead, write down the items you need to buy and split the list. You buy the fridge, he buys the TV. You buy the dishes, he buys the saucepans. If it doesn't work out, you take whatever you bought and there's no messy arguments over who owns what. If you're really sensible, you'll make a list of all your possessions, including books and CDs, before you move in. It's easy to forget who originally owned what.

- **Can you afford to live together?** Sit down together and talk about your existing financial commitments. Can you both *afford* to split expenses evenly? Work out a household budget (see page 217). It doesn't matter whether you plan to keep separate accounts or not—household and entertainment expenses still have to be shared.

- **How will you split the household chores?** See the section above on "Hassles over housework," page 194.

- **How will you handle friends and visitors?** Are you the sort of person who craves time alone while they're the social type? Do you have friends who are prone to drop in for coffee, stay for hours, and maybe even crash the night? How does the other partner feel about it? Set some rules for friends and visitors and stick to them.

The "m" word

If I could give you one piece of advice about marriage it would be this: make sure you both go into it knowing what the other wants out of it. Have a good, long talk about your expectations of marriage. How being married will be different from the relationship you have now. In other words: what does marriage mean to each of you? *Don't* just assume you know because you've been living together for ten years.

Something happens to people when they get married. Everyone has preconceived ideas of how a "husband" and "wife" should behave. What was acceptable for you to do as a girlfriend—wear miniskirts, be independent, have a great career—might not be acceptable once you're his wife. And vice versa. She'll put up with boozy nights with the boys from a boyfriend, but a husband? That's different.

It's also extremely sensible to talk through your attitudes about parenthood and if you both want to be parents. If one's against the idea, it could be the result of a less than idyllic childhood: a few counseling sessions could banish any baby blues. If they don't want children because they're committed to a career, it might just be the timing that's off. But if after long and rational discussions, you're still vehemently arguing for opposite outcomes, reconsider your long-term compatibility. To have or not to have children is an emotive issue that can unglue the closest couple.

Another hot tip from someone who's been there, done that: don't kid yourself it's the same as living together and if it doesn't work out it'll be just as easy to walk out. It isn't. It's

The term "settle down and get married" is truer than you think. Men's levels of testosterone (the hormone that contributes to aggressive, dominating behavior) test high when they're single, drop when married, and rise again on divorce. Other research shows alcohol and drug use decline in both sexes after marriage, probably because it encourages a sense of responsibility. Live-in lovers don't alter their lifestyle habits and neither marriage or moving in stops smokers from lighting up.[19]

hard splitting up when you've been living together—it's devastating when a marriage fails. You don't just have to separate your lives and your hearts, you have to separate legally: handle the pain of filling in those divorce papers (which include delightful questions like "Who ended the marriage?"—not a great feeling when your spouse has already ticked "She did"); you might need to change your name back, make property settlements, sort out the mortgage. You can't just divide up your possessions and get on with your lives—it's a long, drawn out, intensely emotional process to untangle once you've said "I do."

Sorry to sound negative but I'm trying to save both of you from being hurt. For this reason, don't get married because your parents want you to. Don't get married because all your friends are. Don't get married because you've been together for ages and it seems like the logical next step. Don't get married because your partner's pressuring you or even if you want kids together. Get married for these reasons instead: you are both convinced you love each other, for all the right reasons; you're both convinced you want the same things from marriage and can live up to each other's expectations; and the relationship's lasted long enough for you to be sure of all this. In short, you can't imagine being happy without them by your side. Phew! Now I can say congratulations!

WILL THEY EVER ASK?

There's one other thing you need to get married: a proposal. These range from the partner on one knee, serenading violins, and diamond ring popped in a glass of champagne variety to the "I suppose we should get married" muttered while you're climbing into your jammies about to go to sleep sort. If neither is happening to you and you'd like it to, how do you bring up the subject of marriage without feeling like a desperate twit? I'm going to address this section to women, since it's still usually men who do the asking-to-marry bit, despite so-called equality. But I want to make something clear first: there's a perception out there that women get more out of marriage than men do. I'd have to agree women probably get more excited about the wedding *day*, but once all the hoo-ha dies down, men actually get a lot more from marriage than women do. Most surveys show the two happiest groups of people are single women and married men.[20] Men appear to get much more from marriage than women do. Married men drink less, take fewer risks, live longer, and thrive in the network of emotional support marriage provides. Married men also earn more than their single counterparts: seems having "a missus" at home gives them an incentive to work harder.[21] Evidence also suggests men take much longer to get over a divorce than women do. Ironic, isn't it? Here you are reading this, hoping it'll result in him on bended knee, when he's the one who's most likely to benefit from it.[22]

Anyway, here's my advice on working out where your partner's head is regarding marriage, without losing dignity.

- **First, look at your own motives for the conversation.** Are you bringing this up because you want some idea for the future or because you want a commitment NOW. If you'd simply like some feedback because you're curious and deciding whether to hang around long term, just say, "I was reading a story/watching a TV show and it started me thinking about relationships today. What do you think about marriage? Can you see yourself doing it someday?" Get some feedback, then switch topics ASAP. If you want to continue the discussion make it very clear you're talking about marriage in theory, not the two of you skipping off into the sunset.

  You're hoping the discussion will end with a proposal? Check you're up for it before going any further. Are you really ready for this? Have you been together at least two years? Are you wanting it for the right reasons? Do you honestly think your life will be enriched 20 years from now by being with this person? Do you honestly believe they feel the same way about you? Once you're satisfied *you're* sure, work out your own theories on why they haven't asked you already, before putting your partner on the spot. That way you're prepared and able to talk logically rather than emotionally about the issue. Could it be that they haven't asked you to marry them because they're not ready or not sure?

- **Introduce the topic.** Personally, I'd be up-front about this one. You're better off being honest than sending out subtle signals. For a start, most men don't pick up on subtleties, so all that gazing in shop windows while holding his hand is useless. He's checking out the sports watches, not the solitaire diamonds. If you know each other well and talk openly and honestly (and if you don't, you're not ready to make plans for next Christmas, let alone the rest of your life) wait until you're having a particularly good time together and introduce the topic generally. Start with the same point I mentioned previously—but this time, follow it up with, "Have you ever thought about *us* getting married?"

  His response will be one of three. The first: absolute horror. If he shoots you a "you've got to be kidding" look, forget it— and him if you want commitment. This guy's either deleted the "m" word from his vocabulary or you're definitely not his idea of Mrs. Right. The second reaction is one of confusion. He hasn't really thought about it but that doesn't mean he won't in the future. All you need to say then is, "I'd like you to think about it because I'd like to know where we're heading." Unless you're planning on doing the proposing yourself, drop the subject right there. Let him think about it for a few months and see if he wants to take it further.

If you've been together for ages, the third reaction is probably the one you'll get: he has considered it but he's not ready right now because of—whatever reason he has. Resist the urge to jump straight in with, "Oh, for God's sake, that's ridiculous! I don't care if you haven't finished your law degree/built up a bank account/still live with your mother. Let's do it anyway," because it really doesn't matter how trivial *you* think the reason is, it's important to *him*. You'll get a lot further with, "I understand where you're coming from but just for the record, it's not important to me." If you're prepared to wait for whatever it is he's waiting for, again, stop it there. If you're not, you'll need to add another sentence on to the previous statement: "And John, I'm really not happy to put our plans on hold for another five years, so could we talk about this further?" Have the discussion, then:

- **Ask for a time frame** of when he'll be ready to commit, then set your own—the maximum amount of time you'll wait for him. Tell your boyfriend you're giving him six months, a year, whatever, to make up his mind. Don't issue it as an ultimatum; simply say, "John, we've been going out three years now and I'm asking you for a serious commitment. I love you but marriage is important to me. I'm prepared to wait another [whatever] but then I'd like an answer." Drop the subject but stick to the deadline.
- **Mark the date in your diary** and let him know a week or two before D day. If he comes up with a good reason not to commit then, you might want to reconsider. Then it's up to you to decide whether he's worth the wait or not. If you decide he is, mark another date in your diary and make it your personal deadline. Tell him. If he won't commit then and you still need that commitment, it's time to move on. You've given it your best shot but it just isn't going to happen. Hang around after that, and you could be waiting forever.

AND ONE MAKES THREE: KIDS

In our grandparents' day, no one asked questions and just about everyone popped out at least one child by their second anniversary. One minute, the radiant virgin bride, the next, a housewife elbow-deep in dirty diapers and formula. The concept of "waiting" to have children was alien. After all, what were you waiting *for*? Most women didn't work; those that did couldn't wait to escape the mundane tedium of a boring job. Travel was a luxury, and simply postponing motherhood to enjoy your partner and marriage was unheard of. "If you could have babies, you did," says my mom, who was pregnant with twins by 21. "No one thought about putting it off for the sheer enjoyment of life. No one ever, ever talked about how difficult and disruptive children are—which is why we all got the shock of our lives when the babies actually arrived."

Many modern women approach motherhood warily. Not only do we have lots of life options, the mere mention of children is often greeted with a tirade aimed at convincing us *not* to succumb to the maternal urge. As a new mom, you'll not only have no sleep, no time, no money, and no sex, your career will be in ruins and your marriage a mess! The truth is, parenthood *is* a time of emotional turbulence when everything from sleeping and who shops for groceries becomes renegotiable and ripe for argument. Which is one reason why many couples postpone it until they feel they—and the relationship—are mature enough to withstand the pressure.

It's also true that having a child enriches your existence in ways you can't begin to imagine. I've never had a child but I do have a niece and nephew who make my heart pound madly whenever they say "Auntie Trace." Looking into their faces, I believe those stories about mothers suddenly possessing super-human strength and lifting cars off trapped children. Even the most harassed mother has told me one smile can make weeks of torment seem worth it. The joy of being a woman today is you get to weigh the good and the bad and choose what's right for you and when. Not only can you decide not to have children until much later in life—you can also decide not to have them at all. About the only thing that isn't flexible is this: once they arrive, there's no turning back. Children will alter your life utterly and irrevocably. So, if you're thinking of taking the plunge, read on. It ain't *just* about standing side by side with sloppy grins on your faces, watching the little one sleep.

The first shock: a brand-new partner

You'll notice changes in your relationship the moment you break the happy news. Anxious fathers-to-be are prone to lecture on how you should be treating your body: frowning if you so much as *look* at a glass of wine, overloading your plate with "food for two," tut-tutting if you dare to eat curry ("Don't you realize it upsets the baby?"). Your sex life alters. Many couples report no change for the first few months of pregnancy (here's some good news: plenty say orgasms are deeper and more intense).[23] But when the baby grows larger, intercourse becomes uncomfortable and he starts to worry he'll "hurt the baby." He looks at you differently as you change from lover to mother. Then, of course, there's the labor—an experience guaranteed to turn him off sex for at least a few months. For many men, watching their wives writhe in agony is harrowing and upsetting—even if the moment of birth *does* rate as the best in their life. "I must admit I felt really strange about Anna after the birth," confides Steve, proud dad of a six-month-old baby. "Before, well . . . I'd only go down there for pleasure. Then, I'm down there and there's a baby coming out of it. Her vagina changed from a place that gave me great pleasure to a place where babies came from."

You're also loath to leave your baby with just anyone, so may not get the time or opportunity to talk through all these things together and share common fears. Arranging to be alone a few months in— even if it's just for a drink and a quick dinner—can work wonders to revive your relationship and your sex life.

The next shock: where did my life go?

"Mick and I haven't had a decent conversation in months. Before Billy was born, we'd sit out on the balcony and have a glass of wine while we talked about our day. Now when he comes through the door, I push Billy at him and race around doing the million things I'd planned to do that day and couldn't," says Jenny, a 34-year-old management consultant who's been married seven years. "Everyone warned us our relationship wasn't going to be as flexible. But we had no idea just how much it would change."

Jenny put off having children until she was in her mid-thirties because she was worried about the inevitable loss of independence, autonomy, and freedom that having kids would cause. "I liked the world I was in: ordered, organized, child-free. We had such a nice lifestyle." Remember those fabulous, impromptu weekends away? Late-night movies, stimulating dinner parties, strolling down to the local cafe for a cappuccino midmorning on Sunday? Hell, remember being able to go to the bathroom on your own and relax for two minutes? Hold on to those memories because, if you have kids, that's all they'll be for a while. The longer you've become accustomed to a luxurious dual-income, no-kids lifestyle, the longer you're likely to put off having children. Which really isn't such a bad thing. A good marriage needs a strong foundation and a few years child-free, when the two of you can enjoy each other and live life to the fullest, certainly helps keep things on solid ground when you do decide to turn two into three. Besides, unless you've married in your forties, there's plenty of time to hear that pitter-patter later on.

Becoming parents

Having a child dredges up a lot of unconscious feelings about our own parents and hidden expectations about what being a parent means. "Suddenly John wasn't my husband but a *father* and little things that didn't bother me before took on immense importance. Everything from his erratic driving to watching sports took on new meaning," says 26-year-old Mandy. The fact is, all of us have deeply ingrained ideas about how mothers and fathers should act—one very good reason to find out each other's opinions *before* you have children, rather than after, when emotions are raw.

You'll both feel very confused in your first few months of parenthood. You may be unsure of your ability to be a good parent (you're having enough trouble bathing the child without drowning it, let alone guiding it through life while he's just getting the hang of picking her up properly and already panicking about how to explain the facts of life). Often you won't feel love or that magic "maternal bond" for months, until your child develops a personality. Many parents find that quite alarming. While you're coping with these emotions privately, too scared to admit them to your partner, he's feeling left out. Men are often cast aside (quite necessarily) and may resent the attention and affection you're lavishing on your child. You resent him because it seems like his life really hasn't altered at all while yours has been put in the washing machine on a never-ending spin cycle. Your roles have changed dramatically and the transition—however temporary—from equals to carer/provider isn't easy. "Whatever you argued about before, you'll argue about even more," warns one new mom. "Except all the old arguments now become centered around the baby."

You may also find your friendships changing. Suddenly, you understand the automatic bond parents have with other parents and start to see less of childless friends who don't understand the expense of babysitters and the fact that although you once raged all night long, now you need to be in bed by 10:00 P.M. because the baby wakes up around the same time you used to go to bed. You may also feel lonely during the day—especially if you were the consummate career girl and all your friends work. They're out there getting ahead while you're at home pushing a stroller and feeling awfully left behind.

Kids and careers

"I used to run an office of 40 without any problems at all—now I can't organize to get myself and the baby to the mall without bursting into tears," says my friend Elizabeth, struggling to open a pack of disposable diapers with a child on her hip. "No one tells you how useless you feel. My self-confidence is shot." Careers are a source of satisfaction, identity, and self-confidence and giving this up can be

> Since our baby was born, I tend to think about my wife a lot more. My love has grown—it's almost like I'm getting in touch with my emotional side. It's a different type of love, one that includes more respect for everything she has gone through.
> Adam, 36, stockbroker

terrifying for some women. It may also be the first time you've had to be dependent on your partner and the first time you have not felt in control of your life.

Your career—and where you are in it—is often the major factor determining when you'll have children. As a rule of thumb, if you're planning to have a family, it's generally best to postpone doing it until you've at least earned yourself some sort of reputation. The longer you have been in your job, the better your chances of returning to the workforce. But it's hard to say which is the hardest: giving up your job completely for a few years after a child or going back to it within a few weeks or months. For many career women, returning to work seems the most attractive option, but it's difficult. Quite apart from childcare problems, just when the child starts to become interesting, it's time to leave. You may feel confused and not sure you're doing the "right thing" by your child. If, on the other hand, all you're dreaming of are baby-free days back in the office, you'll feel guilty for different reasons. Either way, that first week back in the office is likely to be awful. You'll either feel jealous of the person who's looking after your child and wish you were at home or question what sort of mom you are if it gets to be 5:00 P.M. and you haven't given the baby a thought.

There's also the stress of money worries. Having a baby is horrendously expensive. Not only have you been reduced to one income (even if temporarily), you've had to shell out for a crib, changing table, and bassinet, then dig deeper for a stroller and baby seat for the car. Not to mention diapers, baby clothes, formula, baby food, toys, books, babysitters, and childcare.

Not working also has an effect on your relationship with your partner. If you're ambitious and adored your job but agreed to take time out to stay home and look after the baby, it can be frustrating to see your partner getting ahead while you're feeling horribly left behind. Your end-of-day conversations are different. Your spouse has been out there in the "real world," mixing with all sorts of people; you've been home alone mixing formula. You hear yourself saying, "Marjorie and I took the babies to the park," and feel like a fifties housewife. Which makes you wonder if he sees you as one. After all, you're no longer the sexy, go-getting career girl, dashing out the door with briefcase in one hand, make-up bag in the other. You're a mommy: incapable of dashing anywhere with a baby on one hip and the six tons of baby paraphernalia you now have to lug around.

If the whole parenting thing's starting to sound expensive, restricting, and overwhelming, you're right—it is! Which is why you shouldn't even think about it unless you're prepared to make all these sacrifices. So think long and hard about the ifs before you even start on the whens.

Tick, tock: that's your clock

A woman's fertile life peaks at 25, then declines *slowly* for the next ten years, gathering speed after that. At 24, it takes an average of six menstrual cycles to get pregnant, at 34 it can take ten. Both these figures are averages, which means you could get pregnant after one month's unprotected intercourse at 39 while your 22-year-old sister tries for four years. The only problem with being older is that if you do experience fertility problems, there's less time to sort them out.

As we get older, our eggs get older and our hormones are less efficient. You might have a problem with cervical mucus (which stops the sperm passing successfully through the cervix to meet with the waiting egg) and may not ovulate every cycle. You might also have been a victim of diseases such as endometriosis and pelvic inflammatory disease (PID)—both can cause infertility at any age—or your partner might have a low sperm count. The risk of chromosomal abnormality (such as Down's syndrome) rises with each year after 35, and prenatal screening by amniocentesis is routinely offered to women over this age, sometimes women over 30. Amniocentesis is a procedure that takes a sample of the amniotic fluid around the fetus. You usually have to wait until the third or fourth month of pregnancy before having the test, which makes the decision not to go full-term very traumatic. Older mothers are also more likely to be af-fected by high blood pressure and diabetes, have longer than average labors,

Women who are 35 to 40 years old are three times more likely to give birth to twins than are 20- to 24-year-old mothers.[24]

inductions, or caesareans.[25] In vitro fertilization—IVF—is an option but it's costly, time-consuming, and physically and emotionally exhausting. Having said all that, putting off children until your mid to late thirties really isn't a problem if you've had no major gynecological problems. Plenty of gynecologists will be more than happy to reassure you that you're not putting yourself or your baby at risk. And if you are thinking of delaying having children there are ways to protect your fertility as much as possible. Keep fit and generally healthy. Don't smoke, keep alcohol to a minimum, avoid taking prescription drugs unnecessarily, exercise regularly, and eat a varied diet. If you're single, use condoms every single time. The more people you have unprotected sex with, the more chance you've got of picking up sexually transmittable, fertility-damaging diseases such as pelvic inflammatory disease. Find a good gynecologist early in life and stick with the same doctor for regular Pap smears and general check-ups.

Once you've done all you can to protect your fertility for as long as possible, try really hard to stop panicking. Take a look around you and you'll see plenty of moms who've managed to produce a small army after age 35. Even if you *are* on the wrong side of 35, it's still not a terribly good idea to let your biological clock dictate your relationships. Sure, it's tempting. You celebrate your thirty-eighth birthday, shed a few tears with a girlfriend, sobbing, "Oh God! I still haven't found anyone and time's running out," then you start dating some semidecent guy you'd have ditched in the past and your mind plays tricks on you. You think, *He is nice. Maybe what I'm looking for doesn't exist, so he'll do. He's responsible, dependable, he'd make a great dad,* and before you know it, you're up the aisle and then up the creek. The problem with all this is that, while you might adore the children you create together, it sort of helps if you adore the father as well. Children link you forever, and divorces and break-ups are even more messy and painful when there are children involved. So you've got two choices if you've hooked up with the wrong person: live a miserable life together or bring up the children on your own. Which is probably what you should have done in the first place. If you're *that* intent on having children, time is running out and you're not in a relationship, my advice would be to consider a sperm donor rather than "make do" with a man you don't love.

Another point I want to make is this: when and if to have children is a huge decision and not one anyone else should or can make for you. If you're still happily playing the field in your late thirties with no great desire to "settle down" yet, don't let family or friends change your mind for you. Settle down when *you* want to. If you don't end up finding your perfect partner until it's way too late, well, that's a shame but it's not the end of the world. Plenty of people have happy lives and great relationships without reproducing.

Don't be pressured by existing partners or well-meaning friends and family when you're *in* a happy relationship either. The right time to have children with your partner is when *both* of you agree it's the right time. Get "accidentally" pregnant with a partner who's not ready or doesn't want children, and you risk your relationship. At the very least, you—and the child—are going to be the focus of resentment. It's him that's insistent but you're not? Explain the reason why you're not ready, say when or if you will be, then keep talking until you can reach a compromise that both of you are happy with. If you can't, you might need to get some couples' counseling or admit you've both got different dreams and separate.

THE PLUSES OF HAVING KIDS EARLY

- Your body is in peak physical condition and both carrying and coping with the baby will be easier on you physically.
- You're at peak fertility and able to get pregnant easily and with little fuss.
- You get to "grow up" with your children so you may find it easier to relate to them because you're closer in age.
- By the time the kids are grown up and off your hands, you'll be young enough to enjoy your freedom and do something with it rather than simply retire.

THE PLUSES OF HAVING THEM LATE

- You're more established in your career so your chances of reentering the workforce at a high level are better.

"Sex? Did someone say sleep?"

What really happens to your love life when you've had a child?

My girlfriend Tina was determined to be the sexiest mom around. "So many people said to me, 'After kids, it's just not the same,' eyes averted in a way that suggests the subject is closed. I was determined to prove them wrong. I worried about sleep deprivation, whether I'd ever be able to fit into my Versace miniskirt, how having a baby would affect my career. But I never, ever worried about sex because we were such sexual creatures, my husband and I, I didn't imagine anything could take that away."

And then the baby arrived. Turns out Tina did fit into her mini after a few months but "who the hell wants to wear a mini after having a kid? All I wanted to do was slob around in sweatpants and a

T-shirt stained with baby vomit. I hadn't shaved my legs in three months. I didn't know when I'd last had sex and who the hell cared, anyway?"

Having a child creates a violent upheaval in your sex life. A bouncing baby (emphasis on the word bouncing) is incredibly demanding. Ask any mother how her sex life is three months after the first child and she'll look at you, dazed and bewildered and mutter something like, "Sleep? Can I go to sleep now?" Things do return to normal but it takes effort and a very long time.

It's not surprising neither of you is sprinting to the bedroom when the magic six-week abstinence period is over. You're both tired, she's sore from breast-feeding, both of you are confused about your new roles, she's teary and anxious from all the hormones racing around her body: sizzling between the sheets is about as appealing as wanting to go to an all-night rave party.

No sane women is dying for sex when she's had two hours sleep in six weeks. The gyno says it's okay to do it, but her body is still recovering from expelling (let's face it) something the size of a small watermelon. Postpregnancy hemorrhoids, hot flashes, lubrication problems, scarring from an episiotomy or a vaginal tear—like, *hello!* These are hardly lust-inspiring conditions. A tummy that never quite goes flat, varicose veins, breasts that swelled magnificently during pregnancy and now shrink to the size of grapes—changes like that don't make you *feel* very sexy either. Add a child that needs your attention 24 hours a day, seven days a week and you can see why lots of couples don't resume a regular sex life until a year after the birth. Even then, it's hardly like the old days. Bang goes spontaneity and the freedom to do it in the living room. Weird things happen: like, your child seems to have been born with a well-tuned sex radar. "It's uncanny," says a friend of mine ruefully. "Babies can sense an erection six rooms away. If sex even *vaguely* seeps into your subconscious, they pick up on it and wake up, cry, throw up—do *anything* to demand your attention."

I don't know about you but even researching this makes me wonder if it's all worth it! But there is good news. Plenty of couples get through all the angst to rediscover a new, improved sex life. To up your chances, try doing the following:

- **Do Kegel exercises to tone your vagina.** During childbirth, both the cervix and the vagina stretch. The cervix narrows and firms up again after about seven days but the vagina needs pelvic floor exercises to tighten the muscle. Your gynecologist can advise you on how to do Kegels or refer to any good sex book.

- **Don't stress about it.** Just about all moms lose the desire for sex after having a baby.

- **If you don't want sex, talk.** Your partner's feeling strange, too. He's sharing you with someone else and is probably feeling left out because no matter how involved he is, there's a bond between mother and baby that he can't share. Assure him that your libido and sex life will return, that it's not gone forever. Be loving and affectionate and let him know he's as important as the baby is.

- **Avoid intercourse initially and concentrate on gentle oral and manual stimulation.** Massages, long baths together—even if you don't feel like sex, you can still do sensual things.

- **Experiment with new positions.** What you enjoyed previously might have altered. Try side by side and use bucketloads of water-based lubricant: breast-feeding drains the body of estrogen, which can cause vaginal dryness.

- **Schedule a weekend away, minus the baby**, six months in and then another six months after that. The first weekend, you'll probably drop the bags on the floor and sleep for two days straight. The next time, though, gently re-explore what you enjoyed previously.

- **Plan time for sex.** If you can drop the child off with family or friends for an hour or two on weekends, do it. Be selfish about your sex life. Give it priority. Have sex even if you're not champing at the bit for it: once you start being stimulated, you'll probably be glad you did.

- **Turn your attitude around.** So you've only got three minutes to make love? Great! Turn it into a raunchy quickie.

- **Give it time.** It takes a while to make the transition from two-of-you to three-of-you.

SERIAL MONOGAMY: THE WAY OF THE FUTURE?

There's a relationship pattern emerging that might well become the norm: serial monogamy. Serial monogamists spend years with one person in a committed, monogamous relationship, split, then start another, split, then start another. Instead of matching with one person for life, they might have five or six serious, long-term relationships, which might include a marriage to provide security when having children.

In a sense, most of us already are serial monogamists. Few people commit to marriage without a few long-term relationships under their belt. Plenty of others try hard to stay with one person but end up serial monogamists by default: they start relationships thinking they'll last a lifetime, then when that doesn't work out, they try again.

The difference between true serial monogamy and a series of relationship blunders is the intention behind the partnerships. A serial monogamist believes *all* relationships have a use-by date. "If I'm lucky," they figure, "I'll get a good ten years of true happiness out of it." They don't go into the relationship thinking it will last a lifetime, they *expect* it will end after a period of years. In a sense, it's taking the in-love-with-love phenomenon even further. Lots of people leave relationships when real life kicks in and the fun falling-in-love bit is over. Serial monogamists take it a few stages forward: they move ahead into true commitment and leave when contentment gives way to habit. It probably *is* impossible to maintain a very high level of marital satisfaction over a lifetime together. And if that's what we're after (and it seems most of us are), this is certainly the solution.

One part of me believes serial monogamy is sensible. The other part rebels against it. For a start, it's unlikely both of you will decide you've reached the use-by date for the relationship at the same point, so it won't stop people from getting hurt. Secondly, while being rapturous over your partner does feel fabulous, there's something to be said for pleasant companionship based on shared history. At 50, not everyone wants to go through the drama of moving out, splitting possessions, jumping on the love rollercoaster, and starting all over again with someone new. It takes energy. Most of us are worn out by 30—God knows how we'll feel 20 years later. Last but not least, every time a relationship fails—even if you do split amicably—a little part of your heart and soul go with that person.

There's a difference between being dumped after a few months and being dumped after ten years. I've got several long-term relationships under my belt, including a marriage, and although I'm quite sure none were meant to last forever, I certainly hope it's not a pattern I'm destined to repeat for the rest of my life. I'd rather give all my heart to one person for good than hand over a slice of it once a decade. Perhaps you agree with me.

IF ALL ELSE FAILS: COUPLES' COUNSELING

The room might be cheery but the two people nervously fidgeting on the couch aren't. He's still trying to figure out what he's doing in a "shrink's" office at the ripe old age of 26; she's wondering why she insisted they come. Now that she's here, she can't think of a single thing to say and it all seems a little ridiculous. "It's often uncomfortable to start with," says the psychologist. "Perhaps you'd like to begin by telling me how the two of you met . . ."

Yet another struggling couple seeking help from a therapist to save their marriage? Not quite. Peter and Collette aren't even living together, let alone married. But they are thinking about it *and* have been arguing, and unlike other couples who privately ponder, *Will we make it?*, they decided to seek an expert opinion. It's an increasingly popular trend. After seeing their parents and friends split, today's couples are fighting back. In a bid to understand relationships and learn the skills that will make theirs work, they're detouring to their nearest psychologist *before* they move in or walk down the aisle. It's an option every couple should think about (yes, even you two).

Danger points in a relationship

You might think your problems are individual but the likelihood is the counselor's seen it all before. Most couples hit the same set of problems, around the same time. The first hiccup: when the relationship moves from fun to functional. "Once people decide they're serious about each other, they start getting serious about life: get a house, have kids, get a mortgage," says psychologist Phillip Gorrell. "They stop concentrating on the relationship and concentrate on work and money." Romance takes a back seat and people stop feeling special. It's sobering to realize that real love is more about having things in common and being able to talk than your partner walking in with flowers or champagne. But plenty of couples skid into boring behavior patterns around the two-year mark: often the kiss of death. If you don't take enough vacations and keep the novelty factor happening, you'll soon get bored. This is what usually happens when a person says, "I don't know what happened but I've fallen out of love for no good reason."

The next problem point is based around quality of communication. You feel your partner doesn't understand you, he or she doesn't listen, you can't talk to them. This often slides into the third danger zone: our tendency to focus on the negative. "You say to people, 'What percentage of your relationship is good?' and they'll answer 75 percent." I feel like saying to them, "If that much is good, why are you focusing on the bad?" says Gorrell.[27]

Not only do we focus on the bad we have a tendency toward the grass-is-always-greener syndrome. People compare their relationship with those of their friends and, on the surface, their friends' look wonderful. But how do you really know? You're comparing your internal feelings with their external experience. Don't believe all you see.

Can counseling save your relationship?

The sooner you get help, the more chance you've got and the less damage the problem will cause long term. A big factor in how successful counseling is going to be is how much you both really want it to work—and how hard you're prepared to work at your relationship. It's incredibly difficult to break old habits and to stop from sliding back into them and counseling takes an awful lot of time. It's not just a matter of rolling in there once a week, because there's no point learning skills unless you practice them at home. The average couple is in for anywhere between 6 and 12 hour-long sessions—with homework. It's not a quick-fix solution—which is, of course, why it works long term.

When doesn't it work?

It's not very successful when you're already in the middle of a *huge* crisis. Which is, of course, when most people decide to go. What usually happens is, by the time you've sorted out the mess (usually an affair), you're too exhausted to work on changing, so you settle back into your old ways and the problem starts all over again.

If one of you has already fallen out of love or already decided to leave, again, the prognosis isn't good, though it can soften the blow and your next relationship(s) will benefit from going to counseling. The thing to remember is this: the therapist isn't going to magically solve all your problems for you. They're doctors not magicians: you've got to want to change and work hard at it for counseling to work.

What happens in a typical counseling session?

Usually, you'll spend the first session telling the therapist what your problems are and just by watching you, they can get an idea of your personalities and how you relate to one another. After that, they start problem-solving and teaching you communication skills, like what we've been talking about throughout this book: how to talk to each other, how to listen, and how to make sure the words that come out of your mouth are actually what you're trying to say. Often, simply being able to speak up is half the battle. People will say things in front of a therapist that they wouldn't dream of saying at home because it would start an almighty argument. They'll also delve into your backgrounds and significant life experiences to find out what other influences there are on the relationship (the stuff I talk about in Chapter 8).

Will they tell you if it's best to split up?

No reputable therapist will tell you to go home and pack your bags, but they will say something like this: "We've spent a lot of time on your relationship, I've given you homework exercises and nothing appears to be changing. Is it time now to look at going your own ways? Maybe that's what we should be working on." According to psychologist Grant Brecht, couples have one of two reactions when given this speech. "They'll either say, 'What a terrible thing to say to us! We'll make this work just to show you'—and they do! Or one person will say, 'I'm so glad you brought that up.' "[28] There certainly may come a point where you're working on splitting up harmoniously rather than working to put it all back together. Relationship counseling isn't just about helping couples to stay together—it also helps them break up successfully.

How do you talk your partner into going?

Very tactfully! It's all in the way you approach it. Saying, "You need to get your head checked because we're in an absolute mess," won't get you very far. Saying, "Darling, I love you but I think we need to learn a few relationship skills," might do the trick.

If he's a bit nervous—and it's usually the guy who's not into it— tell him you'll go along on your own to check it out first, so you can reassure him what it's like. If your partner refuses point blank to even consider counseling, it's a pretty good sign the relationship wouldn't have worked anyway. If they're that stubborn, they're not going to change. So like it or lump it and leave. These are the only two choices you've got, I'm afraid.

How do you find a good therapist?

Call the American Psychological Association at 202-336-5500 and ask for a list of qualified counselors in your area. Don't just go to anyone though—call and talk to the counselor first and see whether you like the sound of that person. Counseling's not cheap and it's more effective if you like and respect the person who's helping you. Private counseling is the most expensive, but there are community or religious organizations that may be able to help you find it for free or for a minimum fee.

FIVE COMPLAINTS YOU'LL NEVER HEAR FROM HIM

"Honey, I wish you'd stop bringing home sexy videos."
"Why can't I hang around while you have the girls over?"
"I wish you'd leave the dishes for me to do."
"I can't believe you went Christmas shopping and didn't take me with you."
"Must we? Don't you think sex is overrated?"

AND HER

"I can't believe you didn't look at that girl—she was gorgeous!"
"I'm so depressed your mother's stopped giving me so much constructive criticism."
"Do we *have* to talk about the relationship? I'd rather watch TV."
"I wish you'd stop buying me flowers. They're a waste of money."
"Not more oral sex! I'd much prefer to give it to you."

7

Jealousy and Infidelity

Taming the green-eyed monster and what to do if
your partner cheats (or you're tempted to)

●●

I play it pretty safe with relationships. My dad had an affair so I've had
first-hand experience of the pain of betrayal and would rather stick
red-hot pokers in every orifice than be on the receiving end of *that*.
Any guy who even looks shifty doesn't get to first base. But I did make
one exception.

When I met Jason, all my instincts said, *Run away—NOW!*
Smooth, rich, and oozing sex appeal, he had "I will fool around" written all over his Armani suit. God knows why (okay, it was lust), but I
dated him even *after* he told me he actually did have a problem with
infidelity and had cheated on his wife and every single girlfriend he'd
ever had. I, as always, was to be the exception: I was the only one
he'd ever truly been in love with, after all. With me, it just wouldn't
happen, he said. He *knew* it. I don't know where my brain was at the
time (possibly skiing in Aspen) but I guess I was trying to prove something. That the scars from my parents' divorce really had healed. That
I didn't have a problem with jealousy. That I wasn't so paranoid about
someone cheating on me, I couldn't take a chance.

I wasn't entirely stupid, though. I kept my eyes open and I knew exactly where he hid his stash of condoms (we'd both been tested for HIV and had since stopped using them). There was one unopened packet and two loose. For ten months, they stayed that way. Then three were missing. "I gave them to a friend," he said.

"Which friend?" I asked, and dialed his number. That's all it took for him to confess to a one-night (three times?) stand which, of course, meant nothing. Jason could not understand why I left him. Three years (one for each condom) and a lot of therapy later, he regrets what he did.

> You're far more likely to be jealous if you're less educated, young, and in a new relationship. Men are apt to blame their jealousy on others, women blame themselves.[1]

I simply regret going out with him. It was pointless because I never did trust him and (as I have discussed at length earlier), trust is an essential ingredient in a good relationship. You can have matching libidos, the same interests, dreams, and goals, share a fetish for garden gnomes, and both enjoy wearing green patterned sweaters during oral sex, but if you spend the whole of your life together looking suspiciously at each other through narrowed eyes, it means nothing.

For some people, jealousy and worries over infidelity aren't a problem. They work on the assumption that someone will be faithful until proven wrong. If this is you, count yourself lucky. Sure, you might get an almighty kick in the teeth now and again, but at least you're giving relationships the best chance they've got to succeed. Trusting someone means putting your heart in their hands for safe-keeping. It's a precious present and it takes guts to do it.

Then there are the rest of us: the battle-scarred. If you'd rather sign over your firstborn than trust your partner, one of two things has happened. That person has done something to justify your mistrust—cheated on you or has a history of cheating—or something's happened in *your* past to make you suspicious of *everyone*.

You may find this chapter painful to read because there's a lot in it that isn't terribly pleasant: like the shocking statistics on how many of us *are* sneaking around behind each other's back. And while I'd love to, I can't give any guarantees *your* partner will be faithful. They might well betray you and yes, it will hurt if they do. An awful lot. But what's the alternative? If you never let down your guard, you'll never be able to truly fall in love. So arm yourself with knowledge and by all means look for warning signs, but after you've done that, take a deep breath and take a chance on *someone who's worth it*. Once you've read this chapter, don't look at it again unless you need to. Be sensible, but there's no point in being paranoid.

JEALOUSY: TAMING THE BEAST WITHIN—OR THE BEAST YOU'RE INVOLVED WITH

If you're an extremely jealous person, prepare to hyperventilate. Fact number one: jealousy won't stop people from being unfaithful—it makes it actually more likely they will be. If you accuse someone often enough of having an affair or lusting after so-and-so, they eventually think, *Hey, they believe it, I might as well do it.* Fact number two: the biggest fear of a jealous person is that their partner will leave them, but if you continue to make your partner's life hell, he or she probably will. Feeling completely paranoid? Good. Let these two facts sink in and you might decide it's time to tame that green-eyed monster.

There's another reason why it's a brilliant idea to get jealousy under control. If you're a jealous person and in love, life is pretty miserable most of the time. I've been there. I, like you, spent every minute of every day looking for evidence. A car parked down the street can't belong to a neighbor—it must be a secret lover visiting my boyfriend. His phone's busy at work? He's not talking business, he's whispering sweet somethings to someone else. A girlfriend of mine used to put hairs across the phone to see if her boyfriend was making any secret calls while she hopped out to get the milk. Some people ask their friends to come on to their partners to see if they'd take them up on it. An extremely silly thing to do, since it can spark an unacknowledged attraction that would never have surfaced if you hadn't forced them into it.

Extreme jealousy is an ugly emotion. A doctor friend of mine tells the story of a woman in her thirties with terminal cancer who had to spend a lot of time in bed. She bought some pretty nighties so she could look good for her husband but instead of being complimented, he flew into a jealous rage and accused her of trying to attract the hospital staff. A psychiatrist told me about a patient who wired up his entire house with microphones so he could tape the supposed sex sessions his wife had while he was at work. They weren't rich and he spent their life savings doing it. All he recorded was her doing the dishes and gossiping on the phone to girlfriends. There's another quite bizarre case of a man who was so jealous, he was convinced his wife was being unfaithful during the few minutes he left the bed during the night to go to the toilet.

You can pick the couple where one or both partners are jealous: they don't go out. The only stress-free environment is at home with a video and a bottle of wine because any public place—pubs, restaurants, even shopping—has potential rivals (that is, people of the opposite sex). Some people can't even bear their partners watching attractive people on television. Even the news becomes a problem if the anchor happens to be attractive.

Hah!, I hear you say, I'm nowhere near *that* bad. True (or maybe not). But solve the problem now, while you can. Jealousy is insidious. It grows like a weed and only needs the occasional drop of water to spread. It's dangerous to think you're in control. It's like smoking. One day you're smoking one cigarette, the next week two, then three and before you're know it you're a two-pack-a-day person.

What makes someone jealous?

We all get a bit put out if our partner's drooling over some blonde at a party. But really jealous people have usually had something happen to them in the past. If either of your parents had an affair or you found your partner in bed with the next-door neighbor, it stands to reason you're going to be a tad suspicious.

Experiences like these leave us with cynical attitudes about relationships and we make massive generalizations based on them. If you're female and an ex-lover was unfaithful, you think *all* men will sleep around if given half the chance. That might be true of *some* men, but it's certainly not true of *all* men. Jealous people look at the world through distorted lenses. They see danger where there really isn't any. It's also got a lot to do with self-esteem. If you're happy with yourself, you're much more likely to think, *Why would my partner want anyone else when they've got me?* A healthy ego is great protection against jealousy.

The inability to trust other people affects both sexes, all socioeconomic groups, and all cultures. It doesn't discriminate in intelligence or looks. In fact, a lot of jealous people are actually above average in attractiveness and are often successful. The average person might look at them in astonishment when they throw a jealous tantrum (thinking, *Why would they have any need to worry? Who'd want to play around on them?*), but it's all about feeling like you measure up. We all measure ourselves against a personal ideal that is slightly above what and who we are. The more beautiful/fabulous you are, the higher your ideal. So the reason that gorgeous girlfriend never feels good enough—when she's a million times better-looking than Ms. Average—is because she doesn't measure herself against Ms. Average, she measures herself against the truly extraordinary: the supermodels.

Everyone gets jealous occasionally, but truly distrustful people experience jealousy with *each* and *every* person they go out with.

Insecurity

Jealousy and distrust are often rooted in insecurity. It's logical. And insecure, jealous people react one of two ways. They turn into scared-little-mice partners, convinced their partner's about to run off with the 80-year-old janitor at their work. Or they overcompensate by being bullies. If you're a quivering mess inside, the best way to make yourself feel better is to try to control everything and everyone around you. Playing tough guy and putting down your partner at every opportunity momentarily makes you feel strong. Besides, if you drag them down far enough, they'll become as insecure as you are and won't have the courage to leave you.

Childhood

Middle children are frequently jealous, according to the experts. It sounds like something Freud would say (and probably did), but often the middle child feels left out and over-looked.[2] Similarly, if your mom or dad had an affair, it stands to reason you're going to be suspicious of your partners. We tend to judge our relationships by the relationship we saw our parents have.

The past

If you've been dumped before or cheated on constantly, you've got good reason not to trust a partner. You've learned by experience that (some) people aren't trustworthy and/or your judgment's not so great. If the last time your partner stayed out all night, they slept with some-one else, it's obvious you'll assume that's what your new partner is doing, even if it's actually quite innocent.

Your own history of faithfulness

If you find it incredibly difficult to stay faithful to one person, you may assume others are the same. Psychologists call it "projection"[3]: seeing our own qualities in someone else. You don't trust yourself (now or in the past), so you don't trust your partner. If you've cheated on other people numerous times and gotten away with it, it seems logical that others could be doing the same to you.

> I always kick myself after the rage has worn off. It's like, "Why am I so jeal-ous? How can he stand to put up with me?" Once I've calmed down it becomes painfully obvious that I've ruined a perfectly good evening for nothing. I feel embarrassed and remorseful—and then even more insecure than I was before. It's a catch-22 situation because I'm even more likely to be jealous the next time.
> Sharon, 28, make-up artist

Get a grip! The do-it-yourself jealousy cure

You've got two choices if you've got a problem with jealousy: get pro-fessional help or try to help yourself. Which should you do? Hope-fully, it'll become clear as you read through this section.

1. Identify the reason

Pinpoint the reason(s) why you're jealous by checking the section above. Is it insecurity, your childhood, your past, your own cheating history, or a combination of all four? If the answer's not obvious, force yourself to think outside the box. It might well stem from sitting through all the gory details of when your best friend's heart got smashed to smithereens by a lover who cheated. ("Jesus! I hope this never happens to me!")

If you truly don't know why you're jealous and/or you've grappled with jealousy for years, you need more than this book. Get professional help by calling the American Psychological Association (202-336-5500) and ask for a list of qualified therapists in your area.

2. Work on your self-esteem

The more highly you think of yourself, the less likely you'll believe your partner would dream of risking you and your relationship by playing around with someone else. Chapter 1 discusses self-esteem. If you've already read it and it hasn't helped, again, get help from a professional.

3. Change your behavior

This technique was recommended by one of the world's leading experts on jealousy, psychologist Dr. Nicholas Tarrier. It's hard work and takes an awful lot of time but it solved my jealousy problem. Hopefully, it will help you.[4]

The plan only works if you do it *every single time you have a jealous thought*. You need to follow it faithfully, religiously, and without exception. Doing it every second time or even four out of five times, renders it totally ineffective. It will take over your life for a few weeks or months, depending on how jealous you are. It means you have to carry a notepad and pen wherever you go. It might mean you'll be disappearing to the bathroom a dozen times during a dinner party. But even if it meant taking off your clothes and dancing naked at the local bus stop, it's worth giving it a try.

If you have a good relationship with your partner, it's sensible to tell them what you're doing. If they love you and want the problem fixed as much as you do (believe me, *more* than you do), they'll support and cover for you when you have to disappear. You might also consider telling close friends to explain any long absences when you're out together. But don't make the mistake of turning it into a party trick. It's acceptable to do this exercise with your partner after you've done it alone at least a dozen times. It's okay to work through it with a best friend. But no more than one person at a time: you'll feel silly, they'll make hurtful jokes, and it'll backfire Big Time. Being jealous isn't fun. It's degrading and humiliating. You can do without being teased and trivialized. Ready, willing, and (yes you are) able? Here's how to do it.

Every time you have a jealous thought, write it down and rate how strongly you believe it on a scale of one to ten. For example: *My boyfriend is chatting up the girl behind the bar:* 9 [I'm certain this is true].

Underneath this sentence, list all the reasons why you believe this. Think of as many as you can:

- *He's been talking to her for too long—much longer than necessary.*

- *He smiled at her.*

- *He gave her "that look."*

- *She's his type/she's really attractive.*

- *Everyone else at the table looked really embarrassed—like they knew what was happening and felt sorry for me.*

Even if you know how silly it sounds as you're writing it, write it all down. Wait two minutes and dwell a bit longer on how upset and angry you feel. Deliberately stay at the "rage" point a little while so every single one of those paranoid thoughts comes to the surface for you to write down.

Beside these reasons, now write logical, alternative explanations. Wait another two minutes but this time try to calm down. Breathe deeply, remind yourself of how you felt *after* the last jealous rage (unjustified). Then force yourself to challenge each and every point you've listed with a logical explanation. If you find this difficult, imagine your best friend is there with you. How might she or he challenge those thoughts? Write down the explanations even if you don't believe what you're writing.

- *He's been talking to her for ages.*
  It seems like a long time but it could be that my judgment is way off.

- *He smiled at her.*
  He's friendly and polite. I also smile at people in that sort of situation.

- *He gave her "that look."*
  Let's face it: I'd interpret any sort of friendly expression as "that look."

Don't stop until you've listed a plausible, remotely believable explanation for every single reason you've listed.

Read through what you've written—focusing on the logical explanations—and rerate how strongly you now believe the initial thought. Accept that there's a possibility that this new rating is as true as your jealousy-inspired accusation.

Keep going. The more logical explanations you can think of the better. Try to list at least two, preferably three explanations next to every jealous thought.

Again, rerate how strongly you now believe the initial thought. Don't rejoin your partner until you've reduced your initial rating (example: 9) at least one point. Don't be alarmed if the minute you walk out of wherever you've been hiding, it all comes flooding back and you shoot back up to 9. Just congratulate yourself that you regained a small amount of control when normally you would have stormed out immediately.

Now you're back in the situation, see how you feel. If you have to ignore your partner or look in the other direction to stay calm, do it. If your partner's aware you're following this program, tell them why you've been gone so long. Let them give your hand a squeeze even if you can't squeeze it back, try to smile when they reassure you you've got nothing to worry about, then change the subject.

If you still feel out of control, repeat the exercise or leave. Go back and go through everything one more time. If it's not working, go home—with or without your partner—and try it again there.

Keep repeating this exercise. If you're an extremely jealous person it will have little effect during the first few weeks. A month later, you'll notice a small improvement. In two months, a significant change. And by month three, you're well on the road to living life as nonjealous people do. Please don't give up.

Keep writing things down until you can do the exercise mentally. Follow exactly the same steps but do it in your head rather than on paper.

Congratulations! It worked. One miraculous day, you'll find your brain does the exercise for you—without your even being conscious of it happening! Your brain has been trained to challenge silly thoughts with logic and it starts working through the process subconsciously and automatically. This is how nonjealous people's brains work. Their subconscious sees a potentially threatening situation but before they're even aware of it, the logical side of their brain clicks in and dismisses the idea if it's not based on reality. If there is good reason to be jealous, the thought will filter through anyway. So don't panic: you won't suddenly stop seeing *real* threats, you'll just stop seeing those that aren't.

Your fine, it's your partner who's out of control

A very good friend of mine went out with an intensely jealous guy for one long, miserable year. Before Melissa met him, she was a happy, well-adjusted, fairly typical 24-year-old with no particular problems. Within a month of dating this loser, she suddenly wasn't "allowed" to go out to dinner with me alone. Since the main reason I wanted to see her during this period was to conduct my own one-woman leave-the-bastard campaign, I was more than a little worried when she agreed to do as he said. Once, Melissa did sneak out—and paid for it heavily. He found out, accused her of all sorts of things, and smashed their coffee table against a wall. They argued all night, she was late for work (again), and missed out on the promotion that should have been hers. It was my fault of course—not his. He made sure he convinced her of that.

After six months of virtually no contact, I stopped by unexpectedly. Melissa had lost close to ten pounds—not a good look when she was a size 6 to start with. I had five minutes before the ogre was due home.

"Look at you. *Please* leave this guy," I begged her.

"Logically," she said, "I know you're right. But I don't have the energy or the confidence anymore." Who else would want her when she was obviously such a bad person, someone who couldn't even be trusted to have coffee with a girlfriend at a local cafe? Her boyfriend was okay. Really. He just loved her too much, that's all.

I'm ecstatically happily to report there is a happy ending to the story. When the man who loved Melissa too much decided to show it by breaking her nose in two different places, she finally up and left. But she's still got scars—and I'm not talking about the ones left by plastic surgery.

What was wrong with the girl! I'd never stay with someone like that! you're probably thinking. Don't be too sure. The moral of this morbid little tale is this: be careful, because it *could* happen to you. Don't believe for a minute you're immune to the appeal of jealous, possessive lovers. That's right, *appeal* . . .

Jealous partners come in all sorts of disguises

That intense, wonderfully attentive man who spoils you rotten with impromptu gifts, calls just to say hi several times a day, and wants you "all to himself" seems terribly romantic in the beginning. He hates "sharing" you with other people? Wow! So you cancel that planned girls' night out and secretly feel a little smug about having a boyfriend who doesn't want to go out with the boys. Even his first jealous tantrum seems somehow, well, evidence that this guy really must like you. Tons. Before you know it, you're spending every second together, alone with him.

Early warning signs you've hooked up with a jealous lunatic aren't as obvious as you think. In the "honeymoon" period of healthy relationships, it's normal to live in each other's pockets a little. It's only when you try to return to normality—reestablish your life *apart* from your partner—that you realize they won't let you. You'd like to think this is when you take the nearest exit. But sometimes you feel a bit wobbly and unsure of what to do. *This person loves me so much—and it's obviously upsetting them when I do things alone, so it's best if I put up with it for a little while. Once they become more secure of my love, they'll settle down.* And your perspective starts to get warped. It's around then that Mr. or Ms. Fabulous starts deflating your self-esteem.

Jealous partners erode your self-confidence

They might not even be conscious of doing it, but they start manipulating, trying to make you needy and dependent on them. "I don't know about that haircut," they say. "It doesn't do much for your chin. If Laura was half the friend you say she is, she wouldn't have insisted you cut it so short." The message: *My chin's ugly and I can't trust Laura.* They set the seeds of doubt, then water them regularly. Your family tells you how to run your life, your girlfriends are secretly jealous of you, that colleague is trying to sabotage your success and steal your job. After a while—and if they're clever there's always a grain of truth in there—you start to believe them. You see less and less of family, friends, and coworkers until your social support system is gone. You start to feel unsure of yourself, vulnerable. The only person left in your life is your partner so there's no one to balance those irrational, poisonous accusations.

They've now got you where they want you. Your life revolves almost entirely around them and their opinion counts. It has to—it's the only one you're getting! That's why you don't up and leave when it turns really ugly—your confidence is now even lower than theirs. (Believe me, just about *all* severely jealous, possessive people have self-esteem below rock-bottom.) It suits them for you to doubt yourself because you're less likely to leave. And if someone tells you often enough that being unfaithful to your childhood sweetheart in seventh grade was unforgivable, that you're a *bad* person, you eventually start to believe it. You start to question your own motives for wearing that little black dress, and forget it's not normal for your boyfriend to accompany you to the dentist.

Exhausted from fighting and constantly defending yourself, you haven't got the energy to do much else but hang around and put up with whatever is dished out. You're pushed to the breaking point, your friends are fed up and appear to have forgotten you, your family's annoyed because you don't see them anymore. You feel stressed, emotional, and trapped. All escape routes are effectively cut off: there's nowhere to turn so you stay.

> I used to be jealous until it cost me a great relationship. Now I understand you reap what you sow. If you expect someone to play around, they probably will. Why wouldn't they—you think they are anyway. If you trust them and they know it, they'll try much harder to live up to that.
> Diana, 24, writer

If you're reading this and thinking, *Oh my God, she's talking about me!* please, read the next section that deals with severe jealousy very carefully. If your partner's nowhere near that bad but you recognize it's a problem, skip to the section that follows it.

Your partner's severely jealous and you're miserable but you don't have the strength to leave

Understand the problem

Understand why you feel so bad about yourself and powerless to leave by putting your feelings on paper. Write down how you felt *before* you met this person, how you felt in the first few weeks, two months, six months, and so on. Record when they first started interfering with your friendships; when you stopped seeing friends and family on your own; when you started to feel isolated; when they started to put you and people close to you down; when you began to doubt yourself. If you've managed to maintain any friendships, get that person(s) to sit down with you and jog your memory.

Let the facts sink in

Read your list over and over until you accept what's happened to you. Knowing how you got into the situation will give you the power to get out of it.

Get angry

Keep reading and rereading the list until you start to feel angry. How dare this person have done this to you! It will gradually start to dawn on you that your partner's behavior isn't normal or acceptable. This is not how someone who loves you would treat you. They'd want you to be surrounded by lots of people who love you, who give you compliments and encouragement, not insults and fears.

Get organized

Make concrete plans to leave if you live with the person. Call your friends, even if you haven't called them for ages. Simply apologize for not being in contact and tell them you need help to get out of the situation you're in. It's a good idea to stay with a friend for a few weeks, or your family, rather than try to organize permanent accommodation immediately. Leaving a jealous partner is emotionally draining: just get yourself out of there and worry about a permanent apartment later.

Once you have somewhere to stay, decide *when* you want to leave. If you're female, arrange for a friend to wait outside in the car at a certain time (a male, the bigger the better). If you don't come out within ten minutes, they knock on the door. (If you don't have anyone to call or a place to stay, call the police or a community support group like a women's shelter and ask for their help. They will direct you to the appropriate support service. If you think you're in physical danger, ask your local police to issue a restraining order.)

Break the news and leave quickly

It depends on your partner and how you think they'll react to the news as to when you should tell them you're leaving and it's over. If you're expecting trouble—and it's extremely unlikely they'll let you go without a battle—it's safest to tell them you're leaving two minutes before you walk straight out the door (all possessions packed and removed while they were out). Don't get involved in a long, involved discussion about the relationship. They've had enough chances and there's nothing they can do at this point to fix it. If they swear they'll solve the problem, tell them to make an appointment to see a good therapist and call you through a mutual friend in a few months.

Don't see them

Once you've left, don't see your (now-ex) partner under any circumstances. Surround yourself with good friends, don't answer the door until you know who's there, and hang up if they're on the end of the phone. Forget friendship—if it is possible, it'll be years down the road.

Your partner's got a problem but it's not out of control and you're not feeling threatened

Even if the problem's not severe, constantly defending every move you make and not being trusted to go to the mall takes its toll on the most devoted partner. Jealousy ruins most relationships eventually, so the time to have a serious chat with your partner about it is *now*.

Explain it's their problem

Tell your partner you want to help but essentially, it's up to them to solve the problem. Jealousy is like any other habit—you can't make someone kick it if they don't want to. Your partner's got to want to change and be prepared to do some do-it-yourself therapy (see the program above) or get professional help.

Set a time limit

Set yourself a time limit relevant to how long you've been going out. If you've been dating

> Suspect your partner's not as committed as you are? Women, far more than men, are likely to set "secret tests"—like inventing a love interest or forcing him to choose between a night with her or friends—than men do. The reason? We don't want to be seen as pressuring him, so we try to find out his feelings secretly.[5]

seriously, six months is about right. If they haven't improved by then or are still refusing to get help, bail out. Tell them you're setting this deadline.

Stop reassuring them

Stop reassuring—you're reinforcing bad behavior. If every time they have a tantrum, you run after them saying, "There's no way I lust after that guy in tech support," you're rewarding bad behavior. If a tantrum results in your telling them how wonderful they are, how much you love them, and how you'll never stray, of course they'll keep on hav-

> All men look. If one guy says, "Look at that," we all jump in with a comment. It doesn't occur to any of us to say, "But George! You're happily involved with Mary! What are you checking out other women for?" That's not to say we'd act on it though.
> Stuart, 24, sales rep

ing them—the end result is fabulous. Instead, treat them like a two-year-old. Refuse to be drawn into inquisitions, go to bed early, or disappear until they've calmed down. In other words, leave them alone until logic returns. Do your reassuring *after* the rage has subsided.

Help them make a list

Sit down with your partner and make a list of situations they'd find difficult to cope with. Rate them from nightmare (you out on the town with friends), to hard (you out with an opposite sex friend who's an ex) to relatively easy (you've gone for coffee with a same-sex friend). Put them in order, then try them out—working from the easy end. If you come back from coffee the same loving person who left, they'll probably be fine next time round. Wait until they're comfortable with that situation before moving on to the next, more difficult one. Eventually, they'll realize you're trustworthy no matter what situation you're in. The other bonus: you're working together as a team and can see the light at the end of the tunnel. You'll one day be able to go out without having to come home to a red-faced lunatic.

Build their self-esteem

The better they feel about themselves, the less likely they'll believe someone would want to betray them.

Be reliable but realistic

If you're going to be an hour late, call. But having to call someone three times during a movie is ridiculous.

Be sensitive

Be sensitive to their problem. Don't flirt, even harmlessly, while they're around.

HELP! MY BOYFRIEND'S A PERV!

There's the casual once-over and then there's the look that starts at the top and moves downward very slowly, very obviously undressing someone with your eyes. If your partner's checking out the talent using technique #2, they're out of line.

It's a natural human reaction to look at really beautiful people, and admiring them doesn't mean you don't love your partner or are about to run off with them. But spending all night at a party chatting someone up and leaving with their phone number isn't okay. Even more exasperating is the guy who tries to justify outrageously flirtatious behavior with the old "but I was only being friendly and you're being insecure or jealous" comeback. It's like dog owners who say, "He's just being friendly," while Rover's madly humping your leg: it's *obvious* Rover wants more than just walkies. If your lover's doing the human equivalent of humping but trying to make it seem like *you're* the one with the problem, he's being manipulative. Don't put up with it!

WHAT'S ACCEPTABLE

- **Checking out other women when you're not around.** He knows a comment like, "Look at the chest on that one," is guaranteed to get him a slap on the back from the boys at the bar. It's pretty harmless if you're not with him.
- **Doing a doubletake when a girl walks in wearing a micromini and bikini top and has breasts the size of watermelons.** You can't help but look at people like that. If Tyson Beckford walked in wearing a G-string, you'd do the same.

- **Giving others compliments.** "Sharon looks great tonight," is fine. "Sharon looks fantastic. It's a shame your legs aren't good enough to wear dresses like that," isn't.
- **Lusting after celebrities.** Even if he drools while watching Cameron Diaz on video, it's not something you should feel threatened by. He's just expressing a healthy appreciation of the opposite sex. If he goes on and on about it, tell him it upsets you, and hopefully he'll just gaze adoringly at the screen rather than give a running commentary on how great she looks.
- **Catching your partner exchanging meaningful glances with a stranger across the room.** There's nothing essentially wrong with smiling at someone gorgeous as if to say, "Yes, I find you attractive, too, but we're both with other people," even if few of us enjoy seeing it. If it's not followed through by flirting, it's probably best ignored. After all, you probably do it, too. It's an ego boost, a way of affirming to ourselves that we're still attractive and could get a date if we weren't with our partner. If it seems like your partner's doing it deliberately, they might be trying to give you a good kick in the butt. It's the equivalent of saying, "Hey! Don't take me for granted. I'm not cemented to your side, and other people find me attractive."

WHAT'S NOT ACCEPTABLE

- **Checking out other women in front of you.** If every female gets the once-over and he spends more time looking over your shoulder than looking at you, take a trip to the ladies and don't bother coming back.
- **He's just started drooling over women when he didn't look twice before.** This is a danger sign. It can mean there are real problems in your relationship and he's subconsciously—or even consciously—thinking of leaving and moving into singles mode. Singles scan the room; happily attached people cast a lazy look around but it's not obvious. It could also mean your boyfriend's not getting enough sexually out of your relationship. If he's got a high sex drive and you don't, he might do a lot of mental lusting even though he wouldn't dream of acting on it. Some psychologists call this "leaking": he's got sexual energy that's not being used up, it overflows, and he starts fantasizing

about other people.[6] If you've been fighting a lot, also beware. When people are constantly criticized, they're very vulnerable to temptation. The message you're giving him is, "You're not good enough." He's looking around for someone who thinks he is.

HOW TO FIX IT

- **Check with a trusted friend to make sure you're not being paranoid.** You can't expect someone to totally ignore all other members of the opposite sex, and if you put unrealistic restrictions on people, they will rebel. If you're unable to look at their behavior objectively, ask a trusted friend and get their opinion. Are you overreacting or are they being an insensitive jerk?
- **If you're certain your partner's out of line, call them on it.** The standard answer is, "You're jealous and overreacting." Reply calmly. Say, "No. I've thought about it and I'm not. I won't be treated this way. Look at other women when I'm not around if you have to, but don't do it in front of me. Serious flirting is out of bounds all of the time." End of conversation.
- **Give him one more chance.** See if he's taken your feelings into account. If he hasn't and it happens again, repeat your speech and say you're giving him one more chance. Ask him, "How would you feel if I'd been staring at that good-looking guy over there as long as you have the girl in the black?" It's under-handed and stooping to his level but it will get his attention.
- **If he does it again, give an ultimatum.** This is one of few situations when an ultimatum is necessary—so give him one. Next time he does it, no matter where you are or who you're with, you'll walk out and the relationship will be over. Nothing he can say at that point will change your mind.
- **Follow through and leave if it continues.** He's had three chances to get his act together. If you've rationally and logically explained why you find it unacceptable and he chooses to continue, you're better off without the guy. Put up with him openly drooling over other people at the risk of losing respect for yourself.

AFFAIRS: HOW COULD THEY (OR WHY DID YOU)? AND ADVICE ON THE "OH GOD! WHERE DO WE GO FROM HERE?" PART

Okay, be brutally honest here and imagine yourself in this scenario. You've been married for 15 years. You dearly love your partner, have two wonderful kids, and appreciate how lucky you are. But you're struggling, as most couples are, just a little. Sex is pleasant but all too rare because who's got the energy or the time? The mortgage reminds you of "Jack and the Beanstalk": no matter how much money you pour in, the end's still out of reach. The kids are turning into Incredible Hulks—they're growing up so fast, you're forking out for new shoes every week. Work pressures are mounting, you're arguing, and honestly can't remember the last time you had *fun*. Then your company sends you away on a four-day conference.

It's hot, you're lying by the pool thinking, "Oh my God. I'd forgotten what this feels like." Later that night, you and a single work friend have dinner and he or she convinces you to go for a nightcap in the hotel bar. They start chatting up some gorgeous young thing who also happens to have an equally gorgeous friend. The sort you would have gone gaga over if you were single. You're polite. You tell them you're married, they continue flirting. *Jesus!* you think, *It would be so easy.* But you do the right thing, excuse yourself and go up to your room. Ten minutes later, as you're harmlessly fantasizing about what you'd like to have done if you weren't married, there's a knock at your door. It's one of them.

"Did my friend tell you my room number?" you ask.

"No. I saw your room key," he says. "No one knows I'm here. I know you're married. I'm not interested in a relation-

> He'd check out other women and it was like he had a ten-second orgy with them in his imagination. He'd disappear for a little while and I knew exactly where he'd gone—into fantasyland. He told me it didn't count as unfaithful because he didn't act on it, but it was so destructive to watch, I left him.
> Trudy, 19, promotions

ship, all I want is sex. Now. No strings. I don't even know your last name and I don't want to know."

You've had six too many drinks. You think, *My spouse and the kids are thousands of million miles away, literally. There is no possible way they can find out. I've been faithful for 15 years, I have every intention of being faithful for the next 15. Would it really hurt so much to give in just this once?*

Do you:

a. Say, "Thanks, I'm awfully flattered but I'm married," and shut the door.
b. Start out with every intention to do the above, but instead of shutting the door you invite him in for a drink because you feel a bit rude and immature sending him away like that.
c. Do both of the above, while secretly hoping like hell he'll convince you it doesn't matter and what's the harm. You know you're going to wake up feeling guilty as hell tomorrow, but at that very second, it seems worth it.

Don't think about what you'd like your *partner* to do in that situation—what would *you* do? Go on, admit it—I can't read minds and your partner can't either (even if they are looking at you with an "I know all" look right at this moment). If you're honest, the answer is "c." I don't think too many of us would honestly say no in that situation. We might like to think we would—we hope like mad our partners will—but we probably wouldn't.

If you're like most people, this little self-exploration exercise has left you feeling simultaneously guilty and turned on—and also terribly suspicious of your partner. I wrote this for a reason. Before we start exploring the darker, sinister side of affairs—those that *aren't* so innocent in origin—I wanted you to realize something. We're *all* susceptible to an affair, given the right (wrong?) circumstances. Yes, even you.

I'm quite harsh on people who cheat in this chapter and extremely skeptical about staying with someone who's cheated. If asked the question, "Should I leave if I find out my partner's been unfaithful?"

my knee-jerk—and often correct—answer is yes. That's because *most* partners only find out their partner's been unfaithful after they've fooled around repeatedly. *Very often*, even saying "yes" in the situation above leads to a repeat performance. You get a taste, get away with it once, and continue. The skies don't fall in after all. But I'm the first to admit this doesn't apply to every couple.

I really have come across the occasional person who's strayed—or their partner has—under circumstances like the above. A one-time-thing, never-done-before, never-repeated-again experience. Maybe even two slip-ups over a very, very long period. Do I think couples like this should split if that's the case? Throw away 15 good years, two kids, and what they've built together for a genuinely-not-proud-but-it-happened slip-up? No, I don't. So if this is why you're reading this chapter—you've done similiar or your partner has—there's your answer up front. When I use the word "affairs" from here on, I mean sleeping with someone you shouldn't on multiple occasions. There! Now that I've made myself clear, I'll move on.

Most of the advice in this chapter is aimed at the entirely innocent who want to know how to avoid affairs, people who've been seriously upset by their partner's infidelity—and those of you who don't want to be unfaithful but can't seem to keep your zipper up. (If you're the latter, please read Chapter 8 and forgive me for unashamedly trying to "cure you" by showing how it feels to be on the other side.)

Depending on which category you fall into, the word "affair" will conjure up one of two very different sets of emotions. Some of you immediately think of hot, steamy sex and erotic encounters; others think of pain, betrayal, deceit, and heartache.

If you're in a long-term, committed relationship, affairs are serious stuff, about as serious as it gets for most couples. Plenty of counselors will tell you it's possible to repair the damage caused by serious infidelity; personally, I'm not entirely convinced. So if you're contemplating having an affair, I'd strongly advise that you read the next section *very* carefully. In it, you'll find the latest research on affairs and the effect they have on relationships. A fair portion of the ideas are a result of studies by Shirley Glass, a leading U.S. expert on the subject.

What constitutes an affair?

If you're unsure, ask yourself, "If my partner caught me doing this, would they be upset?" If the answer is, "yes," it's an affair. You don't need to have sex, kiss, or even touch someone to be having an affair with them. You don't even have to meet in the flesh! You can have an affair via the phone, the mail, the Internet, or carrier pigeon if you're creative enough. Basically, affairs are about sharing intimate, romantic, and/or sexual feelings on a regular basis with someone other than your partner.

That's my definition of an affair, but what's more important is that you and your partner agree on your own definition together. Lots of people I know use the old Bill Clinton logic: if you haven't had intercourse, you haven't been unfaithful. Penetration is the unforgivable sin; a bit of harmless "messing around" never hurt anyone (except their partner when they find out).

> I was in a cafe when I noticed a gorgeous guy sitting alone at the other table. I smiled, he smiled back. Two minutes later, his girlfriend appeared from the bathroom. When she turned the other way to talk on her cell phone, he smiled again and shrugged, as if to say, "Hey, if I wasn't with her . . ." I held up my hand to show him my wedding ring. It meant nothing and it made both of us feel good. Attractive people don't go away when you're attached— you just don't do anything about it.
> Mandy, 31, professor

Why do people have affairs?

Both sexes have affairs to get something they're not getting from the relationship they're in—it's that simple. What's not so simple is defining what it is that's missing, because often the cheating partner isn't aware of it.

Sometimes, it is obvious. If you're not particularly interested in sex and haven't been for years, the cute redhead at your husband's office who wears slit-to-the-navel tops and licks her lips is going to be pretty damn tempting. If your partner's a workaholic and your self-esteem's at rock bottom, you might have an affair to prove you're still attractive to the opposite sex and to boost your self-confidence. Other people cheat on "perfect" partners for that reason alone: they're sick of perfection. Some people are searching for something they lacked as a child, others for lost youth. Whatever it is, few of us realize that's what we're really after while we've got our legs in the air in a motel room.

Why do men cheat?

It must be because they're not happy at home: that's what most of us naively believe. Unfortunately, it's not necessarily true. According to Shirley Glass, many men who love their partners and have great sex at home still *never* turn down an opportunity to have something on the side. Fifty-six percent of the men she surveyed who'd had affairs said their marriages were happy (versus 34 percent of women).[8] Men in long-term marriages who have affairs report very high marital satisfaction. Women in long-term marriages having affairs report quite the opposite—they have the lowest satisfaction of all. Everyone's marital satisfaction went down the longer they were married, *except the men who had affairs*.[9] Horrifying, isn't it.

> The female brain is slightly smaller than a male's but it has no significance on her brain's performance. On average, a man has around four billion more brain cells, but women generally test around 3 percent higher in general intelligence than men do.[7]

Why do women cheat?

There used to be a theory that men were genetically programmed to sleep around because their function was to populate the earth. We've evolved since then—like, we don't walk on four legs anymore—and the other thing that blows that theory out of the water is that, these days, women are cheating almost as much as men are.

We have affairs for the same reasons men do. To recapture that "newness." They're forbidden, you're not supposed to have them and it's an unfortunate trait in both sexes that when we're told we can't have something, it immediately becomes more desirable than a family-size block of Cadbury's chocolate. Most affairs don't survive once they're out in the open: the whole point of them is that they're secret and naughty.

One conservative estimate stated that 40 percent of women admitted to an extramarital affair.[10] The real stats are likely to be much higher. Most of us balk at ticking the "yes" box in surveys for fear of somehow being found out, and our definitions of affairs are also dubious. In another poll the resounding majority (67 percent) agreed that an affair does not have to include intercourse, and the majority also ruled that emotional transgressions are just as bad as sexual transgressions.[11]

Why *did* these women feel the need for someone other than their partner? Many said they had an affair as a "reward" for being such a supportive mother and wife. Others believed it was the direct result of a critical life event (like pregnancy, a new job, or a partner changing jobs). Plenty of women said a partner who isn't affectionate, who won't listen or talk to them, and who failed to notice the terrible state the relationship was in was enough reason to justify having an affair. Sometimes, they did it to "get back" at a partner who'd betrayed them. Self-esteem was also right up there. Not convinced your partner finds you attractive? An affair gives a much bigger boost to the ego than a new haircut and a visit to the Clinique counter. Usually, women tend to have affairs with men who are the opposite to their partner, or, actually, just like them but much younger.

We're far more susceptible to having affairs today than our grandmothers were. In the old days, women usually had one sex partner: their husband. These days most of us have premarital sex so it's not such a big deal to share our bodies with another man: we've done it before. We're financially independent and often work, spending our day mixing with the opposite sex.

Both sexes are susceptible to having affairs to fix unhappy childhoods. If we lacked security as a child, we'll often seek out a marriage partner who provides stability. Once we're married and feel secure, we may have an affair with someone like the difficult parent who made us "insecure" in the first place. It's an attempt to rewrite history: if we can make that sort of person love us, somehow it will make the parent love us. Odd, but the subconscious has a habit of working in weird ways.

Your partner dotes on you. Surely they're immune to the temptation of an affair?

More so than most—but *you're* not. The person who gives the most in the relationship—really looks after it and nurtures it—is the person less likely to have an affair. Trouble is, they can become so fixated on the "relationship"—building a nice home and financial future— they forget the person they're having it with. The partner feels neglected, and seeks attention elsewhere. As Glass puts it in a recent article, "A relationship is like a fire. You can let it die down but not out. Even if you're in another part of the house, you have to go back every once in a while to stoke the coals."[12]

You're more likely to have an affair if . . .

- You work in an office where others play around.

- Your parents had one.

- Your culture accepts it's normal.

- You believe affairs are "justified" under special circumstances (you're "in love").

- You work in a high-drama profession.

- You travel a lot.

- You're a high income earner.[13]

How are most people found out?

If you're having great sex, your partner can't possibly be having an affair, right? Glass calls it "the hydraulic pump theory": you only have so much energy for

> My girlfriends don't understand me at all. I've really got no interest in playing around because I know damn well Steve would know the minute I walked in the door. Why throw away all we've got for one hour of what will probably be bad sex anyway?
> Pamela, 23, student

sex, so if you're getting it elsewhere, you won't want it at home. Wrong again. Some people are more passionate at home when they're having sex on the side. The affair sexually arouses them.[14]

It's technology rather than bedroom performance that trips people up. Hit the "redial" button on your partner's cell phone. Look through that nicely itemized cell phone bill and call the number that's called most frequently. Pick up their beeper and see "Darling. Call Me" displayed on the screen. More methods of communication mean more to cover up. Despite this, the fact remains that if you truly *don't* want to be discovered and actively cover your tracks, you probably won't be. If you get found out, you either don't care if you do or aren't being diligent.

Does it mean they don't love you if they're having an affair?

Not necessarily. But it does mean they don't respect you and they have a different value system. Generally, men have sex-based affairs; women have emotion-based affairs. Glass's research shows 44 percent of men who'd had extramarital sex had slight or no emotional involvement. Only 11 percent of women reported the same.[15] A continuing affair for women usually does mean she's not having her emotional needs met and is growing apart from her partner.

Because both sexes have affairs for different reasons, we assume our partners have them for the same reasons. Men assume that if there's emotional involvement, there's sexual involvement. Women assume if there's sexual involvement, there's emotional involvement. Both could be, and often are, wrong. Lots of women have "affairs" that don't include sex: lots of men have affairs that include nothing *but* sex.

Is it ever just about sex?

Some affairs are and most certainly include it. If it is purely a sex affair, it's usually very *hot* sex. Let's face it: if your partner thinks leaving the lights on is risqué, a hint of something more erotic is very appealing. A girlfriend of mine said she was in the park, eating an ice-cream cone at lunchtime and chatting with a guy from her office that she ran into. He told her she had ice cream on her mouth, leaned forward and licked it off with his tongue. That one, simple gesture was enough for her to have an affair with him because her boyfriend wouldn't dream of doing something so spontaneous and sexy. That affair was definitely about sex. Believe me. Spur-of-the-moment, no-strings sex may represent nothing more than a need for it and taking advantage of an opportunity. But it still breaks the trust bond and, if discovered, has the power to destroy a 20-year relationship in one second flat. Women tend to be better at coping with a partner having a one-night stand than men. While few are thrilled, they find it easier to deal with an impersonal fling than a long-term liaison where their partner shared feelings. Men think the opposite. They'd rather you stared lovingly into someone's eyes over 100 romantic dinners than shred the sheets with a stranger for ten minutes. Again, it all goes back to the sex/love, male/female thing.

Is there anything positive about having an affair?

Glass says one of the things people like best about affairs is that they get the chance to start over and be who they want to be.[16] If you've been with the same partner forever, you're usually pigeon-holed into a role. You might have changed dramatically from the person you were when you first met your partner, but they're still likely to see you as you were, rather than the person you've become. If you like the person you've become with your lover, you might not want to return to being "yourself": the "old" you, the "you" your spouse married. (Ironically, plenty of partners would love the "new" you but rarely get the chance to see it. I know plenty of betrayed partners who say, "What! He wanted to be more adventurous in bed? God knows I would have loved it if he had been!")

Glass says she rarely asks about "him" or "her"—the person they had the affair with—when she counsels couples after an affair. "I ask about 'you.' What did you like about yourself in that other relationship? How were you different? What can you do to be that person with your partner?"[17] She says an affair holds up a vanity mirror, the kind with all the little bulbs around it: it gives you a rosy glow to the way you see yourself. The marriage offers a make-up mirror, which magnifies every little flaw.[18] Ironically, it's the make-up mirror type of love that's the real one. It means you're loved *despite* all your flaws.

Why do affairs destroy relationships?

"Thou shalt not sleep with other people" is a pretty standard couple clause. So, for a start, the guilty party is breaking a vow. They've taken what was yours alone—sexual and emotional intimacy—and shared it with someone else. It's not special anymore because it's not something you share exclusively together.

If you love someone and they supposedly love you, you feel safe. It's the two of you against the world. When someone has an affair, everything you trusted is gone and you have to rethink what relationships are all about. If you've been hurt in the past by someone cheating, being hurt by "the one person I finally thought I could trust" is even more devastating.

It's also destructive, because lying goes with the territory and honesty is the basis of most good relationships. Glass says there are two types of lying people use when having affairs. The "lie by omission" is when you say, "I stopped in at Jenny's on the way home." It's the truth but you've omitted the fact that you were at Jenny's for five minutes and licking Brad's thigh (and other parts) at his house for the rest of the hour. The "lies of commission" are those "what a wicked web we weave" type of lies. "My watch stopped on the way home and the jeweler's was shut and I've got a really important meeting tomorrow and needed to be on time so I drove three hours out of my way to find another jeweler and it turned out they were shut as well so I—" The long, elaborate, made-up excuses that get more and more complicated to remember.

Even if you do pull through after an affair, there's a loss of innocence and a scar. It takes years of hard work to rebuild trust, if indeed it can be. Couples who do end up staying together often find the relationship's tinged with resentment, sadness, and guilt. If most people stopped and mentally pictured their partner's face if they found out, they wouldn't have an affair in the first place. If you're tempted, it's a good tactic.

How can you tell if your partner's having an affair?

- Your instincts tell you it's true.

- They're less interested in talking generally. (They're worried they'll slip up.)

- They've changed their routine or habits. Jogging at 7:00 P.M. (with aftershave on) rather than 7:00 A.M.

- They've lost weight/pumped up/revamped their wardrobe with no encouragement from you.

- They want sex more or less than usual. Less, they're getting it elsewhere; more, the affair's boosted their desire for sex in general.

> I'd suspected for a while but the first I *knew* Gary was cheating was when I got a call from his mistress's husband. "Your husband has ruined my marriage," he said, sobbing on the end of the phone, "Do something." I did. When Gary walked in the door, all smiles and, "How was your day, honey?" I handed him a packed suitcase and said, "Leave."
> Shirley, 42, mother

- You've found a clue. A box of matches from an unfamiliar restaurant, unexplained florist bills.

- A new "friend" is suddenly included frequently. In an attempt to cover up an affair, some people pass off their lovers as friends to explain seeing them so often.

- There are too many "wrong numbers" to be a coincidence.

- A friend drops hints. Men tend to cover up for each other, women will often drop subtle hints.

- Your body warns you. You're plagued by yeast infections or feel abnormally tired and teary. You're being exposed to your partner's lover's infections and/or your body's accepted what your heart doesn't want to.[19]

- You find yourself deliberately not thinking about "it." What you won't *know* can hurt you—both physically and mentally. If your partner's not practicing safe sex, you're at risk of contracting an STD or, worse, HIV. If you're crying "for no reason," getting headaches, feeling rundown —again, it's your body's way of saying, "Hey, you might not want to admit it. But *I* know you think they're cheating and I'm suffering for it."

Should you confront a partner who you think is having an affair?

If you truly want to know— and can cope with—the answer, definitely. It's the only hope the relationship has got of surviving. If your partner feels bad about what happened or is still happening, they may well feel relieved to be discovered.

Should you ask for details?

Anyone who's had a long-term affair has led a double life. They've lied. Said they were somewhere when they were actually with someone else. It's natural to want to find out when you were lied to so you can go back, put all the pieces together, and make sense of it all. Another reason we ask for details is because we want to know how good our instincts were. Were we right to be suspicious that night he was late from work? Did her car really break down?

Then there's plain old curiosity. What did this person have that I don't? We don't just want to see the bed where the dreaded deed took place, we want to see the kitchen where the coffee was made afterward.

They're reckless, ruthless, and unreliable. Constantly late, they check their reflection in the mirror frequently, interrupt while others are speaking, leave the lights blazing when they walk out of a room, run up debts, play hurtful practical jokes, and aren't kind to animals. Who are they? According to U.S. sociologists, this is a portrait of people most likely to cheat on their partners. After interviewing 107 couples, they discovered infidelity wasn't the only thing straying partners had in common. They also shared these key personality traits.[20]

Where they both sat, whether she knew he took three sugars and not much milk. If we don't get the details, we make them up. She looks like Julia Roberts, he looks like Brad Pitt. If the partner refuses to give details, our imaginations conjure up the most painful scenario possible. She's thinner/wittier/better in bed/more successful than we are. The more details we get—good and bad—the more the affairee becomes human and less of a threat. Also, as Glass believes, the more our partner will tell us, the more likely we are to trust them again.[21] If they withhold details, they're protecting them. Not a fab feeling when it's loaded on top of all the rest.

Repeating the story over and over until it no longer feels like someone's stabbing at your heart with sharp knives can be part of the healing process. Certain questions definitely need to be answered. Like: Who was it? Are they or were they in love? Why did they do it? Where did they have sex (in the bed you share together)? Is it now over?

Should you confess to an affair?

If your partner has evidence and confronts you, confess. Denying it when there's solid evidence is ridiculous. As for confessing when your partner has no idea, I wouldn't. It might make *you* feel better, like the guilt's been lifted off your shoulders, but all it does is cause them intense pain. If you want to confess because you want to save the relationship, don't. Instead, stop the affair and work hard at doing just that.[22]

Does it usually work out if the two people having an affair leave their partners to be together?

Not usually. Glass estimates only 10 percent of people who leave their relationships for affairs end up with the affair partner.[23] In most cases, the appeal was the affair itself, rather than the person. Doing something secretly. Also, there's often a high level of mistrust. After all, they both know each other is capable of lying and cheating because they've had first-hand experience. Couples that do survive are usually the rare few who had an affair for no other reason but love. They finally found their special person but were unfortunately married or involved at the time.

EIGHT WAYS TO REDUCE THE RISK OF AN AFFAIR (YOURS AND THEIRS)

1. **Make sure you both agree on what monogamous means.** Sit down together and spell it out. Is kissing someone being unfaithful?
2. **Make it very plain, very early on in the relationship that you would leave if your partner cheated, no matter what the circumstances.** If they're 100 percent certain you're not going to hang around to hear the excuses, they'll be much less likely to take the risk.
3. **Have an affair with each other.** Meet during your lunch hours in a hotel room and pretend you're being naughty. Play the part: say, "Darling, how did you manage to get away?" The couple that plays together, stays together.
4. **Don't give in to impulses.** If you're tempted, picture your partner's face if they could *see* you sharing parts of yourself you'd promised to reserve for them exclusively.
5. **If your partner says they're unhappy, take it seriously.** If your partner says they don't feel loved, *do something about it*. It doesn't mean the problem's gone away if they stop complaining, they've simply given up. You have been warned.
6. **Do a once-a-month check on your partner.** Ask them "Are you happy? Is there anything you'd like me to do more of or less of, both sexually and emotionally?"
7. **Do things as a couple, even if you've got kids.** The most precious gift you can give to your children is for them to see mom and dad happy. Plenty of experts say time is one of the biggest relationship killers today—as in lack of it. Couples who spend time together are less likely to stray. It's logical: the more fun you have together, the less inclined you are to seek it elsewhere.[24]
8. **Concentrate on what's good about being together as well as solving what's bad.** It's great to isolate problem areas and work on solving them, but don't forget to acknowledge the areas you're doing well in, too. Make an effort after an argument to point out a "plus" of being together.

Are they worth another chance? How to decide whether to stay with someone who's betrayed you

Some couples do survive infidelity but *only if both of you honestly think the relationship is worth it and the guilty person is prepared to do everything it takes to win back your trust and love.* If your partner has cheated on you, I want you to think long and hard about whether it's worth staying with them. A lot of the time, cheating partners don't deserve to be forgiven. Sit down for a few hours, somewhere quiet and private, and ask yourself the following questions:

Have they cheated on other people in the past?

If your partner's got a history of being unfaithful and they've just done it to you, forget it. You gave them a new chance and they failed dismally. They've always cheated, they've cheated on you, chances are they'll do it again (and again) until someone—hopefully you—tells them to go to hell and they realize they can't get away with it. Even then, they're a far worse bet than the average person.

Why did they do it?

This is crucial: it's your best indicator of whether someone deserves a second chance. A one-time incident with seemingly genuine reasons is a lot easier to forgive than repeated slip-ups or a long-term affair. Perhaps it was very early in the relationship and there was an unspoken rather than verbal commitment between you. An ex showed up at their house, they ended up drunk and in bed together. You might decide it's not worth throwing a perfectly good relationship away over this. I'd agree with you in this case. If they're sorry, they accept what they did was wrong, and there's no evidence it's been repeated or ever will be, hang in there. But if it happened *after* the relationship became serious, and both of you knew it was, that's a different story.

Do their reasons justify their behavior?

Put yourself in their shoes. If you were them, feeling the way they did, in the situation they were in, what would you do? Can you understand it? Could you see them being in the same predicament in the future? How would they react then? What's your gut reaction? Does it seem out of character or aren't you really surprised? Knowing all this, do you think, with time, you could trust this person again—or would you always feel insecure? What guarantees can they give you that it won't happen again? What would be different next time?

Also ask yourself this: Why do I want to stay with someone who behaved in this way? Why did I deserve to be treated this way? Or do you think there's a good, justifiable, I-can-live-with-this reason? Don't cling on just because you're scared of being alone. Don't let fear rob you of logic and dignity.

> **Monogamy is rare in mammals and almost unheard of in primates. Zoologists say it's a relatively recent—and somewhat idealistic—invention of certain human cultures.**[25]

What state was your relationship in when it happened?

As we touched on earlier, you'll be much more likely to forgive (if not forget) if you were aware your partner was unhappy, the relationship wasn't great, and you were suspicious. If, on the other hand, you didn't notice a single sign that anything was wrong—they seemed happy and affectionate and you thought you were living *The Brady Bunch*, it's incredibly hard to trust again. If there were no clues last time round, how will you know in the future if it happens again? What sort of person are they if they can sleep with someone behind your back and not show the slightest hint of guilt?

If the relationship was struggling, sometimes (very, very rarely, but it does happen), an affair can bring problems to a head and you finally solve them together.

Do they obviously regret what they've done?

I mean *really* regret it. A cut-off-their-right-arm-if-they-could-take-it-back kind of regret. Are they as miserable—if not more so—about the pain it's caused?

If you decide to stay

Leave them—if just for a few weeks

If you understand why they've cheated and don't honestly think it will happen again, by all means give it another go. But don't make it easy.

Your first reaction will be to cling to each other like limpets. Don't. If you live together, get them to move out for a few weeks. It'll show you mean business and give you a chance to sort through your emotions. If you don't live together, say you don't want to see them for a while. If you don't trust them enough to behave themselves without you for a few weeks, forget it now. Keep in touch with phone calls during the time apart, but that's it.

Write down all the questions you still need answers to

Keep a notebook handy and write down every single thing you don't understand about the affair or want further explanation on.

Meet after two weeks (minimum) or when you're feeling calmer

If they don't show up with black circles around their eyes, looking like they've camped out at Jenny Craig's, forget it. You've been torn apart by this—they should be, too. They should spend the time apart worrying themselves stupid whether they've lost you for good. If they don't think there's a good chance of it, they haven't taken it seriously and probably will do it again.

This won't be a pleasant meeting. Warn your partner there are lots of questions you still need answered, then whip out that notebook and hit them with all of them. This will be incredibly painful. When you see each other again, you'll probably both burst into tears. The reality of what they've done will hit both of you all over again. But you need to spend a few hours thrashing it all out so you can clear the air as much as possible.

Don't be surprised if you end up storming out when you hear some of their answers. Take five minutes to calm down, then try again. If you can't, arrange to meet in a day or two and try again. Don't go home together whatever the outcome.

Wait for the anger to subside

That might take a day, a week, a month, or longer. When you're feeling logical, rethink the situation. Now that you have *all* the facts or at least all the answers you're going to get, how do you feel? Are you still sure you want to try again? Still reasonably confident you'll both pull through and there's enough to work with? Now's the time to move back in or start seeing each other regularly again. You're ready to start healing. Read this book cover to cover, especially the parts on building good communication skills. Get your partner to do the same: you need to talk and listen to each other to get through this.

LEAVE OR STAY?: THE CHECKLIST

Does the unfaithful person:

- Understand what sparked the affair and believe any problems can be rectified?
- Accept what's happened rather than deny it's happened?
- Realize how much pain they've caused you—and show it?
- Accept full responsibility for the betrayal, no matter what shape your relationship was in? The onus is on *them* to fix it, *not you.* As Glass says: it's not what the betrayed person can do to make the wandering partner happy, it's what the unfaithful person can do to make their partner happy.[26]

Do you:

- Feel confident you'll know when your partner is lying again?
- Feel confident they won't do it again?
- Think, with time, you could trust them again?

Healing: when will the pain go away?

"How long will it take before the pain goes away?" Louise asked me, one month after she found out her much-loved husband had a year-long affair. She had lines on her face that weren't there last time I saw her. Her eyes were weird: she had the look people get when they've just witnessed a horrific car accident and can't forget it. She'd lost at least ten pounds and had on one brown shoe and one black shoe. The pain she was feeling was so intense, if you reached out you could touch it.

It's pretty hard to answer a question like that. My honest response would have been "never." As it turns out, the pain went away after two years—when she left her husband. The wound was too deep to heal. How quickly *you'll* heal depends on the level of betrayal. The more intense and intimate the relationship, the harder an affair hits. If someone cheats after they've been together three months, it hurts, but if someone cheats three years into a relationship, it hurts horribly. For this reason, I've directed this section to couples who've been together for a couple of years before the incident—and want to stay together a long time.

> The absolute, total indignity of it all was that I suffered through two months of couples' counseling, trying to work it all out with him. Two months of pain and heartache and at the end of it, he dumped me anyway.
> Kate, 25, nurse

Some people recover quickly from an affair, others will take longer. Your personality has a lot to do with how quickly you'll heal. If you're a happy, "up" type of person who recovers from life's knocks easily, it will take you less time to get over a betrayal than someone who tends to dwell on the negative—or has been betrayed before.

Taking blame

One of the most common questions after an affair is, "Will our relationship ever be the same again?" The answer is no. Your old relationship is dead and you need to build a new one. That's not necessarily a bad thing. The new relationship might be even better than the first in lots of ways, but make no mistake about it, it's never going to be as "pure" as it was. The innocence and trust are gone and can never be resurrected. The aim is to replace it with other qualities, like, "We are survivors—even this didn't break us up."

You will feel angry and insecure for months, maybe longer if you've been together a long time. Your natural inclination will be to take it out on your partner—and rightly so. If they're truly worth giving another chance, they'll put up with whatever you dish out and reassure you each and every time you get upset. If they don't do this, tell them, "You caused this. You're the one who betrayed me. You're the one who broke the trust. It's up to you to get us through this." Again, the onus is on the person who strayed to fix the relationship—not the innocent victim.

Working together

According to Shirley Glass, one of the goals of healing the damage from an affair is to let the unfaithful person express all the parts of themselves they were able to satisfy within the affair.[27] This might be the freedom to be the "new" them, or reworking the relationship to satisfy something they were craving. Lots of men married to super-competent women, she says, have affairs with weak women so they feel needed. This doesn't mean you have to ditch the business suit for an apron, but letting him see more of your vulnerable side might be a good idea. If she had an affair because you spent every waking hour at work, set limits. Take weekends off, bring work home rather than working late in the office.

Rebuilding trust

The only way to regain trust is to be honest—about everything, but most particularly about anything relating to the person involved in the affair. If you work with them, that means coming home and saying, "I saw Rachel today and she was hassling me to have a drink. I told her 'I'm so *not* interested it's not funny. I'm going home to the person I love.' " If you don't reveal things like this, you run the risk of your work friend, John, seeing the two of you talking intimately, going home and telling his wife, Joan, it's all on again. Joan tells Shirley, her best friend, who happens to work with your partner's best friend. Get my point?

Your partner shouldn't have to ask for information like this, you should offer it freely—and follow it up with tons

> I got propositioned by a real babe once. There was no way Karen would find out but I didn't care. I loved her so much I didn't give it a moment's serious consideration.
> Ian, 33, architect

of reassurance. Eventually, you'll talk about the affair and events and people relating to it, less and less. But it will always crop up again in conversation, even if it's once every five years.

A well-on-the-way-to-recovering couple, says Glass, will have moved past the basic details ("Did you have oral sex?") to searching for meaning ("If you knew it was wrong, why didn't you stop?").[28] Work on taking the positive view that your relationship could be better because of what happened. It's forced you to talk more openly, to spell out needs and expectations clearly.

The signs of recovery

Psychotherapist Mira Kirshenbaum puts it perfectly when she says time heals all *healable* wounds. In other words, if you're not feeling better after a period of time, it's not going to work—ever—with the person who betrayed you. These are some signs time is healing your wounds. I've included some of Kirshenbaum's ideas in this realistic timetable for positive healing.[29]

After the first month

- You have moments when you can calmly discuss couple issues (not relating to the betrayal) with your partner without dissolving into tears or feeling angry.

- You have a feeling things will work out in the end.

- There's some sign of "cooling off." You're still as angry as hell, but it's not consuming your life.

- The cheating partner shows obvious signs of guilt and accepts blame.

After two months to one year

- You can discuss the incident for a few minutes, quite rationally, before you start feeling upset.

- You forget about it for hours at a time.

- You've gone back to doing some of the things you used to enjoy together before "it" happened.

- You find yourself being affectionate, like you used to, for a day or so, "forgetting" to punish them by withholding affection.

- You can imagine trusting them 90 percent.

- You don't feel like vomiting every time you think about what happened.

After the first year

- Your relationship reverts back to "normal" for months at a time. There are still rough patches when the pain resurfaces but it goes away again.

- You can listen to your partner's explanation of how and why it happened without getting very upset. The intensity has eased to a "livable" level.

After the first five years

- You both feel you've learned from your mistakes and are confident they won't be repeated in the future.

- Your partner still accepts responsibility for what she did but you've stopped pointing the finger of blame.

- You feel good about yourselves as a couple, despite what happened.

8

Bad Love Habits

Always falling for people who are wrong for you or treat you badly? Here are the reasons why and how to fix it

••

By the time we've got our heads down the toilet, throwing up our first Jell-O Shot, most of us have a pretty good idea of who we think we are and how we think the world's going to treat us. By 18 years old, we're already 95 percent emotionally programmed: a trillion life experiences have molded our personality.[1] If all *your* life experiences have been wonderful, you're liable to be bursting with self-confidence, optimistic, and enviously free of any emotional baggage. Relationships will be a breeze for you. You'll be able to trust, love, and commit without a problem; go on to marry, raise children, and die happy. Good for you—if you exist.

It's a rare person who has a dream ride along life's highway. It's practically impossible to avoid the potholes, detours, traffic jams, and road blocks, and all of them leave their mark. Every time we have a bad or good experience or relationship, it affects our perception of the world. Unfortunately, just as good life experiences tend to set you up for more (happiness makes others happy), bad life experiences do the same (misery loves company).

What's *really* unfair is that you can't control all of the things that happen to you in life. Death and love are two obvious examples. We can't stop people from dying and we can't make people fall in love with us or stop them from falling out of it. We also can't stop people from treating us badly when we're a child. What you *can* do, though, is analyze what's happened to you so you understand the influence it may be having on your life now. The next step is to challenge those destructive attitudes, either by simply being aware of them or by seeking professional help.

Whatever's happened to you in the past doesn't *have* to dictate your future. Whether you had doting, fabulous parents or a mom and dad fresh from hell, loving, long-lasting relationships or a series of horrendous disappointments, you still have the power to be the person you'd like to be and live the life you want to live.

> **How you feel about yourself is strongly linked to how nurturing your parents and siblings were to you when you were growing up—mom especially. Stable, healthy mothering is great protection against most emotional problems.[2]**

KID STUFF: THE MESSAGES ABOUT LOVE AND LIFE YOU GOT FROM YOUR FAMILY

Parents are often given all the credit—and the blame—for how their children turn out. You get accepted into college, your parents are congratulated on producing such a smart child. You decide you'd rather be a Goth and do weird things with goat's blood, people say, "I wonder where George and Martha went wrong?" We all do it. If some snotty brat's wiping chocolatey fingers all over your skirt in the supermarket line, it's the parent you glare at, not the child. As adults, plenty of us blame our parents for any (or all) of our shortcomings. But how much is their fault—and what can you do to change it?

What nature gave you: genes

The genes you inherit influence your personality and thus your relationships with other people. One of the longest, most thorough studies of child development showed genes have a much greater effect on your personality than previously thought.[3] They're responsible for how well you do in school, how you get along with others, whether you choose a career as an executive or a life of crime. There's zilch you can do about genes, except be aware of what you've inherited and consciously fight against those that don't work for you.

What your parents gave you: environment

We don't just hatch out of an egg and raise ourselves. We're dependent on people around us, and no matter how much our parents love us or how good their intentions, they're human and make mistakes. After all, they have *their* own set of genes inherited from *their* parents, and how *their* parents brought them up influences the way they brought you up. Unless you've done some serious soul-searching (which is what this chapter is all about), we're all products of the generation before.

Ideally, parents are loving, supportive, and affectionate while simultaneously encouraging their children to be independent and make their own decisions. That's the theory. Unfortunately, not too many of us grow up with Mike and Carol Brady as parents. Some parents are cold and distant, others cruel and abusive. Most muddle their way through, alternating between Parents of the Year and "Oh, for God's sake, what do you want *now!*" parents, depending on how far behind on the mortgage payments they are. All parents have some flaws, and as a little child, you are like a sponge, soaking up whatever their attitudes were and reacting to the way they treated you.

Mom and dad in the bedroom

One of the most important influences on the romantic relationships you have now is the relationship your parents had. We learn how men treat women, how women treat men, and how a relationship functions by the way our parents behaved toward each other.[4] Scary thought, isn't it. Now here's the really scary part: *no matter what sort of relationship your parents had, you'll subconsciously search to find a replica of it, or (if you've consciously thought about it) the complete opposite.*[5] Sometimes that's healthy. If you admired your parents' partnership, it's sensible to look for the same. It's also sensible to want something completely different if you didn't. The problem with all this is that we're naturally pro-grammed to look for mom and dad clones. As I said, unless you're intensely aware of what your subconscious is up to, you aren't even aware of what's going on.

I went out with a guy once who said the most attractive thing about me was my independence. Yet what did we fight about the most? My independence and his feeling like he wasn't needed. When I met his parents it all fell into place. Look up "door mat" in the dictionary and there was a picture of his mother: he spent the entire visit telling her to stick up for herself. So while he admired me because I was capable and strong, he was *used to* the opposite scenario. Intellectually, he thought it was great; emotionally, it felt uncomfortable. Being aware of influences like these can make sense of those confusing conflicts.

> **I hated my father for years—it's only now I realize he did the best he could. He wasn't around as much as he should have been because he had to work seven days a week to pay the bills. No one can be purely a parent 24 hours a day. I now accept it wasn't choice that stopped him from being there for me, it was necessity.**
> Sven, 24, physiothera-pist

Your opposite-sex parent: who you're modeling your future partner on

 FOR HER

The way you feel about your father affects the way you feel about all men.[6] He's the first man you met, the first you got close to, so we tend to judge all men by him. My father is a good-looking, successful businessman. He's always impeccably groomed, has traveled the world, and mixed it with the best of them. He also happens to be refreshingly down-to-earth, has always looked out for the underdog and couldn't really give a damn about money so long as he's got enough to brew his own beer. Growing up, I thought all men would be like him. It's only now I realize you don't often find all those qualities in one person, and measuring boyfriends against this ideal is unfair.

If your father was successful, you go out there thinking all grown-up men will be. If he was nice, all men will be nice to you. If he wasn't so nice, you think quite the opposite. In fact, if you don't trust men, dad's usually got something to do with it.[7]

The old theory that women who love their fathers marry a man just like him does have some truth to it. If dad looked like Sean Connery on a good day, you probably are attracted to good-looking men. If he looked like Franken-

> **If you had a doting father, you're likely to reject men who don't adore you. If your father wasn't the hugging, affectionate kind, the message you got was: I'm not sexually attractive.[8]**

stein's monster on a bad day, you'll probably be less impressed by looks and more attracted to personality. But your partner doesn't have to *look* like dear old dad to be similar to him—he might be similar in personality.

Often, it's the *type* of relationship you had with your father that you're trying to replicate.[9] If he was warm and wonderful and loved you no matter what, you'll probably try to find a guy who'll do just the same. If dad was distant and didn't show any love or affection, unfortunately, the same thing can happen. You may find yourself drawn to guys just like him—cold, uncaring men—*because that's what you're used to.* That was your first male–female relationship, so it feels normal to you.

 FOR HIM

It's worth reading the "For her" section above because most of it also applies to mothers and sons. If your mom was a stunner, she could well be your blueprint for what you consider attractive in a partner. Again though, it's more likely you'll seek out the same *type* of relationship.

If you had a good relationship with your mom, it's likely you'll choose to settle down with someone who has the same personality

YOUR OPPOSITE-SEX SIBLING

For her

Women learn a lot from a close relationship with a good brother: it can set you up for a lifetime of easy, comfortable relationships with men. Having a brother means you've got a walking, talking, live specimen of manhood to study, experiment, and practice on during those angst-ridden, sexually formative years. As an adult, you've got the male perspective covered by someone you know and trust.

If you grew up with a brother you admired, you're likely to relate better to men in general. It's because you've seen men as real people rather than knights in shining armor. Women with brothers tend to have a more realistic, rational view of men because they've spent time around males they're not sexually involved with. You've seen that men can be competitive and seem to think more highly of their guy friends than their girlfriend, but also that they cry and have bad-hair days. If he puts a brotherly arm around your shoulder now and then, you'll also learn that men can be supportive. There's lots of nice messages a brother can give you about how men treat women.

If you didn't have a brother, it's hardly your fault. Just be aware that you'll be more likely to view men as future boyfriend or marriage material rather than potential friends. If you attended an all-girl school and didn't have friends with brothers, your contact with men was even more limited. Men were—and still may be—mysterious creatures who made you giggle, blush, and hide your face. Very often, the only males you may have mixed with were those who asked you out. Because of this, you've got higher romantic ideals: men bring flowers and chocolates and smell of aftershave and hair gel. Girls with brothers know what teenage boys really smell like (and it ain't pleasant!).

Feeling sorry for yourself if you're brotherless? Sure, you missed out in some areas but you're still better off than the girl who grew up with a not-so-nice male sibling. Some brothers are outright cruel or unbalanced. They drill holes in bathroom walls to watch their sisters shower, get drunk and make sexual passes at them. Trusting your brother is important, and if he breaks this trust, especially with sexual boundaries, you can end up with long-term difficulties and bad messages. Often you'll shut down your sexual side altogether, to be safe.

Brothers who are cold or dismissive of sisters also leave their mark. If your brother treated you as a second-class citizen, ridiculed you, criticized or ignored you, he sent a strong message about how other men will treat you. If you're lucky enough to go on to date caring and sharing type of boyfriends, it will dilute the effect. Date a bastard and your initial impressions will be confirmed. A good brother–sister relationship celebrates the differences between men and women; a bad one reflects the age-old battle between the sexes.

For him

While your sister was surreptitiously studying you, you were doing the same with her. When your sisterless friends were still trying to figure out how to get to first base, you were way ahead in deciphering what makes girls tick. You saw that women tend to be more emotional, noticed that she talked a lot, took a long time to get ready, and that her girlfriends were important. When you went out with a female, you understood her a little better. Later in life, your sister's often the one you'll turn to for clues on why your girlfriend's upset when you wouldn't have the foggiest notion why.

As with women, if you didn't have any sisters, the opposite sex may seem a bit confusing. If your pals were sisterless as well, you may have grown up to be one of those men who are fond of saying, "I just can't figure women out." As a child you probably ran around the playground passing "girl's cooties" on to others; as an adolescent you were probably shy on dates, the shoe-shuffling, blushing guy with a constantly bobbing Adam's apple.

If your sister was an out-and-out bitch, you grew up being highly suspicious of women. The message you got from her: men are the enemy. That doesn't seem true (you're nice, your friends are nice), so you reinterpret it to read: women are the enemy. Again, a few experiences with understanding, open girlfriends can break the mold. Dating ice-queens reinforces your worst fears.[10]

type as hers. If she was a homebody and dad reveled in being looked after, you'll probably be attracted to a traditional girl who's happy to stay home, bring up the kids, and warm your slippers by the fire. If you thought mom sold herself short, you may consciously search for someone who's kicking ass in the boardroom.

The way your father treats your mother is your blueprint of how you'll treat women. You learned from dad when and how often to send flowers. Mom's response will dictate just how far you think wooing will get you. The more carefully you look at the dynamics between your parents, the more you'll discover about your own relationship strengths and weaknesses.

The parent – partner checklist: how much influence do your parents have on your love life?

B **FOR BOTH OF YOU**

It's worth analyzing the effect your parents have, to make sure your instincts are guiding you in the right direction. Spend an hour or so doing this exercise—you might be surprised what it turns up!

How do you feel about their relationship? Do you want the sort of relationship your parents have or had for yourself? If you do, follow your instincts: you're already programmed in the right direction. If you'd rather stay single than endure a carbon copy of your parents' marriage, write down all the qualities you dislike about it and be on the alert. That's what you'll subconsciously try to turn *your* relationships into, because it's familiar to you. It's a good idea to show serious partners what you've written down and to ask them to do the same with their parents' relationship. Both of you can then watch that the other doesn't lapse into unwanted behavior patterns.

How did your parents treat each other? Was it an equal relationship or was one partner dominant and the other submissive? It doesn't matter which sex was which: your brain's already chosen which role *you'd* prefer to play and is seeking out the matching bookend.

Did either parent have affairs? Pay particular attention if the answer is yes. Parental affairs have a dramatic impact on your future relationships. If you're female and dad had affairs, you've learned not to trust men like him. If mom was the one getting more than just tennis lessons, you might find yourself severely tempted to play around when you're given the opportunity.

If you're a male, watching dad cheat as a young boy sent you this message: this is how men treat women. You'll grow up thinking that's what all men do—or, if you were disgusted with him, turn out to be as faithful as old Rover (perhaps, hanging around when you actually *shouldn't*). Work out what attitude their affair left you with and decide if you like what you discover. If you don't—it's left you overly suspicious or scared of getting close—again, you'll need to actively fight against it.

Did your parents split? If your parents split up, you've learned how to leave. When your own relationship hits a problem patch, you may well bail out rather than stick around and try to sort out the mess. If your parents stayed together even though they were miserable, you're likely to stay put, even if you're as unhappy as they were.

How do your partners measure up? Write down ten adjectives to describe your opposite-sex parent, then do the same for past or current boyfriends or girlfriends. Are they unerringly similiar or completely the opposite? You should be able to work out from this whether you're trying to find a partner just like mom or dad—or steering clear of anyone like them.

Let go of the blame. Once you've done the deep analysis and know what legacies they've left you, stop blaming your parents for making you this way. The quicker you accept that it wasn't intentional and forgive them, the quicker you'll reduce the influence they have. Take responsibility for your life. It's pointless blaming your mother for being attracted to bad boys even if she did marry one. She had

> I stopped looking at my parents as mom and dad and started relating to them as friends. I let them into my life and stopped censoring conversations, gave them a chance to see who I really was. They surprised me by how interested they were— then *they* started opening up.
> Judy, 26, writer

her own influences. Instead, count yourself lucky for recognizing the pattern *before* you name your first child. Look for the positive things your parents gave you. Even if dad was an arrogant son of a bitch, maybe he taught you how to stand up for yourself. Your mother may be clingy and dependent but she *was* always there for you when you were a child. Recognize that, despite their flaws, your parents did their best.

GO OUT WITH WHO YOU WANT TO, NOT WHO YOUR PARENTS EXPECT YOU TO

Everyone who's close to their family would prefer to get the golden seal of approval on their partner and sometimes they *can* see things you can't. But part of growing up is a healthy emotional distance from your family—their opinion matters, but ultimately you should make up your own mind about who you go out with, and they should allow you to do that.

If they don't, it's up to you to make a stand.

If you're serious about someone, that relationship should come first, family second. If they don't like your choice, it's tough luck for them. You're well within your rights to say to your family, "I've chosen this person and I like them. I expect you to treat them with respect and if you can't behave politely, I can't involve you in that part of my life. I want you in my life but not if you can't respect my decisions and my judgment." If you feel silly saying this face-to-face, write your family a warm but firm letter along the same lines:

"Mom/dad/brother/sister, I felt you made X feel uncomfortable when we came over for dinner. I want you to understand how important he/she is to me" then add the speech above, putting it into your own words. Yes, it is formal but emotions run hot in situations like these and, in my experience, you're better off handing over a carefully worded letter than trying to talk it through.

If your family refuses to accept your partner, see them less frequently, minus him/her. Make it obvious you won't be seeing them as often as they'd like but if they insist you come solo, that's all you can offer. With time, they might soften.

Now, I've said all this assuming you haven't hooked up with someone who's treating you badly or an obvious bad choice. If your partner showed up drunk or stoned, kicked the cat, insulted your mother, and puked on the living room floor, I'm with your parents. Ditto the girl or guy who doesn't make a real effort to get along with and be liked by your family. It's a two-way street—and it's also a good test of how serious your partner is about you. If they're a nice person and intend sticking around, it's in their interest to get along with everyone. The more effort they make, the more they're showing how much they care.

DESTRUCTIVE RELATIONSHIP PATTERNS—AND HOW TO BREAK FREE

We all know someone who's been in a bad relationship. The girlfriend who married a nice guy, then left for *him*: the loser ex of hers whom everyone else hated. The bright, successful young lawyer who slays them in the courtroom but stays with a no-good girlfriend who's addicted to both drugs and other men. *Why did they choose them? Why don't they leave?* we think to ourselves. How someone so intelligent, attractive, and *normal* could end up in that situation really is beyond us.

When people constantly go out with people who are bad for them, it's usually because they've developed a destructive relationship pattern. It's not rotten luck—they're subconsciously *choosing* people who treat them badly because of something that happened in the past.

How healthy are *your* love habits? Skim through the following to see if any apply to past or current lovers.

You've got bad love habits if:

- **You love your partner, even though your head tells you you're not compatible.**

- **You're putting up with bad treatment.** You keep on loving in the face of abuse, neglect, and clear absence of any feeling on the other person's part.

- **You believe there is only one magic person out there who can make you truly happy.** Obsessive lovers have no safety net because they're convinced their partner is the only person who can make them happy. That's why they cling on so hard.

- **You've tried to leave in the past but can't.** Even though you're miserable in the relationship, you're unhappier without it.

- **They've left you but you won't accept they're gone.** Many people switch into denial. Even if their partner's married someone else, it means nothing ("They're living with them but their heart belongs to me").

- **Your relationships are always bad but the sex is fantastic.** Because emotions are stretched to screaming point, sex can be nothing short of spectacular. "I had sex every day for four years and loved every minute of it," says Jan, 22. "Even in the end, when I hated him, I still craved his body."

- **Your friends and family often don't like the partners you choose.** If you get along with your parents and friends and respect their opinions on everything else except your love life, pay attention.

- **You sometimes feel like you're on an emotional rollercoaster.** Settled isn't a word that describes your relationships.

- **Other relationships suffer when you fall in love.** You stop seeing friends, family, and other people who were important to you.

- **Your work and health also take a dive.** Does work come last when you're in a relationship? Do you become increasingly reliant on addictive substances like alcohol and cigarettes? Eat much more—or less—than you used to?

- **People who care about you often say your partners don't treat you as well as you deserve.**

- **You constantly think about a past lover whom you haven't seen or heard from in years.**

- **You find yourself returning to the same lover time and time again—even though it never seems to work out.**

- **You live for the day when you'll meet a perfect person and live happily ever after.** Your life won't officially start until then.

Feeling a little uncomfortable because most points are ringing true? Here's how to up your chances of making the next person you meet different from the last.

Ten steps to kicking the addiction

I'll go into specifics a little later, but whatever your particular destructive relationship pattern is, these general rules apply to you.

1. Work out what your pattern is

Think like a shrink. All therapists do is get you to think past the surface and pinpoint what's really happening below. Try this do-it-yourself therapy.

Write down what usually goes wrong with your relationships at the top of one page. For example:

Problem: I always go out with men/women who treat me badly.

On a separate sheet, do the parent–partner checklist exercise (above). Take a long look at what's in front of you. Can you see a connection between your childhood and your relationship problem? Try to tap into the emotions you felt as a child. If your parents fought fiercely, you might have thought, *I have to be really good or they'll start shouting at me.* Twenty years later, you're still sugarcoating every sentence and timid about upsetting people.

Is that the reason why you don't stick up for yourself and let people treat you badly?

Underneath your relationship problem, write down any influence your childhood has had. For example, for the problem list above, you might write:

Childhood influence: Because I grew up surrounded by anger, I avoid expressing anger now. I'm too scared to stick up for myself.

> **The rough times are there for a reason. Learn from them, toughen up if you need to, but don't carry around baggage for the rest of your life.**
> Sue, 42, flight attendant

Underneath those two statements, write down your aim: what you want your relationships to be like in the future. For example:

Aim: I want to be treated well. I deserve to be treated well.

Next, write down the sort of person you think would be able to achieve the aim you've written:

The sort of person who would be treated well in relationships:

- Has respect for themselves: doesn't let others take advantage of them, has a high self-esteem, and sticks up for themselves.

- Walks proud and tall: has friends who admire and respect them.

Try to list as many personality traits you can think of and add to the list whenever you think of more. Watch friends who are in relationships you admire. What is it about them that makes their partner respect them and treat them well?

2. Play pretend

Every morning, look at these personality traits—this is the person you'd like to be. Now you're going to pretend you *are* that person by acting the part. That's right, pretend the person you'd like to be is a character on TV and you've just won the role. Walk the way they would, dress the way they would, interact with people the way they would (and only the people they would). At the end of each day, record what happened. How did you feel? Probably like a complete idiot to begin with! Did people react to you differently? Close friends probably thought you were a little weird. If they do question the "new you," simply say, "I've turned over a new leaf." Keep friends who say, "Good for you!"; ditch those who respond with, "You'll never keep it up."

Continue "acting" for a few months and you'll notice two things start to happen. First, you're only acting part of the time because you're so used to the role you're playing, it's starting to feel more natural than the "real" you. Second, people are reacting to you differently, as though you *are* this new person.

No prizes for guessing what happens next: you *become* this person and no longer need to act at all. You attract partners who treat you well because the new you doesn't put up with any less. Easy, wasn't it!

3. When you next meet someone, don't have sex too soon

Sleep together before you get to know someone and you risk being emotionally bonded to a person you really have nothing in common with.

4. Don't slip back into old habits

Try hard to see people as they really are, not as you'd like them to be. Every single time a partner doesn't come through with a promise, think long and hard about if it's worth going further. They said they'd phone on a particular day but didn't? Challenge them. No one's so busy they can't make one phone call, even if it's just to say, "The market's crashed. I can't talk now but I'll call the minute I can."

5. Spell out your needs

Say, "I understand why you couldn't call for a long talk, but next time, a two-second explanatory phone call would be appreciated."

6. No second chances

One warning, then they're out. You need to be tougher on partners than the average person is, to break the doormat habit. Once you start giving second chances, you'll give third, and fourth, and so on.

7. Listen to your instincts

If you feel uneasy and not quite right about your relationship, sit down and work out why. Is it something they've said? Something they've done? A flirtatious look followed by a guilty one when you caught their eye? A comment by a friend of theirs, which they quickly glossed over? Do they seem like they're hiding something from you?

Keep analyzing until you pin down the source of that funny feeling and have a good idea where it came from. Then look for evidence to back up whatever theory it is you've come up with. If you find evidence, challenge your partner with it. Listen to their explanation but if you're not satisfied, leave.

8. Watch your self-esteem

Low self-esteem is nearly always the reason why people get stuck in obsessive, destructive relationships. Choose partners who make you feel like a million bucks.

9. Avoid drugs and alcohol

They skew your judgment.

10. Shift the focus from worrying about the relationship to worrying about yourself

Become obsessed with *your* needs and desires instead of your partner's. Have your own life plan, which doesn't include a partner but is flexible enough to involve one if they're special. This time, they're coming along with *you* for the ride, not the other way around.

Now, let's move into more specific problems and solutions.

Why do I fall for the same type over and over (instead of learning from my mistakes)?

Kate looked hard at the man sitting in front of her and wondered, as she had so many times before, why she didn't find him attractive. Tim was a close friend of hers who'd made it clear right from the start that he'd like more. Tall, blond, and athletic, he certainly didn't lack for female attention. Tim was intelligent, gregarious, and liked the same clubs and restaurants she did.

He made her laugh, he listened to her problems, he had everything she was looking for, except . . . "I guess he's just not my type," Kate sighed. "Pity."

Her friends would certainly echo that sentiment. Kate's "type" are dark, olive-skinned, handsome men who all have one thing in common: a tendency to stop calling once the relationship gets serious. At 28, Kate wants to settle down, maybe even start a family, except the guys she likes

Do you dwell on bad past events and find it hard to talk about your feelings? You could have a toxic personality—one that literally, makes you sick. Researchers found people who "bottle things up" suffer far more health problems than those who let it all out. Yet another reason to work through any negative emotions.[11]

don't share her enthusiasm. A case of looking for daddy, who also happens to be a dark-haired bad boy? Low self-esteem from being dumped time after time? Or the end result of one hot night in Greece when Kate, a 17-year-old backpacker, happily lost her virginity to a dark, handsome local bartender who gave her more than free drinks? Knowing Kate's background, my guess is it's a combination of all of the above.

As more and more people are seeking help from psychologists to solve relationship problems, the more counselors are discovering what shapes our sexual psyches. Why is it you think Robert De Niro is sex-on-legs and all your girlfriends see is an aging movie star with moles on his face? This is what researchers have come up with so far:

We lust after people who look or act like other people we love or loved

Ever met someone and struck up an instant friendship because you feel like you've known them for years? That sudden familiarity is usually because they have similar features or gestures to those of people you've gotten along with in the past. They might laugh the same as your best friend does or have the same shaped eyes as your much-loved aunt.

It's the same with sexual attraction. From the moment we're born, we continuously feed physical data about people close to us into our subconscious. The brain divides these physical characteristics into "people I like and were nice to me" and "people I don't like who hurt me"; then it tries to generalize. If two-thirds of the people you've disliked have big noses, you'll be suspicious of those who do. When we meet a potential partner, our subconscious checks it against the "liked people" list in our heads and tries to find the closest match. The more "chemistry" we feel, the more matches we've found.[12]

We do the same with gestures. Maybe a yearned-for ex had a habit of smoothing back her hair with the palm of her hand. If a girl standing next to you at the bar does the same thing, you'll look twice without knowing why. Your brain's telling you, "Hey! Remember Maria? She did that, so maybe you could fall in love with this girl as well!" The more "liked" gestures and physical characteristics a person clocks up, the more attractive we find them.

It's cute, but one that seriously can lead you to all the wrong people and stop you from meeting the right ones. Why? Because you're on dangerous ground when you choose partners based on looks and gestures—and that's exactly what your brain is trying to do. Like Kate, my internal "lists" constantly guide me to dark-haired, European-looking men. Blonds don't get a look. When I meet a blond guy, I instantly throw him into the "friend" basket rather than consider him as a potential partner, simply because when I was at college, every single blond guy I fancied didn't look twice at me. They didn't like me then so I don't lust after them now. Who knows how many potential Mr. Rights I've passed up simply because of their hair color!

If you're convinced you've got the same problem, deliberately date against type to break the stereotype. One great love affair with a blond would probably break my subconscious fixation on hair color (and if the dishy fair-haired guy in the Calvin Klein underwear ad is reading this and wants to volunteer, please feel free to write to my publisher). Ask your friends what they think your "type" is—you might not be as eclectic in your tastes as you imagine.

The first person we had sex with strongly influences who we're attracted to

Who we lost our virginity to, what they looked like, and how much we enjoyed the experience was a strong influence on who does it for us in the future. If your first experience was with someone blond and pretty and it was pleasurable, you'll unconsciously seek out people with the same build and looks over and over—even if they're not nice people. That's your "type." If it was a bad experience, you'll avoid anyone who looks like that—no matter how nice they are.

Again, it doesn't get you very far because we're being influenced by physical characteristics rather than choosing partners for healthy, logical reasons like compatibility, shared goals, and respect. Our personalized "sexual blueprints" are also responsible for choosing "bad" people who physically or mentally harm us. If the first time you had sex, it was a traumatic experience, sex may have become associated with violence. Even though the experience was horrifying and you have absolutely no desire to repeat it, you might find you can't get turned on when you're made love to in a gentle way. That first time set the blueprint.[13]

If *your* first-time sex involved rape or extremely violent or unorthodox sex and you think there's a pattern emerging, get help from an expert. If you're having minor relationship problems because you can't seem to break free of a "type" and think your first time might be responsible, try the following:

- **Be aware of your "type" and actively challenge it.** Pick partners for reasons other than looks. If they treat you with respect, seem like great company, and are interested in you, give it a go.

- **Work on your self-esteem.** A bad sexual encounter can leave us seriously doubting our sexual appeal and attractiveness.

Why do I fall for people who need rescuing?

Some people continually and repeatedly choose partners with problems. Women are particularly good at playing rescuer (a lost puppy brings out all those maternal, look-after-him instincts), but both sexes are guilty of it.

Why the need to play doctor and shrink? Because rescuers truly believe that if they love enough, give enough, and do enough, they'll save their lover from their problem. In return, their partner will be eternally grateful and (the pièce de résistance) never leave because they're dependent on them.

Not surprisingly, saviors often come from homes where at least one parent had problems. They saw the other parent devote their life to fixing the problem, so that's what they go on to do. (It's quite common, for instance, for women who marry alcoholics to have a daughter who marries an alcoholic.)

Children who've been through divorce and had a mother or father rely heavily on them are also prime candidates, as are kids who took on mom or dad's role and looked after the family because that parent was too busy or didn't care. You've learned to equate love with being needed. In order to feel loved you have to nurture and solve problems.

Fix-its

- **Screen all potential partners.** If they start pouring out their troubles on date one, two, or three, you've done it again—picked someone who needs rescuing.

- **Deliberately keep conversations with people you've just met on a lighthearted level.** Don't ask deep, personal questions. Don't invite confidences.

- **If someone tells you a problem, offer sympathy rather than a solution.** Say, "How awful for you," suggest they contact a support group or therapist to get help, then change the topic.

- **Only help people who'll also be there for you.** Be aware you attract people who'll take you for granted. Instead of being the first to jump up and say, "I'll do it," let others volunteer first.

Why do I fall for people who are married or involved with someone else?

Falling in love with one person who's married could just be bad luck, bad timing, and bad judgment. But if you've had more than one affair with a married lover, you're deliberately picking them for a number of reasons. Top of the list is self-esteem. It's a boost to the ego to be able to lure a married person away from someone they supposedly love. You *must* be special if they're in your bed. If you rapidly lose interest the minute your married partner does decide to leave their spouse, it's definitely a self-esteem problem. You don't want them, you want a person who is attached to someone else. It's a power game that's over when you're the official winner: you could have them if you wanted to.

> When your partner reacts strangely, they're often not reacting to you but to a parent's voice playing inside their head. Mom and dad are the hidden audience who constantly watch our lives.[14]

Another common influence: your childhood. If one or both parents abandoned you—they split, died, or seemed to forget you were there—you're repeating the pattern by finding adults who can't be there for you either. A married lover who's always running away from you—home to a spouse—feels nicely familiar. Similarly, if your parents put you down or criticized you, the message you got was, "I don't deserve to be loved." Sharing a partner with someone else—and getting the bum end of the deal—is all you think you deserve.

A third possibility is you're scared of intimacy. People who've been physically or emotionally abused by their parents or betrayed by past lovers often end up chasing married people. If you've decided—consciously or unconsciously—not to let someone get close to you in case you get hurt again, married people seem a great option. You've got a built-in excuse for not committing—they already have, to someone else—and the rejection factor is also lower. If they don't choose to continue the affair, it's not *you* they're rejecting. They're simply doing the "right thing" by their spouse.

Fix-its

- **Look hard at your childhood and past.** If you can fathom a reason, constantly be aware of it. The next time you're attracted to a married person, think, *It's not them I want, I'm really looking for—*. Or consider getting therapy. A few sessions with a no-nonsense counselor could uncover what you're really trying to get from these relationships.

- **Work on your self-esteem.** Let's be honest here, it's degrading to be "the bit on the side" and no fun spending Christmas and holidays alone while the person you love is playing happy family. Why anyone would voluntarily choose to be in this situation is beyond me. Why *should* you share someone you love? Don't you deserve to be number one, instead of in second place?

Why do I feel more confident dating people who don't quite measure up to my level?

You're scared of being hurt. If you're always better-looking, more successful, financially superior, and an all-round better package than your partner, you only feel comfortable in the power position. You'll never get dumped, because you're such a good catch.

Again, first look at your past. Did your parents divorce? Did you watch mom or dad go through agony trying to get over it? Did you see a best friend fall to pieces after a much-loved ex left? Has someone in *your* past betrayed you? This is why you'll only go out with people who are guaranteed to hang around.

Next, rate your self-esteem. Why don't you think you're good enough to hold the interest of someone on your own level? Are you trying to boost your ego through "sure-thing" relationships? Every time you leave someone heartbroken, your ego's getting fed. It's quite common for people who've been badly hurt in the past to climb back up the self-esteem ladder by dating from the bottom of the heap. The more superior they are to their partner, the less likely they are to be dumped. Each success (they dated but didn't get dumped), gives them a little more confidence to try someone "better" until, eventually, they're back to dating people who are the equivalent of themselves.

> Mom always said she'd wasted her life by staying home to look after Dad. In a sense, I got the law degree for her, because she didn't have the opportunity to. She's proud of me, but I think I got the message too clearly. I cooked dinner for my boyfriend the other night and I was gritting my teeth. It's like I'm not allowed to look after people or else I'll end up like her.
> Debbie, 34, lawyer

Fix-its

- **Have faith in your own ability to survive.** Imagine the worst possible scenario: you took a risk on someone and they left you utterly heartbroken. Sure, it would hurt for a while but you would survive—most of us do. Convince yourself you'd be okay even if your nightmare becomes reality, and you'll have the courage to take the risk.

- **Consider the alternative.** Dating an equal is far and above the most satisfying relationship of all. Do you want to share your life with someone who truly fulfills and stimulates you, or have a series of insipid, luke-warm love affairs that do little but make you feel guilty when you break it off, yet again?

Why do I always choose the bad guy over someone who adores me?

For a start, they're forbidden. When you were young, your mom said, "Don't eat all the cookies," so that was the first thing you did the minute she wasn't looking. And they tasted damn good, even if you did feel sick afterward. When you're older, she says, "Don't go out with bad boys or girls." So you just *know*. If she says bad boys and bad girls are bad news, they *must* be fun.

Think about it. What do bad people provide that the nice types don't? Excitement. Drama. *Fun*. The freedom to let your hair down, kick your heels up, and unleash *your* bad side. Because even nice girls and boys have one. Bad's always been appealing. Smoking, drinking, eating chocolate—we love doing things that are bad for us.

If your parents were really strict, you might deliberately choose someone who's a little on the wild side as an act of rebellion. If they've controlled everything in your life, bringing home someone with dreadlocks and a nasty tattoo on their tongue is the equivalent of saying, "Up yours! You can't control me anymore. I'm about to turn all your nightmares into reality."

We like "bad" because it's sexy. Put a person with a bad attitude and a great bod into a leather jacket or a short, short miniskirt and our hormones go crazy. We look at people who live on the wild side and think, *I bet they'd be into everything in bed*. We'll do things with them that we wouldn't dream of doing with a potential Mr. or Mrs. Right because *it doesn't matter if they judge us*. If you're not interested in a long-term, serious relationship and simply want a hot, sexy fling, you don't really care if they think you're wicked (in fact, it's better if they do). It's incredibly liberating to be able to unleash the erotic side of yourself and let loose, without someone looking down on you.

We've fallen for the rescue fairytale. It's also got a lot to do with ego. Not all bad boys and girls are bad underneath, and if you can be the one to change them, how fabulous must you be? We kiss the frog and turn him into a prince. It's the stuff of fantasies.

Opposites attract. If you're a "good girl" matched up with a "bad guy," you're both getting certain needs met—at least temporarily. Good girls usually have stable jobs, a bit of money in the bank, and lead pretty sensible lives. They don't need someone for security, they want someone to spice things up. And that's exactly what bad guys do. The bad guy usually has enough excitement and drama going on—what *they* lack is stability, and that's what the good girl gives them.

The beauty of this relationship is that the good girl gets to live on the wild side—but from a nice, safe distance—and the bad guy gets needed stability, without having to turn into one of those boring, nine-to-five morons they detest.

Short term, it works well. Long term, not so fabulous, because the bad guy's refusal to live by the rules usually wears thin for the good girl. The fact that they've got no money, you're always having to bail them out, you can't take them home to meet your parents—it's annoying. What you once saw as wonderfully spontaneous and unpredictable, you start to see as childish and irresponsible. In short, you want them to grow up—especially if you're thinking mortgages and kids. Even the hot sex loses its appeal over time unless it's balanced with a loving, snuggle-up sort.

Can you change a bad guy into a good one?

It depends. Have they always been wild or are they just going through a rebellious stage? Have they chosen to lead the lifestyle they do because it's their passion—or because they're secretly worried they won't measure up in the real world?

There are bad guys and *bad* guys. Some people appear bad just because they're leading alternative lifestyles. They have trouble meeting the rent and are a little too heavy on the booze and cigs because they're genuinely frustrated. If they're trying to break into a profession that's difficult to crack (like acting or the music world), they might have to live rough to be true to their lifelong dream. This type of bad guy isn't bad at all—but still don't expect to change him. He won't—and neither should he—until he really has exhausted every avenue. The day he comes home and says, "Darling. Guess what? I've just gotten a job as a bank teller," is the day he's given up. It's not a cause for celebration, it's the end of a dream. So if you're involved with someone like this and don't like the lifestyle, opt out now. It's not your right to change them, and if you do succeed, you'll be left with a shell and no substance anyway. Take away the dream and you take away the spirit.

Geneticists now believe there's a gene that makes women attracted to men who are bad for them. Aptly named "PRIC 1," U.S. researchers found women who carried PRIC 1 were 5 times more likely to date married men, 15 times more likely to back down in arguments with their boyfriends, and twice as likely to fall in love with guys who never called. A simple blood test could identify susceptible women in the future.[15]

The other type of bad guy has deliberately picked an alternative way of living through insecurity. If their goals are ridiculously high, they won't be judged too harshly if they don't make it. If they have no goals at all, again, they can't fail. If this is your partner, there is hope. You possibly can change them by giving them the courage to be themselves. But the bottom line is always this: do they want to change? You can't change someone unless they want to be changed.

The third type of bad guy is plain bad. Insecurity probably started it but the only way *he'll* change is with the help of a social worker, psychiatrist, rehabilitation, or possibly all three. If your partner is heavily addicted to drugs, alcohol, gambling, or sex, leave it to the experts to cure them.

If you only ever go out with bad boys

I'm going to mainly address this to women simply because we're more often the suckers in this situation. But keep reading if you're a guy with the same problem: the advice holds true for both.

While just about *all* of us find bad appealing in an odd sort of way, some women seem to find an endless supply of partners who treat them badly. Each time it happens you probably think, *I've learned my lesson. Never again*, but the next guy's just as bad as the last. If you're constantly being ripped off, cheated on, or treated badly, it's time to face some facts.

Here's the first truth: in a way, it's your fault. If you *only ever* date men who treat you badly, it's not simply a case of lacking judgment skills. No one's *that* unlucky. Believe it or not, you're unconsciously but *deliberately* seeking out a particular kind of man—and the most common reason for doing this—surprise! surprise!—stems back to your childhood. The first step to forging healthy relationships is to understand *why* you're choosing the men you are.

There are two basic childhood theories to explain your behavior. The first is that you're attracted to men who break your heart because subconsciously it feels "right" when a man makes you feel unloved. You might think, *Get out of here! Here's another one!* when you meet a bad boy, but your subconscious makes you stay. It whispers in your ear, "Hold on. This seems nicely familiar," and that's why you end up getting involved. This is what's happening when you feel like you can't help yourself.

The second theory is that you're searching for something that was missing while you were growing up: you're attempting to change history. Here's how it works. Say your parents were cruel or unloving. You'll tend to seek out men who are equally callous and try your hardest to make them love you. If they love you, somehow it makes up for mom and dad not loving you because, in the murky depths of your brain, they *are* mom and dad. You're also trying to convince yourself the problem was with your parents, not you. If a guy like your parents falls in love with you, you're effectively saying, "See, Mom? See, Dad? He's just as cruel as you were, and he can love me. It's your fault you didn't, not mine." You don't realize you're doing it, but you're actually not seeking love from the guy, but from one or both of your parents.[16]

Some swear playing out this ritual can actually be good for you.[17] If you can resolve unfinished childhood business by making a person like your father or mother love you, I guess it is a good idea. But it's not the sort of thing you set out doing. Like, "Okay. I'm going to go out there and look for someone who's critical, moody, and disapproving—all the characteristics I most hated in my parents—so I can finish my unresolved childhood business."

A more sensible way to approach it is to work through your problems on paper. For this exercise, you'll need to make three lists.

- **List one:** List ten adjectives that best describe your childhood by writing down this sentence and finishing it for me: *As a child I felt . . .* You might write down *unloved, unwanted, lonely, and sad.* Or you might write *happy, loved, supported, and encouraged.* It could well be a mix of both good and bad things.

- **List two:** Now list ten adjectives to finish this sentence: *The atmosphere in my childhood home was . . .* Was it happy, boisterous, and filled with lots of people? Or deathly quiet, tense, and uncomfortable?

- **List three:** Now write, *My boyfriends usually make me feel . . .* and list ten adjectives to complete that sentence. Your past lovers may have made you feel unworthy of them, criticized or not good enough, but there might be some good stuff in there. Again, it could be a combination of good and bad things.

When you've completed all three lists, have a good look at them. What's your initial reaction to seeing all this written down? Do the lists give you a nice, warm glow or do you feel quite sorry for yourself? If it's the former, your relationships are probably in pretty good shape: your parents made you feel good about yourself, your childhood environment was pleasant and your boyfriends are continuing the trend. You're reading this section because you've had one or two bad encounters with bad boys and are either curious or want to avoid a repeat.

You're also on the right track if you can see negative feelings on the first two lists that have positive matches on the third. For example, if "criticized" appeared on your parent and childhood home list and "accepted" appears on your boyfriend list, you're doing fine. You know what you lacked as a child and need now and are choosing men who'll give it to you.

If reading all three lists makes you want to lie down in the middle of a six-lane highway, keep reading—and have faith, you can break the pattern simply by being aware. Concentrate on comparing lists one and two to list three. Can you see any words that match up? Are the feelings you've described similar. Does it now seem obvious you're choosing men who are making you feel exactly how your parent(s) did? These are the reasons behind your behavior; now let's look at how to break it.

1. **Go back to Chapter 1 and do your partner and relationship wish lists to work out what you want from both.** (Keep the three lists you've just done (above) as a reference point for things you *don't* want from a partner or relationship.)
2. **Stick the partner and relationship wish lists to your bedroom mirror** (or at least somewhere where you'll see them daily). Read them so often you don't need to: they're firmly etched into your brain.
3. **If you're currently involved with someone who doesn't have *at least two-thirds* of the qualities on those lists, ditch them.** I don't care how much you like them, just do it.
4. **Tune your radar to spot men with fatal flaws.** Assume the worst, not the best, of men. Avoid anyone who's addicted to something, men who get angry easily, have extreme mood swings, or lose patience easily. Watch out for men who blame others for everything in their life, rather than take responsibility for their own mistakes, and men who want to control you, hate their family for no apparent reason, and don't seem to have any friends. Be especially careful of anyone who won't open up emotionally. If the guy

can't reveal the most trivial intimate detail, he's emotionally unavailable and off limits. It should go without saying that you should also discount anyone who shows the slightest sign they might be verbally or physically abusive.

5. **You think they're fine so you've been on a date?** When you come home, think hard about what they revealed about themselves. Look at your partner list. How are they faring? Do they have most of the qualities you're looking for? Be absolutely ruthless and refuse to date anyone again who doesn't match at least 70 percent. Pay attention in the beginning of relationships when you're more objective. Ask lots of questions, look for warning signs, and stay focused on what you're looking for in a partner.

6. **Don't have sex or make any commitment until you've known the guy at least six weeks** (and are averaging about three dates a week). I'm deadly serious—sex confuses things. As you get to know them, check your list constantly to make sure they're *still* measuring up.

7. **Enlist the help of trusted friends and family.** Take your partner to meet them at all stages of the relationship, not just in the beginning when they're on their best behavior. Listen to their opinions and answer any questions they have honestly. If you find you're making excuses about how he's treating you, you've slipped back into your old patterns. Ditto if you're knocking yourself out trying to please him.

8. **If your date suspects he's being thoroughly checked out, admit it.** Say, "My last two boyfriends turned out to be bastards and I'm making damn sure I don't make another mistake." If he's a nice guy, he won't be worried: he's got nothing to hide and will be proud of you for looking after yourself. If he's not, he won't bother hanging around. Either way, you can't lose.

> Her father opened the door and I thought, *Jesus!*: I was looking at myself in 30 years. Jenny was totally oblivious to the resemblance until I pointed it out.
> Tony, 31, sales consultant

9. **Don't give second—let alone third—chances if someone treats you badly.** If they turn up on your

doorstep with flowers, don't open the door. He's blown it—move on. Accept you've made a mistake, end it, and don't have any further contact, no matter what he does or promises.

> ❗ Each year, at least 1.6 million American women are beaten by their husbands.[18]

10. **Work ferociously on your self-esteem.** Stop focusing on finding Mr. Right and focus on you and your life. Surround yourself with people who boost you up; get rid of those who put you down. Be nice to yourself and concentrate on what you're achieving every day, rather than your failures. Think you deserve the best and you'll get it.

REALLY SERIOUS ISSUES THAT AFFECT YOUR RELATIONSHIPS

If you've been sexually or physically abused in the past, or are suffering right now, you already know the dramatic and destructive influence it has on all aspects of your life—particularly romantic relationships. It would be ridiculous to write a book on relationships and ignore this serious (and tragically common) problem. Unfortunately, it's such a complex, complicated issue it's equally as ridiculous to claim to offer any real help in one section of this entire book.

Quite frankly, even if my entire book was devoted exclusively to this subject, I think you'd need more than written words to help you heal. You need a qualified therapist who specializes in sexual and physical abuse. Please, if you're a victim of either or have been in the past, call the American Psychological Association (202–336–5500) for a list of therapists in your area. I've seen many people's lives turned the right way up through good therapy, and *know* yours will be, too, if you just make that phone call.

All I've attempted to do here is try to encourage you to seek help by talking a little about the emotions you may be feeling. I've also included some signs to watch for, for anyone who's worried their partner might become abusive.

Sexual abuse

If you've been raped or abused, it's pretty obvious your romantic relationships will be affected, even if it did happen during your childhood. There's a school of thought that says if you experience or grow up witnessing abuse you'll seek out an abusive partner later in life. Opinion divides sharply on the truth of this statement. Some swear a girl who grows up in a violent family relationship will come to see this behavior as normal and unconsciously be drawn to men who'll do the same to her.[19] Others believe it does the opposite: the girl grows into a woman with a very low tolerance to abusive behavior—and a highly tuned radar to spot it.[20]

Whichever reaction you may have had to the experience, it's not uncommon to be struggling with emotions a decade or two after being abused—or to still feel it was your fault. *If I hadn't been walking down that dark street/If I'd been more convincing, people would have listened and stopped the abuse.* It's *never* your fault. We can't always control our lives, particularly in instances like rape and abuse.

If you've been abused as a child or adult and haven't had therapy, sex probably isn't a pleasant experience for you. It brings back memories of feeling powerless, betrayed, frightened, and out of control. You might also feel angry, ashamed, and embarrassed. Understandably, you'll have problems trusting outside the bedroom as well. Many abuse victims put up emotional walls to protect themselves: if they don't let anyone in, they can't be hurt. Unfortunately, it also means they can't love properly—and others can't love them back.

In my experience, it's a rare person who recovers from the deep, psychological damage caused by sexual abuse—either as an adult or child—without help from a therapist. If you haven't been through intense counseling and are having relationship problems, please do yourself a favor and get some—even if it has been years since the event.

Physical abuse

If you're in or have been in a relationship where your partner continually hits you, again, you probably need much more than the do-it-yourself style therapy this book offers. You might be able to fix the problem solo, but you'll fix it faster and more effectively with a trained counselor to help. The aim of this section is to encourage you to seek help because—God knows—you shouldn't be embarrassed about asking for it. Shocking but true: you certainly aren't alone on this one. In fact, you probably already know people in your situation—but they're just as good at covering it up as you are.

Domestic violence can decrease without the abuser getting professional help—but it almost never stops. Because of this, and contrary to the myths, battered women do leave in high rates, despite the increased danger they face by doing so.[21] Although attitudes toward domestic violence are changing—thanks to campaigns like "Real Men Don't Bash or Rape Women"—it's still rife. Domestic violence occurs in every suburb, among every social class.

> Six months into the relationship, I found out my boyfriend had been married before and had three kids. He said he forgot to tell me. He also forgot to tell me he'd served time for assault. I'm ashamed to admit, I still gave him another chance: he repaid me by sleeping with an ex.
> Christine, 29, photographer

In almost all cases of abuse, emotional abuse goes hand in hand with the violence. Being told you're ugly, useless, that you wouldn't get hit if you could only "behave yourself," erodes your self-esteem as fast as he's punching it out of you. Add feeling helpless if you truly haven't got the money or anyone and anywhere to run to—and a faint hope that the last time really was the last time—and it's not surprising you don't know how to leave. Plenty of you are plain terrified to walk out the door because you're convinced your partner will come after you and finish the job completely. It's a fear that is justified: authorities say half of all women who die in domestic homicides are killed when they threaten to leave or actually have left violent partners.[22] That's not a reason to stay because it's still uncommon, but take it as a warning why you shouldn't leave without the help and protection of police, support groups, and/or friends and family.

There are lots of reasons why you're staying with someone who hurts you. You might be financially dependent on your partner, terrified to leave for fear of their "finishing the job," clinging to a promise that he'll "change," or battling your own internal demons that say you don't deserve any better. It's beyond the realm of this book to solve these issues for you; they're best explored through therapy. But here's an action plan to inspire you to seek help.[23]

1. Give up the dream

If he's hitting you now, he's probably going to keep on hitting you. Virtually all studies show that without some sort of intense counseling, batterers are unlikely to change. In one study, only 7 percent of batterers had stopped hitting their partners by the end of the two-year follow-up period.[24]

2. Prepare yourself emotionally

Look up "Domestic Violence" in the phone book, on the Web, or call your nearest hospital or a community center (if you cannot find a resource in your area on your own, call the National Domestic Violence Hotline at 1-800-799-SAFE and they will link you to help in your area). Say you want to organize some counseling. It's more effective face-to-face but you can be counseled via the phone, too. The counselors are well aware that you're in a dangerous situation, and won't ask for your name if you don't want to give one. They will do their utmost not only to protect your confidentiality but to stop your partner from finding out you're getting help by fitting in with your situation. They will also discuss fees with you—plenty provide the service for free.

3. Gather evidence as well as courage

It's strongly advisable to report all attacks—even if you don't want to press charges—rather than just the one that breaks the camel's back (and possibly yours). Tell the police you want it on record but aren't emotionally ready yet to take it further and don't want your partner to know you've reported him. The more they have on record, the more chance you'll have of establishing a history of violence. If you don't want to involve the police, keep a diary and take Polaroids of all your injuries. Obviously, keep them hidden somewhere safe. If you still have good friends that you see regularly, ask them to hold them for you.

4. Prepare to make the physical move

Your counselor will advise you on how to make the move to somewhere safe—or how to remove your partner so your current home is safe. You may need to involve the police and obtain a temporary restraining order which stops them from reentering the house until a formal one is issued by the courts the next day. The number one objective is to get you out of the situation without putting yourself in danger.

5. Don't be dragged back in

Violent men can be exceedingly charming and persuasive—they have to be to keep you hanging on to a shred of hope. Don't stop therapy until a year or so after you've left your partner so he's got zero chance of talking you into coming back. If you have friends or family who weren't aware of your situation, swallow your pride and tell them what happened. The more people around you who know and will protect you, the less likely you are to give in and go back.

THE DANGER SIGNS YOUR PARTNER MIGHT HIT YOU

Violent men come in all sorts of guises. You can't tell by looking at them—but you can watch for signs of potential abuse. A major study on domestic violence found batterers came in two distinct types: men whose temper slowly simmered before erupting into violence, and those who strike out immediately. The study also found men who abuse physically nearly always start out abusing mentally. It's necessary to undermine a woman's confidence before she'll "put up with" being physically abused.[25]

Are you at risk of being abused by your partner? You're in danger if your partner:

- Is intimidating: he'll silence you with a look or angry gesture. You're not quite sure what he'd do if pushed.
- Puts you down: he calls you names, insults you, or plays mind games.

- Controls whom you see and when: the more isolated and friend-less you are, the more likely you are to put up with whatever he decides to dish out.
- Pretends you're "imagining things": you're too sensitive, he didn't insult you, he was just playing around. Later, a punch was a "slap," you weren't pushed, you fell.
- Blames you for any angry arguments: you were to blame for his losing his temper, it wasn't his fault.
- Directly threatens to hurt you, your family, or children if you don't do what he says.
- Cuts off your finances: refuses to let you get a job or demands you hand over your paycheck because handling the finances is a "man's job." You're only allowed small amounts of cash at a time (if you had more, you might use it to leave).
- Seems dangerous to you, even though you've got no evidence to support it. Always trust your instincts.[26]

9

Dumped!

How to get over a break-up and what to do if you're still hung up on an ex

● ●

I remember it vividly, even though it happened about 13 years ago. I was working through my lunch hour in the office at Australian *Cosmopolitan*, when an Italian male model wandered in. It was the fashion editor's job to look through model portfolios, but I gave it a flick through just to be polite (okay, he was the sort you instantly imagined wrapping your legs around in a Jacuzzi). Enrico didn't speak English very well, but we had what passed as a conversation (that is, we both smiled a lot). I watched his butt as he walked out the door, sighed, and went back to work.

About an hour later, the rest of the troops filed back in and when I looked up, he was there again. Walking right up to my desk. Standing in front of me.

"I sorry, but I have to come back," he said. "I say to myself, 'Enrico. You like that girl.' Will you go out with me?"

Ahh, what a glorious moment! Not only had a model asked *me* out but he did it in front of *everyone*. Of course I said yes. Of course everyone rushed over the minute he disappeared. Angels burst into song.

Enrico and I had three dates—every detail faithfully reported back to everyone who worked within a ten-mile radius. Our last date was spent at the zoo. He watched the animals quietly for a while then said, "I think I take you home to see *my* country and *my* animals. You would come?"

Hell, I practically had my bags packed. Forget the job, forget my friends, I was on the next plane out of there if that's what he wanted. The next day, the office was a buzz of activity: the fashion editor worked on my travel wardrobe, I remember someone even called the Italian consulate to find out about a work visa. We all waited excitedly for what would happen next. And waited. And I never heard from the guy ever again. Not one friggin' phone call.

Enrico disappeared into thin air and to this day I have no idea why. Did he fall off his big, red motorcycle? Have to hotfoot it back to Italy to sit at the bedside of his dying mother? Catch some killer disease from the elephant he patted that day? Was Enrico now horribly scarred and disfigured and living with the Elephant Man? I suspect—actually, scratch that—am damn positive it was none of the above. He was smooth, he rode a Harley, he was Italian, he was a *male model,* for God's sake. Some other girl caught his eye, that was all (or maybe even a guy—like I said, he was a *model*).

I felt like a complete idiot. I'd told *everyone* this man had asked me to go to Italy, and now I had to tell them all I'd been dumped. Without even a phone call. The *embarrassment* of it all. The *public humiliation*. I'd never get over it. (I did, of course. Within two weeks, we were all making Enrico jokes: "Where's that story disappeared to? Maybe it's done an Enrico.") But back then, I thought my heart would never mend. I'd never love again (blah blah blah). How could he do this to me? (blah blah blah). How pathetic—and how lucky would I be if that was the only dumping experience I'd ever have in my life?

Because while Enrico was my first taste of being rejected, being dumped good and proper feels twenty billion times worse than I felt back then. It's the difference between accidentally dropping your last quarter down the drain beside the parking meter and losing your life savings on the way home from your retirement party. If a long-term, dearly loved partner leaves, everything you've counted on is gone. You look around the home you once shared and it's as though you've misplaced half your life in it—which perhaps you have.

All your life plans have to be rethought. You don't just lose the person, you lose hope—and also part of yourself. When they go, they take a part of your life with them, the part they were a witness to. Sometimes, they split with real evidence of it—like that photo of you looking tanned and terrific on a beach in the Greek Islands, the only picture of yourself you voluntarily showed people. Broken hearts, broken dreams, a whopping great hole in your photo album. Is it any wonder most people find getting over a serious relationship split one of the hardest things they've ever had to do in their life?

The astonishing fact is, though, most of us not only muddle through the agony and survive, we go back for more. When we're hurting we think, *Not me! No sireee! I've learned my lesson this time. I'm never falling in love, ever again.* But we do—and most of us know we will, even in that deep, dark lonely moment. Broken hearts heal,

❗ Beware the lover who believes you are "destined" to be together. Starry-eyed lovers are far more likely to dump you abruptly when they find out you're not quite the dreamed-for partner they'd imagined. Those who believe relationships are built through hard work are much more likely to stick through the hard times (and have fewer one-night stands).[1]

new dreams replace the old, and a lot of people—including me—look back and realize most relationships end for a reason. If you'd stayed with Stan, you wouldn't have met Greg. (What were you thinking? You'd never have been happy with a man obsessed with model train sets.) If Susan hadn't dumped you, you wouldn't be with Sarah—and just looking at her turns the world the right way up.

Yeah, yeah, I can hear you thinking, *that's all wonderful.* But how do I get from the painful part to the Greg and Sarah scenario? I'd like to say it's easy but I'd be lying. It's a difficult, sometimes long road back to recovery, but there's plenty you can do to make the journey quicker.

BREAKING UP

Ten reasons you're about to split

Sometimes, the writing's so obviously on the wall, it might as well be in bright pink neon. Neither of you could possibly miss it. In other relationships, one person's eagerly planning next Christmas together while the other's planning to leave. There are vulnerable points in any relationship, and all of those listed below scream danger. Take them seriously. How you handle them (and each other) could mean the difference between a relationship hiccup and a death rattle.

1. Circumstances have changed dramatically

Change gives us a new perspective—and forces us to question just how happy we are. A new job, a move to a new city, the death of someone close: any major life change for either of you can put the strongest relationship in jeopardy. Sickness or death causes people to look deep inside themselves and at their partner, searching for true feeling. If you decide they're there for a good time, not a long time, you'll search for someone new. A new job exposes us to new people and, considering most people meet their future spouse at work, changing jobs can turn up more dates than a disco.

2. You're at a turning point as a couple

Everyone's asking when you're going to get married/move in/have that baby/buy a house. One of you is stalling because you're not entirely convinced you want to move the relationship onto a deeper level of intimacy and commitment. Sometimes, a nudge from others can make us push through silly fears and take the leap. But in my opinion, outright pressure and nosy interference can send us in the opposite direction—flying over the edge to freedom. Leaving seems the most sensible solution if you're not allowed the time you need to make a decision.

3. You don't want sex anymore

Psychologist Janet Hall nicknames it "the cringe factor."[2] The thought of your partner touching you makes your skin crawl. You'll pick a fight, get drunk, invent exotic illnesses, *anything* to avoid the bed-room. If affection disappears along with the libido—you or they dive for the armchair rather than snuggle up on the couch—the relation-ship's a hair's breadth away from expired.

4. One of you cheated

Infidelity—discovered or not—means you're not just in troubled waters, the boat's sinking fast. If you're the guilty one and got away with it, you've satisfied your naughty side without the sky falling in. But you'll still feel different about your partner because the "special-ness" has gone. You can't quite meet their eye, feel guilty, then end up resentful for feeling guilty and, before you know it, you're caught in a downward spiral. Lots of people fool around to "test" their feel-ings or have one last, final fling before settling down for good (nei-ther is recommended); others do it because they haven't got the guts to say, "It's over," and think it'll be easier on their partner if they are found out (it isn't).

5. The blinders have come off

It's the "new car syndrome." When you want to buy a car, that's all you see: you're checking out makes and models all over the place. Once you've bought one, you stop looking. When you're in love, you don't notice other attractive people because you're committed and happy. Once you fall out of it, you start "shopping" again. The blind-ers come off and good-looking people appear everywhere.

6. People keep assuming you're single

If you're involved and adore your partner, you can run your fingers up and down the stem of a glass and lick your lips all you want: you'll rarely get asked out by other guys. Whether it's a chemical thing, pheromones, or a wicked glint in your eye, we subliminally give out signals that tell others whether we're playing or dead serious. In other words, we advertise our availability. You may well have a ring on your finger or *appear* to be settled but, take my word for it, the minute you decide you want an affair, someone tempting will appear in front of you. As the saying goes, "When the student is ready, the teacher arrives."

7. You talk less

Your boss gives you a glowing review and you find yourself picking up the phone to call—anyone but your partner. Lately, you've forgotten to tell them significant things altogether. We naturally move closer to the person we share our secrets with, and the person who knows most about us is the person *we* feel closest to. If your conversation with your partner is now restricted to "How was work?", they're not number one in your life (or you don't feel you're number one in theirs).

> **Being dumped taught me to think hard about what I really wanted. I've stopped going for looks and put "nice" at the top of the list.**
> Alison, financial adviser, 23

8. You stop arguing

It sounds strange but if you're still arguing—even bitterly and frequently—there's still hope. You're still trying to get your point across and your needs met: once you stop, you've given up. Research on volatile couples—those who have fierce, rowdy arguments—shows the passion and relish of the fight seem to fuel even more passionate make-ups. As intense as their fights are, their good times are that much better.[3] What kills relationships is indifference. Even if you swear you HATE your partner, there's still emotion present and therefore hope.[4]

9. Everything they do annoys you

That cute little habit she has of twisting her hair while distracted seems neurotic. You can't stop looking at his teeth and thinking, *Yuk!* Our tolerance level drops, and sometimes, we deliberately look for faults to try to justify why we're going to be mean and nasty and dump them. When we like someone, we think their imperfections are cute. When we fall out of love, it's like someone got up during the night and turned the "nice" switch off. Suddenly, you don't see the fabulous broad shoulders and washboard stomach. You see hands that somehow seem too small and feminine for a man, lips that seem thin and mean—get my drift?

10. You're seeing less and less of each other

Going out alone and leaving your partner behind because you feel more comfortable solo? Inventing excuses why they shouldn't "bother" coming? You're either testing the waters to find out what it would be like to be single, or things are so tense, it's a relief to escape. Doing less together is one of the tail-end signs that you've drifted apart.

The four fatal fall-out signs for long-term couples

Psychologist John Gottman is a world-respected relationship expert who's spent 20 years studying what makes a marriage last. In his book *Why Marriages Succeed or Fail*, Gottman pinpoints four warning signs that he says signal a serious relationship is headed for disaster.[5] They usually run in this order, with each feeding the next.

Criticism

All couples squabble, and complaining about your partner's behavior is usual and pretty unavoidable. It's when, "Honestly, John, you spend too much money," turns into, "You're such a selfish person. All you think about is yourself," that you're in trouble. Attacking someone's *behavior* is different than attacking their *personality* or *character*.

Contempt

One step past criticizing someone's character is intentionally insulting or verbally abusing them, says Gottman.[6] Calling your partner selfish isn't great. Calling them a stupid, irresponsible pig is worse. If one of you starts flinging insults, the other throws back—if not with words, with body language. We've all been to dinner parties where one partner's telling you all about their latest achievement, while their other half is rolling their eyes and looking bored and disinterested.

Defensiveness

By now, you're both starting to feel understandably defensive. You feel victimized by each other and quite upset about it since you're (obviously) totally innocent. If you feel you're being picked on, the natural reaction is to defend yourself with, "What are you picking on me for? It's not my fault." It's the old "Yes, but." He says you never invite his friends over for dinner. You say, "Yes, but I would if you'd help clean up afterward." Neither of you hears the other, no one's happy.

Stonewalling

Exhausted by constant arguments, you both wearily stop having them—and give up altogether. If he shouts at you, you say, "Yeah. You're right. You always are," and pick up a book. You pick a fight with him and he says something similar and walks out.

All four of these warning signs create a cycle of negativity, says Gottman.[7] There's still hope even if your relationship has already progressed to stage number four but only if *both* of you want to work on it. If your partner's not willing, expect a "Dear John/Jane" letter sometime soon.

WHY MEN DUMP WOMEN

Short term

- **You tried to change him.** In the beginning, you admired everything about him. Then you realized his table manners need fixing, he could do with a haircut, half his wardrobe is just *wrong* . . . The message he gets: I'm not good enough for her (so I'll find someone who thinks I am).
- **You're not interested in sex.** If you've been together four months and are already feigning headaches, he sees the rest of his life stretching out before him. One of intense frustration.
- **You know him too well.** Some men guard those walls with machine guns. A girl that knows him better than he knows himself makes him feel emotionally exposed. Add immaturity and a battle-scarred past and he's out the door.

Long term

- **It's time to tie the knot.** Hell, even his pals are asking when he's going to make an honest woman out of you. He knows it's expected but the old ball-and-chain image keeps popping up. He's convinced he'll never get to play golf on Sundays again.

- **He meets someone else or realizes you're not "the one."**
Women aren't the only ones with expectations about what marriage will be like. He loves you but you're *so* comfortable together, he hardly notices you're there. Then a new girl starts at his job. She's bright, sexy, attractive, *interesting*. She talks to him and asks him questions. He thinks, *There's more to a relationship than watching videos on the couch. This girl makes me feel alive.*

WHY WOMEN DUMP MEN

Short term
- **You don't turn out to be the person she thought you were.** Women are optimistic creatures and she'll think you're Mr. Perfect for as long as she can kid herself. If it becomes painfully obvious you're not ever going to turn into the man she was hoping you would, she'll move on to a new project.
- **The timing's wrong.** She was just offered a great job—in another city. Her girlfriends are about to head off for a six-month trek around Southeast Asia and she doesn't love you enough to stay behind without them.
- **You don't treat her well.** She'll give you a few chances—maybe more than you deserve. But persist with bad behavior and she'll realize you're bad news.

Long term
- **You're—still—not ready to commit.** Sure, she knows, you need time before you're ready to (take a deep breath because I'm going to say the "s" term) *settle down*. But honestly, ten years is long enough.
- **She loves you like a brother.** Sex is important to her, too, but she sometimes gets so caught up in the emotional side of things, she forgets to look closely at that as well. If, after two years, she finally realizes as much as she loves you emotionally, physically it just ain't happening, she knows as well as you do: it's not going to work.
- **She catches you.** Once or once too often, any girl worth her Clarins leaves when it's painfully obvious you're sleeping around.

How to dump someone nicely

There are ways to kick someone out kindly. "Sorry, but my gyno agrees with me—your penis is just too big," would work wonderfully on most men (if only they'd believe it). "Sorry, but you're just so beautiful I can't bear everyone gazing at you," would do the trick for most women (ditto). Another alternative: if Hallmark came up with a series of terribly nice and well-worded dump cards. All you'd have to do then is sign your soon-to-be ex's name at the top, yours at the bottom, and shove it under his/her door. Alas, they're not yet available (actually, I have seen some but they were more of the "blow off" variety) and, even if they did exist, I still wouldn't seriously recommend dumping someone via the mail (or e-mail or phone—so forget those options immediately).

Telling someone you don't love them anymore *must* be done face-to-face. It's necessary for the person to see you saying the words "It's over," so they can have some sense of closure. Your feelings are secondary in this situation—the idea is to make it as painless as possible for *them*. For this reason, do the deed as soon as you're sure it's finished. *Don't wait for their permission to leave.* It's normal to feel upset at the prospect of hurting them, but staying until you think they're "ready" isn't helping either of you.

 FOR HER

Women *hate* hurting anyone. Dumping some guy who's madly in love with us is like shutting the door on that cute stray dog that followed you home to your no-pets-allowed building and licked your nose when you bent over to see if it had an ID tag on its collar. Actually, it's worse, because at least with the dog you can bring it inside and call your mother to convince her one more pet won't matter. Unfortunately, it's not acceptable to ring all your single friends and ask if they'd like to adopt a house-trained boyfriend. Though it is a thought.

Look, you will feel guilty and like a bitch with a capital "B" while you're telling him. But leading someone on is even more cruel. What's the alternative anyway? You don't want to share your denture glass with this guy, or even another Saturday night blowing him off. So get to it.

Decide what you're going to say

Work out *exactly* how you're going to word it and put the plan into action *pronto*. Otherwise, you'll end up mothering the guy because you know what's coming. You say, "You really are sweet, you know? Any girl that ends up with you will be very lucky," thinking you're sending him a clear warning signal because it's obvious that girl's not going to be you. He thinks the opposite (she must want a commitment). So play it cool. Act off-hand. Don't be too nice. Do whatever it takes to get the message across to him that *you are not happy*. In other words, make sure he's had at least a few days (if you can manage it, a few weeks) warning he's about to be dumped.

Sit him down and deliver the speech

Most men react one of two ways to a dumping: they gaze at you with a hurt, glazed expression on their face, listen to what you have to say, then leave without saying much at all. Or they get angry and accuse you of all sorts of nastiness. (If he's the angry type and you're worried he'll become violent, do it in a public place with a male friend sitting outside in the car. Move in with friends or family for as long as you think it'll take for him to calm down and you to be safe.)

If he didn't say much, call him the next day

Women think on their feet and tend to ask the "but why?" questions there and then. We're more in touch with our emotions and used to expressing them instantly. He may not be as articulate and/or he may be in shock. He probably only heard half of what you said because "I can't believe she's doing this" took over his brain. It could take a few hours to sink in, and often he'll call you then or the next day to find out the whys. If he doesn't, and he didn't say much when you delivered your speech, you call him. Ask if he's okay and if there's anything he doesn't understand. If he doesn't want to talk and tells you to take a flying leap, fine. But he might need to know some answers, and could be too proud to pick up the phone.

Call one of his friends

The one you got along the best with. No need to go into details, just say, "Look. I just thought you should know I've just broken it off with X. He might need a bit of cheering up."

 ## FOR HIM

Men hate dumping women because women cry. Most of you would rather go to a poetry reading than dole out the tissues—and that's why you always try the silent dump before anything else. This involves beam-me-up-Scotty type of behavior, that is, pretending you just don't exist anymore. Trying to contact you is like trying to serve a summons, and when she finally *does* track you down (with sniffer dogs), you pretend she's imagined the whole thing. "Honey, I told you. I'm busy at work," you say, all wide-eyed and innocent. Coward! The silent dump will work eventually. It has to. If she hasn't seen you in two months, even the thickest of us know it's over. But it's not playing fair, and if you truly do want her out of your life for good, there are quicker, kinder, and more effective ways.

Women need reasons for things. If you give us a pretty plausible reason why you don't want to go out anymore, we'll still be upset, but at least we'll *know why*. We need to make sense of things before we can move on. That doesn't mean we won't cry and scream and call you names. But we're much less inclined to follow you around with mascara streaked down our cheeks, desperate to figure out why you gave us roses two months ago and can't even give us the time of day now.

First up, decide on a reason

If you don't want to tell the truth (you're sleeping with someone else) or your reason is so petty and trivial even *you* think it makes you sound bad (her new haircut is just awful), come up with a plausible lie. Even clichés like, "I'm too busy at work for a relationship," or, "I must be commitment-phobic because I just can't make a commitment to you," are better than nothing. If it's possible, make it something that makes us believe you did once love us, even if you don't now.

Choose your time

Make it sooner rather than later, but be sensitive. If her father's just been rushed to the hospital with a suspected heart attack, the emergency room is not the time or place. Avoid significant dates like Christmas, her birthday, the anniversary of when you first met. Don't do it in a public place, and if you're really nice, check her best friend's not on vacation the weekend you choose.

Hang around long enough to answer her questions

She'll throw them at you like dinner plates (those, too, possibly). "Did you ever love me?" "Is there someone else?" Then, "How could you do this to me?" "How could you hurt me like this?" There's not much you can say to a lot of this, though you can ease the blow by at least looking suitably upset. Tell her the truth as much as possible. If you didn't ever love her, say, "X, I loved you in lots of ways but not in the way you wanted me to."

When it becomes clear there's nothing more to say, leave. If she's in a real mess, ask her if you can call someone to come be with her. Even if she says no, get on your cell phone the minute you're out of the door and call her best friend. Yes, they will give you a hard time, but that's all part of it, I'm afraid.

> Guys are better at covering up feelings. We form an emotional scab a lot quicker. But the hurt's still there and the scab gets knocked off pretty easily.
> Andrew, 30, sales rep

After the break

Some people are out of your life before you've even finished reading the riot act; others have real problems accepting that it's over. Help reduce the risk by keeping the following in mind.

Refuse to feel guilty

It's not a criminal offense to fall out of love with someone.

Stop being their girlfriend or boyfriend

If you really like the person, it's natural to want to help them when you see they're hurting. You can't: after all, it's *you* they're trying to forget. Don't solve their problems after you've left. It's not your job and it's perpetuating their dependence on you.

Stop seeing them if there's absolutely no chance of a reconciliation

That harmless coffee "just to see if they're okay" will set them back months. If it was serious, wait a year or so after the break to suggest friendship. Semiserious? Wait at least three months.

Beware of manufactured excuses to see you

If they're desperate, they'll come up with all sorts of imaginative ways to get together—and play on your guilt to force you to turn up.

Don't give them hope

Be cruel to be kind: tell them you don't love them and you're not going to change your mind.

Exes that won't go away

You've tried all the above and they're still hanging around? Time to pull out the big guns!

Write them a letter

Say that the relationship is well and truly over, there is no hope, and their following you around is making you dislike them, not regret what you've done. Repeat certain sentences throughout: "I don't love you anymore," "There is no hope," "There is nothing you can do that will change my mind," and, "It is over for good." It's better to write it down rather than say it over the phone. If they're in denial, it's much harder to dismiss something that's before them in black and white.

Ask mutual friends to back up what's in the letter

If your ex is constantly calling them for news, ask them to say that they have indeed spoken to you and they're afraid it really is over. Have a good chat with any super-nice friends you share. They might be giving them hope because they can't stand to see someone so upset.

Keep a diary

If it continues and they start getting heavy, keep a diary of what's happening. Record when, where, and how they're harrassing you, especially any threats that are made.

Send them a letter from your lawyer

Explain to the lawyer that you're being hassled and would like them to send a letter on your behalf. It should be formally worded on official letterhead and state that you will seek a restraining order unless they stop calling/following/harrassing you. It won't cost very much, it shows you mean business, and it'll scare all but the most stubborn exes into giving up.

Get a restraining order

If a letter from a lawyer doesn't help, you've got little choice but to visit your local police station and ask them to help arrange a restraining order. You'll need to go to court to get one. Take your diary with you so you can provide concrete evidence of how you're being stalked.

THE GET-OVER-IT GUIDE: DAY BY DAY, STEP BY STEP TO MENDING A BROKEN HEART AND WHY IT'S NEVER EASY

You knew it was coming. But hearing them say, "It's over," and imagining it are two totally different things. In your fantasy, they take both your hands in theirs and deliver the tragic news in a voice cracked with emotion. Invariably, they're leaving for a reason that has nothing to do with you (the army needs them, they've decided to devote their life to God). You nod quietly, delivering one, hauntingly touching parting line ("Go—but you take my heart with you"). They head for the door then stop dead as they hear you catch a sob. Their back still turned to you, one hand on the doorknob, they say (struggling for composure): "I have to do this. I can't ask you to wait for me but . . ."

Reality is somewhat different. You both sit awkwardly on the couch because you know what's coming. "It's just not working," they blurt out. "FINE!" you say, "That's just WONDERFUL!" Then you start screaming, "You CAN'T *LEEEEEAVE* ME!" fall in a pathetic heap at their feet, wrap both arms around their legs, and burst into a hysterical sobbing fit punctuated with unattractive hiccups and snorts. They start to head for the door, you're forced to endure the indignity of being dragged across the carpet because you won't let go of their legs. Desperate to get away, they kick you free and sprint for the door, slamming it behind them. You're after them immediately, throwing yourself and anything else you can get your hands on in their general direction. Their parting words aren't "Wait for me," but, "Get away from me, you psychopath!" You follow with a supremely clever "Go to hell, you bastard/bitch! I hate you!"

Then the anger goes and you go back inside, slide down the wall, hit the floor, and give in to total panic. You're crying so much you can't breathe. You feel dizzy, think you're going to be sick and are, right there on the carpet. Stumbling toward the bathroom, you visualize the razor blades in the cabinet and sensibly do a detour to the kitchen in search of vodka. One swig and you're sick again. You think, *This is what dying must feel like.* Because that's exactly how you do feel: dead. What's the point of life if they're not going to be there to share it with you?

Getting through the next 30 seconds seems impossible when someone's put your heart through a blender. But you *will* get through the next minute and the next hour and the next day and the next year. However painful it is now, *you will survive.* How do I know? Because I've been there, everyone I know has been there, and I'd bet money on it that you could fit all the people who *haven't* been there into one small, sad little room. You loved, you lost—but at least you loved. We all came out the other side—so will you. Clear the tears long enough to stop the page from blurring and I'll tell you how it's done.

How to use the get-over-it guide

I admit it. The time frame of this guide is ridiculously optimistic, deliberately so. It's not just designed to give you practical advice on how to get through, it's designed to give you hope. The time frames I've organized it under are probably irrelevant, anyway, because every split-up is different and every person heals at a different rate. But most of you will go through all the different stages, usually in this order:

- **Stage 1:** is the intensely painful part. This can last anywhere from two weeks to two months, depending on your relationship. Getting through each day is difficult and you think you'll never be happy again.

- **Stage 2:** is spent adjusting to being single again. It might take a month to six months to stop yourself from saying and thinking "X and I," and come to terms with being "one."

- **Stage 3:** is when you start truly healing. If you went out for a year or so and thought it was forever, this will probably happen about six months after the split. If it was longer, it could take up to a year. You feel normal most of the time but are still battling memories or analyzing what went wrong every week or few weeks.

- **Stage 4:** is when you've made it! Official recovery can take anywhere from one to two years.

Don't panic if you appear to move on to the next stage, then slip back one for a few weeks—it's normal. But that's what you're in for. Hopefully, the following guide will help get you from one to four in record time!

Week one

 FOR HER: THE DAY IT HAPPENS

Get on the phone as quickly as possible, the minute he walks out of the door. Call your closest friend, your mom, big brother, the *butcher*, if you have a special bond: anyone who will understand. Ask them to come over immediately, stopping only for supplies (tissues, alcohol, chocolate, poison to drop into his drink the next time you see him out). While they're hot-footing it to your house (allow time for speeding tickets), call another friend and let "Oh, poor darling," and, "I always knew he'd hurt you," drone on in the background while you hiccup and create a mini tidal wave of tears on the floor. Don't put the receiver down until the doorbell rings, then (and only then) you're allowed to lose it completely. Cry, beat the wall, cling on to your friend for dear life, but let out as much grief as possible. When you feel remotely calm, sit down, have a drink, and pour out the whole sad, sorry tale over and over until they not only know what happened, they're living it with you. He said, then I said . . . Did I tell you he said then I said? Keep going until you can't analyze it any further or your friend falls asleep. If they can't stay with you, let them bundle you up and take you to their house. Tonight is not the night to be alone.

 FOR HIM: THE DAY IT HAPPENS

Initially, you're in shock. You keep thinking, *She'll get over it. Any minute now, she'll call me to say sorry and everything will be fine.* You consider sending flowers—that's worked before. Except you know this is different. She doesn't call, and when you call her four hours later, she says, ever-so-gently, "I meant it. I'm sorry. It really is over."

If you can do it (yes, you can), let yourself have a good cry. When you're done, pick up the phone and call someone. If you've got a close female friend, she's first on the list. Tell her your girlfriend's left you and you're feeling down. Could she come over and cheer you up? She'll be over at your place in a nanosecond, dispensing hugs and all sorts of soothing there-theres (and no, she won't tell everyone how pathetic you were, so drop the macho act). No close female friends? Call a pal. He'll drag you down to the local bar for a game of pool, give you a slap on the back, and say, "You'll get over it—I did." It's not much, but it is true. Whatever you end up doing, tonight is not the night to start the Liver Cleansing Diet. If a few beers make you feel better, have them but keep it under control. The idea is to send you to sleep—not stumbling over to her house drunk.

 BOTH CLING TO THIS

Think back to when you helped someone get over a painful break-up. Remember how they said they'd never smile again, but you knew they'd get over it? They did—and so will you.

Day two

 FOR HER

The first thing you realize when you open your eyes the next day is that you can't: they're swollen shut from so much crying. Reality starts to seep through when you get out of bed and stand on a mound of crumpled tissues. Instant tears. It hits with full force: he's gone, you're alone. Day two (sorry) is even worse than day one, so aim to simply get through it.

It's a weekend

Spend the day repeating the story (for the forty-fifth time) to a friend, any friend. You'll feel raw, miserable, and so sorry for yourself it's not funny, so surround yourself with people who care. True friends will let you tag along wherever they go: take them up on it. If they're cleaning the toilet, hand them the Pine Sol; if they're shaving their legs, the razor (actually, maybe you'd better skip that one). It's wallow-in-it day, so don't feel guilty about dominating the conversation totally and not having brushed your teeth for 24 hours. The only no-no today: DON'T call him and don't persuade your friends to call him either. Resist the urge to park outside his house, do a drive-by, *or* turn up at his best friend's hoping for some inside info. Make a pact with yourself that you can call him in one week if you still need to and get a friend to help you stick to it. (The deal: you have to call your friend before you call him.)

> **Listen to friends but be careful. If they'd secretly prefer you single, they'll think up a million different ways to convince you he's a bastard, even if he's not.**
> Christine, 27, journalist

It's a work day

Get up, put your make-up on and get out that door. You'll be tempted to call in sick and pull the sheets over your head, but you're not doing yourself any favors. If you feel so traumatized you honestly can't make it, call in sick, but get yourself to a friend's house—don't stay at home alone. You've dragged yourself into the office? Great—but it's unlikely you'll be Ms. Efficient, so tell your immediate boss what's happened. You know you won't perform well, but would prefer to be there, and you'll make up for lost time later and so on. If you're on friendly terms with your coworkers, let them know you're hurting (and accept all offers of lunch, Devil dogs, and cups of hot, sweet tea).

If it's a brisk, professional team and you don't feel comfortable blabbing all, put on a brave face and make calls to friends and family during your lunch hour. If you can't hold it together, disappear into the ladies' room and take your make-up bag to do a quick repair job. Call a friend for dinner tonight: their place or yours. If you can't face sleeping alone, crash in front of the TV with the sound turned *up*.

FOR HIM

Read the "For her" section because you'll feel exactly the same. If you picked up the phone and someone said, "Congratulations, you've just won Lotto!" your first thought would be, *I wonder if a million dollars would change her mind?* Fill up your day with activity. Play sports, watch reruns of old sitcoms, strip the car engine then put it back together again: anything to keep yourself busy and keep your mind off it.

It's the weekend

Get on the phone and don't get off it until you've organized nonstop entertainment for the entire weekend. Tell people you've split up, even if you do play it cool and insist you don't care (they'll draw their own conclusions). If you don't want to talk about it, tell people. Say, "It's over. I don't want to talk about it. I'll tell you the details later." People will want to spoil you: let them. It's not being "weak" to accept offers to dinner, it's what friends do. Your main aim today: convincing yourself that turning up at her front door with enough red roses to fill her entire apartment really won't work. If she's serious about splitting, she'll just feel sorry for you.

It's a work day

You're one up on your female equivalent: chances are you'll get through the day without dissolving into tears. If you think you can get through on autopilot, do it. If you can't, tell your boss what's happened. If possible, arrange to meet a friend for lunch, but steer clear of the nearest pub. I don't care how fabulous she was or how bad you feel, she's not worth losing your job over by going back to work drunk.

 BOTH CLING TO THIS

Before you finally go to sleep, tell yourself, "I'm okay. I'm just upset. I will get through this. I survived today, didn't I?"

Day three

 FOR HIM AND HER

Okay, enough of this namby-pamby wimpy stuff: today is toughen-up day. I'm being cruel? Humor me, anyway, and give it a try. You've got nothing to lose except a day of feeling powerless. Today it's time for some action: I want you to gather up all those relationship reminders and put them out of sight. That's right: books, cards, letters, photographs, CDs with your song on them, cute little notes, anything at all that connects your ex to you. If Special K brings back memories, toss it into the garbage. (If *everything* does, perhaps you'd better wait a week.) Put all that memorabilia into a big bag and either throw it all out (best), give it to a friend to look after (okay), or shove it in the back of a cupboard where you can't get to it without a huge effort (a cop-out, but better than leaving it in sight).

Wash the sheets and towels (yes, you must), then go through your datebook and cancel any events where you're bound to run into each other. Stay away from all your old haunts: the secluded

Seven out of ten young women define success as wealth and career, rather than being happy in a relationship or married. Ambitious? You bet! The women surveyed were prepared to risk their health and let family, friends, and lovers fall by the wayside to get to the top.[8]

beach you both discovered, the great little Thai restaurant that was your favorite. Avoid anything that reminds you of your ex. Why? Because you really are kidding yourself if you think lying around listening to "your song" and rereading old love letters is going to help you heal or magically get them back. It won't. In fact, if there honestly *is* any hope of a reconciliation, their seeing you get on with your life is far more likely to do it. The old adage has been proven over and over: act like you don't need them (even if you do want them) and they may well realize they want you, too.

So if they come over to beg forgiveness and notice their picture's been removed, you'll win respect not disapproval. *The quicker you accept they're gone for good—even if they aren't—the quicker you'll get over them, and the more likely it is they'll want to return.* It's a win–win situation. You're not only upping the chances of getting back together, you're upping your chances of happily getting on with your life if they don't. The reverse is also true: send letters begging another chance, pester them with phone calls, follow them around, and they'll thank God they got out when they did. Besides, your ego's been bruised enough, it can't take any more knocks right now, so don't set yourself up for them.

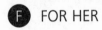 BOTH CLING TO THIS

There are whole minutes—perhaps even two or three together—that you don't think about your ex. You are recovering.

Day four
F FOR HER

From now on, you're only allowed five minutes crying time a day. Yup. It sounds bizarre but I want you to try really hard to hold it all in until you're allowed to let it all out. Schedule a time and once the floodgates open, set the timer because in five minutes you have to stop and reward yourself. Follow every crying session with something that makes you feel good. Slap on a face mask, some empowering music (Alanis Morrisette, *Jagged Little Pill*, The Corrs' "I Never Loved You

Anyway") on the CD player, and soak in a bubble bath with your favorite mag. If you're reading this and thinking, *I can't stop crying for five minutes, let alone restrict it to that*, you're officially allowed to move this step back a little. (And if you're feeling seriously out of control, get yourself an emergency appointment with a good therapist.)

FOR HIM

If you're a typical guy, you probably haven't spoken too much about how you're feeling. Now's a good time to call that female friend and pour it all out to her. If you don't have one, or feel uncomfortable talking about your feelings, write it all down. Get yourself a beer (or coffee) and take an hour or so to write down everything you're feeling and going through. No one's going to see it (burn it afterward, if you're paranoid), so be totally honest. Record how you seriously thought she was the one, the plans you had, how you started reading the fine print at the bottom of the diamond ads. What you miss about her, how she made you feel ten feet tall, and now you feel about one inch high. Why you think you broke up, how you'll never, ever trust anyone ever again or fall in love. Ever.

Yes, it sounds pathetic and you'll feel pathetic as you're writing it all down. But it truly will help. So just keep writing and let it all come out. You'll cry a lot and feel exhausted when you've finished but at least you've released some of the pain and it's not festering inside. Face your emotions *now*, feel the pain *now*, and you'll give yourself a chance to recover. If you push them to some dark place deep inside you, you risk their resurfacing when you next meet someone you really like. It's hard enough making new relationships work without having to grapple with all the old stuff Jayne left behind at the same time.

FOR BOTH OF YOU

Keep as busy as possible and *don't sit by the phone*. Let's be logical here: if the former love of your life suddenly decides they want to live forever in your pocket, they're not going to give up if you're not home when they call. If they do, it was a spur-of-the-moment (they didn't score last night) thing. Or they're simply calling to see how you are.

Don't return the call or pick up the phone if you're pretty sure that's all they want. Hearing their voice will send you straight back to longing-for-them land. Call a friend and ask them to relay a message: you're hurting but you're okay and don't want to hear from them for a little while.

By day four you're still utterly miserable—though more in a depressed than out-of-control way. Nevertheless, keep surrounding yourself with understanding friends and protect your heart. If a sappy song comes on the radio, switch stations. Ditch any novel that has love scenes for gutsy thrillers, choose your movies very carefully, and buy some party music to replace those banned CDs.

B BOTH CLING TO THIS

All this heartache has made you remember how awful you felt when you split with another ex. You got over that person—maybe, just maybe, you'll survive this one, too.

Day five

B FOR BOTH OF YOU

Today you officially take back control of your life by doing some spring-cleaning. If it's a work day, start with your office. Spend your lunch hour going through every single "to do" pile and organizing it properly. Clear out your drawers, ruthlessly throw out everything you don't need or file it where it belongs.

When you get home that evening, turn the CD player up full blast (boppy music, not sad stuff) and do the same at home. Empty all the cupboards and throw out or donate anything useless or stuff you haven't worn or used in the last two years. Rearrange the furniture. Make a list of things to buy that'll brighten up the place. You've just started on the kitchen and it's midnight already? Who cares? You're not sleeping that well anyway—you might as well completely exhaust yourself and have something to show for it in the morning other than knotted sheets. Tomorrow you'll wake up to a clean, organized home and office and feel a sense of satisfaction.

BOTH CLING TO THIS

Believe in fate. Everything happens for a reason. Perhaps you broke up with your ex because someone even better is out there waiting for you or you're about to get that promotion and need all your energy for work. Trust in your future.

Day six

 FOR BOTH OF YOU

Okay, you're still down and feeling terrible but after five or six days should have a little perspective on the situation. You did some physical spring-cleaning yesterday; today we're going to do some emotional spring-cleaning. If you're a guy (and did as you were told), you will have already written down all the emotions you're experiencing. If you're female, you've no doubt verbalized them to your friends. This list is different.

The best strategy to accept someone is gone is to collect as much evidence as possible to prove a) you're a wonderful person who deserves better, and b) they weren't as fabulous as you thought. I'm not being nasty or vengeful, just realistic. After all, if they were *that* perfect for you, they wouldn't have dumped you in the first place. There were obviously areas where you didn't see eye-to-eye and things you didn't like about them. They were human, weren't they?

Start with list number one: get a good friend to help you write down everything great about yourself, all your successes and achievements. You're a great friend. Popular. A terrific listener. Your family adores you. You were crucial in helping your team win the championship. You can sink 12 beers and still stand. Write down big achievements, serious things, silly things—as many as you can come up with.

List two: set to work on your ex. It doesn't matter how much you did or do love them, no one is perfect (not even them). Write down every single flaw and weakness you can think of. How they didn't share your passion for the sea, how your mom never really liked them, the time you caught them admiring themselves in the mirror, how they flirted at parties, the embarrassing green sweatpants that made their

butt look six times bigger, how they'd give you a hard time for wanting to watch "crap," how he vomited all over the bathroom floor after
a night with the boys, how she used to leave little hairs from shaving
all over the tub.

Every time a friend calls, ask them to help you add to the list—
but make sure you explain your motives. Friends will be suspicious if
you ask them to bag the person, because they're worried you'll use it
against them if the two of you get back together. Explain that it's a
silly little exercise you want to do to get on with things right now, and
you'll be amazed what nasties they'll come up with!

BOTH CLING TO THIS

Look at yourself in the mirror every morning and evening and say to
yourself, "It's over. They're not coming back. I will survive." Keep on
doing this until you can look yourself straight in the eyes, speak con-
fidently and believe it.

Day seven
FOR BOTH OF YOU

Get out your diary and phone book and spend the day calling all the
people you've neglected during your relationship. Prepare what you're
going to say when they ask about your ex (a simple "It didn't work
out" is fine). Make dates with everyone until your diary looks satisfy-
ingly full. Give opposite-sex friends preference: they'll give you the
ego boost you need, but be careful with exes. It's extremely tempting
to convince yourself they really were "the one" when you're feeling
vulnerable and lonely. (They weren't.)

I wouldn't accept invitations to go out and party just yet—you're
still too raw. Instead, plan evenings with good friends and happy couples. No, you won't look at them and feel envious—you'll see living
evidence of people who've been through what you're going through
and had the courage to fall in love again. Ask them (separately) to
recount the details of their past break-ups. How they never thought
they'd love again but here they are, doing just that.

B BOTH CLING TO THIS

Do I honestly believe I'm not going to meet anyone else in the next ten years?

Week two

Congratulations! Here you were thinking you couldn't make it through a minute and you survived an entire week without a) joining the French Foreign Legion; b) joining a cult; or c) moving back to the country to live with your parents. A shred of self-respect should be resurfacing. By now, you're probably making about three "God, I feel awful" calls to friends a day and are able to spend half an hour on your own without feeling suicidal. Now's the time to cut the umbilical chord completely. Ask mutual friends not to report back every piece of gossip about your ex—and vice versa. Don't spend your life trying to find out about theirs. If they're depressed, it'll give you false hope. If they're out dancing until dawn—your ego will take another dive.

Beware of friends who encourage you to believe your ex will "wake up" and come back: they're not doing you any favors, just trying to make you feel better. If your ex seriously does think they've made a mistake, they'll call you themselves. Don't believe it unless the words come out of *their* mouth.

On the subject of friends, remember they have lives, too. Make sure they know how much you've appreciated their support and put up with your knocking on their door at 3:00 A.M. and phoning 65 million times an hour. It's okay if your conversations are still largely dominated by your break-up, but make an effort to spend even a quarter of it asking about them. As for striking up a friendship with your ex, it's too soon. Leave it a few months or longer to put some distance between you.

Week three

Okay, you cried when you found his old T-shirt at the bottom of the laundry basket or an old lipstick of hers under the hamper in the bathroom. But you may find sadness being replaced by anger—white-hot, good-thing-you-don't-own-a-gun type of anger. By all means, fantasize about taking revenge, but don't do it. Instead, get rid of the anger in a constructive way. A girlfriend of mine started running. "I was so angry, I didn't know what to do with it so I started pounding the pavement." She now has the best legs in town. Join a gym, take on extra work, get your hands dirty in the garden: just do *something*!

By now, a certain amount of logic should be creeping in. Even if they came back, could you trust them not to leave you again? Even if you did call and beg for another chance, wouldn't you always wonder if they did it just because they felt sorry for you? Your brain's exhausted from diagnosing and dissecting the break-up and quite frankly, you're a bit sick of thinking about it. You stop taking all the blame for the split and realize it's rarely, if ever, one person's fault. Your friends stop worrying you're about to jump off a bridge and call less. Their eyes start to glaze over when you mention your ex's name. By week three, you're forced to spend nights alone and you feel okay about it. Not great, just okay. You still feel an overwhelming sense of loneliness and still wonder (for the 600th time) what they're doing at that moment, but it shouldn't be the focus of your existence. If it is, again, get yourself to a therapist.

Week four

Life goes on. You're surviving without them, your heart is mending but this makes you feel despondent rather than satisfied. True love? Yeah, right. Forced to watch a sappy film, you scoff at the romantic parts and your friends accuse you of being cynical. You are—but that's normal. We all lose faith for a little while. If you're feeling depressed and unmotivated, take a good look at your health. You've probably been eating little and grabbing takeout when you do. Resolve to eat healthily, cut back on the alcohol and cigs, and get a solid eight hours' sleep a night. The better you feel physically, the better you'll be able to cope emotionally.

If you find you can't stop thinking about your ex, try some aversion therapy. Put an elastic band around your wrist and flick it each time you think about them. You'll literally snap yourself out of it because it *hurts*. Your brain will start to associate thoughts of your ex with physical pain and subconsciously stop you from thinking about them. When you flick the elastic band, say to yourself, "I don't need you. I have my own life. I'm over you."

The next month

Take a long look at yourself in the mirror. Are you happy with your appearance, your image, and your wardrobe? The sort of person you are? If not, do something about it. Indulge in a personal trainer, get a friend with great style to help you shop for new clothes, treat yourself to a massage and let a professional get rid of the tension of the last few weeks. Work on areas you'd like to change. Start being a better friend, work harder, take some evening courses. Get back in touch with your sexual side as well. Start masturbating again, if you've stopped. Once your libido kicks back in, you'll find yourself checking out others in the gym (on the street, in your office) even if your heart and brain aren't interested in following through.

I still wouldn't suggest you hit the local nightclubs but you are ready for a restaurant, cafe, or bar. You're not out there to meet anyone, just for the experience of going out single. Don't take it personally if no one checks you out, chats you up, or appears even remotely interested. You're still exuding "poor me!" vibes, even if you don't realize it.

By the end of the month, you begin to feel remotely normal. The word's out that you're single and everyone's inviting you to this party or that dinner. Your calendar is nicely packed full of dates and you've got things to look forward to. You feel rightfully proud of yourself for having coped and think you're well and truly over them until—a song comes on the radio and suddenly it all comes flooding back. You're laughing with friends and *she* walks past—only it's not her at all, just some girl with the same haircut. You go to dinner with friends and your eyes slide down their bookcase and see a travel book on Bali and a memory of the two of you poring over that vacation brochure hits you smack between the eyes. It hurts *intensely* and you think, *Oh God, I'm kidding myself. I'm not better at all.* But you are because the pain does fade—even if you feel faded from the experience.

It's most unfair but you'll probably find all the memories of the two of you are good ones. Blame your brain. We idealize past relationships because our brains are programmed to throw up pleasant memories rather than painful ones. It's an instinct that usually works in our favor (to keep us as happy as possible)—but not in this case. Beat it by consciously dragging up a really unhappy, unpleasant memory about the two of you every time your brain throws up a good one. It puts things into perspective and helps ease the pain. Don't panic too much if you're still having the occasional daydream about your ex months and months later. It's natural to think fondly of your last lover if you're a lonely single.

Two months later

You're laughing again. You're noticing things—like that great shirt or dress in a shop window (and the cute assistant standing at the counter). Life feels full of possibilities and after all those weeks of mooning around, you desperately want to *get on with it.*

It's around now that you suddenly feel the urge to meet someone new IMMEDIATELY! You still miss your ex but wonder if it's more the relationship you miss than the person. By all means get out their and flirt your butt off but do yourself (and them) a favor and keep any relationship you have on a casual basis for now. Give yourself time to grieve and heal and sort through all the baggage. The right time to start a fresh, new, serious relationship is when you honestly believe you understand what went wrong the last time and—even more important—feel confident of your judgment to pick someone who really will be good for you. Even then, take it slow and keep both eyes *wide* open. Not just to protect yourself, but to see the new love of your life. Because if there's one advantage to breaking up, it's this: you get to go through that delicious falling-in-love stage all over again!

If you lived together or were married

If you lived together or were married, the pain of separation is more intense, and you'll take longer to get over it. The above guide applies to you, but you need to multiply the time frame by about a thousand.

Live-in lovers don't get as much sympathy as marrieds who split, but if living together is a trial marriage, then splitting up is a minidivorce. And it's obviously going to hurt more if you lived together rather than simply went out. You shared the rent, the bathroom, and the cat: you're not just losing the relationship, you're losing a life that you've built together. One of you has to move out, you have to decide who gets the fridge. His parents feel like your parents. Your big brother is now his best friend. You're used to sharing your life with someone, and it's difficult to close the gap when they're gone.

If you were married, it's even more heartbreaking. You've got the divorce to face. A whole house full of furniture to split up, bank accounts to divide. If you have children, you need to work out custody and visiting arrangements and accept the fact that, despite what's happened, you have to live with this person in your life forever.

It's beyond the realms of this book to delve too deeply into the serious psychological fallout of a divorce or major separation, and I would strongly suggest you see a counselor to help you get through the first few months. At the very least, buy a few books that deal specifically with this topic and lean on your friends, specifically those who've been through divorce also.

But even after the toughest break-up there is light at the end of the tunnel, and I've included a real-life story to prove it. Nick is a friend of mine whose "happy" marriage came to a rude and distressing end two years ago. He seriously thought his life was over—and I can honestly say I've never seen anyone suffer quite as much over a break-up as Nick did. The reason I want you to hear his story is because he *did* come out the other side. And how. Nick's still single but judging by the bevy of (I'm not kidding here) truly amazing women vying for his attention at a dinner party recently, he won't be for long. He wasn't just smiling—I thought his face would split.

Later, I asked him privately, "Better now?"

He nodded and said, "Actually, better than when I thought I was happily married. I feel brand new."

Have faith in yourself. If Nick can do it, so can you. Nick, 38, was married and has two children. Here's his story:

I lost my virginity to Andrea and she with me. We got married when I was 17 and for twenty years I thought I had the perfect life. Andrea's extremely attractive and I loved her utterly and totally. She wasn't concerned about looks, herself. She didn't care when my hairline started doing the old receding thing—not that I was ever up to her standards anyway. I'm sure people used to look at us and think, *What's she doing with him?* It's not like I'm rich or anything, but she was the model wife. She didn't look at other men, didn't flirt.

We both worked odd hours and sex wasn't a big deal for us. My sex drive isn't high and I just figured hers wasn't either. People said to me after the divorce, "Didn't you realize something was up when you weren't having sex?" but I honestly didn't. We had enough to bear two children, who are a gift from God. They are my life, and if it wasn't for the boys I would have killed myself.

My parents live on a farm and I'd often pack the kids in the car and stay a few nights there to give Andrea a break. She worked most weekends anyway. On one occasion, I told her I'd be home on Monday but decided to come home early. I can't remember why, though I know it wasn't for sinister reasons, like not trusting her. After 20 great years with no signs of unhappiness or straying, you forget about all that stuff.

I remember it was exactly 11:00 A.M. on the Sunday when I let myself and the kids into the house, because I looked at my watch and thought, *We'll have to be quiet because she'll be asleep from working a night shift.* The kids were outside running around and I came in through the living room and went straight to the bedroom. The door was closed. I opened it and from then on, it was like my mind registered everything in flashes.

The first thing I saw was a man's jacket thrown across the bedside table. Then I saw two people having intercourse on our bed. The man turned around slightly but I didn't know him. My first thought was, *Oh my God. Someone's broken in and been using the place to have sex in.* Then I saw her hair, all spread out on the pillow like it always is. At that point, she saw me and screamed, "Jesus Christ!" They froze and stayed like that for what seemed like minutes: this guy's penis still inside my wife. I don't think any of us knew what to do.

I heard the boys racing up the stairs and opened my mouth to shout "No! Stop!" but nothing came out. They stopped in the doorway but didn't go in, so they could see legs but not much else. They looked at my face and sensed something was wrong, though they didn't know what. I moved instinctively toward them and one of my sons said, "What are you doing, Mommy?" and then he came and held my hand and my other son hid behind my legs. I remember holding their hands and leading them down the stairs, then calling my best friend, Stuart. Then I put my head in my hands and just sat there.

I don't know how the guy got out but he managed to escape without running into me or the kids. Andrea took control of the situation. The kids were packed off to the neighbors, my friend arrived, and she sat there with the two of us. I'm dead certain Stuart would rather have been anywhere else in the world than sitting between two people whose marriage has just crumbled, but we needed him. So he stayed.

Andrea told me the guy was someone she'd picked up and they had casual sex once in a while. He wasn't the first one. Turned out she'd been having sex affairs for around ten years. Why? It had nothing to do with her love for me, she said. She just needed good sex, and I wasn't interested and this way, she got what she wanted, I wasn't hurt and everyone was happy. Until she was found out.

Some husbands, I guess, would have forgiven Andrea. Maybe turned a blind eye or tried everything they could to turn her on and make sex great. I couldn't. I left for a while and sat for hours, in a motel room out of town. I was very calm and logical. I knew what I wanted—access to the kids. And I knew she'd give it to me because the courts wouldn't look favorably on her as a fit mother. Now, we have joint custody so the kids spend equal time at her home and mine.

The pain of all this was unbelievable. My sister pushed me into the dating scene and I felt like a complete idiot because I got married so young, I didn't know how to do all that singles stuff. I don't want another serious relationship right now, but I would like to have the life I had with Andrea. I loved being married and I would love to have another child, one I could have full-time, and to feel whole and happy again. I'm gun-shy, and all the women I've met know it and steer clear, but I can feel my confidence returning, and if I met the right girl and trusted her, I know I'd try again.

WHY NOW? YOU CAN'T POSSIBLY DUMP ME—IT'S CHRISTMAS!

"I opened my eyes and thought, Hey! It's Christmas," says Fiona. "I kissed my boyfriend on the mouth and thought, Maybe he'll choose today to ask me to marry him. We swapped presents (mine was perfume—which should have warned me) and went to his parents' house for lunch. Afterward, he asked me to come and sit by the pool with him. My heart did a flitter-flutter and I beamed at his parents, who gave me sad little smiles. They knew what I was thinking, and they also knew what their son was about to do. He told me it was over the minute we sat down.

"I asked him, 'Why now? We're expected at my parents in an hour.'

"And he said, 'I know and that's what made me realize I can't live this lie. I can't face going to your parents' house and having your family ask when we're going to get married, so I had to tell you now.' "

I personally know three people who've been dumped on Christmas Day. I know another two who were dumped on their partner's birthday (*after* the present, I might add). Add about a dozen who've become suddenly single during their thirtieth or fortieth year and at least three couples who didn't make it to midnight on New Year's Eve. That's just in my circle of friends.

You don't need to be Einstein to figure out something's going on here. But why is it that people seem to have particularly bad timing and dump their partners at certain stages, ages, and dates in their lives?

The answer is simple. Birthdays, anniversaries, Christmas, and New Year's Eve force us to think about where our lives are going— and where we've been. Clever people appraise their progress constantly; others get so caught up in the daily rituals of living, that's *all* they do. They go through life on autopilot. For people like this, significant dates are like a wake-up call. They finally reflect on what happened the year before and decide they can't bear another one like the last. It's the equivalent of someone screaming at them through a loudspeaker, "For God's sake. You've been unhappy for ages. DO SOMETHING ABOUT IT!" So they do. Right there and then.

Turning 21, 30, 40, 50—any milestone birthday—is also a time of introspection. We all have a life plan, things we want to have achieved by a certain age, even if we don't religiously stick by it or are particularly conscious of conforming to a timetable. And out of all our goals, marriage and children are by far the most likely to have a deadline attached to them. It's sensible for starters, because women have a fertility cut-off point. If you're a female about to hit 38, want children, and your partner won't even consider moving in (let alone marriage or kids), your birthday present to yourself might be to get rid of him. Give yourself the chance to meet someone who does want to start a family. Time waits for no man and, unfortunately for us, it doesn't wait for women either. Other life events also affect relationships. If your best friend gets married, it forces you to think about it. Realizing you could never get up there and say the sickness and health thing to *your* partner can make you realize the

Revenge: ex-*tremely stupid!*

The best revenge is living well. *No it isn't*, you're thinking. The best revenge would be taking a sharp knife and making deep, satisfying scratches all over the gleaming paint job on his brand-new car. Or cutting off one arm of each of his suits with scissors. Or maybe poisoning those outdoor potted plants she loves so freakin' much. Better still, the cat. That'll wipe the smile off her smug, arrogant face!

Damn right it would. I can't deny the temptation to hit the person who hurt you straight where it hurts them is appealing. Let *them* feel pain for a change. Let *them* see how it feels to have your heart ripped out. For at least a minute, you'd feel like justice had been done.

But here are five good reasons why revenge *won't* make you feel better in the long run:

1. They might retaliate by doing something even worse.
2. They might report you to the police, sue you, or even get you thrown in prison.
3. They might tell everyone what you did (including your mother).
4. They'll have the satisfaction of knowing you're still hung up on them.
5. They might feel sorry for you.

> I sent hate mail to his boss, to his mother, to his friends, and anyone else I could think of. I blabbed every secret he'd ever told me, repeated everything bad he'd ever said about them. A mutual friend called me to say she'd read one of the letters and wanted nothing more to do with me. "No wonder he left you," she said.
> Angela, 23, shop clerk

What do you honestly think would give you the most satisfaction one month from now? Running into your ex at a party and a) being abused in front of all the other guests, and their new girlfriend/boyfriend, for behaving like a psychopath, or b) not even noticing they're there because you're too busy smooching *your* new partner. As they're gazing at you in shock, a total stranger interrupts to tell you how drop-dead gorgeous you look. And a friend shouts across the room, "Hey, Susie! Congratulations on that promotion!"

I rest my case.

THE DREADED EX: YOURS—AND THEIRS

I adore just about all my exes. Come to think of it, almost all my male friends *are* exes. Ask me to tell you the benefits of having an ex-lover as a friend and you seriously can't shut me up. About the only time I do is when I've first started going out with someone new. Strangely enough, not all men initially applaud my talent at being able to recycle old boyfriends as friends. Researching this chapter, I now know why.

Exes are a *huge* problem for many people. Either you've got one you can't stop obsessing about or an ex is hassling you. Or your partner's got an ex they're not quite over or one who's hassling them. Either way, it's bad news. Exes can stop you from moving forward and can cause havoc in new relationships. If you need evidence of this, look no further than *Ally McBeal*. The entire TV show is based around the relationship between Ally and her ex, who also happens to work with her and also happens to be married to another coworker (and of course she's blond with long legs. Don't you just love TV?).

The final section of this chapter is for anyone who's stuck on an ex or convinced their partner is. Plus there's some answers to the age-old question: do relationships ever work the second time around?

> Men carry the scars of divorce long after the relationship collapses—and it's all their wife's fault. Most men blame their wives not just for the problems that caused the split, but for the divorce as well (they did it because "that was what she wanted").[9]

IS YOUR PARTNER REALLY OVER THE EX?

How to tell for sure? There are danger signs and you're wise to watch for them. Because if your partner hasn't let go of their ex, they're not ready for a serious relationship with you.

The break-up was sudden and they weren't prepared

"I think Mike was still in shock when I first met him," says Jenny, a 23-year-old student. "We went out for three months but it was like dating an empty shell. He was about to propose to his old girlfriend, wasn't aware of any problems, but came home one evening to find she'd cleared her things out. She gutted him so effectively there was nothing left for anyone else."

Most of us assume the length of time our partner and their ex were together is the most important issue. But while it's relevant, it's far more crucial to find out if they were emotionally prepared for the split. If they had no idea it was coming, they're probably having a tougher time dealing with it. In other words, it doesn't matter if they were going out six weeks or six years, if they genuinely cared, it's still traumatic to have that rudely taken away from them.

The reason for the split seems trivial

Nikki's new lover had only been single two weeks. He'd had a massive fight with his long-term girlfriend over something silly and hadn't spoken to her since. Nikki felt she was in her boyfriend's bed but it was the ex that was still in his head. And guess what? She was right. He went back.

If you can possibly help it, steer clear of anyone who's just split, and make sure enough time has passed so it looks permanent. It could well be just a fight. Also, be on guard for signs of "rebound." Are they genuinely interested in you or just want someone around?

It's like they never left

"It was almost as if he'd never left," says Carl, still bruised after a short but intense affair with a newly single girl. "The ticket stubs to that special concert were still pinned on the bulletin board. There were photos of him everywhere, all lovingly framed. There was even a shot of the two of them wrapped around each other next to the bed."

You feel like an intruder because you are. The ex isn't out of their life until they've removed the evidence. The same way mothers who've lost a child will sometimes leave their bedrooms untouched, turning them into shrines, some people do the same with their exes. Now if their ex did die, fine. Leaving photos around is all part of the grieving process. But if they're sitting around surrounded by paraphernalia from an ex who's very much alive and left three months earlier, it's not a great sign. It means they can't let go, don't want to erase them from their life, and secretly hope they'll walk back in one day. Do yourself a favor and walk out.

They talk about them constantly—even if it's to criticize

Anne suggested tuning in to an old *Seinfeld* repeat. "Sally used to love this show," Peter said with a sigh.

She came back from the hairdresser with a new, short cut. "That looks terrific," he said. "When Sally cut her hair off, she said it was much easier to look after."

Peter chose to eat at "their" restaurant, played sappy CDs that were obviously significant, and told Anne Sally's opinion on everything. "I couldn't have cared less if Sally was the first female to set foot on the moon. In the end, I couldn't stand it."

Equally nauseating and twice as dangerous is the person who takes great delight in constantly saying, "It's so nice to be with someone who doesn't get jealous/criticize my driving/loves my clothes. John/Jane was such a bastard/bitch." You think, *If you're so happy to be rid of them, why do you still care what they thought of you?*

They won't commit past Saturday night, even though you've been together a few months

This one's a little tricky. While their ex may well be the reason they're not keen to get involved again (they want them back), it could also be the whole experience has left them a little commitment shy. Alternatively (and this is *not* what you want to hear), they might love to settle down but just not with you.

Catherine found this out the hard way. "I hung in there for years with Alex, all the time thinking once he trusted me and got his ex out of his system, he'd come around to the idea of living together. He didn't. Instead, he dumped me, met another girl two weeks later and moved in and married her within a year."

Should you give it another try? What to do when the dumper dares to come crawling back

"Hi, uummm, it's me," they say on the phone. "Please don't hang up. I'm calling because I'm sorry. I have to see you. I think I made a horrible mistake . . ." Your heart practically bursts through your chest. You feel sick and elated simultaneously. This is the call you didn't dare hope for. The call your friends said wouldn't happen. The call that somehow makes the tears, the debilitating misery you've experienced now seem unimportant. They want to come back, they *do* love you. Life, once more, will be perfect.

Or will it? Before you tape together the ripped up photos and cancel that trip to Europe, before you even agree to see them, sit down and do some serious thinking. Second-time-around love affairs are risky business and, more often than not, that "one last try" simply breaks your heart one more time. Is it really worth the heartache?

Beware the first flush

It's your (second) first date. He comes over for dinner.

"Wow, that looks great," he says, snuggling up behind you as you cook his favorite meal. "And so do you."

> My girlfriend got pregnant accidentally and wanted to keep the baby. We were so young, I talked her into having an abortion but she never forgave me. I didn't see her for years. Then one day I looked her up on a whim. She thanked me for being sensible. I told her maybe it would have been the best thing that happened to me. We've been together two years now—and she's trying to get pregnant.
> David, 26, manager

After a glass of wine, he tells you he had to change hairdressers because she wore your perfume and it upset him too much. You confess to six Saturday nights in succession spent sobbing on your bed. He swears he doesn't know what possessed him to let you go and promises he won't go out with the boys so often. You say, "No, don't be ridiculous. I was being silly. Of course you should see your friends." All around, it's the perfect evening.

The initial euphoria of being reunited is heady stuff—and by all means, enjoy it, because it won't be long before reality rudely intrudes. Within a couple of weeks, you'll probably start falling back into old patterns. He remembers how argumentative you were; you discover he still spends every Tuesday night and Sundays with his mother. You're at the make-or-break point—again.

> I went out with a girl for three months and ended it because it was getting too serious. Two months later, I found I missed her friendship, called her up, and we got back together. Within a month, I wanted to leave again. A friend of mine once said: never go back and repeat your favorite vacation, you'll always be disappointed. He was right.
> Tom, 27, fitness consultant

Why? Because problems don't disappear just because you've had time apart. If your "let's get back together again" talk consists of simply telling each other how miserable you were apart, the relationship is destined to fail for the very same reasons you broke up in the first place. Unless you have a good idea of what led to the break-up and have some realistic solutions to the problems, *it's not going to work.*

When it's worth a second try

- **The circumstances have changed—or the person has.** You can make a sensible assessment of your chances of success by looking at the reasons why you split in the first place. If you separated because of outside stresses—their job demanded too much time, they had family issues to sort out, someone close to them died and they lost perspective—it's worth going back if the situation has now been resolved. Stress affects people's ability to think clearly and make good decisions. If they've sorted out whatever was stopping them from committing to you, it could have a chance of succeeding.

- **You think you can trust them again.** It's a key issue. Even if they didn't leave you for someone else, they still walked out and left you hurting. Can you trust them to stick around the next time you hit a rough spot? What would she do if you got sick and were bedridden for months? What would he do if you got accidentally pregnant? Will they stick around for the hard stuff?

- **You're sure you haven't idealized the past.** Are you 100 percent certain you want to try again? Look realistically at your old relationship. Was it truly as wonderful as you remember?

- **Give it a test run before you get too involved.** If you can test their commitment to change, do it. You broke it off because he was insanely jealous? Deliberately put him in a situation that previously would have caused fireworks. She was an outrageous flirt? Take her to a party and let her loose.

- **You need to go back to move forward.** Sometimes, letting an ex come back one more time, even if you *don't* think it will work, is a good idea. If you're haunted by "what ifs," give it one last go. That way you can finally convince yourself that you did give it all you had and it still didn't work. Some therapists call it "reality testing": going back to check you really have done the right thing.[10]

- **You're certain you can protect number one.** You genuinely believe things will be different. They seem like a changed person and you're prepared to take the risk. Terrific! By all means give it a go—but give it time before you give them your heart. Keep an objective eye on things and proceed with caution. Look after number one—yourself! If they haven't changed or the changes don't last, break up quickly and for good. This is one situation when "third time lucky" doesn't apply.

When you should forget it—and them

- **You forced them into giving it another go.** If you've threatened suicide or pleaded and cajoled until they've given in, your chances of success are close to zero. You can't force them into loving you.

- **They treated you badly.** If they were cruel—mentally, physically, or emotionally abusive—don't even think about it.

- **They try to sleep with you the first night you get back together.** They're horny, not sorry.

- **You're lonely and there's no one else around.** Please.

- **They've just been dumped themselves.** Everyone decides their ex wasn't that bad when they've been dumped. They're coming back for a confidence boost and will be off again the minute they feel secure.

- **They say they're willing to change but you suspect it's all talk.** People will say anything to get what they want and if they know you well, they'll know how to win you over. Promises to change are just words—it's their behavior that's important.

Can you ever be friends with an ex?

"Let's be friends." Let's be honest: it's the oldest cliché in the world. Few people mean it but we're all guilty of saying it in those last dying throes of a relationship. When you can't pledge undying love, friendship seems the next best thing, slipping in nicely after the "I'm sorry, but I don't want to go out anymore" speech. Never mind that you'll be crossing the street to avoid them from now on. Saying you'll stay friends leaves both of you feeling warm, fuzzy, and terribly adult.

But then there are times when you really *do* mean it. Okay, so you aren't working out as a couple but the thought of never seeing them again? It's unbearable. You say, "Let's be friends," and actually call them the day after the split to check they're okay. You leave it at phone calls for a few months, then when you think they've got you out of their system as a lover, meet for coffee. It's all a little strange to start with but kind of nice. Love changes into caring and before you know it, your boyfriend has turned into a best friend.

Ask anyone who's ever had one: friendships with exes are special. There's a comfortableness and familiarity male and female friends only ever achieve when they've gotten sex out of the way. If you're sick, he's the only one you'll allow to see you with unwashed hair and pink, fluffy slippers because *he's* seen it all before. You're a bit snappy? No need to explain: he's suffered through enough of your PMS episodes to recognize the symptoms 20 paces away. She understands how significant losing that promotion was because she knows your dreams. It's her shoulder you'll cry on because you don't need to explain yourself. You can touch and hug each other without fear of it being taken the wrong way, so when your new lover dumps you at 3:00 A.M., it's their doorstep you turn up on and their body you snuggle up to that night, feeling comforted but not obligated sexually. New lovers may hate them, your parents may never understand, but just because you don't love someone anymore doesn't mean you don't still love them.

Of course exes can be friends! But there are two golden rules you must abide by. Friendships with exes only work if you a) give each other time to make the transition from lovers to friends, and b) the split was pretty mutual. In other words, neither of you is still in love with the other or has a hidden agenda of wanting to take it further.

Another word of warning: be wary of using exes as substitute boyfriends or girlfriends. If you're such good friends you rarely venture out without the other, your chances of meeting someone new are slim. Everyone who knows the two of you will assume you've still got something going and strangers always assume any male/female combo is a couple. Then there's the sex thing.

Sex with an ex is awfully tempting when you're both single, climbing the walls for it and—the clincher—you've done it before.

> **Do you hate your ex with a passion or count him as one of your best friends? Surprisingly, neither matters when it comes to your ability to get over the break-up: it's how often you think about them that's the key. Intense but infrequent bursts of hatred are better for you emotionally than constant, cozy conversations and reminders.[11]**

Sometimes it works. I went through a period where I didn't want a relationship but still wanted regular sex. I told an ex, he said he was in the same boat and it seemed silly not to paddle together for a while. We did exactly that for a few months and managed to remain friends at the end of it. But I know plenty who drowned the friendship in the

JUGGLING AN EX AND YOUR NEW LOVER

- **Let them meet each other early on.** If it really is just friend-ship—on both sides—your partner will see firsthand and won't be threatened.
- **Include them.** Not every time but enough. If you want to see an ex alone (which is natural—after all, you want their opinion on your new lover!) do it during your lunch hour or on week-nights. Not date nights.
- **Don't take trips down memory lane if your partner's there.** This is the one area everyone slips up on: the tendency to slip into the "wasn't that weekend fabulous," "didn't we have a good time" stuff. Even if it is all over and you do just appear to be friends, it's not fair. That's called rubbing your partner's nose in it.

If you're on the other side

- **Get the full story on what happened between them.** Listen carefully and use your judgment.
- **Ask to meet them.** If it truly is just friendship and your partner's serious about you, the ex will be over the moon they've found someone to make them happy. If they're offhand or unpleasant to you, they're still hoping for a reunion or worried you'll hurt them. If you're genuinely in love, allay their fears. If they're still chilly after that, assume it's the former.
- **If they want to see each other minus you, ask for reassur-ance.** Get your partner to call you when he or she gets home. It's normal to feel a little paranoid to begin with, even if you're convinced there's nothing going on.
- **If the ex is an ex-wife or husband and they have children together, accept reality or leave: this ex is not going away.** If your partner and their ex-spouse are adult and sensible, they'll try damn hard to get along for the sake of their children. It is not your place, or your right, to interfere with or jeopardize any friendship they have.

process. Falling into bed with a comfortably familiar body often seems like the perfect solution, but just make sure it's not going to reignite any hopes you're unaware of. If they're still holding a candle for you (or you for them), you're not just fanning the flame by sleeping with them, you're pouring gasoline on it.

I don't want them but I don't want anyone else to have them either

Naughty. Very naughty—though, I have to admit, I also suffer the occasional, irrational, jealous pang when a significant ex finds someone they're serious about. It's natural. After all, they once held *your* hand like that, looked at *you* with *that* expression on their face. It used to be you brushing the hair out of his eyes and holding on to his arm and—oh, for God's sake, if she got any closer, she'd be in his pocket. I mean, she's all over the guy! How does he stand it?

Most of us become illogical about much-loved (maybe even still loved a little bit) former boy- or girlfriends. If we're single, it's a blow to our ego that they dared to find someone else before we did. Even if we dumped them and are shacking up with Christie Brinkley or Matt Damon, the idea of an ex liking (let alone loving) anyone more than us is unthinkable! Seeing them happily in love with someone else is like giving your friend a dress you never wear, then seeing them in it and wishing you had it back.

> I once went out with a model. Everywhere we went, guys eyed her up and my ego dived. I slept with an ex to boost my self-esteem, she found out, and it was all over. The irony is, I think she really did love me.
> Nathan, 20, student

If you're like most people, the first thing you'll do when you get home after seeing the happy couple (*Grrrr!*) is rummage through your drawers to find the old love letters and cards. *We were good together*, you think, flicking through photo albums and dreamily idealizing every good time you ever had. If you're realistic and mature, you'll wake up the next day and realize you feel a bit funny simply because the door is closing on a nice part of your life.

Or you'll feel like renting *My Best Friend's Wedding*—to find out where Julia Roberts went wrong, so *you* can get it right.

Help! I'm stuck

It depends on the length of the relationship and the level of commitment as to how long it'll take you to truly get over a break-up. After all, if you were married for ten years, you're obviously going to take longer to heal than someone who went out with their ex for a few months.

But if your friends and family are starting to look worried, the pain is still intense and unbearable, and it's been a few months, you might need to seek help. A few counseling sessions really can help you see things more clearly. They will help you work through the pain and get on with your life.

Alternatively, these are some reasons why you might not be able to move forward.

The relationship drifted apart for no apparent reason

If you're not quite sure what caused the break-up, you can't help but keep dwelling on it. Apart from not being able to learn from your mistakes, curiosity alone can drive you crazy.

Solve it by: If you're the sort that can handle feeling vulnerable, contact your ex (if you know where to find them). Explain you're having trouble getting over them because you don't have a clue why you split. Ask them to tell you, straight out, without sparing your feelings, what it was that caused them to leave. Take it on the chin, analyze it for a week, then drop it. If you still can't, get help from a pro. If you're too embarrassed to do this or your ex moved to Saudi Arabia to escape you (and, funnily enough, didn't leave a forwarding address), ask a close friend whom you trust to give you their opinion, *without sparing your feelings*.

The break-up was your fault and could have been prevented

The relationship was going wonderfully and you had a one-night stand and got caught, or you didn't give them enough time because of work pressures, or the timing was wrong for you. You can't stop thinking, *If only I'd done this or that.*

Solve it by: Giving it a second try, if you can. If you honestly think it could work if you changed your behavior, call your ex and ask for another chance. Explain the reason why it didn't work last time for you and your reasons for thinking it might now. If you cheated, chances are they'll hang up in your ear. If it was something forgivable, they still might hang up in your ear (their new lover is listening). Or they'll agree to try again. Whatever happens, you'll get rid of that "if only I tried harder" feeling. Even if they end up dumping you again, you've given it your best shot *now* and that's all you can do. You can't turn back time.

Reminders are everywhere

You're still living in the house you bought together. They're still best friends with your best friends and you run into them constantly. Even worse, you work together.

Solve it by: Removing the reminders. If it seriously is ruining your life, it's worth changing jobs, selling the house, even changing cities if you have to. Drastic measures, I agree, but necessary if it finally gets you over them and into a fresh, new life.

You can't stop spying on them

You know it's ridiculous but you find yourself parked outside their building, watching the window. You walk three miles at lunchtime to watch them eat a sandwich in the park. Every time you see them, the pain hits you again.

Solve it by: Keeping a diary. Write in it before you're tempted to play Sherlock and when you get back again. One of three things will have happened: a) you've seen something that's upset you (that is, they've found someone else); b) they caught you and you feel like a complete idiot; or c) nothing happened and you just feel empty and lonely. Record all these feelings and when you're tempted again, use the old smoker's trick of putting it off for five minutes. Spend that five minutes reading about how awful you felt after the last episode.

Resisting the rebound

Replacing an ex with another warm body will make you feel temporarily better. You've got someone to go to the movies with, a human hot-water bottle, your self-esteem gets a boost, and it *will* take your mind off your ex. And that's essentially the problem. Jumping straight into a new relationship means you won't heal from the last one. No one can sort out the hurts from an old relationship while simultaneously giving a new relationship the energy it takes.

Another point to consider is judgment. When you're hurting and desperate for someone to love, even the elderly walking their dogs in the park look good. You throw yourself even more enthusiastically into this relationship than you did the last one because you're even more desperate for this one to work. Invariably, the person you chose turns out to be so wrong for you it's not funny. You're forced to dump them (never fun) or they dump you (even less). So anything other than *casual* relationships are out, and you're only allowed those when you're starting to feel remotely normal and follow these rules:

- **Only have casual sex if you're the type that can handle it.** In other words, if you're going to wake up feeling guilty, don't do it. If you're the sort of person who can't help but turn anything sexual into a "proper" relationship, don't go there.

- **Make it plain to the person you're seeing that you're there for a good time, not a long time.** If you think there might be potential, tell them you're still getting over an ex and want to take it really slowly. Tell them you don't quite trust your feelings yet—so neither should they.

When you're ready to take it further

- You're absolutely certain you're not going to make your next partner pay for the crimes of your last.

- You stop comparing all new partners to your ex.

- You're prepared to take it slowly.

- You're confident in your judgment. By now you've had a few dates with Mr. or Ms. Wrong but got out of there the minute you saw the danger signs.

- You realize not all men or women are like your ex. Just because they did the wrong thing, it doesn't mean others will. You're able to trust a little.

- You can watch a romantic movie without wanting to hurl your popcorn at the screen.

- You don't *need* to change the radio station when "your song" comes on (even if you want to).

- You run into your ex and forget to tell your friends about it.

- You run into your ex and think, *That's weird. They don't look like how I remembered them at all.*

When you're nowhere near ready for a relationship

- You still run out of coffee shops because you think you saw your ex walk past.

- You have spare copies of your song stashed away just in case CDs actually can wear out.

- The labels on the canned food in your cabinets are all neatly aligned, you've reorganized the cutlery drawer three times this month, and mopped under the fridge twice.

- Your ex has a security guard posted at his front door.

- You care so little about your appearance, you bought five of everything, all in the same color, so wear the same outfit every day.

- You still drink yourself silly every weekend.

- You're so cynical about love, your best friend didn't even invite you to her wedding.

- The last time you saw your ex they were pushing a stroller, but you still haven't given up hope.

- You don't find this list funny at all, just intensely painful. (*Please*, get professional help. It really will help.)

10

Dear Diary

Four lives, four relationships: how does yours stack up?

••

In my previous book, *Hot Sex: How to Do It*, I asked six people to keep sex diaries for one month. Some took a bit of convincing (like, how detailed are we talking here? Are you sure my boyfriend won't recognize it's me?) but everyone I approached agreed. (Hell, once word got out, I was beating back volunteers!) Not so with the relationship diaries.

Singles refused: "Say I don't meet anyone? I'd look like such a loser." One married man refused: "I think if I was forced to write it all down, I'd have to leave." The same girl who'd provided me with a highly explicit sex diary refused point blank to even consider committing her feelings about her relationships to paper. "No way. That's too *personal*," she said. "Sex is sex. Love is private. I don't care if people know I had bad sex, but say my boyfriend cheated on me? I'd feel humiliated if everyone knew how devastated I really was." I agree with her. Revealing feelings *is* more intimate, and if a relationship is suffering, it is painful to record.

Finally, I found four people who I felt represented a broad cross-section of relationships and their different stages. Jason was having real problems with his girlfriend of six years. Jodie, a career girl, was happily cruising along and convinced she not only wouldn't meet anyone, she didn't want to. "If you're happy for me to talk about relationships generally, fine. But I'm telling you now, it'll be more about past relationships than current ones." (Amazing what can happen in six months, isn't it?) I chose Carla, married and trying to "make babies," because she represents a very traditional model of marriage. And then there's Brad. Brad, well . . . let's just say (hope?), he represents a small minority of single men (though if you read between the lines, he's actually not as bad as he likes to think). I'll give him this: he's certainly honest.

Each person was asked to keep a diary for six months. They were permitted to use false names for themselves and others but not allowed to alter or exaggerate any details of their lives. They could write about their current relationships, any significant past relationships, or their views on relationships in general. Each diary is recorded in their own words.

Jason

Jason, 32, is a journalist. He wrote his diary at the tail end of a six-year relationship and is currently (by choice) single.

The beginning

I can't just present you with a diary for the last six months because I need to go back to the beginning to make sense of it all. The whole thing was like something out of *The Celestine Prophecy*. Like, we were never in control, just two people being blown along and together by other forces. It was through a string of coincidences that we met and they lent a fairy-tale feel to the relationship. I think that's what made me lose perspective on what was really happening. Whenever things went wrong and I was tempted to bag it all, I'd think, *Believe in fate. This is meant to last forever.* I'm such a strong believer that people meet for a reason, I found that one of the toughest things to accept in the end. It was like, "Why did God go to so much trouble to put us together if it wasn't meant to be forever?" Idealistic, naive, stupid: maybe I was all of those things. Even by writing this down, I realize that the coincidences weren't *that* amazing, but at the time they seemed unbelievable. Such is the benefit of hindsight.

I was traveling around America with a friend when I first saw Christine on a train. She was totally absorbed in a novel. We spoke briefly, the usual stuff like where we were headed and so on. I found out she lived in Boston and was traveling with a girlfriend. That was the extent of it. The next day, we all ran into each other again, walking around the tourist traps. A few hours later, my friend and I walked in to have lunch at a cafe and there were Christine and her friend. We all said the "we've got to stop meeting like this" stuff and ended up going for a drink. Christine mentioned she was having a party when she got back to Boston and invited us. We said, "Great! It's where we're headed but we have to meet up with some other people and unless you want ten of us . . ." But (due to *another* string of coincidences), the rest of the crew didn't turn up. We had nothing else planned so we called Christine when we got to Boston and said, "Hey, about that party . . ."

At that point nothing was happening. I wasn't really into her—if anything I was into her friend—but we got along well. I was staying in a backpacker's place in town and we saw lots of each other. She was shy but interesting and for two nights we stayed up all night talking. On the second, without any warning at all, she kissed me. It was exactly midnight. I had no romantic feelings for her whatsoever before then, but when she leaned over and her lips touched mine it was like *bing*! I said, "Why did you do that?" and she said, "Because it's been exactly a year since I broke up with a guy who almost ruined me. I survived to meet someone like you." It was such a heavy, vulnerable statement yet I knew she wasn't attaching any strings to it: it was more an acknowledgment of the moment. I admired her courage so much then; now I realize there was something odd about it. She didn't know how I felt about her but she jumped right in there. Later, when it was safe for her to do so, she couldn't.

We made love that night and she cried when she came. At the time I was blown away but now I see it was the beginning of things to come. The wall went up—or maybe it never came down—because she never, ever told me why having an orgasm made her cry and while at the time I thought it was a happy cry, in reality it was bitter and sad and messed-up.

She went back to work, I continued traveling. I met someone else in the meantime and forgot about Christine for a little while. Then the new girl had to leave for a few days and I had the choice of waiting for her to come back and seeing her a second time or calling Christine again. I decided to wait for the girl, but again, something happened that meant she couldn't meet me. So I called Christine instead and it turned out she had two weeks' vacation, so we met in San Francisco. I remember we were in a jazz bar and I was at the counter, buying drinks. I watched her, sitting there, looking self-conscious and gorgeous and innocent and so much like a little child that I fell in love with her. (Her? Or who I thought she was?) When the two weeks were up, I went home with her and didn't leave for a year and a half.

The middle

It's weird when I look back. I thought I was so in love with Christine the whole six years yet friends remind me of conversations when I confessed I didn't think it was going to work. But I had nothing to judge it against. I'd slept with my fair share of women but she was the first to claim my heart.

She was the first girl I lived with, the first one I said "I love you" to. I had such a sugary, romantic idea of love. I used to think that once you were in love, truly in love, that was it. I'd see people split up and think, *Ahh! Well, they weren't in love after all.* Now I know it doesn't mean they weren't, they just fell out of it. It should last forever, but it doesn't always.

Again, in hindsight, there were clues I'd never really know her. She'd have nightmares, *real* nightmares, and wake up screaming in the middle of the night. But she'd never tell me what they were about. Ironically, she thought she was very open with her feelings and used to give me a hard time about not being expressive enough. It was like she put up boundaries, not realizing that she had. I didn't know it at the time but I think maybe my subconscious figured it out and that was why I didn't show her what was in my heart. It often felt like she was there with me in the flesh but her soul and spirit were somewhere else. Some bad place. There were times when we'd have a discussion and her interpretation of it was so completely different to mine, I'd question my hearing and my sanity. Maybe she drifted off to the same place during arguments.

I had to return to Australia and it seemed natural for her to come with me. She lined up work and then I was among my friends again. I started looking at other people's relationships and they seemed a lot more grounded than ours was. The couples would talk, laugh, rib each other, and smile and you could see they *liked* each other. Christine and I, I think we loved each other but I'm not entirely sure we liked each other as lovers. We liked each other as friends, but as lovers? I don't know. Yet for the first two or three years, I'd see her across a crowded room and know there wasn't anyone else. I'd think, *We're meant to be together.* No matter who was there she was always the one I wanted to wake up next to the next morning. Every morning. Forever. There was that feeling, then there were the nagging doubts. One or the other: never both simultaneously.

I feel I grew from a boy to a man when I was with Christine. I felt confused as to how much she was responsible for and how much I would have achieved on my own. I really wanted to stay with the person I'd traveled that journey with. She was a witness to an integral part of my life.

The (long, drawn-out) end

I was in love but who was I in love with? I knew what Christine had for breakfast, I knew that if she crinkled her nose she was thinking hard about something. I knew where to put my tongue to bring her to orgasm, I knew what writers she admired, what movies she hated. But she was still a mystery to me—and not in a good way. More a really frustrating, "hey, if we're going to get closer, you have to let me in" sort of way. I tried so hard to make her feel safe enough but it didn't happen. And so the blinders crashed to the floor and in that crowded room there were suddenly other attractive people. She might still be the one I wanted to wake up with but she wasn't necessarily the one I wanted to go to bed with.

I finally put my finger on it: the passion was missing. She'd never truly let go with me sexually. She didn't get passionate about life like I did. I wondered if she found me sexually attractive at all. I went to the gym. I built muscle. "Do you realize why I go to the gym?" I asked her once. She shrugged. "Because I want you to look at me and want me." I can't remember what she said, it was probably something really nice, but it wasn't the right answer, because she didn't understand. Sex trickled from sporadic to nothing. We talked a lot about doing things to improve our sex life. We tried this and that but it didn't work because it was me trying this and that, she never really did.

I worried that maybe she wanted marriage and kids and that was responsible for the coldness, because I hadn't asked. But whenever it came up, she gave the impression she wasn't ready. She'd say airily to friends, "Oh, I'm not ready for *that*. I'm not sure I ever will be." Yet, after we split, she told a close friend that's what she really wanted. She wouldn't talk about long term. That would mean one of us choosing to leave our country permanently. We were both tense but still in love. If I had to say what emotion I felt most at that point it was confusion.

There was a girl I worked with whom I knew I would have asked out if I hadn't been with Christine. I really liked her. I tried to avoid liking her. One night after work, we went out to dinner. I knew I was putting myself in a dangerous situation but I wanted to prove to myself I could get through it: my love for Christine would be protection. The other part of me knew why I was really there. I wanted to feel someone melt in my arms and kiss me like they meant it. We had dinner, we went back to her place and played CDs. Nothing happened. I kissed her goodbye at the front door and walked to my car then thought, *No!* and went back and she was still standing there, watching me, and we went inside and it was so amazing to hold someone and know they wanted to hold me and touch me and make love to me as much as I did them. I savored the feeling but broke it off before anything of consequence happened. I got in the car and had a half-hour drive ahead of me and I knew the minute I got home I was going to tell Christine what happened. Sure enough, she was in bed, awake. Every other time I'd gone out with friends, she was asleep when I got home. I told her and she said she knew. She'd picked up the vibes. Did she? Or was it another metal door clanging down, the key thrown away forever?

It all basically disintegrated from there, but I honestly don't think it was because of that kiss. The separation was happening way before that happened. I wanted to go on vacations together, she didn't. We agreed to separate for two weeks and live life as single people. Implied in that was if we met someone else, we'd act on it. See if we *could* make love to them. See how it felt, how it made us feel about each other. At least, that's what I *thought* we agreed on. It was yet another of those conversations where I thought we said one thing and she thought another. As it turned out, I did meet someone when I was away. I thought she was special. Alison made me think there was someone else out there for me, that Christine wasn't the only one.

I came home and Christine and I tried again. After six weeks, she asked if I'd slept with anyone while I was away. I told her the truth: we'd agreed to be honest about whatever happened. But all of a sudden, I was a bastard. I'd betrayed her. The conversation we'd had hadn't occurred as far as she was concerned. Again, I wondered if it was me, stupid me, me who couldn't even listen properly. About one week later Christine went home to the States to see her family and we decided it was time to pack up shop and split permanently. She'd found somewhere else to live, I was going to move out of the apartment we shared.

You know what? I didn't care less at that point. I'd had enough. The first thing I did was call Alison and invite her down for the weekend. Again, coincidence.

"You won't believe this," she said. "My boss just told me I have to take vacation—I've got too many days built up. I can come down for two weeks."

Two weeks was a lot different than a weekend. I freaked out. It had all started to hit me: Christine and I had split. I picked Alison up at the airport. She didn't look the way I remembered. I took her out and she started touching me and I could feel myself flinching. I hated myself for that. It wasn't Alison's fault: she was emotionally fragile, too, she'd had lots of bad stuff happen to her. If she'd come for a weekend, it would have been fine. But two weeks was way too much for me. Bad karma.

Alison left after three days and that was when I had what felt like an emotional breakdown. I collapsed emotionally. I felt no connection with anything or anyone. I'm a social person, but for two weeks I didn't contact any friends. I felt like someone had scooped out my insides and forgotten to stuff me with straw. I felt completely hollow. It was a nonemotion. I could get through the day but I couldn't reach out to people.

It passed and I moved in with friends. The emptiness translated into a "let's screw the world" feeling. I had one one-night stand with someone but it wasn't great. Then Christine came back and we started seeing each other as friends. We didn't know what else to do, so it seemed logical. There was talk of getting back together. I remember crying with her and wanting to be with her. She wrote me a letter and I still don't know if it said it was over or to give her time. I had no idea what she was feeling. I asked her if she loved me and she said, "How can you ask that of me?" And I felt bad, like I shouldn't have asked. I kept wondering what was wrong with me. Why was I so inappropriate all the time? That's one thing I won't tolerate in my next relationship: when you're in love with someone, you do have a right to answers.

The bottom line though was I thought she *did* still love me. I thought all this aloofness was a test that I was meant to pass. All I had to do was change and get to the point where I was ready to say, "No one else but you Christine," forever. I even read fucking John Gray: *Mars and Venus*. I thought maybe that's what she wants: a guy like that. I reached the point where I thought: I'll never meet anyone better than her. I'm willing to put up with what she doesn't give me and take what she does. I was ready to take the leap: marry her and have kids.

I planned to tell her on New Year's Eve. We were at a friend's place. She was predictably cool, which started me wondering if there was some-one else. So I asked. I said, "Look, is there someone else?" and she looked at me and said, "I don't think I want to be with you," and it was like she ripped my heart out and threw it against the wall. And before I started cry-ing, I said to her, "I wanted to marry you. I thought you were the one. I thought we were going to have children together. I thought we were going to have that perfect life. I always thought once I was ready for that with you, you'd be ready for me." She looked sad but her eyes were like a stranger's eyes. I found out later there was someone else. Who knows for how long.

I went home that night, lay in my bed in the new apartment we were meant to start a new life in, and looked at the four walls. I cried like a babbling idiot. I had to work the weekend and couldn't get out of it. So I'd cry all the way there in the car, wipe my eyes, do the job, get in the car, and cry all the way home. I woke up crying, I went to sleep crying. I cried like that for a month and even after that it didn't let up completely. Ironi-cally, I quite enjoyed it in a bizarre sort of way. It was the opposite to how I'd felt before. Before I felt nothing; now I felt everything.

But I still wanted her back. For four to five months I wanted her back. I've only *not* wanted her back for the last month or so. My fear used to be that I'd find someone else and start to feel something for them and *then* she'd come back and I'd let her and all the crap would start over again. Now I know, that won't happen. I saw her the other day with mutual friends and for the first time, I felt nothing but pity for her. I think maybe something really bad happened to Christine and until she deals with it, no one will get close. She's with another guy, the guy she was seeing while I thought she was still connected to me, and I wonder if their relationship is different to the one we had. For his sake, I hope so.

Jodie

Jodie is 36, single, and works in an advertising agency. She's divorced, has lots of short-term relationships, and, although she's not ready to settle down again, finds the tick of her biological clock quite alarming.

Month one

Everything is just brilliant right now. I secured a major, major client for the agency and I'm flavor of the month. Whoever said success breeds success was right. Before, I'd work so hard on clients and not get anywhere. I'd take them to lunch, do that whole wining and dining thing, and then they'd buy one piddling page in a cheap newspaper and complain if it didn't double their business overnight. This isn't the only major account I've won but times have been tough lately and I could feel myself slipping down a rung or two on the career ladder, the younger executives biting at my heels. Now I'm back on top: enthusiastic, motivated, and want more, more, more business.

I know this diary is meant to focus on relationships but they're so low on my priority list at the moment. I don't have time, I've only got so much energy and I want to devote all that to my career. By the time I'm 40, I want to own my own ad agency, so I'm spending most weekends working: reading, making plans, and organizing my finances. All I want to do on Friday and Saturday nights is flop in front of the TV with a trashy video. Only one problem: I'm as horny as hell. Power, winning, feeling so alive, it makes me want to have fierce, passionate sex. I've got a male friend whom I sleep with now and then in situations like these but I don't really want to call him because he's now involved with someone. I guess it's just me and the trusty vibrator.

Month two

This month started with a bang—literally. I rang my male friend and turns out it's not serious with this new girl, so we spent a whole day shacked up. Afterward wasn't so hot, though. I think maybe he felt bad about cheating on his girlfriend, which makes me think it probably is serious, he just couldn't resist a bit on the side. That makes me feel cynical about men and myself. Are men capable of being faithful? What if I was involved with some guy: would he say no to no-strings sex? And what does this say about me: what sort of woman am I to steal someone's boyfriend, even if just for a day? I keep reading that women find it difficult to have sex with men they're not in love with, yet I can quite easily. To me, there's two different sorts of sex: sex for fun and sex you have when you're in love with someone. They're totally different. I wouldn't dream of having sex for fun if I was involved with someone and loved them, but what's wrong with satisfying yourself in the meantime? I can rationalize it but still: what was meant to be fun ended up being tinged with guilt.

That nasty feeling continued, not helped by the fact that I turned 36 on the 20th. Wonderful—now I'm the wrong side of 35. Stupidly, I passed up the offer of dinner with friends for dinner with my family. My sister was there, also single at 32, and Mom went to town. "What's wrong with you?/Why can't you find a nice man and settle down?/Steve was such a nice man, I can't understand why you divorced him." I wanted to say, "Well, Mom, it's this simple. I found out he'd had a two-year affair with the office slut. God knows why, but it upset me since I was trying to get pregnant at the time." Mom has no idea why I left: most people don't. I kept quiet, not out of respect for him, but for myself. I was embarrassed that I didn't suspect, just kept on loving him. I felt like a fool and still do.

Turning 36 also dragged up that whole kids dilemma again. I know I've supposedly got years to think about children. I've seen girlfriends churn out their first at 40-plus but it makes me nervous, this constant ticking. Say I've got fertility problems? Say I have an early menopause? Each month I inspect my tampons and worry because there seems to be less and less blood. I asked my gynecologist whether that meant time was running out and he said it didn't. But I'm not sure I believe him. It feels like someone's set the timer and I have to find someone I want to spend the rest of my life with really soon. And I'm not ready yet. I don't know if I'll be ready before I turn 40: there's so much to focus on career-wise. If I were a man, I'd set the agency up first, get it running smoothly, then find someone, spend a few years getting to know them, then have kids. But I can't do that because I'm female and I'd be closer to 50 by the time that's all happened. I love being a woman but it makes me angry that I can't control my own body.

Month three

Fabulous! Just brilliant! Just when I'm starting to crawl out of this mini-depression and enjoy being single again, my ex-husband knocks on the door with flowers. He forgot my birthday. No, he didn't forget, he was just so busy with work and wanted to see me when he could give full, 100 percent attention to me blah blah blah. Like, save it for someone who gives a damn. Save it for someone who believes you. I hate him and it hurts that he can still muster up such a powerful emotion in me. I lie in bed some nights, imagining him with her, and it's still so painful. The pain's lessened but it hasn't gone away, and seeing him brings it all back, sharply into focus again.

I slept with my friend again and this time it made me feel better. He's broken up with his girlfriend so it wasn't serious after all. I like Alan—he's warm and funny and makes me laugh at myself. He knows all about my ex and helped put that into perspective.

An agency client asked me out today at a work function. He's a client of a coworker of mine and he's actually really nice. I think he'll do well once his business has a few years behind it. But it's agency policy not to date clients, even if he's not my personal client. I told him and he laughed and threatened to transfer his business to another agency unless I said yes to dinner. I laughed and changed the subject and he didn't push it. Still, it was a nice ego boost and made me forget about exes and babies for a few hours.

Month four

So much for my deliberately cultivated office image as the hard career woman who only lives for work (to get ahead in this firm, you can't afford to act female). The agency manager called me in with the biggest smirk on his face and thrust a letter at me. It was from Martin, the client who'd asked me out. Martin wrote to ask official permission to ask me to dinner, wanting assurance that it wouldn't affect my position within the firm. His argument was that since I didn't work directly on his account, the policy of not dating clients shouldn't apply. It was wittily worded, struck just the right tone, and couldn't possibly offend. I was ridiculously pleased but still my stomach turned over. My boss is moody and unpredictable: some days, he'd find this funny, others he wouldn't. Turned out to be my lucky day.

"Do you want to go out with this guy?" he asked.

"I guess so," I said, rather nervously.

"Then I think it's best you do."

He swore he wouldn't tell anyone, but I knew it'd be around the agency within an hour (and it was). My boss called Martin and gave him the go-ahead. Then Martin called me, suitably nervous. We arranged to have dinner that Saturday (a date night!).

Getting ready I felt all girly and silly, like I was 18 and going to the prom. Three girlfriends called to wish me luck, which instead made me feel annoyed and righteous. Like, did I look desperate? I was hardly hard up for dates.

"It's just because he wrote that letter," said my best friend. "It's like we all want something to come of it because of it."

Well, it didn't. Dinner was nice but I think the expectation was too much. We'd lost that easy flirting we'd had at the function and it was all stiff and horrible. He said he'd call but I don't think he will.

He called the next day. Early. Like I was still in bed. "Jodie, it's Martin. I'm calling to say what a disaster last night was and to see if you've got enough of a sense of humor to see the funny side or whether you never want to see me again."

I saw the funny side so we went out for lunch, drank, and laughed ourselves silly and ended up back at my place. The booze helped but it seemed totally natural to climb into bed (underwear on) and watch the late-night movie snuggled up. He made no moves on me, I made none on him. It was possibly the nicest night I've had in years. It worried me plus I was late for work. I'd forgotten why I didn't want a relationship: it's because it always ends up interfering with my career.

Month five

I so much wanted my diary to be that of a fast-paced career girl without any romance in it at all. I wanted it to show women don't need men. Like, we really like you, but you're not essential, you know! We can live quite happily without you. And that's still true: the best years of my life have been the single ones. But now Martin and I are very definitely a couple and I'm enjoying that as well. He's the first guy I've gone out with that doesn't mind that I'm so work-obsessed. He accepts I don't want to see him every night and that I work most weekends. He's not a hindrance to my career, he's a help. I find I'm using him as a sounding board for my ideas and he's as excited about me starting up on my own as I am. The sex is great but I think good sex is easy to find. It's the partnership thing I'm most impressed with. I'm more vulnerable with him than I have been in the past. One night I got drunk and told him all my fears about the child thing: worried that if I have kids, I'll hate the effect they have on my life; worried that if I don't, I'll regret it later. The next morning, I was so embarrassed. But instead of making me feel exposed, he said he felt the same things. He's 45 and though he doesn't have a time limit on his fertility, wonders about all that, too. Don't panic: we've only been going out a month and aren't going to do anything rash. But I think when you've had a few long-term relationships under your belt, you recognize early on which are going to be special and skip through those initial stages more quickly. This is one of the special ones.

Month six

Work's going well, my relationship's going well. Life's settled in a nice, easy, contentedness that I've never experienced before. I have no idea whether Martin and I will be together by the time this book is published. I'd like to think so but won't fall in a heap if we're not either. We've had our fair share of arguments (feisty ones, too!) but more than our fair share of good times. The best thing about it is, for once, I feel I'm getting the best of both worlds. My career is enhanced by my relationship because Martin's so supportive; my relationship is enhanced by my career because I'm smart enough to help him with his, too. I guess what you can take from my story is this: it is possible to have both.

[Author's note: Jodie and Martin are still going strong.]

Carla

Carla is 25 and was born in Italy. She came to Australia when she was ten years old and married a year ago. She is currently trying to get pregnant.

Month one

I am, perhaps, a typical Italian girl who's grown up in Australia. I've adopted Australian ways but retained things from my own culture that I truly believe in. I love my parents and my husband and I spend most week-ends at their home. My husband's parents live in Italy but we call them on weekends so we're close to them also, just in a different way. My parents' opinion of me is very important, even though I'm now married. They strongly influence me, but in a good way. I respect them and I respect their advice and opinions. I ask them, "What should I do about this or that?" and nearly always follow their advice. My Australian girlfriends don't understand this. They think it's weak, that I should grow up and distance myself, make my own decisions. I think, *Why not benefit from their wisdom? They love me, they've been through what I'm now going through and I know they won't lead me astray.* I consider this sensible. But I have a different value system from my friends. They believe they are different from their parents, that a generation between them means they can't under-stand. I don't believe this is true, but I accept their views and don't criticize them. I wish they would accept mine as readily.

My Australian friends think I married too young. My Italian friends and family believe I married late. Such is the curse of being a little of one, a lit-tle of another. I think I married at the right time. My Australian friends think my husband, Marco, is chauvinistic. My Italian friends think he is too Australian. He's like me: a little of both. He is warm and supportive, but likes a woman to be a woman. I put on make-up and dress up so I look pretty when he walks in the door after work. He appreciates it and compli-ments me. I like this, I don't find it demeaning or unliberated.

I consider myself as liberated as my friends: if my husband beat me or cheated or treated me badly, I would leave. But my husband and I still believe it's the woman who should be the one to look after the home and cook the meals and have babies and look after them, too. I try to make my friends understand that I'm not being forced into this role, I want it. I like it. It makes me very happy and him, too. So what's the problem?

Month two

I am trying to get pregnant. We stopped using contraception two months ago but nothing has happened yet. My mother is already looking anxious but she has no reason to be. I've read good books on pregnancy and know it takes longer, and neither Marco nor I is interested in turning sex into something we have to do at a certain time. We're just having sex like we normally do and waiting to see. Sex is different because we're now trying to make a baby. Marco is more affectionate and tender during it. Afterward, he cuddles me and says, "There! That made a baby!" I love him. He's like a man and a boy all in the same person. At home, he's affectionate and playful. At work, he's boss and people are a little scared of him. He's got a temper and can't understand that Australians aren't as volatile as we are and take his temper very seriously. If Marco and I argue, we shout and throw things and slam doors but ten minutes later, it's forgotten. I'm used to it but my friends aren't. Once, a girlfriend was here when Marco came storming in and she practically hid under the table when he shouted at me. But it was nothing. He was upset because the fridge was empty and I hadn't been shopping. There was nothing for him to eat and he was hungry, that's all. My friend told me his behavior was unacceptable. That if the fridge was empty, *he* should go out and do the shopping rather than shout at me about it. But it's my job to make sure he has things to eat. His to make money for us. I'd shout at him if he didn't do his job; it's fair he shouts at me when I don't do mine. Besides, it only lasted five minutes.

The same friend is worried that when I have a child, my husband won't help me. She means changing diapers and helping with housework. I don't need or want help with that. What I want Marco to do is play with the baby and give it lots of love and attention. I know he'll do that and I think that's more important.

Month three
My best Australian girlfriend is sick. She has meningitis, which means she can't work or look after herself. Her family lives far away and I'm worried about her. She doesn't have a husband and I don't understand why her parents don't come to look after her. She says it's because they've both got careers and can't afford the time away. I find that hard to relate to. If Marco's parents, who live in Italy, found out he was sick and he didn't have me, his mother would come over immediately. I asked Marco if she could stay with us until she gets better (she's the girlfriend who thinks he bullies me). He knows she doesn't like him but said fine. So I offered but she refused. I guess I'll just help by taking her food.

Marco and I have sex lots but still nothing. What started as a "let's wait and see and not stress" thing, has turned into pressure. My mother asks me every day if anything has happened; my father keeps telling me not to worry—I'm Italian! Of course I'll be able to have children! I wish maybe I hadn't told my parents we're trying. But they kept asking and asking when we would have children and I thought this would stop them from nagging me. It hasn't. It's made it worse.

Month four
Still no baby. I went to my gynecologist, who suggested Marco and I get some simple fertility tests done. Marco won't hear of it. I know why. He couldn't bear it if there was something wrong with him. He wouldn't be a "real man" if there was something wrong with his sperm. For once, I agree with my girlfriends that he's carrying the macho thing too far. Another part of me worries that there's something wrong with me. If I couldn't provide Marco with children, I would be devastated. I know he loves me but I know he also wants a family. A friend of mine, her husband left her when he found out she couldn't bear children. She understood but now can't find another husband. All men want children. I would feel like such a failure as a woman and a wife if I couldn't give Marco a son.

Month five
My period was late. I told Marco and he immediately called our families to announce I was pregnant. I wasn't. My period was two days late, that was all. It really upset me. I told Marco he was a stupid pig for doing that. I made him call everyone back and went to the bedroom and cried and cried. He came in afterward and said he was sorry and we both cried together. I asked him, "What if we can't have babies? Will you still want to be married to me?" He told me I was crazy, that he wanted children badly but would never choose them over me. I told him I was frightened there was something wrong with me and he said he was worried there was something wrong with him. I asked him again if he'd come with me to get fertility tests done and this time he agreed.

We got the tests done yesterday and now wait, impatiently, for the results. Marco is quiet and anxious. We didn't tell our parents we'd had the tests because we didn't want to worry them.

Month six
Celebration! Both Marco and I are given the all clear! We're both normal and healthy and all we need now to make babies is patience. We are both so happy and the relief is enormous. In a sense, though, I'm glad we had problems and I didn't get pregnant right away. Our marriage is better for what happened. I feel closer to Marco, knowing that he must truly love me to want to stay with me even if I couldn't have babies. There's a tenderness and togetherness that wasn't there before. We are now relaxed and making love happily again. My parents still nag, nag, nag, but it's okay now. I don't mind because I think it will happen soon.

[Author's note: Carla is now two months pregnant.]

Brad

Brad, 28, works in his family's business. He is single and enjoying living in a city of "desperate thirtysomethings."

Month one

My life is pretty routine. It has to be because I work 6:30 A.M. till 6:30 P.M., six nights a week. Monday nights I spend getting over the weekend, Tuesday nights I play sports and have a few beers with the boys afterward. Wednesday nights, who knows, Thursday maybe I'll see my semigirlfriend. Friday night is boys' night. No girls allowed. We get drunk, scope chicks, play pool, tell lies, tell jokes. Saturday night and Sunday day is girlfriend time, usually spent seeing her friends who bore me stupid because all they do is talk about work. Sunday night I'll go drinking again. The boys always get priority.

I wrote "semigirlfriend" because my girlfriend's a headcase. Headcases always seem to find me, I attract them. This one can't handle her booze and she calls me three, four times a day at work. She'll say, "I love you . . ." and it's like, "Look, can this wait? I'm busy here . . ." Every time we go out, she gets a few drinks into her and then she's off. I don't mind a woman with a temper—it shows she's got guts and soul—but Jesus!

Month two

The boys and I moved last weekend. As we were unloading our stuff, this old biddy from the unit next door said, "I hope you're quiet. We've had a lot of rowdy people up there in #9." Like, yeah right, lady, we'll try to be quiet. The first night, I had a blow out with my girlfriend down at the pub. She lost it again and I told her to wake up to herself, leave me alone, and don't come near me. Half an hour later, I'm at home, watching TV and I hear her outside, yelling obscenities at me at the top of her voice. I'm like, "The neighbors are going to *love* this." I got her inside, made her sleep on the couch, and told her not to come near me. This is the kind of girl who'd get up in the middle of the night and slash your penis off. I'm not joking, she's seriously weird. She's a psycho. But I woke up later that night to find her mouth wrapped around my penis telling me how much she loved me. A great way to wake up, but it's over.

She wanted to be friends and I thought: why would I want a woman as a friend? What have guys got in common with women, really? I'm 28, I play sports. What would we talk about if we weren't screwing? I've got my friends, why bother? Don't get me wrong, I love women. I grew up in a household of women: my mom, my sister, and my grandmother. I'm good friends with all of them—I just don't need any more female company.

Month three

I've been in love once, when I was 18. Her name was Nicole. When I met her, she was going out with someone else and so was I, so we'd see each other on the sly, whenever we could. She'd come over every Friday night while my other girlfriend was at work. I'd go to sleep with one girlfriend, wake up with the other: Nicole would come over and leave that night; then Trish would come home so I'd wake up with her. It was forbidden, which made it better.

Nicole had "it": everybody's got someone who does it for them. She had the body, she was great in bed, she was funny. She was also selfish and a bitch, but I'm selfish and an asshole so we got along well. We were a good couple. We'd walk in somewhere and kick ass all night. We went out secretly for four years, then moved in together for a year. I loved her but I found out she'd been screwing someone else. She did the sly on me. I lost it because it fucking hurt. It was tough for me money-wise, so we decided to keep living together until the lease ran out. That was hard. It was bad.

I haven't been in love since then but I say it. Girls say, "I love you," a month into the relationship. I'll say, "I love you," back. I do love them in a way, but not the way they mean it. I never lie to people but to women? That's different. I have no qualms about it. I just say whatever it takes to get whatever I want. I told you, I'm an asshole.

I was an idealist, now I'm a pragmatist. I look at other people slog through relationships and I think, *I don't need this. I've got enough hassles with work, let alone a relationship.* I guess a part of me is scared of getting hurt, but I think it's got more to do with not meeting the right girl. All I want to do with my life is meet a really nice girl, have kids, have fun. Who's my ideal girl? I like women with brains, but they're smart enough to steer clear of me. She can't be stupid, though. She's got to be a good sort, she's got to be good in bed. If she's not good in bed, there's no point to it, really. She's got to be independent. She's got to like sports. She's got to get along with my friends and family. And she's got to let me have at least three nights a week out with the boys. If I met a girl like that there's no way I'd cheat. Not at all. Not if I was totally in love with the chick.

Month four

I'm seeing a girl who's a good sort but all she does is keep up this constant, inane chatter about her career. She's a model/actress/dental nurse. Another nut job—and so dumb!

She called me one night—for the sixth time that day—while I was cooking dinner and it was really giving me a headache so I hung up on her, or at least thought I did. The phone in the living room was off the hook and she stayed on the line because she could hear everything we were saying. I'm saying to my roommates, "That stupid bitch. She's driving me mental. If she wasn't a dental nurse, I wouldn't even talk to her. I just want my teeth done for free." Then we started talking about one of her friends who we all want to screw and what we'd do if we could get our hands on her. About 20 minutes into the conversation I hear, "I can hear you," from the phone receiver. I hung it up immediately and thought of what to do next. I decided to pretend we'd done it deliberately. Like, we knew she could hear us and were trying to get to her. She fell for it. Like I said: dumb.

Month five

There was another girl I liked. She was lovely but not a good sort at all. Once, on Valentine's Day, she booked us into a really nice hotel as a surprise, spoiled me the whole weekend, and paid for the whole thing. That was the nicest thing a woman's ever done for me. No girl's ever paid for me when we go out for dinner. I always pay if I'm earning more. If she earned more, we'd go halves. But I'd never expect her to pay for me. It doesn't sound like it but I do treat women nicely when I like them. Flowers now and then. Take her out to dinner all the time. Go to the movies. Hold her hand.

But it's too much fun being single right now because this is a city of desperate thirtysomethings. Desperate unless she's a good sort, of course, then she'll get the pick of the room. I like older women, though. They know what they want, they don't giggle every five seconds. They're good in bed, comfortable in bed. It doesn't worry me if a woman's older than me. I don't think many guys are hung up on age these days. It's 2000: women can have babies when they're 43. Age is irrelevant.

Women should know that if they're a good sort, men find them unattainable. Which is silly because if you've got the gift of the gab, you can get them all. I don't usually approach women, I wait for them to approach me. One of my pals, he's always saying to girls, "Hi. Want a fuck?" Nine times out of ten, he'll get slapped across the face. But the other time, he'll get something. Some of the girls I've seen come out of his bedroom are horrendous. Another friend walks around all night looking at the good sorts, then at 3:00 A.M. he'll say, "I've got to find a pig." Because he knows, the uglier the girl, the more likely she is to put out that night. I don't do one-night stands, I don't like them. I've had about five in my whole life.

Good sorts are different. But you don't have to be good-looking to be one. It's about sex appeal. You can have a very ordinary girl who's got sex appeal, *oozes* it, and she's gorgeous. It's the way she holds herself, the way she walks, the way she'll give some other guy the brush, the way she looks at you.

Month six

I can't meet a nice girl with my lifestyle. I work 70 hours a week. When I'm not working, I'm either playing sports, watching sports, drinking, or carrying on like a yahoo. There aren't too many women around here who'd put up with that.

But I'm not chauvinist. Relationships now aren't like what our parents had. They're more like a business partnership. You can't expect a woman to come home from working all day and cook the meal, and do all your washing—it doesn't work like that these days. Most men my age know how to do all that shit anyway. Plenty are better cooks than women. I love cooking. I'll come home, cook for the boys, do the laundry. But I never iron. If I have to go somewhere and we're going out with her friends, the chick has to iron whatever I'm going to wear.

We still have roles, though. It's still the guy who has to put the garbage out, the guy who has to kill the spiders, the guy who has to go around and hassle the neighbor. The girl still buys the furniture and pictures to hang and makes the place look nice. Guys aren't interested in that stuff. But if my woman was earning more than me and we had kids, I'd stay home and look after them. No drama at all. I'd love it. Kids are easy. I think they're great. Every guy wants kids, you've got to have someone to carry on the name. And speaking of names, why don't women take the man's name anymore? I'd take it as an insult if a girl didn't take my name in marriage. We can't give up everything. We've given up being the breadwinner. We've given up coming home to dinner on the table. At least take the guy's name, for God's sake.

I don't know if I'll find the relationship I want. I'll probably end up marrying some slut, we'll have two or three kids, then three or four years later, we'll get divorced. Just like my parents. I hope I'm wrong but it worries me I'm going to be right.

Notes

CHAPTER 1

1. Deborah Blum, "Making Faces," *Psychology Today*, Sept./Oct. 1998, p. 34
2. Tara Barker, "Not Tonight Dear, I've Got Cellulite: How Your Weight Affects Your Sex Life," *Cosmopolitan* (Australia), Feb. 1998, pp. 58–59
3. Susan Quilliam, *Women on Sex*. London: Smith Gryphon Limited, 1994, pp. 78, 81
4. Hara Estroff Marano, "A New Focus on Family Values," *Psychology Today*, Nov./Dec. 1997, pp. 53, 54
5. Katie Aston, "Love by Numbers," *Company* (U.K.), July 1997, pp. 43, 45. (Based on theory of Dr. Peter Todd, a psychologist at the Max Planck Institute for Psychological Research in Munich, Germany)
6. "A Reason to Smile," *Psychology Today*, April 1999, p. 18
7. Study by Dr. Richard Wiseman, University of Hertfordshire, Hatfield, Herfordshire, U.K. As reported in "Women's Instincts" by Sasha Slater, U.K. *Cosmopolitan*, Aug. 1997, p. 80
8. Dr. Maryon Tysoe, *The Good Relationship Guide*. London: Piatkus, 1995, p. 9

CHAPTER 2

1. Flic Everett, "The Look of Love," *Company* (U.K.), June 1997, p. 57. Statistic quoted by Dr. Julian Boon, a psychologist from Leicester University, U.K.
2. Dr. Maryon Tysoe, *The Good Relationship Guide*. London: Piatkus, 1995, p. 20
3. Flic Everett, "The Look of Love," p. 57. Statistic quoted by Dr. Julian Boon, a psychologist from Leicester University, U.K.
4. Dr. Maryon Tysoe, *The Good Relationship Guide*. London: Piatkus, 1995, pp. 6–7; Rebecca Johnson, "Is He Mr. Right or Mr. Horribly Wrong," *Company* (U.K.), June 1996, pp. 82–83. Direct quote from the American researcher, Dr. Galdino Pranzarone.
5. Barbara De Angelis, Ph.D., *Ask Barbara: The 100 Most Asked Questions about Love, Sex and Relationships*. London: HarperCollins Publishers, 1997, p. 74
6. John Gray, *Men Are from Mars, Women Are from Venus*. New York: HarperCollins Publishers, 1992, pp. 30, 33
7. "Sex Report," *Cosmopolitan* magazine (Australia), Mar. 1998, p. 44
8. Allison Kornet, "The Truth about Lying," *Psychology Today*, May/June 1997, p. 54
9. *Ibid.*
10. Tracey Cox, "Get that Man!" *Company* magazine (U.K.), July 1997, p. 100
11. "Putting Sex in the Shades," *The Daily Telegraph*, June 22, 1999, p. 4. Based on study by psychologist Dr. Glenn Wilson, University of London.
12. Alison Magney, "Office Lust: When It's OK to Take It Further," *Cleo* magazine (Australia), January 1995, p. 76
13. Carol Potera, "Trapped in the Web," *Psychology Today*, Mar./Apr. 1998, p. 66
14. "Confirmed: The Closing Time Effect," *Psychology Today*, May/June 1997, p. 22
15. Cris Evatt, *He & She: 60 Significant Differences Between Men and Women*. Berkeley, CA: Conari Press, 1992, pp. 68–69

16. Allison Kornet, "The Truth about Lying," p. 54
17. Cris Evatt, *He & She*, pp. 29, 132–133
18. Barbara De Angelis, Ph.D., *Ask Barbara*, 1997, p. 171. Also term used by Australian clinical psychologist Eric Fleming, as quoted in "When You Can't Let Go" by Tracey Cox, *Cosmopolitan* (Australia), to be published.

CHAPTER 3
1. Dr. Maryon Tysoe, *The Good Relationship Guide*. London: Piatkus, 1998, pp. 87–88
2. Flic Everett, "The Look of Love," *Company* (U.K.), June 1997, p. 50. Based on views of John Jefferys, Professor of Neuroscience, Birmingham University; "Will You Make It or Break It?" by Yasmin Boland, *Company* (U.K.), March 1997, p. 72. "Looking Back: 30 Years of Sex, Love and Psychology," *Psychology Today*, July/Aug. 1997, p. 35
3. Cris Evatt, *He & She*, p. 91
4. Tracey Cox, "Are You Addicted to Him?" *Company* (U.K.), Dec. 1997, p. 94. Quote from Australian clinical psychologist Dr. Janet Hall.
5. Emanuel H. Rosen, "Think Like a Shrink," *Psychology Today*, Oct. 1998, p. 59
6. Grant Brecht, *Sorting Out Relationships*. Australia: Prentice Hall, 1997, p. 22
7. Barbara De Angelis, Ph.D., *Ask Barbara: The 100 Most Asked Questions about Love, Sex and Relationships*. London: HarperCollins Publishers, 1997, p. 42
8. "Reach Out and Propose to Someone," *Psychology Today*, July/Aug. 1997, p. 16
9. Barbara De Angelis, Ph.D., *Ask Barbara*. London: HarperCollins Publishers, 1997, p. 94
10. U.S. Bureau of the Census, 1992, p. 5

CHAPTER 4
1. Stephanie Osfield, "Confessions of Infidelity," *She*, Oct. 1997, p. 48
2. Study by author consisted of interviewing 28 heterosexual, two gay and two lesbian couples (total 32 couples), varying in age from 24 to 42, who considered their relationship "very happy" and had been together for more than two years. Interviews were face-to-face in 1996 and followed up by phone in 1997. Some results also formed basis of "Relationships in the '90s" by Tracey Cox. *Cosmopolitan* (Australia), May 1996, pp. 92–96
3. Sean Thomas, "Love Fool," *All About Men*, supplement to *Cosmopolitan* (Australia), June 1997, p. 13; "Why Men Don't Listen and Women Don't Read Maps," Allan and Barbara Pease, Sydney: Pease Training International, 1999, pp. 264, 265
4. Cris Evatt, *He & She*, p. 56
5. *Ibid.*, pp. 28, 29
6. Deborah Blum, "Making Faces," *Psychology Today*, Sept./Oct. 1998, p. 37
7. Cris Evatt, *He & She*, pp. 52, 53
8. *Ibid.*, pp. 32, 33, 82, 83
9. *Ibid.*, pp. 62, 63
10. *Ibid.*, pp. 64, 65
11. Dr. Maryon Tysoe, *The Good Relationship Guide*. London: Piatkus, 1995, pp. 60–61
12. Cris Evatt, *He & She*, p. 61
13. *Ibid.*, p. 53

14. John Gottman, *Why Marriages Succeed or Fail.* London: Bloomsbury, 1997, p. 216
15. Tracey Cox, "Want to Know How Many Men She's Slept With?" *Sex Report, Cosmopolitan* (Australia), June 1997, p. 48
16. Dr. Maryon Tysoe, *The Good Relationship Guide.* London: Piatkus, 1995, pp. 35–42
17. Barbara De Angelis, Ph.D., *Ask Barbara: The 100 Most Asked Questions about Love, Sex and Relationships.* London: HarperCollins Publishers, 1997, p. 21
18. Direct quotes from various couples interviewed in study by author, which consisted of interviewing 32 couples, varying in age from 24 to 42, who considered their relationship "very happy" and had been together for more than two years. Interviews were face-to-face in 1996 and followed up by phone in 1997. Some results also formed basis of "Relationships in the '90s" by Tracey Cox, *Cosmopolitan* (Australia), May 1996, pp. 92–96
19. Katherine Billie, "When Couples Compete," *Psychology Today,* Sept./Oct. 1998, p. 14
20. Dr. Maryon Tysoe, *The Good Relationship Guide,* p. 84
21. *Ibid.,* p. 85
22. *Ibid.,* p. 89

CHAPTER 5

1. Allan and Barbara Pease, "Why Men Don't Listen and Women Don't Read Maps," Sydney: Pease Training International, 1999, p. 219; John Gray, Ph.D., *Mars and Venus in the Bedroom.* Sydney: Hodder Headline, 1996, pp. 3, 4
2. Allan and Barbara Pease, "Why Men Don't Listen and Women Don't Read Maps," p. 230
3. Dr. Maryon Tysoe, *The Good Relationship Guide.* London: Piatkus, 1995, pp. 132–33
4. Joann Ellison Rodgers, "Flirting Fascination," *Psychology Today,* Feb. 1999, p. 45
5. Durex Condoms, *Durex Global Sex Survey,* 1998, p. 30. The survey investigated the sexual behavior and attitudes of 10,000 men and women across 14 countries. Commissioned by London International Group PLC.
6. *Ibid.,* p. 9
7. Joann Ellison Rodgers, "Flirting Fascination," p. 67
8. Dr. Miriam Stoppard, *The Magic of Sex.* London: Allen and Unwin, 1991, pp. 196–99
9. June M. Reinisch, Ph.D., and Ruth Beasley, M.L.S., *The Kinsey Institute New Report on Sex.* New York: St. Martin's Press, 1990, p. 89
10. *Ibid.,* pp. 88, 89
11. Josephine Fairley, "Dream Lover," *Cleo* (Australia), Feb. 1995, pp. 82, 84. Anne Hooper quoted directly in article.
12. *Ibid.*
13. Dr. Maryon Tysoe, *The Good Relationship Guide,* p. 141
14. "Porn Again," *Cosmopolitan* (U.K.), Nov. 1998, p. 113
15. June M. Reinisch, Ph.D. and Ruth Beasley, M.L.S., *The Kinsey Institute New Report on Sex,* p. 153
16. *Ibid.,* p. 107
17. "The Pleasure Quota" study by psychologist Bob McBride for the Associates for Research into the Science of Enjoyment. McBride surveyed 4,000 people in eight

countries on their most enjoyable activities. As reported in "Pleasuring Women Not Always Music to Men's Ears" by Catherine Chisholm, *The Daily Telegraph*, Sept. 18, 1998, p. 11

CHAPTER 6

1. John Gottman, *Why Marriages Succeed or Fail*. London: Bloomsbury, 1997, p. 57
2. Nancy Kalish, "Tell-tale Signs of a Rocky Relationship," *She* (Australia), Oct. 1998, p. 92; Dr. Maryon Tysoe, *The Good Relationship Guide*. London: Piatkus, 1995, pp. 66, 67; John Gottman, *Why Marriages Succeed or Fail*. London: Bloomsbury, 1997, pp. 181–89
3. Dr. Maryon Tysoe, *The Good Relationship Guide*, p. 68
4. John Gottman, *Why Marriages Succeed or Fail*, p. 110
5. *Ibid.*, p. 178
6. Susan Quilliam as quoted in "Tell-tale Signs of a Rocky Relationship" by Nancy Kalish, p. 92
7. Lisa Tolin, "A New Look at Nagging," *Psychology Today*, July/Aug. 1997, p. 16
8. Marcus Wynne, "From the '70s to the '90s," *Psychology Today*, Dec. 1998, p. 8
9. Opinion of Ellen Galinsky of the Families and Work Institute, U.S. As reported in Cris Evatt, *He & She: 60 Significant Differences Between Men and Women*. Berkeley, CA: Conari Press, 1992, p. 145
10. John Gottman, *Why Marriages Succeed or Fail*, pp. 154–155
11. *Ibid.*, p. 157
12. *Ibid.*, p. 155
13. Rosemary Desmond, "Speaking of the Sexes," *The Daily Telegraph*, Oct. 1, 1998, p. 9. Based on a Ph.D. thesis by Dr. Jennifer Peck, University of Queensland, Australia.
14. Hara Estroff Marano, "A New Focus on Family Values," *Psychology Today*, Nov./Dec. 1997, p. 53
15. "Before Taking Your Vows," *Top Info* page, *Top Sante* (U.K.), June 1997, p. 5. Based on research from the University of California.
16. "Before Taking Your Vows," *Top info* page, *Top Sante*, p. 5. Based on research from the University of California and opinion of Denise Knowles of Relate, the relationships counseling service, U.K.
17. Keith Blanchard, "The 7 Deadly Sins of Living Together," *Cleo* (Australia), July 1995, p. 76
18. "What Makes Divorces Go Bad?" Statistic from *www.infidelity.com*. Reprinted from Accord Mediation Services, Sept. 15, 1999.
19. "The Ups and Downs of Testosterone," *Psychology Today*, Nov./Dec. 1997, p. 18
20. Laura Marcus, "Single and Loving It," *Cleo* (Australia), Nov. 1994, p. 112. Statistics quoted within article are from The Morgan Gallup Poll, Australia, March 1993–April 1994; Hara Estroff Marano, "A New Focus on Family Values," *Psychology Today*, Nov./Dec. 1997, p. 54
21. *Ibid.*
22. Direct quote from counselor Peter Jordan, speaker at the national conference "Men and Family Relationships," held in Canberra, Australia, on June 10, 1998. As reported in *The Daily Telegraph*, June 10, 1998, p. 23
23. Dr. Miriam Stoppard, *Conception, Pregnancy and Birth*. New York: Penguin Books, 1993, p. 210

24. Frederic Golden, "Making Over Mom & Dad," *Psychology Today*, May/June 1999, p. 72
25. Dr. Miriam Stoppard, *Conception, Pregnancy and Birth*, pp. 26–27, 32–34; Dr. Miriam Stoppard, *What to Expect When You're Expecting*. Sydney: HarperCollins Publishers, 1992, pp. 25–27; Dr. Jane Macquarie, *Below the Belt*. Melbourne: Reed Books, 1994, pp. 154–60
26. Dr. Maryon Tysoe, *The Good Relationship Guide*, pp. 107–8
27. Tracey Cox, "Two's a Couple, Three's Counseling," *Elle* (Australia), pp. 48–52. Comments from interview with Phillip Gorrell, an Australian psychologist.
28. *Ibid.* Comments from interview with Grant Brecht, an Australian psychologist and author.

CHAPTER 7

1. Cris Evatt, *He & She: 60 Significant Differences Between Men and Women*. Berkeley, CA: Conari Press, 1992, pp. 90, 91
2. Tracey Cox, "Jealousy: Why Some Women Need Help," *Cosmopolitan* (Australia), pp. 50–54. Article based on interview with British psychologists Dr. Nicholas Tarrier and Richard Beckett.
3. Emanuel H. Rosen, "Think Like a Shrink," *Psychology Today*, Oct. 1998, p. 58
4. Tracey Cox, "Jealousy," *Cosmopolitan* (Australia), pp. 50–54. Article based on interview with British psychologist Dr. Nicholas Tarrier.
5. Dr. Maryon Tysoe, *The Good Relationship Guide*. London: Piatkus, 1995, p. 27. Based on work by U.S. researchers Leslie Baxter and William Wilmot.
6. Term used by Australian clinical psychologist Eric Fleming.
7. Allan and Barbara Pease, "Why Men Don't Listen and Women Don't Read Maps," Sydney: Pease Training International, 1999, p. 51
8. Shirley Glass, Ph.D., "Shattered Vows," *Psychology Today*, Aug. 1998, p. 36
9. *Ibid.*
10. Statistics from the DearPeggy.com advice website (www.dearpeggy.com/affairs.html#), cited 6 November 1999), p. 3.
11. Statistics from the Women.com Relationships Poll: "Cheating, Infidelity, and Affairs" (www.womenswire.com/forums/back talk/E0113/results.html), pp. 1–2.
12. Shirley Glass, Ph.D., "Shattered Vows," p. 78
13. *Ibid.*, pp. 68, 69, 79
14. *Ibid.*, p. 36
15. *Ibid.*, p. 38
16. *Ibid.*, p. 42
17. *Ibid.*
18. *Ibid.*
19. *Ibid.*
20. Cherry Norton and Chris Hastings, "Tell-tale Signs that Betray the Adulterer," *The Sunday Times* (U.K.), Sept. 21, 1997, p. 10. Based on research by Dr. David Buss, a sociologist at the University of Texas. Buss interviewed and correlated the educational and class backgrounds of 107 couples, who answered 40 questions to establish their personality traits. Spouses were then interviewed separately about the nature and history of their relationship and the likelihood of whether they would be, or had been, unfaithful. Personality traits were found to be a more

accurate way to predict potential infidelity than social status or the nature of the couples' sex lives.

21. Shirley Glass, Ph.D., "Shattered Vows," p. 40
22. Stephanie Osfield, "Confessions of Infidelity," *She* (Australia), Oct. 1997, p. 50. Opinion of Anne Hollonds, director of services for Relationships Australia, NSW, Australia.
23. Shirley Glass, Ph.D., "Shattered Vows," p. 72
24. Tracey Cox, "Two's a Couple. Three's Counseling," *Elle* (Australia), pp. 48–52. Opinion of Phillip Gorrell and Dr. Janet Hall, both Australian clinical psychologists.
25. Cris Evatt, *He & She*, p. 97
26. Shirley Glass, Ph.D., "Shattered Vows," p. 74
27. *Ibid.*, p. 42
28. *Ibid.*
29. Mira Kirshenbaum, *Too Good to Leave, Too Bad to Stay*. New York: Penguin, 1996, pp. 230–32

CHAPTER 8

1. Barbara De Angelis, Ph.D., *Ask Barbara: The 100 Most Asked Questions about Love, Sex and Relationships*. London: HarperCollins Publishers, 1997, p. 30
2. Emanuel H. Rosen, "Think Like a Shrink," *Psychology Today*, Oct. 1998, p. 56
3. Annie Murphy Paul, "Kid's Stuff: Do Parents Really Matter?" *Psychology Today*, Jan./Feb. 1998, p. 46
4. Emanuel H. Rosen, "Think Like a Shrink," p. 56
5. Barbara De Angelis, Ph.D., *Ask Barbara*, p. 42
6. Adrienne Burgess, "Fathers and Lovers," *She* (Australia), p. 62. Opinion of Dr. Petrushka Clarkson, psychologist, quoted directly in article.
7. *Ibid.*, p. 66. Opinion of U.S. researcher Seymour Fisher and U.S. psychiatrist William Appleton.
8. *Ibid.* Based on study of 225 women by Victoria Secunda, author of *Women and Their Fathers*, Sydney: Transworld, 1996.
9. *Ibid.*, p. 62. Opinion of Dr. Petrushka Clarkson, psychologist, quoted directly in article.
10. Based on author's own research of interviewing couples and individuals for magazine articles and radio show; opinions of Australian clinical psychologists Dr. Janet Hall, Grant Brecht, and Eric Fleming, interviewed by author for this book; Tracey Cox, "Big Brother Is Watching: How Your Siblings Affect Your Sex Life," *Australian Women's Forum*, June 1995, pp. 67–71; Emanuel H. Rosen, "Think Like a Shrink," p. 56
11. Study by clinical psychologists including Dr. Bahman Najarian at University of York, U.K. As reported in "Hold It In and You'll Put Your Health at Risk" by Emily Wilson, *The Daily Telegraph*, Aug. 10, 1998, p. 77
12. Direct quote from Dorsey Cartwright, relationship therapist, as quoted in "Relationships Are a Lot Like Mountain Climbing" by Emma Stephens, *Living Now!*, July/Aug. 1998, p. 38
13. Tracey Cox, "The First Man You Slept With: Why He's Still in Bed with You Today," *Cosmopolitan* (Australia), March 1997, p. 88. Based on research by professor of psychology Marita McCabe.
14. Emanuel H. Rosen, "Think Like a Shrink," p. 56

15. Tracey Cox, "Good Guys, Bad Guys," **Sex Report,** *Cosmopolitan* (Australia), July 1997, p. 45
16. Barbara De Angelis, Ph.D., *Ask Barbara,* pp. 41–44
17. Shirley Glass, Ph.D., "Shattered Vows," *Psychology Today,* Aug. 1998, p. 70
18. Neil S. Jacobson, Ph.D. and John M. Gottman, Ph.D., "Anatomy of a Violent Relationship," *Psychology Today,* Apr. 1998, p. 60
19. Opinion of Gerard Webster, Australian clinical psychologist who specializes in abuse.
20. Theories of other Australian domestic violence experts as reported in "Domestic Violence: Would You Leave Your Partner If He Hit You?" by Stephanie Osfield, *She* (Australia), pp. 36–43. Survey based on poll of 616 women aged 16 years and over.
21. Neil S. Jacobson and John M. Gottman, "Anatomy of a Violent Relationship," p. 62
22. *Ibid.*; Stephanie Osfield, "Domestic Violence," p. 42
23. Neil S. Jacobson and John M. Gottman, "Anatomy of a Violent Relationship," p. 60; "Stephanie Osfield, "Domestic Violence," pp. 42, 43
24. Stephanie Osfield, "Domestic Violence," p. 42; Neil S. Jacobson and John M. Gottman, "Anatomy of a Violent Relationship," p. 81. Statistic based on study by Jacobson and Gottman of 63 battering couples who were measured against a control group of couples who were dissatisfied with their marriage but had no history of violence.
25. Neil S. Jacobson and John M. Gottman, "Anatomy of a Violent Relationship," p. 62. Research based on same study as cited above.
26. Based on opinion of author; opinion of Gerard Webster, an Australian clinical psychologist specializing in abuse; theories detailed in "Domestic Violence," p. 42

CHAPTER 9

1. Nadia Hohn with Annie Paul. "Does Fate Make Mates," *Psychology Today,* July/Aug. 1998, p. 16
2. Opinion of Dr. Janet Hall, Australian clinical psychologist. As quoted in "10 Signs You're About to Split" by Tracey Cox, *Cosmopolitan* (Australia), July 1996, pp. 112–14
3. John Gottman, *Why Marriages Succeed or Fail.* London: Bloomsbury, 1997, p. 41
4. Study by University of Utah and Duke University Medical Center, North Carolina. "Importance of Difference," *Psychology Today,* Sept./Oct. 1997, p. 20
5. John Gottman, *Why Marriages Succeed or Fail,* p. 79
6. *Ibid.,* p. 72
7. *Ibid.,* p. 97
8. Monica Melki, "Women Put Health Second," *The Daily Telegraph,* July 19, 1999, p. 17. Based on a British survey of 950 women aged 18–24, conducted by the Bread for Life health campaign.
9. "Men to Confront Role in Failed Relationships," *The Daily Telegraph,* June 10, 1998, p. 7. Direct quote from counselor Peter Jordan, speaker at the national conference "Men and Family Relationships," held in Canberra, Australia, on June 10, 1998. "Men Lose More from Divorce," *The Daily Telegraph,* Dec. 4, 1997, p. 31. Result from the London conference "The Chaos of Love."

10. Opinion of Australian Professor of Psychology, Dr. Marita McCabe. As quoted in "He's Back but Will He Stay?" by Tracey Cox. *Cosmopolitan* (Australia), Aug. 1998, pp. 86–90

11. Study by University of Utah and Duke University Medical Center, North Carolina. "Importance of Difference," *Psychology Today*, Sept./Oct. 1997, p. 20

Index